HISTORY *of* ST. PE'

HISTORICAL AND BIOGRAPHICAL

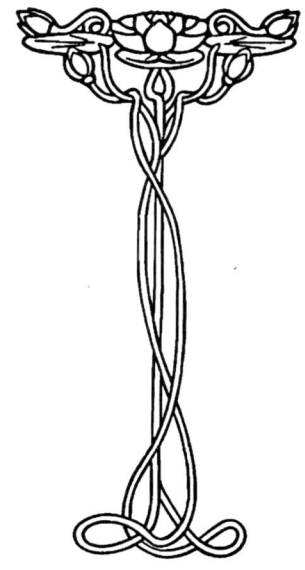

By KARL H. GRISMER

PRINTED BY THE TOURIST NEWS PUBLISHING COMPANY
ST. PETERSBURG, FLORIDA

Copyright, 1924
By Tourist News Publishing Company

A birdseye view of St. Petersburg in 1924, looking northwestward from above Tampa Bay

HISTORY OF
ST. PETERSBURG

CONTENTS

	PAGE
CHAPTER I—GENERAL	
IN PREHISTORIC TIMES	1
EARLY SETTLERS	3
CONCEPTION OF ST. PETERSBURG	5
HOW ST. PETERSBURG WAS MADE	8
THE FOUNDING OF ST. PETERSBURG	9
EARLY GROWTH OF ST. PETERSBURG	14
FIRST PUBLIC IMPROVEMENTS	16
TOWN GOVERNMENT	19
CHAPTER II—EVENTS OF THE YEAR	27
CHAPTER III—RAILROADS	45
CHAPTER IV—WATER FRONT DEVELOPMENT	55
CHAPTER V—F. A. DAVIS COMPANIES	67
CHAPTER VI—CITY GOVERNMENT	81
CHAPTER VII—PINELLAS COUNTY	93
CHAPTER VIII—CHAMBER OF COMMERCE	99
CHAPTER IX—FISHING AND BOATING	109
CHAPTER X—SCHOOLS	115
CHAPTER XI—REAL ESTATE	123
CHAPTER XII—GREEN BENCHES	139
CHAPTER XIII—POST OFFICE	141
CHAPTER XIV—CITY LIBRARY	145
CHAPTER XV—HOSPITALS	149
CHAPTER XVI—PUBLIC UTILITIES	151
CHAPTER XVII—STREETS AND ROADS	155
CHAPTER XVIII—FESTIVALS AND CELEBRATIONS	163
CHAPTER XIX—GOLF CLUBS	165
CHAPTER XX—PROHIBITION	169
CHAPTER XXI—BANKS OF ST. PETERSBURG	172
CHAPTER XXII—PUBLICATIONS	179
CHAPTER XXIII—BASEBALL	183
CHAPTER XXIV—SOCIETIES AND CLUBS	185
CHAPTER XXV—PARKS	197
CHAPTER XXVI—POPULATION	202
CHAPTER XXVII—CHURCHES	203
CHAPTER XXVIII—WORLD WAR	213
CHAPTER XXIX—WHO'S WHO IN ST. PETERSBURG	215

APPRECIATION

The author wishes to take this opportunity to express his sincere thanks to the following:

W. L. Straub, A. F. Bartlett, Roy S. Hanna, Ed. T. Lewis, Reese Moffett, H. H. Richardson, Josef Henschen, Mrs. Annie McRae, Arthur Norwood and Mrs. T. A. Whitted, who assisted materially in the preparation of this history.

A. H. Phinney, who helped in many ways. Mr. Phinney spent many months gathering data for a history of St. Petersburg, with no hope of financial gain. When he learned the author was engaged in the same task he kindly consented to turn over his manuscripts, together with a number of very valuable photographs.

Doherty & McMahon, commercial aviator photographers, who supplied several bird's-eye views of St. Petersburg, and the F. A. Davis Publishing Company, of Philadelphia, which loaned a number of old cuts.

Lew B. Brown, who granted the use of the old files of the *Evening Independent,* and the publishers of the *St. Petersburg Times* for the same courtesy.

PROLOGUE

Out of the sea rose the land. Dazzling white sand, the vast expanse of encircling waters, and the sky above—nothing else. Ages later came plant life, and reptiles, and birds, and strange monster creatures unlike anything on the earth today.

Eons passed.

Then came man—savages from out of the North. Their needs were simple, and the land supplied them. They lived largely on oysters and clams, and they piled up the shells in huge mounds which serve as a mute reminder of their existence. Rival tribes came in, fierce battles were waged, their strength was weakened. Finally, they were succeeded by another race—the Indians.

Then came the white man, the Spaniard, resplendent in costume and relentless in his determination to conquer the land and wrest from it its riches.

Such was the beginning of Florida as we know it today, and such was the beginning of Pinellas Peninsaula. Just the beginning—nothing more.

Upon this peninsula of Pinellas, a favored part of a favored land, there has grown a city—the city we call St. Petersburg. It is the story of this city that we are going to tell—the story of St. Petersburg, the Sunshine City, the city of prosperity, and health, and happiness.

THE HISTORY OF ST. PETERSBURG

I

IN PREHISTORIC TIMES

EVIDENCE that Pinellas Peninsula was inhabited long before the coming of the white man is furnished by the numerous shell mounds which can still be found in or near St. Petersburg.

Ethnologists who have dug into the mounds say there is no doubt but that they were made by man. Carved shells, weapons made from wood and stone, crude jars and bowls and numerous other articles have been unearthed, along with human skeletons.

It is evident that the mounds were made for various purposes. A number were apparently built as fortifications. Others were used as burial places for the dead. Still others probably were nothing more than places where the savages gathered to eat their shell fish, the heap of discarded shells being built up through the countless years.

Old settlers say there were originally six or seven mounds in the vicinity of Sixth street and Sixth avenue south, where Shell Mound Park has been established. All except the present mound were destroyed when the early city fathers hauled away the shells for use on streets and sidewalks. Although most of the mounds within the city were leveled, many still remain on Weedon's Island, Pinellas Point, Maximo Point, the Jungle, Pine Key and elsewhere.

John A. Bethell, in his *"History of Pinellas County,"* tells about an old fort, made entirely of shells, which was found on the north side of Big Bayou. One side of the fort faced the water; the others were walled up, the walls being several feet high. Large trees were growing in the walls, indicating that the fort had been there for many generations. In describing the fort, Mr. Bethell surmised that it was built by the Spaniards as a protection against the Indians. Whether that is the case or whether the mounds were built by the Indians themselves, or a race which preceded them, will never be known.

At all events, the many other mounds on the peninsula prove that the savages at one time must have been very numerous, and must have lived here for hundreds of years. Perhaps they lived on the peninsula the year round; perhaps they migrated here each winter from the North, seeking a balmy climate. In either case, they evidently found the peninsula to their liking and lingered, just as the tourists do today.

Discoveries made recently seem to prove beyond doubt that both Panfilo de Narvaez and Ferdinando de Soto set foot upon the lower end of Pinellas Peninsula in their explorations of the West Coast of Florida early in the sixteenth century. This contention is partly based upon the writings of Cabeza de Vaca, a lieutenant of Narvaez, who was one of the four survivors of the ill-fated expedition. De Vaca wrote: "We anchored near the shore in the mouth of a bay near the head of which we say some habitations of Indians. The next day we landed with as many as the boats would contain. The houses were abandoned, the Indians having fled at night in the canoes. The day following the governor resolved to make an incursion into the land and see what it might contain. We took our way toward the north until the hour of vespers (traveling about eleven miles), when we arrived at a very large bay that appeared to stretch very far inland. We remained there that night and the next day we returned to our people."

The place described by de Vaca apparently was on the west coast of Pinellas Peninsula, probably near the Jungle. The descriptions he also gave of the bays, bayous and rivers seem to tally exactly with the topography of the country as it is today. Some persons argue that nowhere else in this section of the state is there a large bay eleven miles north of another bay, and that, consequently, the place of the landing is fixed definitely.

Excavations made during the winter of 1923-24 on Weedon's Island under the direction of Dr. J. Walter Fewkes, chief of the Bureau of American Ethnology of the Smithsonian Institute, provide convincing proof that at least one of the Spanish explorers must have landed on the island. Many dishes and crocks of Spanish origin, as well as Spanish weapons, have been unearthed, together with a number of skeletons of white men. The positions of the skeletons indicate that the men must have been murdered by the Indians and their bodies thrown together in a heap, and later covered with earth.

Although there are no records available, it is believed that a number of Spaniards later lived on Pinellas Peninsula and gave Spanish names to some of the islands and some points on the mainland. Point Pinellas, for instance, was called Punta Pinal, meaning Point of Pines. These names might have been given, of course, by the Spanish explorers and map-makers, but the belief that they were named by early Spanish settlers is equally possible.

Early Settlers

The first known settler on the lower end of Pinellas Peninsula was Antonio Maximo. In 1843 Maximo secured a land grant from the United States government for services during the Seminole War and established a fish "ranche" at the lower end of the peninsula, now called Maximo Point. Three years later another fishery was located on one of the keys below the peninsula by William Bunce. Maximo and Bunce did a good business in supplying fish for the Cuban market until both of their ranches were destroyed by the hurricane of 1848.

After the storm blew over, Maximo and Bunce discovered that all their possessions had disappeared with the high waters. They left and never appeared in this section again. However, the point was not doomed to remain long uninhabited. A few years later other settlers began coming in. The majority just "squatted," fencing in a few acres and raising farm products and cattle. A few started small citrus groves.

The first house on the lower end of the peninsula was erected by James R. Hay, who came here in 1856 to look after the cattle and hogs of the old Tampa stockmen. He fenced in a small tract at what is now about Lakeview avenue and Twentieth street to truck farm for the Tampa markets. A little later he built his home of hewn pine timber, the strips being about four feet long, six inches wide and three-quarters of an inch thick.

In 1857 Abel Miranda settled at Big Bayou and in 1859 John C. Bethell* at Little Bayou. Miranda, John Bethell and William C. Bethell shortly afterwards established a fishery at Maximo, thereby reviving a business which had been dormant since the disastrous termination of the experiment of Maximo and Bunce.

The value of property on the point in those early years is indicated by the fact that in 1860 Hay sold his house and part of his other improvements to William T. Coons for $25 and a gold watch. Perhaps Hay disposed of his possessions at such a low price because the Civil War had started and he wanted to leave. He was a Northerner and at the first opportunity he joined the blockaders at Egmont Key.

Pinellas Point did not play much of a part during the Civil War. The only event of which there is any record was the shelling and destruction of Miranda's home at

---
*See Life of John Bethell.

Big Bayou by the Egmont Key blockading fleet. The Federals manned a smack which had been captured from Key West fishermen and in February, 1862, paid a visit on Miranda. They fired a few shells over the home and then came in to get provisions. They killed the hogs, cattle and poultry and loaded the smack with syrup, pumpkins, bacon, corn and sweet potatoes taken from Miranda's storehouse. Having accomplished this, the invaders burned the buildings on the farm and killed the orange trees. Miranda and John Bethell returned later and, seeing what damage had been done, decided to leave the point. They found a rowboat, which the invaders had overlooked, and proceeded to Tampa, taking two days for the trip. There Miranda secured a team and went back for his family. When he returned to the peninsula after the war he bought the Hay place, several miles inland, because he did not want "to take any more chances of having his home bombarded from the water." John Bethell, upon returning, purchased the Coons' property and resumed farming. William C. Bethell also came back to the point and lived here for many years.

The Civil War ended, settlers began drifting to the point again. Truck farms were started and orange groves planted. A number of newcomers went into the raising of hogs and cattle. Land was very cheap, and if a person lacked the money to buy, all he had to do was settle on as much as he wanted, and he could stay as long as he desired.

Many of the new arrivals settled at Big Bayou or Disston City, near what is now Gulfport. The settlement at Big Bayou, called Pinellas Village, became quite important and boasted of seven stores, a good harbor, a hotel and a score or more homes. A postoffice was established there in 1876, John Bethell being the first postmaster. The office did a flourishing business until an office was opened in St. Petersburg—in one quarter the cancellations amounted to $74 and the stamp sales to nearly $100. The main business of the village was in shipping farm products and in supplying the needs of the settlers. It also was a popular objective for excursionists from Tampa.

Disston City came into being as a result of a real estate promotion, engineered by the officials of the Disston City Land Company and the Florida Land and Improvement Company, which owned thousands of acres of land on the peninsula. A large area of land was platted into five and ten-acre tracts with wide streets and avenues and a boulevard along the water front. Disston City was to be the center of this development. The town plat was recorded in 1884. The promoters launched an extensive advertising campaign in many cities throughout the North, heralding the brilliant future of Disston City. Some of the advertisements were even published in England, and, as a result, a number of English families came to the point to settle, including the Watson family, William A. Wood, Rev. Watt and three sons, R. L. Locke and Hugh H. Richardson. The actuality of Disston City was not as alluring as the advertisements, however, and many of these newcomers left after a short time. Mr. Richardson remained in Florida and later achieved a reputation in Chamber of Commerce and harbor work. In 1923 he made a report for St. Petersburg on its harbor development.

For a few years Disston City made a hard fight for existence. A number of homes were built, a few stores opened and even a newspaper established. An effort was made to get a postoffice. As there was another postoffice in the state called "Disston," the postoffice department frowned upon "Disston City" and called the office "Bonifacia." In 1890 the Diston office was abandoned, and Disston City was permitted to take its own name in mail matters. But by that time the decline of Disston City had set in. The railroad to St. Petersburg passed it by, and the dream of the promoters was shattered. Disston City breathed a few last gasps and then expired. Today few traces of it remain.

Conception of St. Petersburg

The first settler on the land included in the original plat of St. Petersburg was Dr. James Sarvent Hackney, who bought 600 acres of land from the state for twenty-five cents an acre. He built a home at what is now Fourth street and Fifth avenue south in 1873, and made extensive improvements, reclaiming the sawgrass ponds and clearing the land for farming and groves. The Manhattan Hotel now stands on the site of Dr. Hackney's home.

The next settlers on the land included in the original plat of St. Petersburg were Judge William H. Perry and his brother, Oliver. They built their home on the block south of the Atlantic Coast Line tracks between Second and Third streets. With them they brought all implements needed for farming and sugar-making. They entered forty acres, planted three acres in sweet potatoes, corn and melons and set out some sweet-orange seedlings.

Neither the Perrys or Dr. Hackney became very enthusiastic about the farming possibilities of the peninsula, and when W. F. Sperling appeared late in 1873 and offered to buy all their improvements, they readily consented. In this way, Sperling secured about 640 acres with a mile frontage on Tampa Bay. He added a few acres to the grove started by Dr. Hackney and also reclaimed the pond north of the Hackney home by putting in drain pipes.

John A. Bethell,* in commenting on the Sperling domain, said: "When Mr. Sperling located with his family in his new home he was surely monarch of all he surveyed, for there was not another family within a radius of one and one-half miles of his home. Here is a curious incident of his settlement: After Mr. Sperling bought the Perry place he took his wife one morning for a drive to look over the improved portion of his purchase. While there he found a piece of railroad iron brought there by the Perrys. He picked it up and planted it in the ground near where the Atlantic Coast Line tracks are now laid, remarking to his wife, 'I have laid the first piece of iron for the railroad!' not realizing at the time how nearly prophetic his words were to prove."

St. Petersburg may be said to have had its beginning in 1875, for it was in that year that General John C. Williams,† of Detroit, Mich., first visited the peninsula.

---
*Bethell's History of Pinellas County. †See Life of J. C. Williams.

Many stories are told about why General Williams first came to Florida. Some say that, having disposed of almost all his realty holdings in Detroit, inherited from his father, he set out to find new fields to conquer. Others say that General Williams was suffering from asthma, and that he came to Florida for relief. Whatever the reason, he came, and after traveling over almost all of Florida, he finally arrived on Pinellas Peninsula.

According to one account, General Williams was in Cedar Keys on his way back North when he first heard of Pinellas. He had seen nothing in Florida which suited him, so the story goes, and was ready to leave for good. While waiting for the train, a chance acquaintance boosted Pinellas Peninsula so effectively that he decided to go back and see this wonder place. He returned to Clearwater, hired a team, drove here—and found what he sought.

It is problematical whether General Williams, upon his first visit here, had any idea of founding a city. But at all events, he lost no time in acquiring property. He traveled over the peninsula, looking at all the large tracts which had water frontage. Of them all, he liked the Sperling tract the best, believing that it had the greatest possibilities for development. This was evidenced on March 4, 1876, when two deeds were executed in Alabama to the general from W. F. Sperling. The deeds show that General Williams paid $3,000 for the tract. In March and April of the same year he received deeds from the State of Florida for 712 acres adjoining his other purchase. Later he bought about 200 acres more, making his total holdings about 1,600 acres. To the state he paid on an average of a dollar an acre.

In 1879, General Williams, his wife, two daughters, one of his sons, B. C. Williams, and his nephew, F. W. Tilden, started out for Florida. At Cincinnati, Mr. Tilden left in advance to get here and make some repairs on the property. The rest of the party went on to Gainesville by train. The general had brought with him four horses, two wagons, farming tools and household goods. At Gainesville he hired two additional wagons, covered all four wagons with canvas, and the cavalcade started out to drive to the future St. Petersburg—a wagon journey of 250 miles through a thinly-settled country. At places the road was nothing more than a trail, and then again it was not even that. Almost a month was required for the trip.

Upon his arrival at his Pinellas estate, General Williams started work clearing about forty acres. He tried farming, but met with the usual success of men who try Northern farming methods in Florida. One of his sons later said that every potato he raised cost him a dollar. After a time he gave up the venture, left a few employes on the land to look after his property, and returned to Detroit.

It is believed that General Williams conceived the plan of founding a town on the peninsula after he learned he could not make his land pay by using it for farming purposes. Possibly he had had the idea in mind from the beginning—no one knows exactly. At all events, his subsequent activities were centered on devising ways of bringing a railroad to his property and making a town possible. In 1886 he shipped his furniture, horses and dogs from Detroit to Tampa and built a home in Hyde Park, a suburb of Tampa. He lived there until he completed negotiations with the Orange Belt Railway, which resulted in the building of a railroad to his land.

The Orange Belt Railroad* was fathered by Peter A. Demens†—his correct name was Petrovitch A. Demenscheff—who came to Florida from Russia in 1880. For several years Demens operated a sawmill at Longwood, about ten miles southwest of Sanford. To get logs to his mill, he built a small railroad out into the timber lands. This probably gave him the idea of building a railroad on a larger scale. He interested a number of men and got about $35,000 in cash, in addition to a few thousand he had himself.

His first venture was to build a road, narrow-gauge—from Lake Monroe, on the Jacksonville, Tampa and Key West Railroad, near the St. Johns River, to the southern edge of Lake Apopka, about eighteen miles west of Orlando. Judge J. G. Speer, who owned much land in this locality, gave the railroad one-half of a townsite of 200 acres and the town of Oakland came into existence. It was the headquarters of the Orange Belt Railroad—and the Orange Belt Investment Company—for a number of years.

Demens wanted to extend the railroad on to the Gulf. One of his partners objected, but the others outvoted him. Donations were secured all along the proposed route. The Disstons, of Philadelphia, who owned large tracts in that section of the state, agreed to give the railroad about 60,000 acres. At first, Demens had no intention of coming to this particular part of Pinellas Peninsula. He wanted to go to a point near where Gulfport now is. But his negotiations for this site fell through and arrangements were made with General Williams through Henry Sweetapple, his treasurer, to come here.

Writing to his brokers, Demens said: "Gentlemen—Just received a report from our Mr. Sweetapple that he succeeded in making an arrangement with a certain Williams about getting one-half interest in 500 acres, with a mile frontage on the Gulf, where we will have our terminus in case the 'key' cannot be had. There is eighteen feet of water right at the shore and a splendid townsite there."

Construction work on the railroad was started early in 1887, but Demens began to get into difficulties from the very start. His shipments of rails did not come as fast as he expected. The rainy season was very bad. And then, late in the summer, Florida had an epidemic of yellow fever, and his force of workmen was demoralized.

To make matters worse, Demens was unable to get money as fast as his underwriters had promised. He began to get behind, and the contractors and workmen started clamoring for their money. At one time 500 Italians gathered in Oakland and threatened to lynch him unless they got their money at once. Early in September, the creditors attached all the property of the company and the engines were chained to the rails. This proved such a shock to Henry Sweetapple, the company's treasurer, that he suffered a stroke of apoplexy and died almost instantly.

Demens managed to get enough money from his brokers and personal friends to tide him over for a short time. He worked eighteen to twenty hours a day. His health began to break down. Every few weeks he went to New York to beg for more money. At every opportunity he went out to the construction gangs, urging them to hasten the work. Speed was essential, inasmuch as many of the land donations were contingent upon the road being completed by December 31, 1887.

*See Railroads. †See Life of Peter A. Demens.

A month or so before the time limit, Demens succeeded in getting support from a syndicate of capitalists in New York and Philadelphia. It came too late to get the road completed on the date specified. It was not until June 28, 1888, that the first train came into St. Petersburg from the eastern end of the line. Many of the land donations were lost.

The financial condition of the Orange Belt was in a bad state, and it grew steadily worse. The income from the road was negligible, and only a few small tracts of land could be sold. Early in 1889 the affairs of the company reached a crisis. It had $750,000 worth of bonds outstanding and $55,000 in interest was due in July. Most of the bonds were held by the syndicate; the syndicate wanted the road as its own, so it proceeded to make terms with the original stockholders—Demens, Taylor and Henschen. Demens went to Philadelphia to handle the negotiations. He came back with a check for $25,500—and $8,500 of that belonged to Henschen and $2,000 to Taylor. All that Demens got for his three years' work, and all his original capital, was $15,000. He had counted on making millions—but he ended with less than he had when he started.

How St. Petersburg Was Named

The old familiar story regarding the naming of St. Petersburg runs somewhat as follows:

Both Demens and General Williams wanted to name the town they had founded. They couldn't agree as to which should have the honor. To end the dispute, they drew straws. Demens won, so he called the town St. Petersburg, after the town in Russia which he loved the best. As consolation, General Williams was given the privilege of naming the first hotel, and he called it the Detroit, after his birthplace in Michigan.

It is possible that this story is incorrect. Josef Henschen, the only one of the original Orange Belt group who is still living, says it is only a figment of someone's imagination. The true story, he says, is less romantic, and runs something like this:

Early in 1887, when construction work on the Orange Belt was getting well started, and postoffices were being provided for all along the right-of-way, E. R. Ward was appointed postmaster for the town at the end of the road, on the Williams property. Even before the railroad reached here, Ward had occasion to write to the postoffice department. And, inasmuch as the town had not yet been named, he was in a kind of dilemma—he didn't know what to call the town. He talked with Williams, and the general told him that the town should be named after one of the four original backers of the Orange Belt—Demens, Henschen, Sweetapple or Taylor.

So Ward went to Oakland—the headquarters of the Orange Belt. No one was there except Henschen, so he talked with him about the matter. He asked Henschen to decide on a name. This is the way Henschen tells the rest of the story:

"They wanted me to name the town, and I didn't know what to call it. We'd already named a town along the road after Taylor—called it Taylorville. And we couldn't call a town Sweetapple very well—it would be doomed from the start. And my name—Henschen—wouldn't be good—no one could spell it.

"However, I knew that Demens wanted a town named St. Petersburg. He had tried to have Oakland named St. Petersburg, but Judge Speer, who gave half the townsite, didn't like the idea and insisted upon Oakland. So I thought to myself—why not call this town down there on the Gulf St. Petersburg—it will never amount to anything anyhow, so its name doesn't make any difference.

"So I told Ward we'd call it St. Petersburg. And St. Petersburg it became. I signed a petition, got four or five others to sign it, and we sent it to Washington, where it was approved by the postoffice department. That is the way that St. Petersburg got its name."

There is no way of proving which of these two versions is correct—possibly it is immaterial. It is a matter of record, however, that Demens, in letters to his brokers, referred to the town as "St. Petersburgh" as early as September 6, 1887, some time before the construction of the Detroit Hotel was even planned. Consequently, it would not seem as though the town could have been named co-incidently with the naming of the hotel, and if the two were not named at the same time, the story about drawing straws loses some of its weight.

The Founding of St. Petersburg

During the early part of 1888 the townsite was surveyed and platted by A. L. Hunt, chief engineer of the Orange Belt Railway. General Williams was on hand to supervise the work, having come over from Tampa and taken a home at Big Bayou at the outbreak of Tampa's yellow fever epidemic.

Contradictory stories are often heard regarding whether it was General Williams or Demens who gave St. Petersburg the wide streets and park. Some say it was Demens who insisted upon them, and that the early negotiations were almost broken off because the general was reluctant in "giving away" any more land than he had to. Others say that General Williams was the advocate of plenty of room, and that when Demens threatened to balk at such prodigal waste, the general replied: "It's my land, and I'll do with it whatever I damn please!" Probably the truth is that the whole matter was worked out without friction. Land was "dirt cheap" in those days and it did not make much difference whether the streets were fifty feet wide or two hundred. Some of the general's friends declare that if he had known that St. Petersburg would become the city it is today he would have insisted upon even wider streets and more parks.

The railroad reached Ninth street on April 1, 1888. It was not until June 8, however, that the first through train came in from Oakland. According to Ed. T. Lewis,* the only passenger was a traveling man for a shoe house in Savannah, who had heard of the new city, and decided it might be good business to come here and try to open an account. There is no record of this salesman having become so impressed with St. Petersburg that he cast aside his outside connections and settled down here for life. In fact, it is doubtful whether he even got an order for shoes.

---
*See Life of Ed. T. Lewis.

Other authorities fix the date of the arrival of the first train as May 1. They say that two persons came in on it, Demens and H. H. Kinyon, a helper of General Williams. It is believed, however, that this train was just the private train of Demens and that it did not come all the way from Oakland. Matters like this probably never will be decided definitely—there are no accurate records available and the tales of eye-witnesses differ.

Regardless of the date of the first train's arrival, it is certain there were no cheering crowds on hand to welcome it as it puffed into the town limits. In fact, there was not even a town—the maximum population of St. Petersburg was not more than thirty, including the children. There were about six homes, a general store and several tumble-down shacks where the track laborers were living. All that—but nothing more.

The agreement between General Williams and Demens regarding the division of the town, each to take half, resulted in complications during 1888. The railroad was to get its property, according to the agreement, when it had laid the tracks through the town and built a pier out to twelve feet of water. The tracks were not laid down to Second street until December, 1888, and the pier was not completed until more than a year later. In the meantime, Demens became impatient and on August 11, 1888, he recorded the plot under his own name. Still the general held off from making the division, evidently fearing that if he did so the railroad could not be forced to complete its work.

St. Petersburg's Water Front in 1888

A memorandum of January 20, 1889, made by R. C. M. Judge, General Williams' stepson and clerk, read: "Mr. Demens is anxious to get the lands divided with Mr. Williams as he wants to have things in shape so that when Armour, Drexel & Company come down he could get another appropriation for the road." It was not long after this that Demens sold his interest in the road and left Florida. On February 28, 1889, General Williams deeded to the railroad a good many blocks, probably one-half of the town, and also the Detroit Hotel.

The hotel was built during the second half of 1888. Another of Mr. Judge's memorandums says: "June 14—Mr. Williams, Mr. Kinyon and myself met with Mr. Demens on his private car. We located the depot and the hotel and agreed upon clearing the streets. The hotel is to be built by the railroad and Mr. Demens, each paying half and the cost not to exceed $10,000."

During the period between June 8, 1888, when the first train came into St. Petersburg, and February 28, 1889, when the division of property was made, neither General Williams or Demens could legally sell any of their joint holdings without the other's consent. As a result, only two lots were sold, the first, a lot to Hector McLeod, on August 9, and the second on August 11, the lot on the southwest corner of Central avenue and Second street, to J. C. Williams, Jr., for $700.

Meanwhile, the "old town" up around Ninth street had a chance to boom. In fact, it had started booming even before the railroad was completed. The first settler in this district was Jacob Baum, who located on the south side of Reservoir Lake, now Mirror Lake, in 1876. He built a home on the lake and set out the orange grove later known as the Jackson grove. Part of his grove extended across Central avenue from Ninth street east to a point about half way between Seventh and Sixth.

In March, 1888, Fred Lewis came to St. Petersburg with his family from New Mulford, Pa., and bought one acre of land from Mr. Baum for $50. It was located between Eighth and Ninth streets south of Central. On it was built the first house of the new town by Mr. Lewis' two sons, Ed. T. and Tracy G. Lewis, and T. A. Whitted, who came to St. Petersburg about this time from Disston City.

When the completion of the railroad was assured, E. R. Ward came to the Ninth street section from Big Bayou, where he had opened a store in 1885. He obtained the use of an old, ramshackle building at Ninth street and First avenue south, which had been built as a gathering place for the settlers of the peninsula, and established a general store—the first store of St. Petersburg.

In April, 1888, Mr. Ward made a partnership arrangement of some sort with Mr. Baum, and five acres were platted as the Ward & Baum addition of St. Petersburg. The plat was recorded April 4, 1888. Ward & Baum gave clear titles, something General Williams or the railroad could not do, and they did a lively business after the railroad came in. Later a sharp rivalry developed between "uptown" and "downtown" and the first factional feeling was created.

The subdivision of Ward & Baum did not conform in any way with the plat of St. Petersburg as made by General Williams and the railroad. The lots were smaller and the streets were only fifty feet wide. Central avenue was not even laid out correctly. It was narrow and there was a jog in it between Seventh and Sixth streets.

Not until many years later was this jog removed and the avenue widened, at a cost of several thousand dollars to the city and inconvenience to the property owners.

The first lot in the Ward & Baum subdivision was sold to W. A. Sloan, who was afterward postmaster. The prices for the lots ranged from $20 to $60, considerably less than was asked a little later for lots "downtown."

Although "downtown" St. Petersburg was slower in getting started than the Ninth street section, it began to forge ahead after the propery was divided and the sale of lots started. Late in 1888 the Detroit Hotel was built at Central avenue and Second street and the depot was completed. A little later J. C. Williams, Jr., opened a general store directly across the street from the hotel. Another building was erected between Third and Fourth on Central to serve as the combined offices of the Orange Belt Investment Company, the land department of the railroad, and General Williams. These were the first buildings of any importance. D. S. Brantley previously had erected a small shack near the railroad to use as a restaurant for the railroad employes. Brantley was the contractor who furnished ties for the railroad. He settled in St. Petersburg and a few years later built a bathhouse on the water front.

Following the birth of the downtown section, General Williams placed some of his property on the market and the Orange Belt Investment Company also opened up for business, the office being in charge of Col. L. Y. Jenness,* who had come with the railroad as land agent. Both the general and the investment company offered lots for sale on liberal terms, allowing the purchaser nine years in which to pay for

*See Life of Col. L. Y. Jenness.

The Detroit Hotel as it was in December, 1888.

them. The only restrictions regarding the use of the lots were that all buildings must be erected on brick or stone piers and be painted. The general insisted particularly upon the paint. "Unpainted buildings make a town look as though it's going to the dogs," he asserted.

Fourth street south from Central avenue was opened up by General Williams late in 1889. When the necessary surveys were made it was seen that the street, if laid out according to the town plat, would come within a few feet of the front steps of the new home which the general had just completed where the Manhattan Hotel now stands. In order to provide a little larger front yard, he decided to move the street over ten feet toward the east. To do this, a new plat had to be made. It was recorded on November 12, 1890, as "The Revised Plat of St. Petersburg." The plat was prepared after all property owners had given their consent. The agreement, dated August 18, 1890, showed that those who had bought lots up to that time were J. C. Williams, Jr., D. D. Klinger, Mary T. Howard, E. Powell, J. R. Barclift, J. Douglas Jagger, A. P. K. Safford, A. Maltry, Theodore Maltry, E. Ward, Sr., and the trustees of the Congregational Church.

The federal census of 1890 showed that St. Petersburg had 273 inhabitants, most of whom lived around Ninth street. St. Petersburg had started to grow, but its growth at the start was slow.

The Detroit Hotel as it is at present

Early Growth of St. Petersburg

The initial growth of St. Petersburg was due solely to the fact that it was on a railroad connecting it with the outside world, and that it was at the end of this railroad. Trains laid in the town over night, and the railroad employes naturally found it advantageous to establish their homes here. Many of the original Orange Belt men are still residents of the city.

The railroad gave St. Petersburg a big advantage over Disston City and Pinellas, and it was not long before it was recognized as the shipping and trading center for the lower end of the peninsula. A number of far-sighted merchants in the other settlements realized how things were going and moved their stores to St. Petersburg. Some of the farmers and grove owners also came into the town in order to enjoy the community life.

St. Petersburg received its next impetus through the summer excursions run by the railroad. The low rates induced many persons in the central part of the state to visit the town for the first time. A number were so pleased with what they found that they later returned here to live. It was as a summer resort, in fact, that St. Petersburg gained its first fame. The inlanders learned that St. Petersburg, because of its being surrounded by water, was cooler during the summer months, and they came here to be comfortable. The excursions were run for a number of years. The first was held on July 4, 1889, and the visitors were welcomed at a celebration attended by everyone in the town.

The big freeze of the winter of 1894-95 proved a tragedy to thousands of persons in Florida, but it resulted in good for St. Petersburg. Many of the citrus groves on Pinellas Point survived the low temperature and a number of growers in other parts of the state who had been frozen out came here to make another start. They played an important part in developing the town.

It might be opportune at this point to mention the big boost given Pinellas Point by Dr. W. C. Van Bibber, of Baltimore, Md., who was an advocate of the establishment of a "Health City." Such a city was first suggested by Dr. B. W. Richardson, of London, in 1874. With the idea of finding the best location for such a city, surveys were made of the climatic conditions of places in all parts of the world. After long investigations, it was decided that Florida offered the best advantages and observers were stationed in various parts of the state to see which was the best. One of the observers stayed a year on Pinellas Point, keeping accurate records on the temperature, humidity, prevailing winds, amount of sunshine and other health factors.

During the thirty-sixth annual meeting of the American Medical Society, held in New Orleans in April, 1885, Dr. Van Bibber read a paper embodying the reports and conclusions of all the observers. In part, he said:

"Where should such a Health City be built? Overlooking the deep Gulf of Mexico, with the broad waters of a beautiful bay nearly surrounding it; with but little now upon its soil but the primal forests, there is a large sub-peninsula, Point Pinellas, waiting the hand of improvement. It lies in latitude 27 degrees and 42 minutes, and contains, with its adjoining keys, about 160,000 acres of land.

"No marsh surrounds its shores or rests upon its surface; the sweep of its beach is broad and graceful, stretching many miles, and may be improved to an imposing extent. Its average winter temperature is 72 degrees; that its climate is peculiar, its natural products show; that its air is healthy, the ruddy appearance of its few inhabitants attest. Those who have carefully surveyed the entire state, and have personally investigated this sub-peninsula and its surroundings, think that it offers the best climate in Florida. Here should be built such a city as Dr. Richardson has outlined."

At the time the report was made, Point Pinellas was isolated from the rest of the world so far as adequate transportation facilities were concerned, and nothing was ever done about the proposed Health City. The report was given wide publicity, however, and when the railroad came to the peninsula, talk about the Health City was revived. Many physicians visited St. Petersburg. They found that the climate of the peninsula was all that Dr. Van Bibber had claimed for it, and they boosted St. Petersburg far and wide. It is impossible to estimate the result of all this favorable comment, but certainly it had some bearing on St. Petersburg's future growth.

During the early nineties the number of winter visitors to St. Petersburg was negligible. The tourist tide barely touched the town. For one thing, the railroad service was not what it might have been, and the trip was anything but pleasant. Sometimes, when conditions were perfect, the rickety old engine bumped along over the uneven rails at a twenty-mile gait, but more often it crawled along with aggravating slowness. And every so often something broke, and then the passengers had to spend

The Orange Belt depot, on the site of the present A. C. L. depot, with the Detroit Hotel in the background

hours looking at the scrub palmettoes and scrawny cows. No wonder the tourists did not include St. Petersburg on their itinerary.

During the latter part of the nineties, however, St. Petersburg began to come into its own. The railroad service was improved and trains began coming in on scheduled time. The tracks were made standard gauge and better equipment was secured. Simultaneously, the St. Petersburg Land & Improvement Company (the successor to the Orange Belt Investment Company), spent considerable money advertising the town throughout Florida and in the North. The results were apparent—tourists began coming in.

Many of the first tourist visitors came to fish. And they found St. Petersburg a veritable fisherman's paradise. From the railroad dock they made big catches of trout, mackerel and sheepshead, and when they took boats and went out into deeper waters they tired themselves in fighting with the battlers. Anglers who came to stay a week remained for the entire winter. And when they went North in the spring they told their friends about the spot they had found, and the next winter the friends came too. So spread the fame of St. Petersburg. The fine fishing, coupled with the ideal climate, proved an inducement which could not be denied.

First Public Improvements

The St. Petersburg of 1891 was graphically described by John A. Churchill, of Council Bluffs, Iowa, when he visited the town again in 1911 and was interviewed by a reported of the *St. Petersburg Times*.

"The only way you could get into the city by land was over the narrow-gauge Orange Belt Railway," Mr. Churchill said. "The engine used to jump the track about once a week, but I never heard of any one being killed or even injured seriously—the train didn't go fast enough. Wood was used as fuel and, in wet weather, when the wood got wet, you could keep up with the train by walking.

"Fishing for Spanish mackerel on the railroad dock was great sport in those days and the market contained venison, wild turkey and Mallard ducks. The farmers brought in wagon loads of oranges and sold you a hat full for a nickel.

"Two large alligators made their home in the lake and basked in the sun on the shores undisturbed. Where some of the business buildings stand at present there were ponds. Good building lots could be had for $50 to $100 each. There were no paved streets or street lights at that time. The only barber was a big negro who carved you at 15 cents per head and then rubbed turpentine into the cuts to stop the flow of blood."

Unquestionably, St. Petersburg was a primitive place in those early days. The first public improvement of which there is any record was the construction of a wooden sidewalk along Central avenue. This sidewalk was started at Ninth street in 1889 and built toward the bay. After about two hundred yards were laid, the money ran out and the work was temporarily abandoned. Baum's grove extended across Central and on both the east and west sides of the grove fences had been erected to keep out the wandering cows and hogs. Stiles were built over the fences and Arthur Norwood, one of the pioneer merchants, relates that when he used to take his baby out for a ride in her carriage, "down the sidewalk," he had to lift the carriage over the stiles.

This sidewalk, the first improvement, was started largely through the efforts of the women of the town. They objected to walking through sand up above their shoetops and, besides, they were inspired by the dawning town beautiful movement. Banding together, they raised a small fund by selling ice cream and lemonade, giving entertainments and picnics, and used the money in building the sidewalk. It was not until 1891, however, that they saw the sidewalk completed down as far as the Detroit Hotel. Between Second and Third streets the sidewalk was elevated like a bridge over the swale which used to extend through this section.

The construction of the board walk used up all the energy and money of the town builders during the period of 1889 and 1891. The avenue was not even opened all the way through to Ninth street. Between Sixth and Seventh streets Baum's grove intervened and the road jogged over to the alley on the north side of the railroad tracks. T. F. McCall, whose home used to face this alley, said that it was the main thoroughfare of the town, and that as many as eight or ten teams passed by

Brantley's Bathhouse near the site of the present Municipal Pier

there daily. Central avenue was not opened through Ward & Baum's addition until 1893.

The swale across Central between Second and Third streets proved a knotty problem to the town builders in the early days. The water was several feet deep during the rainy season and teams could not get through. The swale could have been filled in easily enough if there had been money available to pay for the work, but in those days money was scarce in St. Petersburg.

Even after the town was incorporated and a few dollars began rolling into the public coffers, nothing was done about the swale until another year had elapsed. The first money available for road work was used in grubbing out a clump of palmettoes north of Central on Ninth street. The work was done by a Confederate veteran named Calhoun, commonly known as "the last private."

It was not until the latter part of 1894, during the administration of H. W. Hibbs, that the swale was finally filled in. T. F. McCall, C. Durant, J. C. Hoxie, T. M. Clark and T. A. Whitted, then members of the town council, signed the notes so that the work could be done. Later the notes were paid out of the taxes. The work was done by Ernest Norwood.

The completion of this work gave an added impetus to the growth of the lower end of town. More stores were opened there, and in the course of a few years it became the real business center of St. Petersburg. The Ninth street section became the manufacturing district. George L. King's lumber mill, the St. Petersburg Novelty Works and other enterprises were located there. Many of the Ninth street merchants moved down town or went out of business.

The streets of St. Petersburg were almost impassable during the early nineties. Horses loosened the sand and during the dry seasons teams had a hard job getting through. To help matters a little, sawdust was obtained from King's sawmill and scattered along the ruts.

Realizing that road improvements were essential, the council, on September 13, 1892, passed an ordinance providing that "all able-bodied males over 21 and under 45 and residents of the town for twenty days, shall be subject to work on the public streets." Ministers of the gospel and all town officers were exempted. No person could be called for more than six days' work in a year. So far as known, this ordinance was never enforced and the roads were not improved until the town had money to pay for getting the work done.

During 1893 and 1894 the town council was deluged with complaints from residents regarding the bad condition of sidewalk crossings over intersecting streets. Finally, enough money was scraped together to put a layer of shells on the crossings along the important streets. The first contract for this work was awarded to C. W. Springstead,* who agreed to do the work for 24 cents per lineal foot. The shells were obtained from the mounds in what is now Shell Mound Park. Shells from the same source also were used at some of the most sandy places along Central.

Real road improvements did not come until 1897. On June 24 of that year the council awarded contracts for paving Central with pebble phosphate, 25 feet wide from the bay to Second street, 50 feet from Second to Fourth, 25 feet from Fourth to

---

*See Life of C W. Springstead.

Seventh, and 20 feet from Seventh to Ninth. It was about this time that the famous "race track" came into being. This was a pebble phosphate road which made a loop through the business section and around the north side of Mirror Lake, including Second street north, Central avenue and Ninth street north. Boys used to race over this course on their bicycles, and in the evenings when young couples went out buggy-riding, this is the route they always took. It was St. Petersburg's first Lovers' Lane.

Work on the sidewalk crossings and streets comprised about all the public improvements in St. Petersburg during the decade from 1890 to 1900. A start was made toward improving the channel leading along the railroad pier so that small boats could dock at the foot of Central, but the work stopped before anything worth while was accomplished.

The famous wooden sidewalks along Central gave way about 1895 to shell sidewalks, and the shell was replaced about 1900 with an asphalt preparation. Later came the cement blocks. The town was becoming very prosperous, and the dawning prosperity was reflected in the better sidewalks and streets. It was not until 1903, however, that any real movement was started to pave the streets with brick.

Town Government

During the first three years of its existence, St. Petersburg managed to labor along without any government. Residents could do just about as they wanted to, so far as the law was concerned. There were no ordinances to obey, or no officers.

Several attempts were made during 1890 and 1891 to incorporate the town, but they were blocked by a small faction which was opposed to any town government,

Fishing was the main attraction of St. Petersburg in the '90s

partly because it meant the curtailment of "personal privileges" and also because incorporation would surely be followed by town taxes.

Early in 1892, however, a group of town boosters renewed the fight and called for an election Monday morning, February 29, in Cooper's Hall. An account of this election was carried in an issue of *"The Weekly South Florida Home,"* dated March 4, 1892, as follows:

"Pursuant to a call, issued thirty days prior, the citizens met at Cooper's Hall Monday morning, February 29, to vote on incorporating the town. After considerable discussion, a vote was taken on the question, which stood 15 for incorporation to 11 against, and St. Petersburg laid off her swaddling clothes and donned the more comely garb of an incorporated town.

"The question of incorporation having been settled, the judges and clerks were duly elected and the polls opened for voting.

"There were two tickets in the field. The winning one put up by the conservative, temperate, sturdy, working property owners, generally understood as the Anti-Saloon faction, and the other was put up by what is generally understood as the Open Saloon faction. The Anti-Saloon ticket received the following vote:

"Mayor: David Moffett,* 21. Councilmen: George L. King, 22; Charles Durant, 18; Arthur Norwood, 25; Frank Massie, 22; J. C. Williams, Jr., 27. Clerk: Wm. J. McPherson, 26.

"The other ticket received the following vote:

"Mayor: J. C. Williams, Sr., 10. Councilmen: H. W. Hibbs, 6; H. Martin, 9; G. W. Anderson, 7; T. A. Whitted, 7; J. Baum, 1. Clerk: J. Torres, 5. Marshal: S. A. Sloan, 18; C. M. Gill, 13.

"The officers elected have the confidence of the entire community, and with the reins of government in their hands, a new era of faith and confidence in the future town is established.

"That the government will be conducted economically and with the best interests of every property owner in view, and also for the general good and prosperity of the town, every one feels assured."

An analysis of this newspaper story reveals a number of interesting facts about the early town. In the first place, it shows that the prohibition question already had become an important issue in the community, and that the "drys" outnumbered the "wets" two to one. Moreover, the result of the election shows that the people of St. Petersburg did not feel as grateful toward General Williams, the founder of the town, as might have been expected. Instead of electing him first mayor of the town he had made possible, they defeated him by a substantial majority. Whether this was due to an unfriendly feeling toward General Williams or to animosity against the party he represented will always be a matter for discussion.

Less than two months after the election General Williams died.

It cannot be said that everything ran smoothly directly after the election. It did not. The question of incorporation had resulted in bitter strife, and after the election the fires of contention did not die down. Williams' party was disgruntled and Judge Wm. H. Benton secured an injunction to prevent the councilmen from taking office.

---
*See Life of David Moffett.

Inasmuch as there were no town funds to fight the injuction, the councilmen dug down in their pockets and contributed five dollars each to present their case in the courts. The legality of the election was sustained and in June, 1893, at the next session of the State Legislature, a bill was passed legalizing the incorporation.

The first meeting of the town council was called by Mayor Moffett on the evening of March 1, in the office of the South Florida Home. All the councilmen were present. George L. King was chosen president of the council. The term of office of the various members was determined by lot, the result being that King and Durant were to serve one year and the others two.

At the next meeting, held March 4, the council got down to business and passed nine ordinances. Ordinance No. 1 was designed to preserve the peace and morals of the town and was as follows: "Be it ordained by the town council of St. Petersburg, that any person who shall violate good order in the town of St. Petersburg, first, by a breach of the peace, or second, by the use or utterance of indecent, obscene or profane language, or third, by indecent exposure of person, or fourth, by disorderly conduct, or fifth, by drunkedness, shall, on conviction, be fined not less than one nor more than one hundred dollars, or be imprisoned not more than sixty days."

The second ordinance passed prohibited the sale of goods, wares or merchandise on the Sabbath Day unless to persons in need of the necessaries of life. Drug stores were excepted from this Blue Sunday law. Other ordinances passed at this meeting prohibited the firing of guns in the town limits, provided for the punishment of "bad characters," prohibited gambling, and fixed license fees for various occupations, including a $100 license fee for saloons.

The General Store of J. C. Williams, one of the first buildings erected in "lower" St. Petersburg, and the Opera House—picture taken in 1896

At their third meeting, on March 8, the councilmen kept up their good work and passed an ordinance to halt the wandering of hogs over the streets and through the gardens. Said the ordinance: "Be it ordained by the town council of St. Petersburg, that the running at large of hogs within the corporate limits of the town of St. Petersburg is hereby prohibited, and all hogs found running at large within the aforesaid limits shall be impounded by the town marshal, and shall be released only on payment of one dollar per head and costs. If the fine is not paid within six days the hogs impounded shall be sold at public auction by the marshal." This was Ordinance No. 10.

The councilmen then turned their attention to the "speed demons" who were racing their horses through the town. They decreed that anyone who drove recklessly or raced would be punished upon conviction by a fine not exceeding ten dollars or imprisonment not exceeding ten days. The speed of trains also was limited to six miles an hour in the town limits.

After the first burst of ordinance passing, the council settled down to the drab existence of providing for the many needs of the town with the small means at its disposal. No taxes could be levied the first year and the only funds received by the town were part of the fines paid by law-breakers and the license fees. A report made by the finance committee on July 7, 1893, showed that the town had run more than $100 in debt during the first year.

In April, 1892, Marshal W. A. Sloan called the council's attention to the fact that there was no place to confine law-breakers after he had captured them. Thereupon the council voted "to erect a town calaboose," eight by twelve feet and ten feet high, with two-inch plank walls. When the bills came in it was learned that this "calaboose" cost $37.68.

Salaries for the various town officers were fixed at the council meeting on May 3, 1892, the councilmen at the same time voting to serve one year without pay. The salaries were as follows: mayor, a fee of $1 for each conviction before his court and such other fees as allowed him by ordinance; marshal, $20 a month and a fee of $1 for each conviction before the mayor; collector of revenue and assessor of taxes, 5 per cent of first $2,000, 2½ per cent of next $2,000 and 1 per cent of all other sums so collected and turned into the treasury; clerk, $2 for each day's attendance at council meetings, $1 for each conviction before the mayor, 25 cents of each license issued, and other fees as are allowed clerks of the circuit court in Florida; treasurer, 1½ per cent on all monies received by him; town policemen, not more than $1.50 a day.

Early in the summer of 1892 the council took up the problem of raising money by taxation. J. P. Pepper was appointed first town assessor. He submitted a report on September 6, 1892, showing the total valuation of all personal and real property in the town to be $123,352.92. The council thereupon fixed the tax levy at 10 mills. When the assessor's report was made public and residents saw how much their property had been appraised, a storm of protest arose. Many requests for a reappraisal were made.

A change of feeling toward General Williams must have occurred during the year following his death because, on March 8, 1893, at the second election, Judge

Wm. H. Benton, the general's right-hand man, was chosen as mayor. Judge Benton served less than a month, however, as he died suddenly of apoplexy while getting ready to go to Tampa. On April 28, David Murray was elected to succeed him.

St. Petersburg's first bond election was held on July 18, 1893. The council decided at first to ask the town to support two bond issues of $7,000 each, one for grading and paving the streets and the second for building a school house. Later on, however, the councilmen became convinced that the voters would never approve two issues for such large amounts at one time, and they dropped the $7,000 for streets. With only one bond issue confronting them, the voters rallied to its support and it was passed, 39 to 1. It would be interesting to know the identity of the lone resident who opposed the issue. Possibly it was the same man who moved just outside the town limits a short time later because he "didn't want to be robbed of everything he had."

During the next few years the town fathers occupied most of their time with routine matters. Their greatest difficulties were encountered in keeping the town's expenditures within its very limited income. On several occasions the councilmen gave their personal notes in order to raise money to pay for vital improvements. From all quarters of the town came demands which could not be met.

St. Petersburg took another step forward on April 5, 1895, when the council boldly defied the "cattle barons" and passed an ordinance which prohibited cows carrying bells from meandering hither and yon within the town limits. Previous to this action, the residents were awakened at all hours of the night by the jangling of bells.

St. Petersburg in 1901, from painting by W. L. Straub

Despite this ordinance, the cow problem kept bobbing up time and again during the next few years. A number of large herds of cattle grazed all over the peninsula and even though the cattle industry was of comparatively little importance, the cattle barons were so well organized and had such powerful friends in the ranks of the county politicians that little could be gained by fighting them, regardless of how much the cattle damaged property. Finally, however, the era of cow supremacy was ended. The residents of the town brought such pressure that the council passed an ordinance providing that "no cow, calf, heifer, bull, steer or cattle of any description shall be permitted to roam at large within the town limits between sundown and sunrise." Mayor Edgar Harrison signed the ordinance on May 19, 1899. The prediction of the cattle barons that the peninsula would be ruined never came true.

That the voters of those days wanted to shun bond issues was indicated on March 8, 1899, when they were called upon to approve or defeat a proposed issue of $5,000 to build sewers. The issue was defeated, 9 to 10. However, a $5,000 issue for building a water works was approved on the same day, 17 to 5. The election later was declared illegal on account of irregularities, and another election was called for May 23. This time $10,000 was asked for the water works and the issue was approved, 31 to 9.

Another bond election was held on August 27, 1901. Issues of $11,000 for the schools, $3,000 for the water works and $5,000 for a channel were approved by substantial majorities.

St. Petersburg's mayors during the period from February 29, 1892, when it became a town, and June, 1903, when it became a city, were as follows: David Moffett, 1892; Judge Wm. H. Benton and David Murray, 1893; H. W. Hibbs, 1894 and 1895; J. A. Armistead, 1896, 1897 and 1898; Edgar Harrison, 1899; J. A. Armistead, 1900; Edgar Harrison, 1901; R. H. Thomas, 1902, and George Edwards, 1903.

The councilmen during this period were: G. L. King, 1892; J. C. Williams, Jr., 1892, 1893, 1899 and 1900; F. Massie, 1892 and 1893; C. Durant, 1892, 1893, 1894, 1895 and 1896; Arthur Norwood, 1892, 1893, 1896 and 1897; B. F. Livingston, 1893; J. C. Hoxie, 1893, 1894, 1895 and 1903; T. M. Clark, 1894 and 1895; T. F. McCall, 1894 and 1895; T. A. Whitted, 1894 and 1895; J. T. Hearn, 1895; S. A. Burrier, 1896 and 1897; R. T. Daniel, 1896, 1897 and 1898; David Moffett, 1896 and 1897; J. G. Bradshaw, 1897 and 1898; B. C. Williams, 1898, 1899, 1900 and 1901; T. R. Chapman, 1898 and 1899; H. P. Bussey, 1898 and 1899; A. P. Avery, 1899 and 1900; George Edwards, 1899, 1900, 1901 and 1902; A. Welton, 1899 and 1900; W. A. Sloan, 1900 and 1901; A. P. Weller, 1900 and 1901; W. L. Ainslee, 1901 and 1902; F. E. Cole, 1901 and 1902; W. C. Henry, 1901 and 1902; B. T. Railsback, 1902 and 1903; C. C. Wilder, 1902; J. B. Wright, 1902 and 1903; F. R. Chapman, 1903; F. E. Cole, 1903; J. C. Hoxie, 1903; F. P. Klutts, 1903; W. A. Coats, 1903.

The necessary moves for St. Petersburg to become a city were made by the town council, acting with Mayor George Edwards, early in 1903. No intimation of the plans or any details about the proposed city charter were divulged to the public until after the State Legislature had acted favorably. Everything was done with the utmost secrecy, according to an editorial in the *St. Petersburg Times,* in the issue of

June 6, 1903, which stated: "St. Petersburg's new city charter has been passed by both houses of the Legislature and signed by the governor. This would call for a column editorial, but the fact is, the Times, like everyone else but the city council, doesn't know anything about the new charter." Members of the council at this time were B. T. Railsback, J. B. Wright, F. R. Chapman, F. E. Cole, J. C. Hoxie, F. P. Klutts and W. A. Coats.

II

EVENTS OF THE YEARS

PRIOR to 1900, the growth of St. Petersburg was slow, but each year the town became a little larger as a few new residents came, attracted by the many natural advantages of this section of the state. Few events of unusual importance occurred during this period. Mention must be made, however, of the establishment of the first electric light plant by a company fathered by F. A. Davis of Philadelphia. A franchise was secured from the town council early in 1897 and the plant was moved here from Tarpon Springs, where it had been located, and set up at the foot of Central avenue on the water front, where the Yacht Club now stands. The power was turned on August 5, 1897. The event was described in the September, 1897, issue of *The Medical Bulletin*, as follows:

"The latest improvement of magnitude in St. Petersburg is the completion and inauguration of the electric light system. By this enterprise every part of the town is brilliantly illuminated. A formal inauguration of the new undertaking occurred in St. Petersburg on August 5, and was the occasion of much rejoicing among the inhabitants and invited guests. The trial illumination was a success in every particular. No pains had been spared by the company to provide themselves with the latest scientific devices, and the appliances connected with the work are of the most improved construction."

As might have been expected, *The Medical Bulletin*, which was published by Mr. Davis' company in Philadelphia, did not hesitate in praising the new plant as much as possible. Later, however, this early plant was described by one of the officials of the company as "a wonderful collection of junk." But it served the purpose for a number of years and helped materially in lifting St. Petersburg out of the village class.*

During those early years, as at present, St. Petersburg was a peaceful, law-abiding community. In this connection, the following paragraph of an article which appeared in the *St. Petersburg Times*, July 20, 1901, is interesting: "City Marshal Wickwire has devised a rather unique plan for the keeping of the peace. He has purchased a pair of bloodhounds with which he proposes to catch any culprit who flees from justice. These hounds are in training and not a single arrest has been made since their arrival, the criminally inclined being evidently more afraid of the dogs than they are of the law. St. Petersburg is remarkably free of lawbreakers."

---
*See F A. Davis Companies.

The Woman's Town Improvement Association, which worked industriously for the beautification of St. Petersburg for many years, was founded on May 1, 1901, with twenty-eight charter members, merging with the Park Association. Mrs. A. P. Weller, wife of the manager of the electric light plant, was elected first president; Mrs. W. L. Straub, first vice-president; Mrs. F. E. Cole, second vice-president; Miss A. A. Michael, secretary, and Mrs. G. B. Harris, treasurer. The W. T. I. A., as it was commonly known, led the work of beautifying Williams Park, clearing out the undergrowth and weeds and planting plants and flowers.*

During the fiscal year ending June 30, 1901, St. Petersburg experienced its first building boom, acclaimed by the newspapers as the first substantial evidence of civic greatness. During the year, 130 buildings were erected at a cost of $131,000. The most expensive building was the Wood block, which cost $12,000. The population of the city at the time was 1,600, so the building program represented a per capita expenditure of about $82.

The first definite step toward improving the water front was taken by the town council on December 7, 1901, when it appropriated $2,250 for digging a channel from the foot of First avenue north, at the King & Chase dock, to deep water, the channel to be thirty feet wide at the bottom, fifty feet wide at the top, and with a minimum depth of seven feet at low tide. The work was to be done within sixty days after the contract was awarded. Permission had to be secured from the War Department, however, and it was not before the summer of 1902 that the channel was completed.

St. Petersburg's first tourist society was organized by the winter residents from Illinois on January 1, 1902, at a meeting called by Capt. J. F. Chase, Rev. J. P. Hoyt and M. Arter. Mr. Arter was elected president. Two weeks after the Illinois Society was formed tourists from the New England states formed a similar organization with Rev. J. P. Hoyt president. Meetings were held regularly by both societies for the remainder of the winter.†

The Sanford & St. Petersburg Railroad, owned by the Plant System, was absorbed by the Atlantic Coast Line in April, 1902. In commenting on this change the *St. Petersburg Times* stated: "St. Petersburg has no reason to feel disappointment over this big railroad merger—the policy of the Plant System has never been helpful to growing industries and new settlements in this section and it is not very difficult to believe that if any change at all occurs it will be for the better."‡

The people of St. Petersburg were able to talk over the telephone to Tampa for the first time on June 28, 1902, when the Bell Telephone Company completed its Tampa line and announced that a toll of twenty-five cents would be charged for calls.

The first booklets to advertise St. Petersburg were ordered by the Chamber of Commerce following a meeting held on July 21, 1902, at which the members pledged themselves to pay $125 for having 10,000 booklets printed by the F. A. Davis Publishing Company, of Philadelphia, the work to be done at cost and the cuts to be furnished free. The cost exceeded the original estimate by $25. Records of the F. A. Davis company show that the booklets were not paid for until several years afterward.

---

*See Woman's Town Improvement Association. †See Tourist Societies. ‡See Railroads.

St. Petersburg suffered a severe blow on August 9, 1902, when the St. Petersburg State Bank, organized in 1892, failed to open its doors. Residents of the town had $51,000 in deposits in the bank at the time and this amount represented a large part of the town's wealth. Great excitement prevailed and there was talk of a lynching. A guard was placed around the bank vault, but this was later found to be a useless pre-

A bird's-eye view of downtown St. Petersburg and the Water Front in 1903, as seen from the Tomlinson Tower, Fourth street and Second avenue south

caution, inasmuch as the vault was empty of everything except more or less valueless papers. John A. Bishop, the bank president, explained that the bank had become involved in the affairs of a phosphate company in Pasco County, and when the phosphate company collapsed, the bank collapsed with it. John Trice, president of the Citizens Bank of Tampa, was named receiver. The case was in the courts for years, and in 1914 the final payments were made to the depositors, who received altogether about twenty-five cents on the dollar.*

Members of the Chamber of Commerce recommended at the annual meeting held June 1, 1903, that the city appropriate $500 for municipal advertising. After care-

*See Banks.

fully considering the petition at their next meeting, the councilmen voted it down on the grounds that $500 was too much money to spend for such a purpose.

The avenues of St. Petersburg were renamed by the city council during 1903, preparatory to the publishing of the first city directory by the *Times* Publishing Company. In the original town plat what is now Fifth avenue north was called First avenue, and the avenues to the south were numbered in rotation. Sixth avenue, now called Central avenue, was the main business street. This system of naming was unsatisfactory for many reasons, and the council decided, upon the solicitation of a number of residents, to change the name of Sixth avenue to Central avenue, and to make it the dividing line of the city, naming the avenues in accordance to their location north and south of Central, as First avenue north, First avenue south, and so on. Inasmuch as few of the houses had been numbered up to that time, the change caused little inconvenience. The names of the streets were not changed.

The first contract for brick pavements in St. Petersburg was awarded by the city council in July, 1904, to Henry & Wishard, the city to pay $1.75½ per square yard The work was delayed, however, by a number of property holders along Central avenue, who secured an injunction against the city to prevent it from assessing them for the street intersections. After much haggling, the work finally was resumed and Central was paved from Second to Fifth streets. The delay necessitated another contract with Henry & Wishard, and this time the city to pay $1.82½ per square yard.

The St. Petersburg & Gulf Electric Railway, founded by F. A. Davis, of Philadelphia, and his associates, started in operation on September 28, 1904. "The first trip over the completed route," said Mr. Davis' *Medical Bulletin,* "was made the occasion of an appropriate celebration by the people. It is as delightful an urban ride as may be found anywhere, and not so short either for a little city." The franchise to the company had been granted by the voters, 108 to 48, at an election held February 4, 1902, but more than two years was required by Mr. Davis to obtain the necessary amount of money. The original line, as operated at the beginning, extended from the foot of Central avenue west to Ninth street and south on Ninth street to Booker Creek. In the spring of 1905 the line was extended to Disston City.*

St. Petersburg escaped from the heavy freeze of January, 1905, with very little damage. Seventy-five per cent of the fruit in the state was killed, according to reports, but the fruit on Pinellas Peninsula escaped with little damage. The thermometer registered 28 degrees at the worst period of the cold wave.

The Board of Trade was organized on February 14, 1905, to succeed the Chamber of Commerce, which had accomplished little during the preceding years because of a lack of money. F. A. Wood was elected president at a meeting held in the office of Mayor R. H. Thomas. Other officers elected were: A. F. Bartlett, vice-president; R. H. Thomas, secretary, and J. Frank Harrison, treasurer. Although considerable interest was shown in the Board of Trade at the beginning, the first year passed without any important achievements. Early in 1906, however, a campaign was launched to raise $2,000 by popular subscription for advertising and the fund was oversubscribed within a week.

---
*See F. A. Davis Companies.

Veteran City, the dream of Capt. J. F. Chase, was dedicated with impressive ceremonies on April 5, 1905. Rev. J. P. Hoyt delivered the dedicatory prayer and Hon. E. R. Gunby, of Tampa, gave the principal address. The city was founded by Capt. Chase, working in conjunction with the Florida West Coast Company, as a place where veterans of the Civil War could spend their last days. Descriptive folders, praising Veteran City to the skies, were sent to veterans in all parts of the country. A few responded and bought land, but Veteran City never prospered. Today none but the old residents know such a town existed.

The E. H. Tomlinson residence on Fourth street south was purchased by Joseph C. Sibley, who represented the Twenty-eighth District of Pennsylvania in Congress, on April 8, 1905. Mr. Sibley lived in the city a number of years and took a keen interest in the various activities.

A bitter fight over whether brick or marl should be used on the streeets of St. Petersburg followed the approval by the voters of a $35,000 bond issue on July 18, 1905. This issue included $10,000 for street improvements and the council was divided on the momentous question of what kind of paving material should be purchased with the money. A few held out for brick and put up such a hard battle that they finally secured brick for the business streets. Marl was used on the residential streets. The brick lasted; the marl soon went to pieces. After that the marl advocates kept well in the background, and brick was used almost exclusively.*

The St. Petersburg Reading Room and Library Association was formed during the summer of 1905. The organization meeting was held late in July, with Arthur Norwood chairman and Miss Pauline Barr secretary pro tem. Eloquent speeches were made by some of the leading citizens and the association was started with 122 members. The library was established in the schoolhouse and a few months later was moved to a room in the Bussey building on the south side of Central between Third and Fourth.†

A hotel register published by the *St. Petersburg Times* on November 25, 1905, showed that the hotels of the town could then accommodate 675 guests, as follows: Detroit, 100; Manhattan, 100; Colonial, 150; Huntington, 100; Wayne, 75; Chautauqua, 50; Paxton House, 50, and Belmont, 50.

An organized effort to acquire the water front for the city was launched at a meeting of water front boosters held on the evening of December 20,

The Tomlinson Tower, built by E. H. Tomlinson at Fourth street and Second avenue south, to aid Marconi in his wireless experiments

*See Streets and Roads. †See Public Library.

1905, in the home of Col. J. M. Lewis. Eight men attended—the same men who led the fight until it was won, years later. The plan adopted at the meeting was the plan which finally was used by the city, only a few changes being made. On April 24, 1906, the city council authorized the water front committee of the Board of Trade to acquire four water front lots at a cost of $5,120 and to hold them in trust until such time as the city could take them over; also, to acquire as much of the remaining water front as possible. With this endorsement, the committee bought the lots, the deeds running to C. Perry Snell, A. F. Bartlett and Roy S. Hanna. This proved to be the real beginning of St. Petersburg's water front development.*

New fire apparatus, ordered by the city council some time previously, arrived during the week of May 26, 1906. It consisted of a hook and ladder truck, a steam fire engine, a chemical engine, and a new fire hose. The offer of the Woodmen of the World to organize a fire department was accepted, and J. Frank Chase was elected chief and Will Longman assistant chief. A month later the personnel of the department was complete, the men being assigned as follows: Steam fire engine: Said Klowie, engineer and captain; George Boyer, assistant; W. J. Jones, E. J. Branch, G. Harrod, W. E. Patterson, Verne Goodwin, J. J. Eiland, linemen. Hose reel company, No. 1: John Beard, captain; H. H. Renfroe and J. E. Howell, nozzlemen; Robert Mitchell, Fred Pellerin, Fred Barden, Tom Brown, Carl Brown and Joe Kletts, hosemen. Chemical engine: Assistant Chief Will J. Longman in charge; W. A. Roberts, engineer; George Ainslee, assistant; E. R. Matchett and Ira Taylor, nozzlemen. A paid fire department was installed during 1907.

Poor service given by the Atlantic Coast Line Railroad resulted in an indignation meeting of citizens held December 4, 1906. Postmaster Roy S. Hanna produced records which showed that not one of the trains carrying mail had come in on time during the preceding month. One train had arrived only fifty minutes behind scheduled time, he said, but that had been an unusual occurrence.†

The St. Petersburg Land & Improvement Company, originally the Orange Belt Investment Company, sold all its remaining holdings in St. Petersburg on December 15, 1906, to C. Perry Snell, Albert Hoxie and J. C. Hamlett. The holdings included the Detroit Hotel, a number of water front lots and lots in the business section, and also considerable property in the residential districts. The St. Petersburg Land & Improvement Company, during its existence, helped materially in the growth of the city and at one time was the only agent for advertising the city's attractions.

Early in 1907 the people of St. Petersburg had their first taste of artesian water and they found it not to their liking. Prior to that time the city's water had been obtained from Reservoir Lake, now called Mirror Lake, but as the city grew, the supply proved insufficient, particularly during the winter months, when the population of the city was largest and the rainfall least. In casting around for a new supply, the city council in November, 1906, employed W. W. Jacobs to drill an artesian well. A twenty-foot reservoir was struck 450 feet below the surface of the ground and a short time later the well was connected with the city mains. The housewives soon learned that the water was hard, very hard, and they objected strenuously. Later more wells were dug and better water was secured.‡

---
*See Water Front Development. †See Railroads. ‡See Public Utilities.

The Tarpon Club of St. Petersburg was organized on November 10, 1907, at a meeting of anglers held at the home of Roy S. Hanna. The purpose of the club was "to encourage the use of the rod and reel in fishing, promote social intercourse among its members, aid in securing the protection of game fishes, elevate the sport to the highest standards, and to do all the things proper and necessary to attain these objects." George E. Downey was elected president, W. H. English vice-president, and W. L. Straub, secretary and treasurer.*

The first motorboat regatta was held in St. Petersburg on Monday, January 20, 1908. Nineteen boats took part. A trip was made to the clubhouse of the Pinellas Boating and Fishing Club off Pinellas Point.

Advocates of a wide business street through the center of the city won their cause in 1909, when $9,000 was voted to widen and straighten Central avenue through the Ward & Baum addition, between Sixth and Ninth streets. A. C. Pheil was one of the leaders in this movement.

Upon the recommendation of a special committee, composed of L. C. Hefner, A. F. Bartlett and W. R. Howard, the Board of Trade in March, 1909, decided to reorganize and incorporate under the name of the St. Petersburg Chamber of Commerce. A. F. Bartlett was elected president, S. D. Harris first vice-president, and W. L. Straub second vice-president.

On November 16, 1909, the first through Pullman from New York City arrived in St. Petersburg over the Atlantic Coast Line. It was the "Salome." The arrival of the

*See Tarpon Club.

Looking east on Central from Fourth street in 1907

Pullman was heralded as an event of the greatest importance for St. Petersburg. "In a few years," prophesied one of the local newspapers, "many through Pullmans will be coming into St. Petersburg each day from the North, bringing hundreds of tourist visitors. St. Petersburg is now on the threshold of its greatest development."

St. Petersburg received a valuable Christmas present on Christmas eve, 1909, when the water front committee of the Board of Trade turned over to the city the deeds for all the remaining water front properties except those owned by the electric light company and the Atlantic Coast Line Railway. The railroad lots later were leased on favorable terms to the city, while the electric light company's lot was obtained when the company went bankrupt.

A movement to make St. Petersburg a model city was launched by some of the Protestant ministers at a meeting in February, 1910. They unanimously adopted resolutions against the evils of card playing, dancing, intoxication and cigaret smoking. "We deplore the increasing use of tobacco and cigarets by our youth and children," they said, "believing that the use of tobacco in any form is unnecessary, expensive and harmful. . . . . We ask that the sign on a cigar store on Central avenue, which is considered disgraceful and even blasphemous, reading 'You had better smoke here than hereafter,' be removed by the council or public protest."

The dredge "Blanche," named in honor of Blanche Straub, daughter of W. L. Straub, started work on the water front improvements on May 2, 1910, amid the cheers of a large crowd of spectators. Mr. Straub pushed the lever that started the machinery. Many of the city's prominent men were on the dredge when the work began.

The new city hospital, called the Good Samaritan, was opened for public inspection on July 28, 1910, a reception being given by the Woman's Auxiliary. Prior to that time the only hospital in the city was a private institution on Second street north near First avenue, owned by Dr. J. D. Peabody and A. P. Avery. The Good Samaritan soon proved to be inadequate and steps were taken to provide a more suitable building.*

Gulfport was incorporated as a town at a meeting of the residents held Wednesday night, October 12, 1910, in the Gulf Casino. Of the thirty-eight residents in the territory, thirty were present. Rev. J. P. Hoyt presided. Twenty-three voted for incorporation and seven against. E. E. Wintersgill was elected mayor; S. J. Webb, clerk; John C. White, marshal, and A. C. Stefanski, H. C. Slauter, Henry Withers, Joshua White and L. M. Wintersgill, councilmen. Commenting on the incorporation, the *St. Petersburg Times* said in the issue of October 14, 1910: "Gulfport is perhaps the largest town in Florida, territorially speaking, and for population per square mile it is undoubtedly the largest on earth—and for good hard American cheek it perhaps will compare with any in the country, the taking in of large areas of valuable lands that can never receive any benefits of the corporation whatsoever and are taken only to be taxed, being nothing more nor less than a hold-up. But hold-ups are seldom satisfactory to anyone in the long run and the thing probably will right itself in time."

*See Hospitals.

The nickname "Sunshine City" was given to St. Petersburg as the direct result of a promise made on September 1, 1910, by Lew B. Brown, publisher of the *St. Petersburg Independent,* to give away all copies of his newspaper every day that the sun failed to shine. Up to January 1, 1924, the paper had been given away only seventy-one times. This novel offer has attracted the attention of the entire country to St. Petersburg, and from an advertising standpoint it has been invaluable. The *Independent* is the only paper in the world that makes such an offer.

As a result of persistent agitation by Blue Sunday advocates, the city council on November 10, 1910, authorized the city attorney to draw up an ordinance prohibiting the sale of all kinds of merchandise on Sundays, except the prescriptions ordered by physicians of the city. "This will be a severe blow to the people who are compelled to purchase their meals on Sunday," commented one facetious newspaper writer, "as they will have to eat enough Saturday night to last until Monday morning." At the next meeting, the councilmen killed the Blue Sunday ordinance by a four to one vote.

Pinellas County was born on Tuesday, November 14, 1911, when the division bill passed by the State Legislature during the session of 1911 was ratified by a vote of 1,379 to 505. All evening the streets of St. Petersburg were filled with a joyful crowd celebrating the greatest victory Pinellas County ever had achieved. The county division movement, started a number of years before, had been bitterly opposed by the Tampa politicians, who did not want to see Pinellas Peninsula lost from "grand old Hillsborough County."*

The Poinsettia Hotel, one of the first modern hostelries of St. Petersburg, was opened Saturday evening, December 23, 1911. The proprietors were Dr. G. W. Williamson, Arthur L. Schultz and Mrs. E. M. Vroom.

The first airplane flight in St. Petersburg was made on February 17, 1912, by L. W. Bonney, the "dare-devil aviator," brought here by Noel A. Mitchell. A crowd of more than 5,000 persons gathered at Bayboro to watch the flight. Only a comparative few, however, paid the twenty-five cents admission charge to the grounds. The others stood on the outside and watched the flight for nothing. It was reported that Bonney collected only $182, and that his expenses were more than twice that amount, the deficit being made up by Mr. Mitchell.

The movement to secure good roads for Pinellas County resulted in the formation on February 19, 1912, of a Good Roads Association in St. Petersburg. Ed. T. Lewis was elected president; A. W. Fisher and Glen Taylor, vice-presidents; Joseph W. Taylor, secretary, and F. A. Wood, treasurer. G. C. Prather, A. T. Blocker, P. J. McDevitt and C. M. Roser were appointed to serve on the executive committee. As a result of the activities of the association a favorable vote was secured on a good roads bond issue about a year later.

St. Petersburg got its first white way lights during the summer of 1912, the first white way pole being installed on April 11, 1912, in front of Noel A. Mitchell's office at Fourth and Central. During the next two months the system was extended from Second street to Fifth.

---
*See Pinellas County.

During 1912 St. Petersburg experienced its first real estate boom. Property values soared and many new subdivisions were opened, particularly in the West Central section, backed by H. Walter Fuller and his associates. The sale of lots on West Central was started on March 12, Charles R. Hall opening the first subdivision after purchasing a tract from the Fuller interests. Another subdivision closer to town was sold at auction by the Florida West Coast Company on March 18, 19 and 21. The demand for business sites was as great as the demand for lots in the residential district and lots on Central between Second and Sixth streets more than tripled in value during the year.*

On a wager made with D. W. Budd, G. B. Haines drove to Tampa on June 11, 1912, in five hours and fifty-nine minutes. Mr. Budd bet him that an automobile could not get through on account of the heavy rains and bad roads, and Haines said he could make the trip in six hours. He left at 11 in the morning and arrived at the Tribune office in Tampa at 4:59, with one minute to spare.

*See Real Estate.

The Congregational Church, Fourth street and First avenue north, where the Post Office is now located

HISTORY OF ST. PETERSBURG 37

The people of Pinellas County took their first action for a system of good roads on December 3, 1912, when they approved, 489 to 505, a bond issue of $375,000. Marl roads were built with the money. For a time they held up well, but finally deep ruts were made by the rains and it was seen that more durable roads would have to be provided. A bond issue of $715,000 to build seventy-three miles of nine-foot brick roads was approved on November 16, 1915, 827 to 754. The roads were finished by November 15, 1916.*

The first special train of tourists reached St. Petersburg Thursday night, January 9, 1913, bringing more than two hundred winter visitors from Cleveland, Akron, Mansfield, Steubenville, Niles, and a number of points in Indiana. The train was met at the depot by a cheering crowd and a band.

The Plaza Theatre, built by George Gandy, was opened on Monday night, March 8, 1913, with Cammaranos' "Il Trovatore," played by the Royal Italian Company.

*See Streets and Roads.

This view connects with the view on the opposite page and shows Fourth street and First avenue north as it was in 1910—The Mason Hotel has since been built on the far corner

The site for the theatre was purchased by Mr. Gandy from Mrs. A. Dew on January 27, 1912, for the announced price of $34,000. The completed theatre represented an investment of approximately $150,000, the owner stated.

The West Central trolley extension was completed out to Twenty-eighth street by February 10, 1913. A group of city officials and officials of the various Davis companies made the trip on the first car and later a luncheon was served at the Poinsettia Cafe.

Saying that too much speculation in lots was injuring the business of the city, a number of real estate dealers took steps on February 12, 1913, to limit auction sales to one a week.

St. Petersburg and the rest of Pinellas County went "dry" for the first time on July 2, 1913, 778 voting in the county for prohibition and 668 against it. St. Petersburg split even on the issue, 359 votes being cast on both sides. The saloons were closed on Saturday night, July 5. The election was contested and after a bitter fight in the courts it was declared illegal on October 13. Licenses could not be secured by the saloon keepers and the saloons were not opened again until March 4, 1914, after another election had been held on February 3 and the wets won, 902 to 798. The Davis package law was passed by the State Legislature during the session of 1915, and the last saloon closed in St. Petersburg, voluntarily, during the summer of 1917.*

The Municipal Pier was opened in December, 1913, being accepted by the city officials on December 18. Contractor E. W. Parker paid a forfeit of $600 for not having it done on time. The pier was built after a long controversy between the Bayboro and anti-Bayboro factions. The original intention was to build the pier to twenty-eight feet of water and make it St. Petersburg's permanent freight pier. Later, however, it was decided to build a shorter pier and use it for freight purposes only until the Bayboro Harbor project was completed.†

The Spa, St. Petersburg's first modern bathhouse, was completed late in 1913. Bradford A. Lawrence, the owner, employed T. J. Rowland, of New York, to serve as swimming instructor. A lease to construct the bathhouse on the North Mole was granted to Mr. Lawrence by the city council on June 19, 1913. Under the terms of the lease Mr. Lawrence was to pay $500 a year from 1913 to 1917, $750 a year for 1917 and 1918, and $1,000 a year from 1919 to 1923. The buildings were to revert to the city at the end of ten years.

The St. Petersburg-Tampa Airboat Line, the first commercial airboat line in the country, was established in St. Petersburg late in 1913 by the Benoist Company, brought here through the efforts of P. E. Fansler and L. E. Whitney, secretary of the Board of Trade. The first trip with a passenger was made on January 1, 1914. An auction was held to determine who would make the first trip and A. C. Pheil won, paying $400 for the privilege. Tony Jannus, the company's star aviator, piloted the plane, and the trip to Tampa was made in twenty-three minutes; return trip in twenty minutes. The airboat company, while not financially successful, brought much publicity for St. Petersburg.

The Washington's Birthday celebration, held for nineteen years in St. Petersburg by the school children, was called off by the school board in 1914. The members of

*See Prohibition. †See Water Front Development.

the board, T. A. Chancellor, A. F. Thomasson and W. A. Holshouser, decided that the celebration interfered too much with the work of the children, months being spent in preparation for the event.*

The first election under the new commission form of government, approved by the voters on March 5, 1912, was held on July 1, 1914. J. G. Bradshaw was elected commissioner of public affars, T. J. Northrup commissioner of public safety and C. D. Hammond commissioner of public works. Although the new charter was not considered perfect, even by its staunchest supporters, it was an improvement over the old charter and provided, among other things, that the cost of paving could be assessed against the property owners. St. Petersburg's good road work might be said to date from the time the charter became effective. Before that, comparatively little paving had been done; thereafter, hardly a year passed without a large paving program. The new charter contained a recall provision, and on July 28, 1914, the city was treated to its first recall election. The three commissioners were charged with numerous more or less serious crimes, but they were retained in office by substantial majorities, indicating that the recall had been instituted on flimsy grounds.†

The completion of the Tampa & Gulf Coast Railroad to St. Petersburg was celebrated on September 22, 1914. The first passenger train, pulling fifteen coaches and carrying 1,500 persons from towns and cities along the line, was welcomed at the depot by a crowd of 3,000 and a barbecue was held in Williams Park. The Tampa & Gulf Coast later was absorbed by the Seaboard Railroad.‡

Edward F. Sherman, a tourist, was murdered on November 11, 1914, at his home at Johns Pass road and Twenty-ninth street by two negroes. Mrs. Sherman was beaten until she was unconscious. John F. Evans, a negro accused of the crime, was taken from the jail on the following night by a mob and hung from a telephone pole at Ninth street and Second avenue south. Ebenezer Tobin, another negro arrested, was taken to Tampa for safe keeping by the authorities. He was tried in Clearwater on September 17, 1915, found guilty of murder in the first degree, and hung on October 22.

The people of St. Petersburg cooked their meals on gas stoves for the first time on December 1, 1914. The construction of a municipal gas plant had been approved, 156 to 27, at an election held May 12, 1914, on a bond issue of $148,000 to purchase a site, build a plant and lay mains. Work progressed rapidly and on Thanksgiving Day of the same year gas was supplied for the home of J. G. Bradshaw, commissioner of public affairs. A few days later, on December 1, gas was turned into all the mains.§

A sixty-room addition to the Detroit Hotel, which cost $75,000, was opened on December 9, 1914. The hotel then accommodated 200 and the dining room 300.

The paving of West Central was completed on March 23, 1914, and was formally opened with a triumphal procession in which 175 automobiles took part. The contract for the "missing link" between Ninth and Sixteenth streets had been let on February 15.

The new Atlantic Coast Line passenger depot between Second and Third streets, which had been started on October 2, 1914, was opened on March 26, 1915. A. W.

---
*See Festivals and Celebrations. †See City Government. ‡See Railroads. §See Public Utilities.

Fisher bought the first ticket, paying fifteen cents for a ticket to Lellman to keep as a souvenir.

The Public Library, made possible by a donation of $17,500 from the Carnegie Corporation, was completed September 11, 1915, and opened to the public on December 1. At that time it had 2,600 volumes. Miss Emma Moore Williams was appointed librarian. The site for the library was donated by the city.*

A new charter, providing for a mayor and seven commissioners, was approved by the voters on December 28, 1915, 487 to 278. At the next election, on April 14, 1916, Al. F. Lang was elected mayor by a substantial majority. Commissioners elected were A. P. Avery, A. C. Odom, Jr., Charles R. Carter, R. L. Davison, A. F. Thomasson, J. S. Norton and J. Frank Harrison. One of the first acts of Mayor Lang was to push through an ordinance standardizing the benches along Central avenue and compelling the owners to paint them green.

St. Petersburg got its first golf course on January 1, 1916, when the St. Petersburg Country Club course was formally opened. The club was first discussed at a meeting of business men on February 9, 1914, the plan being fathered by officials of the Johns Pass Realty Company, allied with the St. Petersburg Investment Company. A year was required to get the necessary support, but by March, 1915, the required bond issue of $60,000 had been subscribed. Work on the course was started immediately under the supervision of A. W. Tillinghast. The clubhouse was started on November 20 and was formally opened on March 10, 1916. The first officers of the club were: Al. F. Lang, president; H. Walter Fuller, vice-president; H. M. Pancoast, secretary, and J. D. Harris, treasurer.†

Forty business men in December, 1916, signed petitions asking for the repeal of the ordinance prohibiting Sunday movies. The petition was tabled by the city commission on December 22 for fear of a "general uprising."

The clubhouse of the St. Petersburg Yacht Club was formally opened on June 15, 1917. Funds to build the clubhouse had been raised in December, 1916. The completion of the clubhouse marked the realization of the dreams of the men who had tried for years to make such a club possible. An effort to form a yacht club was made in 1909, but it was not successful, largely on account of the deplorable condition of the water front, which made yachting almost an impossibility. The movement was started again in 1916, and this time a permanent organization resulted.‡

The financial affairs of the various St. Petersburg companies founded by F. A. Davis, of Philadelphia, reached a crisis in October, 1917. Charles M. Allen, of New York, was named trustee. The assets of the companies were said to be $4,200,000 and debts $2,000,000. The trolley line was bought at forced sale at Clearwater by Jacob Disston, of Philadelphia, and Warren Webster and Horace F. Nixon, of Camden, N. J., for $165,999. They sold it to the city for $175,000. The land owned by the companies was purchased by George C. Allen, of Philadelphia.§

During 1918, St. Petersburg, like all other cities throughout the country, subordinated all things to the main task of winning the World War. Hundreds of St. Petersburg boys went into the service. The solution of civic problems was postponed and work on civic improvements was delayed.‖

---

*See Public Library. †See Golf Clubs. ‡See Fishing and Boating. §See F. A. Davis Companies ‖See War.

The women of St. Petersburg gained the right to vote on July 19, 1919, at an election called on a law passed by the State Legislature on May 31, 1919. The opposition to the law was not based primarily upon opposition to the idea of women being allowed to vote, but to a provision in the law which stated that the women could vote "at any or all elections" regardless of property qualifications. The city commissioners led the opposition, contending that the law would play havoc in bond elections. The law passed, however, by a vote of 154 to 148.*

A publicity tax of 2½ mills maximum was ratified by the voters, 278 to 84, at an election held July 30, 1921. Prior to this time the publicity tax was 1½ mills maximum.

On Tuesday, October 25, 1921, St. Petersburg experienced the worst storm in its history. Only three others are known to have compared with it in intensity. One was in 1848, when there was little in Florida to be damaged; another in 1884, and the third in 1910. The storm of 1921, worse than any of the others except the 1848 storm, developed in the Western Caribbean Sea, swung around the west end of Cuba, proceeded northward to the latitude of St. Petersburg, and then swung inward. The barometer fell to 28.81 by 2 o'clock Tuesday afternoon and the wind attained a velocity of sixty-eight miles an hour. Water from the gulf was blown inward until it rose six feet above mean low tide level at St. Petersburg. The damage was confined largely to the water front, although a few tin roofs and signs were blown away in the city proper. Piers that extended out into Tampa Bay were partially destroyed and a number of small boats anchored in the yacht basin were wrecked or sunk.

*See City Government.

The Jungle Club, formerly the clubhouse of the St. Petersburg Country Club

People who lived in the sections of St. Petersburg nearest the sea level experienced many thrills as the water came in from the bay and and overflowed their lawns, but their lives were never in danger. Within two days after the storm, a plan was worked out by the business men, led by Lew B. Brown, to loan the city $18,000 for rebuilding the Municipal Pier. The work was finished by January. Great excitement was caused when the storm was at its peak by a report that Pass-a-Grille had been wiped out. When a government ship reached there Wednesday it was learned that not one person had been killed or injured.

The opposition to Mayor Noel A. Mitchell, which had been increasing for some time, resulted in a recall election on November 15, 1921. The vote stood 1,374 to 1,033 in favor of the recall. Frank Fortune Pulver was elected mayor on December 24, following a white primary in which five candidates participated. Pulver received 2,172 votes to Mitchell's 1,412.*

Dorothy McClatchie, 18-year-old daughter of Mr. and Mrs. Charles McClatchie, 1475 Thirteenth street south, was attacked by a barracuda while swimming near the

*See City Government.

Looking west on Central avenue from roof of the Pheil Building, between Fourth and Fifth on Central

channel buoy a mile off the Atlantic Coast Line Pier on Saturday afternoon, June 17, 1922, with Mary Buhner. Miss Buhner made a valiant effort to save her chum, holding her up for more than a half hour after she had been attacked. When help finally reached them, Miss McClatchie was dead, having bled to death from a deep wound in the calf of her leg where the fish had bitten her. Miss Buhner later was awarded a Carnegie medal for her bravery. Miss McClatchie was a graduate of the St. Petersburg High School, class of 1922, and had been a member of the school's basketball and swimming teams.

In April, 1922, the heirs of General Williams applied to the circuit court for a restraining order to prevent the granting of the exclusive use of two roque courts in Williams Park to the National Roque Association. The suit was brought by Emilie E. C. Schirp, J. C. Williams, B. C. Williams, J. Mott Williams, Mary S. Fisher and Cornelia Mott Morse against the city, park board, the mayor and the members of the city council. A temporary injunction was granted and later the injunction was made permanent. As a result of this injunction, the park board began making plans for the removal of all games from Williams Park.*

*See Williams Park.

Looking east on Central from the Pheil Building, showing the Water Front

Work on the Gandy Bridge, the twenty-year dream of George S. Gandy, was started on September 24, 1922, the dredge "Tuscawilla" going to work on the west fill. By March 28, 1923, three dredges were working. The construction camp at Ganbridge, on the west end of the bridge, was completed by June 1. All piling had been made and all necessary materials purchased by December 1, 1923. The county commissioners let the contract for the paving of Fourth street extension, the road leading to the bridge from St. Petersburg, on December 14.*

The municipal power plant was completed on July 27, 1923, at the cost of $311,000. It was built to provide power for city purposes and at present supplies power for the trolley lines, car barns, gas plant and City Hall. When contracts with the Pinellas County Power Company expire, power also will be furnished for the water plant and the street lighting system.

A new charter, greatly curtailing the powers of Mayor F. F. Pulver and providing that future mayors should be chosen by an entirely different system, was passed on August 14, 1923, by a vote of 431 to 356. Lew B. Brown was chairman of the board which drafted the charter and A. P. Avery was vice-chairman. When the new charter was put into effect it resulted in a long drawn-out controversy between the mayor and the commissioners regarding their respective powers. The agitation culminated in the circulation of petitions for the recall of Mayor Pulver and Commissioners E. G. Cunningham, O. R. Albright, Charles R. Carter and Paul R. Boardman. The election was held on January 22, 1924. Mayor Pulver was recalled by a vote of 1,136 to 1,999. The commissioners were retained in office by the following votes: Albright, 1,106 for the recall, 1,986 against; Boardman, 1,130 to 1,970; Carter, 1,022 to 2,062, and Cunningham, 994 to 2,099.

A period of unprecedented building activity and growth occured during 1923. Two hotels, costing more than a million dollars each—the Soreno and the Mason—were started in the spring and completed in time for the next tourist season. Four other hotels also were built, as well as scores of apartments and hundreds of homes. St. Petersburg led the entire state in building for the first ten months of the year. Jacksonville and Miami forged ahead during the last two months, but the race for the lead was close. Jacksonville's total was $7,536,537; Miami, $7,228,567, and St. Petersburg, $7,124,460.

Many new subdivisions were opened during the winter of 1923 and 1924, and thousands of lots were sold to investors and home builders. Reports of the Chamber of Commerce showed that 40 per cent more tourists had come to the city than in any previous winter. Confidence in the future growth of the city and willingness to aid in making the growth possible were indicated in the Chamber of Commerce drive in January, 1924, when $65,000 was subscribed to a fund for boosting the city, only $40,000 having been asked for.

*See Gandy Bridge.

III

RAILROADS

PRIOR to the early '80s, when numerous railroad projects were started in Florida, Pinellas Point was isolated from the rest of the world. The nearest railroad point was Cedar Key, about seventy miles north of Clearwater on the West Coast. Cedar Key was the western terminus of the railroad of the Florida Railway & Navigation Company, which extended northwest to Fernandina, a distance of 155 miles. The road was standard gauge but the service was anything but punctual.

Tampa got its first railroad in 1884, but nothing was accomplished toward bringing a road to the site of St. Petersburg until Gen. J. C. Williams completed negotiations with the Orange Belt Railway, of which Peter A. Demens was president.*

Demens was the owner of a sawmill at Longwood, about ten miles southwest of Sanford, and had built a small railroad northward into the timber lands to bring logs to his mill. In 1885 the timber supply in the vicinity of Longwood became exhausted and Demens cast about for something else to do. He conceived the idea of building a railroad across the state, connecting the St. John's River with the Gulf of Mexico. Early in the next year he purchased the charter of the Orange Belt Railway, incorporated in 1885 by T. Arnold, H. Miller and H. Hall. Demens proceeded immediately to construct his road, narrow gauge, making the eastern terminal at Lake Monroe, on the Jacksonville, Tampa & Key West Railroad. To begin with he used the light 16-pound rails from his log road.

Shortly after work started, Demens' funds began to run low and he endeavored to secure financial assistance. Through his attorney, Andrew Johnson, of Orlando, he induced Josef Henschen to put in $20,000. He also obtained $15,000 from Henry Sweetapple, a Canadian, who had come to Florida for his health. A. M. Taylor, Demens' storekeeper, also put in about $2,000. These gentlemen incorporated the Orange Belt Investment Company, whose main business would be to build the Orange Belt Railway.

The railroad received donations of land along the proposed right of way. Judge J. G. Speer gave a half interest in 200 acres on Lake Apopka and the investment company surveyed and laid out a town, the present Oakland, which was made the headquarters of the investment company and the railroad. Demens wanted to call the town St. Petersburg, but Judge Speer insisted on the name "Oakland."

In order to permit completion of the road, $50,000 worth of bonds were issued and sold through Griswold & Gillett, a New York brokerage firm. With this money,

---
*See Life of Peter A. Demens.

25-pound rails were purchased, the lighter rails replaced, and the road completed in to Oakland. The first trains came into the town early in November, 1886. The settlers of the neighborhood gave a dinner to the builders on November 15, which afterwards was called Oakland's birthday and celebrated with public dinners and sports.

The completion of the Orange Belt to Oakland did not satisfy Demens. He wanted to extend it on to the Gulf. Josef Henschen opposed the idea, believing that it would be impossible for the road to make money in such an undeveloped country. But Demens induced Sweetapple and Taylor to support him, and Henschen was outvoted. Arrangements were made with Griswold & Gillett, the New York brokers, to handle the sale of 170 more bonds, of $1,000 denomination. In order to tide over until the bonds were sold, arrangements also were made with L. Lissberger & Company, money lenders of New York, to advance $30,000 a month in cash and the necessary 25-pound steel rails. With the completion of each ten miles of the road, five more $1,000 bonds were to be issued.

Demens met with success in securing large donations of land along the proposed right-of-way. The Florida Land & Improvement Company, the Lake Butler Villa Company, and the Disston Land Company—all controlled by the Disstons of Philadelphia—agreed to give the railroad one-fourth of all their lands within six miles of the railroad and one-half of all townsites. Numerous donations were given by other property holders along the road, all the way from Oakland to the lower end of Pinellas Peninsula. Many of the donations, however, were contingent upon the railroad being completed by December 31, 1887.

In the beginning, Demens had no intention of going to the property of Gen. J. C. Williams at Paul's Landing. He negotiated with the Disstons for a site which he termed as "on the key." In describing this proposed southern terminal to his brokers, he wrote: "The southern terminus of the road is the most important feature of the whole business and is in such a shape that I do not dare to write about it—will only state that we have a chance to have the only harbor which exists in Florida on the Gulf Coast and to build a commercial city of international importance." The negotiations for this site fell through, for some unknown reason, and Henry Sweetapple, treasurer of the company, entered negotiations with J. C. Williams regarding a townsite on his property. These negotiations were completed by Sweetapple on January 29, 1887, and provided that the railroad would be given one-half interest in the townsite of 500 acres when the road had been completed and a wharf built to twelve feet of water. Demens then wrote to his brokers as follows: "Gentlemen—Just received a report from our Mr. Sweetapple that he succeeded in making an arrangement with a certain H. Williams about getting one-half interest in 500 acres, with a mile frontage on the Gulf, just where we will have our terminus in case the 'key' cannot be had. There is eighteen feet of water right at the shore, and a splendid townsite there. Thus that last question is settled very satisfactorily."

The railroad began getting into difficulties from the start. Contracts were let to a number of contractors for grading and laying ties and work was started. But when the end of the first month came around, $30,000 was not received from the New York underwriters as promised, and only a small amount was received during the second month. The contractors and employes of the railroad began clamoring for their money. By borrowing from everyone he knew, and stretching his credit to the limit, Demens managed to continue. Later he met a man who introduced him to Drexel & Company's agent, E. T. Stotesbury, and to H. O. Armour's partner. From these sources the railroad secured $200,000 and the construction work went on. This money, however, gave him only temporary relief. Practically all of Demens' letters during the spring and summer which followed contained pleas for more money. To make the situation worse, L. Lissberger & Company failed to ship the iron as agreed and the entire construction program was delayed. Moreover, the rainy season was unusually bad, and the work of grading was interrupted; and late in the summer, an epidemic of yellow fever broke out in Florida, and the working force was demoralized.

The affairs of the company reached a crisis early in September, 1887. Creditors demanded their money and the property of the road was attached. The engines were locked to the rails. This proved such a shock to Henry Sweetapple that he suffered a stroke of apoplexy and died instantly. Demens succeeded in obtained $10,000 from his brokers and a compromise was made with the creditors. But the financial situation of the company became steadily worse. On September 19, Demens wrote a personal letter to L. Lissberger as follows:

"Dear Sir: I am sorry that you are still unable to comply with my calls for money. The reason I write you this personal letter is to assure you that I *ask only for*

The Orange Belt depot, on the site of the present Atlantic Coast Line depot. Photograph taken in 1888. The depot, the Detroit Hotel and the office building of the Orange Belt Investment Company, shown in the distance, were the only buildings in lower St. Petersburg.

the very least I can get along with. It is impossible to do anything if the money is not forthcoming exactly as I call for—no use to attempt to do the work, as it will only culminate in further trouble and disaster. Everything and everybody is disorganized and disgusted. I can do nothing without cash—all my time at present is consumed in trying to reconcile our creditors. They must be paid in order to have the thing going. When I wrote you that I want twenty thousand dollars between the 20th and 25th, I meant it, have to have it—every day the delay hurts us badly. Am going today to Orlando to try to get the bank not to protest our checks, as you can see from the enclosed letter from them. We cannot expect anything else. One-half of the contractors have quit, threatening lawsuits—we broke the contract by not paying in time and are helpless. A loss of time and money everywhere. I am alone—how can you expect me to go ahead under such circumstances? Have to organize two iron forces anew, send for men—cannot use the former contractor as he is obliged to lay only twenty miles per month and that will not fill the bill at present. In fact, have to organize everything anew, and must have all my time to do it—instead of that have to run to Orlando to reconcile the bank, lose a whole day and certainly tomorrow will be besieged again from morning till evening by creditors. Cannot buy anything for the stores—as invariably comes a reply 'settle your former bills'—and have to buy from stores here, losing all profit.

"In fact, I cannot run the business this way—as I stated to you in my official letter of today. I will have to give up. *It kills me.*

"Give me the money I ask for, see that your mills really roll 150 tons a day, send your son here to help me, and we will see the road through. I shift all responsibility from myself otherwise. I have done all I could, and cannot do more. You ought to understand it. Either we go through or we do not. I know we cannot if the money will not be here.

"I expect a telegram immediately upon receipt of this letter."

Despite this desperate plea, Demens did not get the help he wanted in time. The first of the year passed without the road being completed, and the railroad lost many of the land donations which had been promised. Demens was forced to borrow money at ruinous terms from a syndicate of Philadelphia and Chicago capitalists, and to place the fate of the railroad entirely in their hands.

The railroad was completed to the edge of the Williams property on April 30, 1888, and on June 8 the first train came into St. Petersburg from the eastern end of the line, on the St. John's River. The tracks were laid down to Second street in December and the pier was completed about a year later. The pier was over 3,000 feet long and the water was ten feet deep at the end at low tide, permitting ocean-going vessels to dock. About this time Sanford became the eastern terminus of the road, a connection being made with the town of Lake Monroe.

The Orange Belt failed to make money during the first year of operation. It continued to go deeper and deeper in debt. By the spring of 1889 it owed $900,000 to the syndicate of capitalists, composed of H. O. Armour & Company, of Chicago; E. W. Clark & Company, of Philadelphia; Ed. T. Stotesbury, of Philadelphia, and Drexel & Company, of Philadephia. On July 1, $55,000 was due in interest, and the money was not on hand—not even a fraction of it. The Orange Belt Investment Company owned about 200,000 acres of land, including 79,582 acres which it had obtained from the state, but no one wanted to buy it. There was nothing for the original backers of the Orange Belt to do other than accept what terms the syndicate cared to offer. Demens went to Philadelphia to handle the negotiations. He returned with a check for $25,250. Of this, $8,850 went to Henschen, $2,000 to Taylor and $14,400 to Demens. These payments represented only a small part of the capital which the men had invested in the road. It gave them nothing for their three years of service for the road.

New officers were appointed after the syndicate took over the railroad. They were: Wm. McLeod, president; George A. Hill, treasurer; Frank E. Bond, superintendent; S. H. Dare, purchasing agent; Joseph W. Taylor, general freight agent; A. L. Hunt, chief engineer, and H. H. Richardson, secretary.

Few changes for the better were made on the railroad after the syndicate took charge. When Demens had it, its main claim for distinction was that it was the longest narrow-gauge railroad at the time in the country. In most respects it was a joke. The tracks had been laid in a hurry, and, as a result, they were uneven and needed constant repairs. And no repairs were made for several years, the syndicate refusing to spend any more in the losing venture. It is a wonder the trains were able to get to the end of the line.

Most of the rolling stock was in as bad condition as the roadway. Some of the cars and locomotives had been purchased, second-hand, from the South Florida Railroad; a few locomotives came from an abandoned narrow-gauge road in Alabama, and the Orange Belt had built a few of the cars in its shops in Oakland. Nothing was first-class—hardly a train made a trip without a breakdown. The engines burned wood as fuel. When the wood was dry, and all other conditions were favorable, the engineer could speed up to fifteen or twenty miles an hour. Once, on a test trip, when Demens was showing off the road to Mr. Armour, the train raced along at forty—but that was when the roadway had just been laid. Later on, when the roadbed began to get rough, and when it happened that the fuel was wet, the train barely crawled, the engine leaking just about as much steam as was generated over the hesitating fire.

The train crews consisted of three men—the fireman, the engineer and a general utility man who labored along under the official titles of conductor, baggage master and express messenger. W. F. Divine, now a resident of St. Petersburg, had this last position for a number of years. He says that despite the multiplicity of his duties he was not worked to death during the first few years of the railroad's existence—busy days were few and far between.

When the syndicate took over the railroad it also acquired all the holdings of the Orange Belt Investment Company. These holdings included the one-half interest in the townsite of St. Petersburg, which had been deeded to the investment company on February 28, 1889. To dispose of this property the syndicate formed the St. Petersburg Land & Improvement Company, which secured all the deeds on October 6, 1890. The St. Petersburg office was in charge of Col. L. Y. Jenness, who played an important part in the development of the city. The company continued to sell its property until December 15, 1906, when it sold the Detroit Hotel and all remaining lands to C. Perry Snell, A. E. Hoxie and J. C. Hamlett.

Some of the bonds of the railroad were held outside the syndicate and in 1892 the Farmers Loan & Trust Company, of Philadelphia, to clear up the issue, started foreclosure proceedings in the United States Court at Jacksonville. On June 5, 1893, the road was sold for $150,000 to John P. Illsley and Joseph S. Clark, representing the syndicate. The outside bondholders received about 16 per cent of the face value of the bonds.

Efforts were made by the syndicate to develop St. Petersburg as a commercial port and also to bring settlers on the land along their right-of-way, thereby increasing the business of the railroad. But in both things the officials were unsuccessful and the railroad continued to lose money. The disastrous freezes during the winter of 1894-95, which killed many of the citrus groves in Florida and impoverished thousands of people, dealt the company another blow, and within two weeks after the last freeze the syndicate leased the railroad for ten years to Henry Plant, who operated it as a part of the Plant System, its name being changed to the Sanford & St. Petersburg Railway.

There is nothing to indicate that this change resulted in any material gain for St. Petersburg. It is said that Henry Plant, president of the Plant System, did not want to push St. Petersburg at the expense of Port Tampa, one of his creations, and refused to spend any money in its development. When a storm took about 500 feet off the end of the railroad pier, no effort was made to rebuild it, and St. Petersburg's hope of becoming a seaport went glimmering.

The only important improvement on the railroad during the Plant control was the widening of the tracks to standard gauge from Trilby to St. Petersburg, permitting through traffic of cars from the North. This improvement was made about 1897.

The Sanford & St. Petersburg Railway was absorbed by the Atlantic Coast Line in April, 1902. In commenting on the purchase, the *St. Petersburg Times* stated in the issue of April 12: "The policy of the Plant System has never been helpful to growing industries and new settlements in this section, and there is great room for improvement in this respect. St. Petersburg has no reason to feel disappointed over this big railroad merger. . . . . It is not very difficult to satisfy one's self that if any change at all follows it will be beneficial."

For a number of years the boosters of St. Petersburg agitated for a new passenger depot, asserting that the one then existing was a disgrace to the city, having an inadequate platform, poor lights and being dirty and too small. Late in 1904 the Atlantic Coast Line promised something better and bought the property of the St. Petersburg Novelty Works between Seventh and Eighth streets. The railroad announced it would build a model depot, but in February, 1905, it decided that the site would be used for a freight depot. The officials, however, promised to provide a more suitable passenger depot on the old site by moving the old depot and freight house across the siding, remodeling the buildings and joining them together under one roof.

Commenting on this plan, the *St. Petersburg Times* said in the issue of February 11, 1905: "The building will be—just plain wood—with probably a tin roof—which will be a great disappointment to the people of St. Petersburg, and we think ourselves the company should have treated us better as they had always promised to do, but—you know how big corporations are."

Work on the remodeled passenger depot started in October, 1905, and it was finished during the week of January 27, 1906. Even though it was not as good as the residents thought the city deserved, it was a great improvement over the old building. A short time later the streets leading to the depot were paved and a small park was made on the north side. Work on the park cost about $800 and was paid for by popular subscription.

The service given by the Atlantic Coast Line during 1906 must have been unusually bad, otherwise front-page space in the *Times* would not have been given to a statement made by Edgar Harrison that he was seriously considering the idea of establishing an overland transportation system between St. Petersburg and Jacksonville with a team of burros. "Mr. Harrison's proposed enterprise," remarked the *Times*, "is a most commendable one and should prove very profitable, and the entire community will await its further development with great interest. Mr. Harrison is confident he can easily cut a week or ten days off the time required for the A. C. L. to transport freight between the two points."

Even better evidence of poor service given by the railroad was furnished at an indignation meeting held Tuesday night, December 4, 1906, which was attended by a large percentage of the residents. Many complaints were made and Postmaster Roy S. Hanna produced records to show that not one of the trains carrying mail had arrived on time during the month preceding. One train had come in only fifty minutes late, he said, but that was an unusual record. A committee composed of Postmaster Hanna, R. Veillard and W. E. Heathcote was appointed to ask the postmaster-general to intervene and take such steps as might be necessary to give St. Petersburg "decent" mail service.

The Atlantic Coast Line depot, built in 1915

On December 22, 1906, the Atlantic Coast Line announced that it had authorized the purchase of $5,000,000 worth of new equipment, including 100 locomotives, 3,500 freight cars, 50 passenger coaches and 36,000 tons of 85-pound rails. Several weeks later high officials of the railroad visited the city and promised better service in the immediate future.

This promise was kept and during the next few years many improvements were made in the service. The roadbed was reballasted and heavier rails laid down. Trains began coming in on scheduled time, something St. Petersburg people never had been accustomed to in the past.

An ordinance granting permission to the Tampa West Coast Railroad to enter the city was passed unanimously by the city council on August 11, 1908. The city was restrained from going farther with the matter by a temporary injunction granted by the circuit court a few days later. The injunction was obtained by property owners along the proposed track of the road. They said it would lower the value of their property. Plans for the railroad did not materialize and nothing more was heard about a competitor for the Atlantic Coast Line until some years later.

The first through Pullman, "Salome," from New York City to St. Petersburg, arrived here Tuesday morning, November 16, 1909, over the Coast Line. "This is the first service between these cities ever inaugurated," said the *Times*, "and means much for St. Petersburg."

The Water Front and part of the business section as seen from an airplane in 1924

The first special train of tourists reached St. Petersburg Thursday night, January 9, 1913, bringing here more than 200 winter visitors from Cleveland, Akron, Mansfield, Steubenville, Niles and a number of points in Indiana. It was a big event for St. Petersburg and the train was met at the depot by a cheering crowd and a band.

Plans for a new brick freight depot to cost $100,000 were announced by the Atlantic Coast Line on July 29, 1913. The railroad officials, in making the announcement, stated they would give St. Petersburg the best terminal facilities in Florida. The plans of the railroad provided for the closing of Seventh street and a number of property owners in that section sought an injunction to prevent the company from going ahead with the work. The court decided against them, however, and the freight depot was completed on February 20, 1914.

The Atlantic Coast Line announced on June 2, 1914, that it would erect a new $100,000 passenger depot at once on the site of the old structure. Work of removing the old depot was started on September 16 and the new depot was started on October 2. It was opened Friday, March 26, 1915. A. W. Fisher bought the first ticket, paying 15 cents for a ticket to Lellman, first station out of St. Petersburg, to keep as a souvenir.

Talk of a new railroad to St. Petersburg was revived during 1913, about the time the Atlantic Coast Line announced its new improvements. The Tampa & Gulf Coast, which had built a road to Tarpon Springs in 1911, wanted to come down the peninsula,

St. Petersburg in 1924 as seen from an airplane flying at 6,000 feet

and sought a franchise to enter St. Petersburg. A number of persons in the city fought the new road, contending that it was not fair that another railroad should be allowed to compete with the Coast Line at a time when it was spending so much money on improvements. The issue stirred up a bitter controversy and the city fathers, to play safe, submitted a proposed franchise to the voters on June 2, 1914, giving the Tampa & Gulf Coast permission to enter the city as far east as Sixteenth street. The franchise was ratified by the voters, 343 to 17.

This favorable action of the voters did not end the difficulties for the Tampa & Gulf Coast. Property owners along the proposed right of way threatened to fight the railroad in the courts. After negotiations which ended nowhere, the railroad officials announced that they would do nothing further, and would give up the idea of entering St. Petersburg rather than get into a long, expensive battle in the courts. Realizing that the railroad was not bluffing, a group of St. Petersburg boosters bought in the land necessary for the right-of-way and enabled the railroad to come through to Ninth street. Later this property was turned over to the city at cost plus interest, even though it had increased many times in value in the meantime. The men who bought the land and made the railroad possible were A. F. Bartlett, John N. Brown, J. S. Davis, Roy S. Hanna, J. Frank Harrison, Noel A. Mitchell and A. C. Pheil. Altogether they bought ten acres of land and twelve lots, costing $12,000.

The completion of the Tampa & Gulf Coast, connecting St. Petersburg with Tampa, was celebrated on September 22, 1914. The first passenger train, pulling fifteen coaches, brought in 1,500 persons from points along the line, including Tampa, Tarpon Springs, Clearwater, Largo, Pinellas Park and Gulfport. A crowd of 3,000 was waiting at the depot and when the train pulled in, the celebrators went to Williams Park, where a barbecue was held, costing the city $554.

A double daily passenger service was started immediately by the Tampa & Gulf Coast, connecting with the Seaboard at Tampa. The first trainload of passengers coming from Jacksonville direct to St. Petersburg arrived on Monday, January 4, 1915. About this time the Tampa & Gulf Coast was absorbed by the Seaboard.

The Pinellas Special, through train from Jacksonville, was started by the Atlantic Coast Line in the fall of 1915. A limited train from Jacksonville also was operated by the Seaboard during this season.

During the World War the train service to St. Petersburg was curtailed, as it was in other sections of the country. Since the railroads were turned back to the private owners the service has constantly become better. At present, winter visitors can board their Pullmans in almost any of the important cities in the East or Middle West and come direct to St. Petersburg without changing trains. The excellent service given by the railroads has been an important factor in making St. Petersburg one of the greatest resort cities in the world.

IV

WATER FRONT DEVELOPMENT
(INCLUDING BAYBORO HARBOR)

"WE FOUND that nearly the whole water front was in an insanitary and unsightly condition—decaying seaweed and other vegetable, as well as animal matter, produced obnoxious odors, rendering residence along the front almost intolerable and beyond all question detrimental to health. . . . .

"The general appearance of decay and neglect between the two docks—old boats, rotting piers, all sorts of riff-raff, and especially where the outgoing tide leaves large stretches of sand covered with a variety of animal and vegetable matter in all stages of decay—does not well comport with a live, progressive city such as St. Petersburg aspires and claims to be."

This description of St. Petersburg's water front was contained in a report submitted to the Board of Trade by its water-front committee on July 21, 1908. The contrast between what the water front was then and what it is today indicates what the city has done in the way of development. The change did not occur over night—the Water Front Park of today is the result of long years of constant effort, bitter controversies, and almost endless negotiations. It is a monument to a small group of men who had "water front on the brain" and who fought unceasingly until they made their dreams come true.

The story of Water Front Park is linked up inseparably with the story of the development of Bayboro harbor, and so both must be given together.

St. Petersburg's water front, in the beginning, was a stretch of sand flats, extending several hundred yards out into the bay. At high tide, the flats were covered with shallow water; when the tide went out, the flats were exposed.

In the original town plat, made in 1888, the water front within the town limits was divided into twelve lots, each about 400 feet wide and 1,000 feet deep, numbered from one to twelve, beginning at the north. With the rise and fall of the tide, the shoreline varied as much as several hundred feet in many places.

The first development on the water front, if development it could be called, was the construction of a pier out to deep water by the Orange Belt Railway. This pier was started late in 1888 and completed a year later. At the end of the pier, the water was twelve feet deep, as stipulated in the agreement between General Williams and the Orange Belt officials. Along the north side of the pier was a little channel, made when sand had been taken to form the fill out to where the wooden structure began. For a number of years this channel provided the only way for small boats to get close to the shore. Large boats could not use it at all as the water was too shallow. Its usefulness was limited to a certain extent because the management of the Plant System at one time dumped into it a carload of rock, for the purpose, it is said, of eliminating water competition. The railroad had a steamer, the H. B. Plant, that ran to Tampa, and competing steamers could not use the pier.

As time went on, the water lots were sold to various persons, some of whom built rickety docks, boathouses and other unsightly structures. The flats were covered with decaying weeds and rubbish. The town grew, and the appearance of the water front grew steadily worse. As the Board of Trade committee stated, it did not well comport with a live, progressive city such as St. Petersburg aspired and claimed to be.

In the fall of 1901, Captain George L. King bought a little steamer, the Anthea, and undertook to enlarge the channel along the railroad pier so that his boat could navigate it at low tide, but he was stopped on December 1 by an injunction obtained by the railroad. As a result, the town was enraged and an indignation meeting was held in the Opera House. Upon a motion by A. P. Avery, it was unanimously decided to dig a channel straight in from the bay to the foot of First avenue north. On December 7, the contract was awarded to B. E. Coe, of Tampa, who agreed to do the work for $2,250. A few days after he started, however, he was stopped by a federal officer from Tampa, who said the city would have to get permission from the War Department before it could alter the water front. This permission was secured on February 2, 1902, and the work proceeded.

The disgraceful appearance of the water front at this time gradually aroused the ire of the progressive citizens and a movement was started to do something about a "bulkhead line." W. L. Straub and David Murray, appointed on the committee, sought government aid, but learned that the government would not do anything as long as the water-front property was privately owned, and they so reported to the Chamber of Commerce on July 2, 1902. The chamber then adopted the following resolution: "Resolved, that it is the sense of this Chamber of Commerce that the water front between Second avenue north to the city limits should be a corporate park."

So the idea of a municipally-owned water-front park began to materialize. The *St. Petersburg Times* fought for it incessantly, but it was a long time before it became an actual fact. The chamber appointed W. H. English to circulate a petition praying for the park, but evidently he did not pray loud enough, or the citizens failed to take any interest in the petition, for nothing ever came of the step.

The agitation over the water front gradually began to attract attention, however, and on December 16, 1903, Representative S. M. Sparkman brought St. Petersburg before Congress for the first time with a bill to make a harbor survey. Inasmuch as St. Petersburg did not have a harbor and was not large enough at that time to really need one, the report naturally was unfavorable. And so the matter rested for nearly a year.

The water front question came up again, however, after the Board of Trade was organized in 1905. It was now one of the leading issues of the city. Numerous plans were presented. Some advocated public ownership and beautification, but this plan was not entirely satisfactory, inasmuch as it made no provision for the shipping needs of the city. At that time there was no prospect of a freight harbor, Bayboro being unthought of. Bayboro basin was a mud flat—"Fiddlers' Paradise," the tourists called it.

Inasmuch as the public ownership plan did not solve the freight problem, the Board of Trade dropped it for the time being and approved Barney Williams' plan to build a seawall several hundred feet out from the existing shoreline and fill in the intervening space with sand pumped from a channel in front, this channel to be connected with deep water by another channel. There were many obstacles to this plan, one of the most vital being that all the land so made would belong to the water-lot owners. It was dropped after a while.

The first organized campaign for a municipally-owned water front came as a result of a meeting of water-front boosters at the home of Col. J. M. Lewis, on Second avenue north, on December 20, 1905. Those present were Col. Lewis, W. L. Straub, Ed. T. Lewis, Roy S. Hanna, W. H. English, A. H. Davis, C. Perry Snell and A. F. Bartlett. Col. Lewis presented a carefully drawn plan of the water front as he thought it should be, and all present approved it. Except for a few modifications made later as the town grew, this plan was used substantially as drawn.

The first official action on the water front came on February 2, 1906. A water-lot owner on the north shore planned to build a number of cottages on piers over the

The Water Front in 1905—the smokestack of the electric-light plant is seen at the left

water for rental and the prospect awoke even the sleepiest. On the above date Mayor R. H. Thomas signed Ordinance No. 100, which ordered that no buildings other than boathouses or bathing pavilions could be built on the water front except with plans approved by the building committee of the city council. The councilmen who signed this ordinance were T. J. Northrup, W. E. Allison, A. T. Blocker, F. E. Cole, C. P. Goodwin, Ed. T. Lewis and A. C. Pheil.

The water front became a vital issue in the 1906 election and resulted in a bitter campaign. The water front boosters won out, however, and secured a majority on the council. They also gained control of the Board of Trade. C. Perry Snell, Roy S. Hanna and A. F. Bartlett, strong advocates of public ownership, were appointed on the board's water-front committee. This committee got busy immediately and on April 5, 1906, it made to the city council an offer to buy four water-front properties, upon which it held options, and to hold them in trust until the time came when the city could take them over. These properties comprised all of water lot No. 1, owned in separate parcels by B. T. Quilling, W. H. Adams and C. P. Snell, and valued collectively at $1,320; the south one-half of water lot No. 2, owned by S. W. Bachman, held at $500, and all of water lot No. 5, owned by the St. Petersburg Land & Investment Company, and held at $3,300. On April 24, the council adopted a resolution accepting the offer of the committee and requesting it to go ahead and acquire, as far as possible, all the remainder of the water front. With this endorsement, the committee bought the lots, the deed running to C. Perry Snell, A. F. Bartlett and Roy S. Hanna as trustees, and kept on securing options on the remaining land.

The work of securing the water-front park was complicated by the conception, about this time, of the Bayboro harbor project by C. A. Harvey, "the most prophetic and daring real-estate operator who ever came to St. Petersburg." Harvey's plan was to buy all the swamp lands south of the city and reclaim them, dredging out a harbor, and make valuable land. The plan was visionary, but Harvey succeeded in convincing others that it would work out, and on June 13, 1906, the Bayboro Investment Company was incorporated with a large number of St. Petersburg's most influential citizens as stockholders.

The Bayboro project was destined to be the cause of long years of factional warfare, due to misunderstandings among men in the company and out of it. There were citizens who were opposed to the freight harbor at Bayboro and worked hard to establish the freight harbor where the yacht basin now is, in order to thwart the Bayboro plan. And there were men in the Bayboro company who struggled to delay work on the water front because they believed it was going to head off Bayboro. Still others favored a freight harbor adjoining the Atlantic Coast Line right-of-way on the south side. The result was a tussle between the conflicting interests which delayed and held up all the improvements, both for beautification and for a freight harbor, for a number of years.

An administration opposed to the water-front development was elected in March, 1908, and more time was lost. A $12,000 bond issue was submitted and carried in July, but for crosswalks and sidewalks only. The council adopted R. Veillard's resolution declaring the city's intention to purchase the entire water front, but as this had been done before it did not push along the project. Mayor Murphy sent in a special message urging action on December 1, 1908, but the council did not pay any attention. It was not until the water-fronters adopted new tactics that the council was spurred into action.

The boosters met on December 12, 1908, in the office of Ed. T. Lewis and the St. Petersburg Water Front Company was organized with the avowed intention of taking over the lots already held by the trustees, acquire the remaining property, make a yacht harbor, provide for freight along the south side, beautify the park, and so on, the whole to be turned over to the city, if wanted within a certain time, "on certain terms." Those present at this meeting were C. Perry Snell, A. F. Bartlett, Roy S. Hanna, A. H. Davis, W. L. Straub, W. H. English, T. J. Northrup, C. W. Springstead, Ed. T. Lewis, D. M. Lewis, R. L. Raymond, W. E. Allison, A. C. Pheil, S. M. Eddins and David Moffett.

The effect of this meeting was surprising. When the council learned that a private company was going to take a hand, the members rose up in indignation. Moreover, there was a feeling among some of the water-front boosters that if the company ever took over the property, and developed it, the city might never get it back. The upshot of the whole thing was that the council and a group of public ownership advocates secured the money to secure the lots. The deed, the first to go to the city for water-front property, was dated January 8, 1909. It included the water lots for which the trustees had paid $5,120 nearly two years before.

After the private opposition was squelched, the council kept on with the water-front work. The Little Coe channel, dredged out by B. E. Coe, of Tampa, in 1901, was cleaned out again. On March 23, 1909, $75,000 worth of bonds were voted, $25,000 of which were for the water front. Some time was lost in selling the bonds and more discussing of plans, and it was not until December that machinery for the city dredge was ordered. This was done only after a lengthy battle between those who wanted the city to do the work itself and those who thought the work should be let out on contract.

All the remaining water-front property, except that held by the Atlantic Coast Line Railroad and the electric-light company, was secured by the water-front committee of the Board of Trade for the city on December 24, 1909. This committee, composed of W. L. Straub, Lew B. Brown, Roy S. Hanna, Arthur Norwood and R. Veillard, had been busy for weeks securing options. Money was raised by A. F. Bartlett to buy the properties, the title going to Mr. Bartlett, Roy S. Hanna and Arthur Norwood to hold until the city arranged to take it over. The final arrangements were made on Christmas eve and resulted in what the *Times* termed "the best Christmas present that St. Petersburg ever had."

The dredge "Blanche," named in honor of Blanche Straub, daughter of W. L. Straub, "the persistent and insistent water-fronter," started work on the water-front improvements May 12, 1910, amid the cheers of a large crowd of spectators. Mr. Straub pushed the lever that started the machinery. The dredge was christened by Miss Beth Blodgett, daughter of G. W. Blodgett, president of the city council. The christening, and the starting of the work, was a big event in the history of the city and many of the city's notables were on board the dredge when the work started.

Another appropriation for the water front, $10,000, was included in a $100,000 bond issue presented to the voters on August 30, 1910. The entire bond issue carried by an overwhelming majority and work on the water front went ahead without interruption. On December 5, 1910, the administration, by Ordinance No. 246, formally and legally created the water-front park, establishing the outer line 500 feet from and paralleling Beach drive and First street south in front of the city and providing for the yacht basin.

Money spent on the water-front improvements from March 13, 1910, to March 1, 1911, totaled $22,205.21. It included $11,678.54 for purchasing land, $5,502.60 for building and maintaining dredge, and $5,024.07 for operating expenses.

On June 13, 1911, the voters approved, 113 to 60, still another appropriation for the water front, this one for $35,000. The item was included in a bond issue of $100,000, all of which was passed. The contract for constructing the first seawalls was let by the city council to W. B. Williams at $5.83 per lineal foot on July 20, 1911. By October, 1911, Beach drive and First street south had been paved for the entire length of the city, the foundations had been laid for all sides of the yacht basin, and the park improvements were started, the block between First and Second avenues north being filled, graded and planted with grass and shrubs.

While this preliminary work on the water front was going on, Representative Sparkman was working in Washington to secure a government appropriation for the Bayboro project, vitally necessary for the success of the beautification plan in front

This view and the view on the adjoining page show the Water Front as it was in 1910, before the Water Front improvements were started

of the city. He persuaded the Board of Engineers to have a harbor survey made, and the board instructed Major Spaulding, then district engineer, to make a report. The major came to the city, looked over the proposed harbor, made his report, and, as might be expected, it, too, was unfavorable. However, the major did not deliver a killing blow to the project. He said the harbor was feasible and that, if certain changes were made, he would have recommended it. The city council and Bayboro company took advantage of this phase of the report and immediately got busy, agreeing on the necessary changes. A special council committee, composed of Dr. M. H. Axline, John N. Brown and W. P. Pope, investigated, submitted a report embodying the changes necessary, and the council approved. Councilman J. J. Sullivan was the only one who objected.

W. P. Pope, representing the council, R. H. Thomas, the Bayboro company, and S. D. Harris, the Board of Trade, were then sent to Washington to appear before the Board of Engineers on July 18, 1911, and pray for another survey. Their prayer was granted and Captain Slattery, who had succeeded Major Spaulding, was instructed to inspect the water front again. He came on October 11, 1911, and by request met a large gathering of representative citizens at the Hotel Detroit to learn what they wanted. He was informed, by a unanimous vote to a resolution offered by F. A. Wood and seconded by Lew B. Brown, that St. Petersburg wanted her deep-water harbor at Bayboro and was ready to meet all the conditions prescribed by Major Spaulding's adverse report.

At low tide, in 1910, the boats which came into St. Petersburg's harbor were stranded. Large boats could not come in at all, even at high tide

Despite the promises of the gathering, Captain Slattery did not find the project even yet to his liking and in his report, made October 17, 1911, he refused to approve it. He stated that the harbor, as planned, did not provide for the future growth of the city and had too sharp a turn at the mouth. He also disapproved of it in certain other respects. Representative Sparkman, when he learned that the adverse report had reached Washington, did not give up the fight. Instead, he wired the Board of Trade to send a representative to the National Rivers and Harbors Congress in Washington on December 6. W. L. Straub was sent. When the St. Petersburg project came up, Straub and Sparkman plead for it so successfully that the city was promised that if the required changes were made, the project would be approved.

Mr. Straub hurried back to St. Petersburg, got the council and the Bayboro company together again, and the changes were made. The Board of Engineers then approved the project and recommended an appropriation of $40,000 for the channel and jetty. The appropriation was included in the next Rivers and Harbors bill, was reduced to $32,000 in the Senate, and passed. It was signed by the President in the Spring of 1912.

Despite this favorable action, opposition to the Bayboro project continued to appear in St. Petersburg, even among those who had attended the Detroit Hotel meeting and apparently had approved of the action taken. The city officials elected in March, 1912, were evidently anti-Bayboro. Instead of going ahead with the Bayboro development, they went ahead and began making plans for a big freight pier out from Second avenue north to twenty-eight feet of water. The great cost of such a project finally deterred them, however, and they compromised upon a pier to twelve feet

St. Petersburg as seen across the Yacht Basin—the Soreno Hotel is shown in the center

of water, which would serve as a freight pier until the Bayboro harbor was completed and as a recreation pier thereafter.

The opposition to Bayboro was due, in part, at least, to an honest belief that it would be impracticable to dredge a channel from deep water into Bayboro basin—that the channel would be filling up continually with sand. This contention was based upon a report of one of the government engineers, who stated that "St. Petersburg has no proper harbor. It is a half-mile from the short to twelve feet of water and a mile to a depth of eighteen feet, and any channel dug to deep water would be across the flow of the tide and would surely fill up." The anti-Bayboro faction asserted that it would be better to go out to deep water, rather than to attempt to bring deep water in.

About a year later, publc sentiment crystalized in favor of the Bayboro project again, and the city council employed Henry C. Long, municipal expert from Boston, to make the Bayboro plans. His plans were approved by the Secretary of War on May 24, 1913. They are the plans which are still recognized by the government as the official plans for Bayboro.

The new city commission form of government went into effect July 1, 1913, and the commissioners apparently were farsighted business men who realized the importance of the water-front development, as well as the Bayboro project. One of their first acts was to call an election on October 7 on a bond issue for $227,050, $43,500 of which was to be for the water front and $41,850 for Bayboro. The water-front issue was

Looking east from the Soreno Hotel. The view shows the north side of the Yacht Basin, the Spa and the Municipal Pier

to be used for completing the seawall and the recreation pier. The Bayboro appropriation was to purchase 600 feet of water frontage at the harbor and to pay for dredging the inside of the basin, both required by the government as the city's part of the work. The water-front bonds carried 174 to 34 and the Bayboro plans 173 to 39, indicating the strong sentiment in favor of the development.

The city put up a bond of $50,000 on December 20, 1913, to guarantee that the city's share of the work on Bayboro harbor would be done. The bond was signed by H. A. Murphy, A. P. Avery, T. A. Chancellor, F. A. Wood, G. B. Haines, Cramer B. Potter, W. E. Heathcote, A. Welton, Ed. T. Lewis and H. A. Farmer. The four specific requirements were that the city dredge the basin ten feet deep, keep it dredged out, construct in eighteen months one pier as planned by Long, and connect the pier with a railroad; also, to acquire 600 feet of water frontage at the harbor, and to construct and maintain a municipal wharf and warehouse.

A. C. Pheil, who was awarded the contract for dredging the basin for the city, started in May, 1914. The government dredge "Florida" arrived on August 16, 1914, and started work several days later on dredging out the channel. The work was completed by the government dredge on December 14, 1914, and shortly afterwards the stone jetty was completed.

The government did its share of the project but the city fathers failed to do theirs. Only part of the $41,850 voted in October, 1913, was ever used for that purpose. The one pier required was not completed until the fall of 1922. A trolley connection with the pier was not made until the fall of 1923. Part of the delay was caused by the war; part because of the attitude of the city officials. The $50,000 put up by the city could have been forfeited as a result, but instead, two extensions of time were allowed by the Board of Engineers of the Rivers and Harbors congress.

On September 3, 1921, the city commission and the Chamber of Commerce tentatively approved E. C. Garvin's plans for building a million-dollar commercial pier into Tampa Bay from the south side of Bayboro, approaches along Eleventh and Twelfth avenues south. The harbor committee of the chamber recommended the abandonment of the old Long plan and urged the city planning board to set aside a zone for commercial and industrial purposes in Bayboro section between Seventh and Thirteenth avenues south and east of Third street. Mr. Garvin recommended that the city should complete its part of the harbor project so that the government would dig out the channel to fifteen feet.

Failure to get additional government assistance, coupled with other obstacles, held up this project. In the Spring of 1923, H. H. Richardson, harbor expert of Jacksonville, was employed to make a survey of St. Petersburg's requirements and determine what should be done. He recommended a modification of the Long plan.

Although St. Petersburg made slow progress on the Bayboro project, it never slackened in its efforts to complete the water-front development. The recreation pier was completed in December, 1913, and work on the seawalls was pushed steadily ahead. The walls on the north side of the yacht basin were completed even before the recreation pier, and the walls on the south side were completed in January, 1914.

Thereafter, appropriations were made for building seawalls north and south of the basin.

Considerable difficulty was encountered by the city in acquiring a small section of the water front held by the St. Petersburg Investment Company, parent company of the F. A. Davis companies. Negotiations extended over a number of years without success. Innumerable agreements were made, only to be broken by one side or the other. A settlement was made only when the Davis companies got in financial difficulties and were forced to accept any terms the city offered.*

Much less trouble was encountered in dealing with the Atlantic Coast Line regarding its water-front lots. An agreement was reached in 1911 whereby the company leased the lots to the city for ninety-nine years, in return for which the city made their fill out to the present pier, 150 feet in width and 300 feet long. The last section of water-front property was acquired in 1916 when, on December 22, a bond issue of $16,200 was approved to buy land owned by Mrs. David C. Cooke.

The city's expenditures on the water front and Bayboro are indicated by the following bond issues approved by the voters: March 23, 1909, $25,000, water front; August 30, 1910, $10,000, water front; June 13, 1911, $35,000, water front; April 26, 1912, $60,000, water-front and city docks; August 24, 1913, $43,500, water front, $41,850, Bayboro; February 16, 1917, $106,200, water front; November 12, 1919, $35,000, water front. This makes a total of $356,550.

St. Petersburg's water-front and harbor developments are not yet completed, but a good start has been made—a wonderful start, considering the obstacles that had to be overcome. An adequate harbor, or deep-water pier, is still a problem of the future. But the city already has its Water Front Park, more than twenty blocks long, and each year it is becoming more beautiful and a greater asset to St. Petersburg.

---
*See F. A. Davis Companies.

V

F. A. DAVIS COMPANIES

IT IS impossible to estimate how much good was done for St. Petersburg by the various companies fathered by F. A. Davis, publisher, of Philadelphia. Certain it is, however, that the companies played an important part in the development of the city, giving it an impetus at a time when outside assistance was needed badly. For the stockholders many of the projects turned out disastrously, it is true, but for St. Petersburg they helped materially in bringing prosperity.

Mr. Davis came to Pinellas County for the first time in 1890 because of poor health. He spent a few months in Tarpon Springs and was completely cured. While there, he met Jacob Disston, also of Philadelphia, who owned many thousands of acres of land on the peninsula. Mr. Davis had faith in the future growth of this section of Florida and decided to assist in its development. With the financial assistance of Jacob Disston and others, he organized an electric light and power company and built a plant at Tarpon Springs. But the people of Tarpon Springs showed no inclination to help in any way, either in giving a satisfactory franchise or in buying the current, preferring to stick to "the good old kerosene."

Mr. Davis finally became disgusted with Tarpon Springs and turned his attention elsewhere. A short time before he had visited the infant town of St. Petersburg and and had been deeply impressed with its possibilities so, naturally, when he made up his mind to move the plant, he turned toward St. Petersburg. He acquired some land on the water front, near the foot of Central avenue, and applied for a franchise. It was granted at an election held on February 2, 1897, the St. Petersburg Electric Light & Power Company was formed, and the removal of the plant to St. Petersburg was started under the direction of A. P. Weller, who later served as manager of the company.

The lights were turned on August 5, 1897. It was a history-making event. It was described in *"The Medical Bulletin"* of September, 1897, as follows: "The latest improvement of magnitude in St. Petersburg is the completion and inauguration of the electric-light system. By this enterprise every part of the town is brilliantly illuminated. A formal inauguration of the new undertaking occurred in St. Petersburg on August 5 and was the occasion of much rejoicing among the inhabitants and invited guests. The trial illumination was a success in every particular. No pains had been spared by the company to provide the latest scientific devices, and the appliances connected with the work are of the most improved construction."

Evidently *"The Medical Bulletin"* was stretching the facts a trifle, for the plant was anything but perfect. In telling about the old plant, Benjamin F. Measy, later treasurer of the company, stated: "It certainly was the most primitive and out-of-date aggregation of machinery that had ever been collected, as it were, from the four corners of the earth, but after being put together under the able direction of A. P. Weller, manager of the company, the light it gave was certainly wonderful to behold."

The plant may not have been ideal but it was far better than none at all. It gave St. Petersburg a distinction which other towns on the peninsula lacked and for two or three years it served in a fairly satisfactory manner, the machinery running from sunset to midnight. There were no meters and the users paid a flat rate per lamp and could use as much as they wanted to. Naturally, this did not work out for the best interests of the company, and later on, when improvements were made, meters were installed and the people paid for what they used.

The money for financing the electric-light company did not come from St. Petersburg. Mr. Davis put up part of it himself and the rest he obtained from influential friends in Philadelphia. Later on, when Mr. Davis promoted other projects in St. Petersburg, he got the money in the same way. A few St. Petersburg men subscribed for small blocks of stock, it is true, but most of the money came from the Philadelphia capitalists.

The electric-light company was not a success financially during those early years. Checks had to be sent weekly from Philadelphia to cover the deficits. Despite this failure to make a profit, Mr. Davis did not lose heart. He had a vision of a great city and he reasoned that when the growth came profits would come too. So he went ahead and began planning for a trolley line. And, as before, he enlisted the aid of his Philadelphia friends.

Late in 1901, Mr. Davis applied to the town council for an electric-railway franchise. Strange to say, he did not have an easy job getting it. A certain faction was determined that the town should not give away any of its "rights," and endeavored to block the franchise. And this despite the fact that only a "dreamer" would ever have sought to put a trolley line in a town which then had less than 2,000 people. On December 1, 1901, the franchise was passed by the council, but it was an impossible franchise, inasmuch as it bound the company in every way possible and gave nothing in return. Mr. Davis and his associates naturally rejected it. After a heated controversy, a revised franchise, suitable to the company, was submitted to the voters on February 4, 1902, and it passed 104 to 48, even though it was bitterly attacked by the *Sub-Peninsula Sun* on the ground that "it would prevent other traction lines from entering the city." Inasmuch as a traction line from Tampa to St. Petersburg was then contemplated by a Colonel Martin, this was quite an issue. But the interurban never materialized, and not because of the franchise, either. It died a natural death because of a lack of finances.

One of the terms of the franchise was that one mile of track should be laid in six months and two and one-half miles in eighteen months. Mr. Davis, however, encountered great difficulty in getting enough money to go ahead. But no one else wanted the franchise, so Mr. Davis had little trouble in getting a time extension.

Along about 1902, the St. Petersburg Investment Company came into existence. This was the holding company for the St. Petersburg Electric Light & Power Company and the proposed trolley company, the name of which was the St. Petersburg & Gulf Electric Railway Company. The investment company secured options from the Disstons on about 4,000 acres of land west of the city. These options, together with the stock of the power and trolley companies, constituted the basis upon which those who purchased the stock of the investment company were to make "untold profits."

Months rolled by before Mr. Davis could secure enough money to start construction work on the electric railway. He brought all his indomitable enthusiasm to bear

The electric-light plant on the Water Front, near the foot of Central avenue, as it was in 1904

and eloquently presented the glowing future of the city, but even then he had hard work persuading anyone to put up cold cash. Finally, in February, 1903, Mr. Davis succeeded in getting a group of Philadelphia men to visit the city, and when he got them here he won them over. He took them over the proposed route of the trolley line and convinced them that in no time this jungle land would be dotted with prosperous farms, inhabited by a happy people. Members of the group included William C. Haddock, director of public works, Philadelphia; Cyrus S. Detre, senior member of Detre & Blackburn, stationery and blank-book manufacturers of Philadelphia, and director of the Lincoln Trust Company, and Ex-Senator H. C. Hackett. Mr. Detre was one of the first to invest. He put up $5,000. Then Mr. Haddock subscribed. And then a block was sold to George S. Gandy, another friend of Mr. Davis. With these prominent men behind the company, its success was assured. Comparatively little trouble was encountered in selling the rest of the stock.

Work on the trolley line was started on May 30, 1904. The first car was run on September 28, 1904. Like the inauguration of the light company, this was an event of great importance to St. Petersburg. It was described as follows by the *St. Petersburg Times* of October 1, 1904:

"The entire line, equipment and operation of the St. Petersburg & Gulf Electric Railway within the corporate limits of St. Petersburg as described by the franchise is now complete, and the first trip over the completed route was made the occasion of an appropriate celebration by the suburban people at the north end, which was the last point reached in its construction.

"The stop at Booker Creek is only until a bridge can be built, when the line will be extended out among the magnificent orange groves and pretty homes of the Pinellas Peninsula to the Gulf and famous Pass-a-Grille. The completed system will provide for our people and crowds of tourist visitors the ideal trip to be had in Florida, and will be a great factor in the upbuilding and development of the entire peninsula."

And so the first street car was run in St. Petersburg. It was a dinky little thing, holding not more than twenty people, but that was plenty large enough. During those first few years the cars were seldom crowded. Lots of times they ran empty from one end of the line to the other. The town was so small that when the residents wanted to go anywhere they could get there by walking. So the company lost money from the start; but, undaunted, it went ahead completing the line to Gulfport. The town wasn't called Gulfport then; it was called "Disston City." Later on it became "Veteran City," when Captain J. F. Chase had a vision of attracting Grand Army veterans there from all parts of the country. Finally the town became Gulfport, but that is a different story.

Work on extending the line was rushed and early in 1905 it was completed. For the first time people of St. Petersburg could go to Gulfport and thence to Pass-a-Grille without jogging along over impossible roads or making the entire trip by water. The trolley company operated a boat from Gulfport to Pass-a-Grille which met the cars so the entire trip could be made in a little more than an hour. On holidays the line did a rush business. But on weekdays the conductor did not have a hard job in collecting fares.

For the next few years hardly anyone in St. Petersburg believed that the trolley line could live. They labelled it a foolhardy undertaking. It probably was. If it had not been for those weekly checks from Philadelphia to meet the deficits it would have gone under within six months. As it was, it continued to live and continued to be one of St. Petersburg's greatest assets, making future growth possible.

During 1906, the company extended Brantley Pier out 2,000 feet into deep water. The intention was to make this the commercial freight pier for St. Petersburg, the freight to be unloaded from the boats onto the freight cars of the traction company to be delivered to the consignees. This was done. For many years the "electric pier" was the "deep-water harbor" of the city. It also served as the recreation pier. In the wintertime it swarmed with tourist anglers intent on capturing some of the fighters of Tampa Bay.

After the trolley line was in operation, Mr. Davis made a determined effort to enlist some of the local people in his companies. Stock was sold to a number of the biggest boosters of the city. They did not have much faith in the success of the enterprise, but they realized it was a good thing for the city and that it deserved support. So they gave it. On Friday night, July 21, 1905, a meeting of the St. Petersburg stockholders was held, Mr. Davis stating that the enterprises should be controlled as much as possible by local people. An advisory board was elected, J. Frank Harrison being chosen chairman and W. L. Straub, secretary. Other members were A. F. Bartlett, J. H. Craven, R. H. Thomas, W. E. Heathcote, T. A. Chancellor, Ed. T. Lewis, Roy S. Hanna, W. C. Henry, Arthur Norwood, T. K. Wilson, Dr. A. B. Davis, M. L. Stoner and F. R. Singlehurst. One of the first acts of the board was to lower the fares charged by the traction company, the fare to Disston City being reduced from 15 cents going and 10 cents return to 10 cents each way, and the fare to "Denny's Corners" from 10 to 5 cents.

The Tampa Bay Transportation Company was formed in 1906 by Mr. Davis and his associates. An idea of Mr. Davis' plans at that time are given in a news story which appeared in the *St. Petersburg Times,* May 19, 1906. It quoted a story which had been printed a few days before in the *Philadelphia North American,* and read in part as follows: "Capitalists in Philadelphia plan to make St. Petersburg one of the most important ports in the South Atlantic States. . . . Among those largely interested in the project are Jacob S. Disston, Joseph C. Sibley, his son-in-law; Wm. E. Heathcote; B. F. Measey, recently appointed cashier of the state treasury (Pennsylvania); F. A. Davis, George S. Gandy, Dr. John B. Shoemaker, Edward T. Davis, Wm. H. Houston, Wm. C. Haddock and Cyrus S. Detre." The plan was to extend the electric pier to deeper water so that ocean-going vessels could land. The idea was

The trolley line in 1906, as represented by Cartoonist W. L. Straub

to develop St. Petersburg as a port for West Indian, Gulf and South American trade, and to be ready for heavier commerce by the time the Panama Canal was completed.

Although this ambitious plan never materialized, the Tampa Bay Transportation Company went ahead developing freight traffic on the bay, and early in the summer of 1906 purchased the steamer Favorite in New York for the announced price of $80,000. The steamer was brought to St. Petersburg on October 17, 1906, and shortly afterwards it was put on the Tampa run. Early in 1907, the company made arrangements with the Seaboard Air Line Railroad whereby St. Petersburg would be included among the cities served by that road, so that tickets could be purchased direct and freight could be billed through to St. Petersburg from any point on railroads allied with the Seaboard, connections being made at Tampa by the company's boat. During the next year it was found that the Favorite could not be operated profitably and it was sold, the company purchasing the Vandalia, an 81-foot boat, which could carry 100 tons of freight and 150 passengers. About this same time the Tampa Bay Transportation Company was dissolved and was succeeded by the St. Petersburg Transportation Company.

The Independent Line, owned by a company of which H. Walter Fuller was president, proved to be a strong competitor of the St. Petersburg Transportation Company during 1908. This line owned the H. P. Plant, the Manatee and the Favorite, acquired some time after it had been sold by the Davis interests. On March 27, 1909, F. A. Davis announced that the Independent Line had been absorbed by the St. Petersburg Transportation Company and that the capital stock had been increased from $25,000 to $100,000. H. Walter Fuller was elected president; George S. Gandy, vice-president; T. K. Wilson, general manager, and George B. Oliver, secretary and treasurer. Directors were F. A. Davis, George S. Gandy, H. K. Heritage, and Franklin Davis, of Philadelphia, and H. Walter Fuller, T. K. Wilson, George B. Oliver, Roy S. Hanna and C. A. Harvey, of St. Petersburg.

The consolidation marked the entrance of H. Walter Fuller into the Davis organization. Within a comparatively short time Mr. Fuller became as important a factor in the various companies as Mr. Davis himself. He was made president of some of the companies and manager of the others. Although Mr. Davis remained the guiding head, Mr. Fuller was placed in a position of the highest responsibility and was given almost a free hand in directing the companies' work and in trying to reduce the heavy burden of debts the companies then carried.

During the next few years the activities of the various companies became more and more extensive. In addition to the trolley line, the boat line and the electric-light and power business, the organization entered the real-estate business on a larger scale, disposing of lands already in its possession and buying more for development and sale. In order to avoid complexity, it is necessary to discuss each of these activities separately, without going into great detail regarding the separate companies, all of which were closely interlocked. Inasmuch as the St. Petersburg Electric Light & Power Company was the parent of the entire organization, it will be taken up first.

Electric Light Company

As stated before, the service given by the electric-light company was never above reproach during the early years of the company's existence. The equipment was inadequate and had a regretable habit of breaking down at crucial moments. Such a breakdown occurred in August, 1904, while Mr. Davis was in the city with Wm. H. Houston and Frank Meazy, of Philadelphia, to whom he was extolling the merits of the plant. During their talk, both dynamos at the power plant went out of commission, plunging the city in darkness. This did not phase Mr. Davis, as he was used

A busy day for the Veteran City trolley line in 1907—an excursion drew the crowd; most of the time the cars ran nearly empty

to even worse catastrophes. The records show that both Mr. Houston and Mr. Meazy continued to be identified with the company, so Mr. Davis must have drawn heavily upon his reserve store of eloquence. To the townspeople, Mr. Davis offered an apology for the breakdown and announced that the power company had secured new capital and would proceed immediately to get better equipment.

Although some improvements were made shortly afterwards, the service continued to be below the standard desired by the consumers, and many complaints were made. In November, 1909, these complaints crystallized into a movement to organize an independent light and power company. Glowing promises were made by the company officials to provide better service immediately, but it was not until a year later that anything was accomplished, and then it was nothing more than to provide all-night service, something the city had been demanding for years. "After many patient years," remarked the *St. Petersburg Times,* "we have all-night service at last. It is no longer necessary to leave off calling on your best girl at midnight for fear of the lights going out."

The water-front site of the power plant was sold to the city about this time and Mr. Fuller announced on June 16, 1911, that the company had purchased a tract at Central avenue and the A. C. L. tracks as a site for the new plant, which would be completed within eighteen months. Early in 1914, the new plant was in operation and the old plant on the water front was torn down, removing one of the last unsightly structures from the land which then was being converted into a city park. Following completion of the new plant, the service given by the company was excellent.

The St. Petersburg Electric Light & Power Company was sold to the General Utilities & Operating Company, of Baltimore, on April 12, 1915. The name was changed to the St. Petersburg Lighting Company. Shortly after it took over control, the new company had a fight on its hands because of the efforts of the Pinellas Electric Light & Power Company to secure a franchise. After a long fight in the city council, a franchise was drafted and an election was called for June 29, 1915. The franchise was rejected, 339 to 336. The Pinellas company did not give up, however, and another election was called for December 7, 1915. This time the franchise was approved, 374 to 315. Nothing ever came of it. The rising price of materials evidently deterred the company from going ahead. On August 5, 1916, the city entered a ten-year contract with the St. Petersburg Lighting Company to provide street lights at 5 cents per kilowatt hour.

Electric Street Railway

The trolley line operated at a loss for many years. The heavy shipments of fruit and fish which Mr. Davis had so confidently expected would be received were very slow in coming, and the transportation of freight never proved to be profitable, even though it was continued for a number of years. Likewise, the line carried comparatively few passengers, and the revenue was insufficient to meet the expense. The company unquestionably would have gone bankrupt during this period had it not been for large loans made by Jacob Disston, of Philadelphia. The loans probably were made for two reasons: first, because Mr. Disston owned large tracts of land in the vicinity of Veteran City and, consequently, was vitally interested in having that section provided with rail connections to St. Petersburg; second, because he was interested in the welfare of the Davis companies and in the development of St. Petersburg. Whatever the reason, he made the loans, taking mortgages on the company's property, and the company lived.

According to a statement in the *St. Petersburg Independent* of February 7, 1911, the trolley company broke even for the first time during the winter of 1909-10. Simultaneously with this announcement, the company officials gave "absolute assurance" that it would build a seven-mile extension of the Gulfport line to Johns Pass within the next year. However, the plans of the company were changed and the extension was not built.

During 1910, the trolley line was extended to Bayboro at the expense of the Bayboro Investment Company and the first car made the round trip on January 5, 1911, with officials and stockholders of the Bayboro company on board. The line was turned over to the trolley company for operation. An extension to Coffee Pot

Before the trolley line was extended to the end of the Electric Pier, Old Dobbin furnished motive power

Bayou through Snell & Hamlett's North Shore development was built the same way, the first car running over the line on April 18, 1912. The West Central extension (see below) was built out to Twenty-eighth street by February 10, 1913, and completed to the Jungle in the Summer of the same year. The Bayboro line was extended to Big Bayou at the expense of the Big Bayou Railway Company during the Winter of 1913-14 and the first car was run on March 12, 1914, carrying nearly a hundred invited guests. F. R. Kennedy, owner of the Grand View subdivision, was the chief backer of the Big Bayou Railway Company. As in the case of the other extensions similarly constructed, the completed line was turned over to the trolley company for operation.

From 1909 until the final collapse of the Davis organizations, the trolley company was in almost constant negotiations with the city regarding the disposition of its lot on the water front at the foot of Second avenue north. The city needed the lot in its program of water-front development; the trolley company refused to give it up except at a price the city was unwilling or unable to pay. Numerous agreements were made, only to be broken off by one side or the other. In August, 1916, after the trolley company's pier had been replaced by the municipal pier, the city officials endeavored to force the company into an agreement by charging it $100 a month for the privilege of run-

Among its other real-estate activities, the F. A. Davis companies made many improvements at Pass-a-Grille. This view shows the island as it was in 1904

ning its car to the pier-head, and also by charging $50 a month for the docking of the Favorite. The company retaliated by stopping the running of its cars on the pier, much to the dissatisfaction of the people. The lot was not acquired by the city until the trolley line was purchased.

Real Estate Activities

The first important venture of the Davis organization into the real estate field was made shortly after the completion of the trolley to Disston City. The Florida West Coast Company, a subsidiary of the St. Petersburg Investment Company, was formed to sell lands which had been acquired from the Disston interests. Working in conjunction with the company, Capt. J. F. Chase started a movement to establish Veteran City close to Disston City, his idea being to attract veterans of the Civil War who wanted to spend their last days in the Sunny South. Two hundred acres of land were laid out and Veteran City was dedicated with impressive ceremonies on April 5, 1905. Rev. J. P. Hoyt delivered the dedicatory prayer and Hon. E. R. Gunby, of Tampa, gave the principal address. Several hundred persons attended. Despite this auspicious beginning, Veteran City did not meet with prosperity. Only a few veterans could be persuaded to buy property and the whole venture soon fell through. The Florida West Coast Company continued selling its lands, however, for a number of years, with indifferent success.

The next big venture of the allied companies was made in 1911 and 1912, when large tracts of land west of the city were purchased following the conception by H. Walter Fuller of the plan of extending Central avenue westward to Boca Ceiga Bay. During 1912, several large subdivisions on West Central were sold at auction and a number of tracts were sold to other developers. About the same time, Davista (now Pasadena) was laid out, and plans were made for a high-class residential district.

The trolley line out West Central was built during 1912 and on February 10, 1913, the first car ran out to Twenty-eighth street, in Hall's subdivision. Officials of the road, city officials, newspaper men and a number of prominent citizens were on the car. Afterwards, luncheon was served at the Poinsettia Cafe. Those present were H. Walter Fuller, Charles R. Hall, A. P. Avery, F. A. Wood, A. F. Thomasson, H. K. Heritage, R. E. Ludwig, H. C. Case, S. Paul Poynter, Wm. H. Wright, Thomas Dormer, Charles T. Evans, G. F. Hogdon, Henry A. Borrell, Jacob N. Vodges, R. E. Sykes, J. A. Potter, Joseph W. Taylor and George N. Sarvin. The road was opened to the public on the next day.

The paving of West Central was ordered by the city commissioners on December 11, 1913—the biggest contract ever let by the city. The laying of the first bricks, on February 19, 1914, was quite an event. Major J. G. Bradshaw laid the first, then others were laid by Mr. and Mrs. Charles R. Hall, Noel A. Mitchell, F. A. Wood, H.

The Electric Pier, built by the F. A. Davis companies where the Municipal Pier is today

Walter Fuller, C. D. Hammond, Vincent Ridgeley and J. B. Robinson, while a large crowd looked on. Because of difficulties in getting permission of property owners in changing the course of the avenue from Ninth to Sixteenth streets, the paving began at Sixteenth. Originally, the avenue jogged at Ninth. The West Central boosters insisted that it be straightened out so that it could be run straight through from bay to bay. Finally, after months of negotiations, an agreement was reached, and on February 15, 1915, the contract was let for the paving of this "missing link," as it was called. The completed paving was formally opened on March 23, 1915, with a triumphal procession in which 175 automobiles took part. It was a real celebration.

Although the development of the West Central section was apparently a financial success, it was one of the things which helped to bring about the final collapse of the allied Davis companies. At the outbreak of the World War, large sums of money were being spent by the companies for West Central and Davista improvements. More was being spent for improvements at Gulfport, Pinellas Park and Pass-a-Grille. And, although the war affected the real estate market adversely, and the sale of lots was at a minimum, the companies continued with their improvements. The result was inevitable. The financial condition of the companies gradually became more precarious—and in October, 1917, the crash came.

Following a conference of Philadelphia creditors in this city, H. Walter Fuller resigned as general manager of the companies. It was stated that the assets were $4,200,000 and the debts $2,000,000, and that Mr. Fuller owed $800,000 personally. Charles M. Allen, of New York, was named as trustee. Efforts were made immediately to realize on some of the properties of the companies. Lots on West Central were sold at public auction on February 18 and 19, 1918, and at Davista on February 20. The properties brought in more than $100,000, according to announcement by the company officials.

On April 29, 1918, attorneys for the St. Petersburg Investment Company and allied companies applied for a friendly receivership for a sufficient period to work out a bonding plan. On May 3, 1918, Charles M. Allen was named receiver. On May 14, Mr. Allen accepted an offer of $70,000 from the Florida Masons for the Southland Seminary property, built at the head of Coffee Pot Bayou for school purposes and acquired by the Davis companies for a part in its development program.

The receipt of these various sums of money, however, did not prevent the complete collapse of the companies. On May 25, 1918, Horace F. Nixon, of Camden, N. J., applied in the United States Court in Jacksonville for foreclosure on claims aggregating $161,800, comprising sixty-three mortgages. On June 25, the Pennsylvania company, trustee for the bondholders, applied for foreclosure of the trolley company. R. E. Ludwig, Guy B. Sheppard and T. W. Weston were named as appraisers. H. Walter Fuller announced on January 25, 1919, that he had severed all connections with the companies.

The long-disputed waterlot, No. 4, finally came into the possession of the city on February 15, 1919, after the city had placed the company in a position where it was forced to sell at a price fixed at $20,000. The money was paid over to Receiver

Allen, who turned it back immediately for back taxes and paving liens, the payment of which the company had resisted for five years.

On April 7, 1919, the trolley line was bought at forced sale at Clearwater by Jacob Disston, of Philadelphia, and Warren Webster and Horace F. Nixon, of Camden, N. J., for $165,000. They held mortgages totaling $250,000. Under terms of an agreement between the new owners and city officials made in Philadelphia on June 30, the city started operating the trolley system on July 1, with an option of purchase. On August 30, 1919, the city voted 350 to 103 in favor of a $250,000 bond issue, $175,000 of which was for the purchase of the properties and $75,000 for improvements, including $22,500 for car equipment and $28,500 for track construction. Work was started on September 3, 1919, on the removal of the old Favorite Line pier and warehouse, signifying the fall of the Davis empire.

F. A. Davis did not live to see the utter collapse of the companies which he had fathered. He died on January 12, 1917, at his home in Philadelphia ten months before the financial condition of the companies first became really acute. However, it is the shock and worry brought on his death.

VI

CITY GOVERNMENT

St. Petersburg became a city on June 6, 1903, when the bill legalizing the new city charter was signed by the governor. George Edwards was mayor at the time and the councilmen were O. T. Railsback, J. B. Wright, F. R. Chapman, F. E. Cole, J. C. Hoxie, F. P. Klutts and W. A. Coats. On June 18, 1903, the council voted to issue $23,000 worth of bonds, $13,000 to pay all floating indebtedness of the water-works and $10,000 for duplicating the water-works plant and to extend the system On July 2, the council considered a petition to spend $500 for municipal advertising. After due consideration, the councilmen decided that $500 was too large a sum to spend all at one time for such a purpose and the petition was disregarded.

Mayor Edwards declined to run for re-election the next spring and R. H. Thomas was elected, getting 161 votes to J. A. Armistead's 151 and B. C. Williams' 33. Councilmen elected were A. T. Blocker, T. J. Northrup, A. C. Pheil, T. R. Chapman, F. E. Cole and C. P. Goodwin. One of the first problems considered by the new administration was the need for better streets. On July 2, 1903, a $10,000 bond issue was passed for the paving of Central avenue and also "such residential streets as could be paved with the money remaining." This resulted in a controversy which lasted nearly six months and caused considerable friction between the mayor and the council. Three blocks of Central, from Second to Fifth streets, were finally paved.

On April 16, 1905, the city council passed an ordinance calling for an election on a $50,000 bond issue, $25,000 to be used for water-works extensions, $10,000 for streets, $10,000 for sanitary channel and improvement of the water front, and $5,000 for sewerage. The Board of Trade at its next meeting recommended that the issue be reduced to $35,000, the members saying they did not believe a $50,000 issue would carry. The matter resulted in a controversy between the council and the mayor and an amended ordinance, providing for a $35,000 issue, finally was passed over the mayor's veto. When submitted to the voters on July 18, 1905, it carried, 67 to 24. It provided $15,000 for the water-works, $10,000 for streets, $10,000 for sewerage and $5,000 for a new City Hall. Another controversy then arose over whether brick or marl should be used in paving the street. A compromise finally was agreed upon whereby brick was to be used on the business streets and marl in the residential sections.*

T. J. Northrup was elected mayor at the election held Tuesday, March 6, 1906. Mr. Northrup polled 126 votes, F. E. Cole 98 and Edgar Harrison 76. Councilmen

*See Streets and Roads.

elected were A. C. Pheil, Ed. T. Lewis, W. E. Allison, C. W. Springstead, David Moffett, S. M. Eddins and B. C. Williams.

The water-front problem came up before the council at its meeting on April 24, 1906, when a committee of the Board of Trade announced that it had secured options on four keystone water-front properties and would buy them and hold them in trust for the city until such time as the city wanted to take them over, provided the council approved. The council passed a resolution authorizing the purchase and also requesting the committee to go ahead and acquire, as far as possible, options on all the remainder of the water front.

A movement to widen and straighten Central avenue through the Ward & Baum addition to Ninth street, making it 100 feet in width to conform with the remainder of the avenue, was started early in the Spring of 1906. The movement was fostered by A. C. Pheil and met with the approval of the council. It was not until 1909, however, that the project was accomplished.

The city council passed a $63,000 bond issue on October 25, 1906, providing for $29,000 for the water front, $16,000 for the high-school building, $10,000 for widening Central avenue, $5,000 for schools and $3,000 for street crossings. Another controversy followed the authorization of this bond issue. The faction opposed to the water-front development joined with another faction which did not like the site chosen for the high school, and they took their fight to the courts. In December, 1907, the State Supreme Court decreed that the issue was illegal. Immediately there-

This photograph, half of which is shown on the adjoining page, was taken from the northeast corner of Fourth and Central, looking toward the southwest

after the council passed an ordinance calling for an election on a new bond issue of $80,000. It provided $25,000 for the high-school building, $16,000 for the purchase of water-front property, $9,000 for the improvement of the channel, $5,000 for sewer extensions, $4,000 for crosswalks, $12,000 for buying the remaining privately-owned property at Mirror Lake and $9,000 for widening Central avenue. The election was held on February 4, 1908, and all the improvements were defeated by large majorities.

Dr. H. A. Murphy, candidate on the Citizens' Protective League ticket, was elected mayor at the election on March 3, 1908. Dr. Murphy received 158 votes, A. P. Avery 131 and T. J. Northrup 5. Mr. Northrup had retired from the race before election day. Councilmen chosen were F. E. Cole, R. Veillard, S. E. Bodman, A. F. Freeman, H. A. Kellam, J. C. Blocker and James S. Norton.

One of the first acts of the new administration was to call an election July 28, 1908, on a $12,000 bond issue—$7,000 for steam pump and other water-works improvements and $5,000 for crossings and hard roads. The issue passed with scarcely any opposition: for crosswalks, 166 to 29; for waterworks, 161 to 31.

Although the water-front problem was of the utmost importance at that time, the council delayed action until late in December, when the St. Petersburg Water Front Company was formed for the purpose of taking over the water front and developing it. Alarmed at this proposal, the council got busy and immediately made arrangements for acquiring the property in the city's name. Early in January, 1909, the council called an election for March 23 on a $75,000 issue, divided into two

Central avenue, west of Fourth street, in 1910

sections: $45,000 to include improvements on the water front, sewers, Central avenue and purchase of shell mound, and $30,000 for schools. Both issues carried by big majorities: $45,000 issue, 190 to 29; $30,000 issue, 180 to 39. The $30,000 issue later was invalidated by the Supreme Court on the grounds that a city could not issue bonds for school purposes.

Evidently encouraged by the public support of the bond issues in March, the council in May called for an election on July 19 on a $10,000 issue, including $67,500 for paving, $5,000 for sewers, $10,000 for the water front, $10,000 for the water-works and $7,500 for a fire station, jail and police alarms. The proclamation was not made properly and the election was postponed until August 30, 1910. All items of the issue carried by majorities ranging from three to one to four to one.

A. T. Blocker was elected mayor March 1, 1910. Mr. Blocker received 205 votes, Edgar Harrison, 135 and David Moffett 129. Councilmen chosen were M. H. Axline, G. W. Bodgett, John N. Brown, C. B. McClung, W. B. Pope, J. J. Sullivan and R. E. Sykes. An audit of the books showed many errors and a number of shortages. A better system of bookkeeping was ordered and an annual audit recommended. Salaries of city officials were fixed as follows: Mayor, $250; assessor, $450; clerk, $1,020; attorney, $500, and treasurer, $150, plus fees. The tax levy was fixed for the year at 21 mills. The budget for the year was $47,000, $10,042 of this being required for interest on outstanding bonds.

On November 17, 1910, the council passed an ordinance establishing all lands owned by the city around Reservoir (Mirror) Lake as a city park.

Imperfections in the existing form of government were recognized by many of the citizens about this time and on March 17, 1911, a citizens' committee, composed of W. L. Straub, C. W. Springstead, A. F. Bartlett, John N. Brown and W. B. Pope reported to the council in regard to the matter of the city adopting the commission form of government. Copies of the charters of other cities were submitted by the committee. The council received the report, placed it on file, and discharged the committee. A motion was carried to appoint a committee of five to draw up a new charter: H. A. Murphy, G. W. Blodgett, W. B. Pope, M. H. Axline and W. L. Straub.

Another $100,000 bond issue was placed before the voters on June 13, 1911. It included $35,000 for the water front, $5,000 for street crossings, $5,000 for sewers, $5,000 for the water-works, $15,000 for improvement of Reservoir Lake and Lake Park and $35,000 for street improvements. The issue carried by big majorities.

The commission form of government was approved by the voters at the next election, on March 5, 1912, the vote being 361 for and 78 against. A. C. Pheil was elected mayor at the same election. He received 324 votes, C. E. Chambers 252 and Edgar Harrison 82. Councilmen elected were G. N. Sarven, J. J. Sullivan, Cramer B. Potter, R. E. Sykes, R. Veillard, Charles Braaf and Joseph W. Taylor.

The city council on April 26, 1912, called for an election on June 11 on a $200,000 bond issue. It passed as follows: $25,000, water-works bonds, 395 to 81; $60,000, water front and city docks, 303 to 147; $5,000, city park, 389 to 81; $65,000, street paving and sewers, 433 to 51; $10,000 for fire department, 394 to 74; $20,000 for sewer extensions, 413 to 54; $9,000 for city hospital, 402 to 51; $6,000 to buy waterfront lots at Bayboro, 362 to 72.

The charter bill permitting the commission form of government passed the State Legislature during the session of 1913 and was signed by the governor on May 14. Arrangements were immediately made in St. Petersburg to elect the new officials. Due to the fact that certain candidates for the commission, unfavorable to the white people, had strong negro support, a white primary was held on June 25, at which J. G. Bradshaw was selected for commissioner of public affairs, T. J. Northrup, commissioner of public safety, and C. D. Hammond, commissioner of public works. The primary

A celebration was held when West Central was opened in 1913

election was ratified at the regular election on July 1 by a substantial majority. The charter provided that the term of office of the commissioners should be determined by the number of votes cast for them. Mr. Northrup received the most votes, so he was to stay in six years; Mr. Bradshaw, next, four years, and Mr. Hammond, last, two years. Mr. Bradshaw was chosen mayor.

The new government found itself without money. The city accountant reported that all the money had been spent for paving and the water front. The city had been paying a third of the cost of paving and the paving expenditures had reached the total of $465,000. The new city charter, however, permitted the city to escape from the paving burden in the future, inasmuch as the cost was to be borne by the property owners on the streets paved.

On August 24, 1913, the commissioners called for an election on October 7 on a $227,050 bond issue: water front, $43,500; reservoir park, $15,000; Bayboro harbor, $41,850; incinerator, $20,000; woman's building, $7,400; paving, $20,500; waterworks, $41,000; fire department, $11,00, and redemption of revenue bonds, $26,800. The money for the water front was to complete the seawall and make the final payments on the new recreation pier, as well as for dredging out the yacht basin and clearing away the old electric pier. The bond issue carried five to one.

The new city charter contained a recall provision and early in the summer of 1914 petitions were circulated by a number of citizens demanding the recall of the commissioners. One hundred and sixty names were needed and 240 were secured. The election was called for July 28. All the commissioners were retained in office, the election resulting as follows: Commissioner of public affairs, J. G. Bradshaw, 343; Edward C. Allen, 282; commissioner of public safety, T. J. Northrup, 334; R. Lee Davidson, 297; commissioner of public safety, T. J. Northrup, 334; H. A. Farmer, 176, and C. R. Carter, 107.

C. D. Hammond was re-elected as commissioner of public works on June 1, 1915. He received 461 votes and his opponent, George H. Sarvin, 112. Shortly after the election the opposition to the commissioners broke out again, and on August 3, 1915, they were served with warrants charging them with misfeasance and nonfeasance in office. Many charges were made, one of the most important being that they had diverted to other purposes $15,000 of the $41,500 approved by the voters on October 7, 1913, for the improvement of Bayboro harbor. The commissioners also were charged with having failed to have made a full examination of the city books and accounts as required by law. The commissioners, however, were able to prove that they had done nothing illegal and they were found not guilty by Judge LeRoy Brandon on October 28, 1915.

In the meantime, on August 24, 1915, a new charter commission was elected at a special election as follows: A. F. Thomasson, J. Frank Harrison, S. D. Harris, Wm. G. King and John N. Brown. Several months later the commission recommended a new charter providing, among other things, for a mayor and seven commissioners. It was approved by the voters on December 28, 487 to 278.

At the next election, on April 4, 1916, Al. F. Lang was elected mayor by a substantial majority over his opponents, Noel A. Mitchell, J. W. VanDeventer, Ed. T. Lewis and J. C. McNabb. Commissioners elected were: two years, A. P. Avery, A. C. Odom, Jr., Charles R. Carter; one year, R. L. Davison, A. F. Thomasson, J. S. Norton and J. Frank Harrison.

The new city commissioners and mayor took office July 1, 1916. The 1916 budget by departments was as follows: mayor's department, $20,000; financial, $4,135; public works, $38,770; public utilities, $6,452; library and advertising board, $9,500; park board, $7,987; hospital board, $2,000; interest on bonds, $49,608; sinking fund, $8,000; old debts, $8,000. The rise in property values allowed a greatly increased assessment and a levy of only 11 mills yielded a revenue of $176,000.

Mayor Lang started in with a sign-removal campaign, getting unsightly and dangerous overhanging signs off Central avenue. July 15, 1916, was set aside as "Sign Pulling Down Day." Shortly afterwards he forced through an ordinance standardizing in shape, color and size all benches along the avenue. The color selected was green.

On December 22, 1916, the city commission called an election for February 16, 1917, on a $180,000 bond issue including: purchase of property known as railroad lots, $12,000; improvements to Tomlinson Pier, $2,800; septic tank system, $30,000; purchase of water lot No. 4, $20,000; purchase Cooke property on water front,

Fishing from the Municipal Pier in 1924, the Spa in the background

$16,200; brick paving, $4,000; fill and seawall, $90,000; improvement to city buildings, $5,000. The issue passed by a good majority. The sale of the bonds was delayed for many months, however, by a suit brought by Herman Merrill. It was not until October 25, 1917, that the issue was validated by the State Supreme Court. By that time the cost of materials had advanced because of the war and it was stated that the delay cost the city at least $30,000.

Late in December, 1916, forty business men signed a petition asking for a repeal of the ordinance prohibiting Sunday moving pictures. It was tabled by the city commissioners on December 22 for fear of a "general uprising."

At the election held April 4, 1917, J. F. Harrison, J. S. Norton, A. F. Thomasson and R. L. Davidson were re-elected as commissioners. During the next year, W. F.

Smith was appointed to the commission to fill out the unexpired term of A. C. Odom, Jr., who left the city.

Al. F. Lang was re-elected mayor on Tuesday, April 2, 1918, receiving 469 votes to 235 for his opponent, Noel A. Mitchell. A. P. Avery, Charles R. Carter and W. F. Smith were re-elected to the commission without opposition.

J. F. Harrison and A. F. Thomasson were re-elected to the commission on April 2, 1919, and George W. Fitch and Arthur Norwood were chosen to succeed J. S. Norton and R. L. Davison. Members of the charter board elected were George S. Gandy, Sr., L. D. Childs, A. R. Welsh, C. W. Springstead, W. L. Watson, Ed T. Lewis, R. H. Thomas, John H. Thorn and A. R. Dunlap.

The right to vote was given to the women of St. Petersburg on July 19, 1919, at an election called on a law passed by the State Legislature on May 31, 1919. The vote in favor of equal suffrage was 154 to 148. The opposition to the measure centered on a provision which stated that the women could vote "at any and all elections." The city commission, of which A. P. Avery was chairman, contended that this would invalidate bond issues, inasmuch as the state law required that voters on bond issues must own a certain amount of property. To leave the women vote "at any and all elections," regardless of property qualifications, would cause serious results, it was stated. Despite the opposition, the bill passed, and for some time thereafter bond elections were complicated by having the votes divided into two classes, the property owners and the non-property owners. Those who led in the fight for equal sffrage were Mrs. Nellie R. Loehr, president, and Mrs. E. G. Porter, secretary, of the Equal Suffrage League.

Eleven out of twenty-one amendments to the city charter suggested by the charter board were approved by substantial majorities on August 12, 1919. The amendments which passed were the ones which had been approved by the commission; the others failed.

A $100,000 bond issues, the first after the war, was carried on November 12, 1919, as follows: $10,000 for bandstand and comfort stations in Williams Park, 72 to 24; $35,000 for waterfront, 76 to 23; $5,000 comfort station, 77 to 22; $15,000 bridge at Booker Creek, 74 to 24, and $25,000 sewer system, 75 to 23.

Noel A. Mitchell was elected mayor on April 6, 1920. Mr. Mitchell received 875 votes; L. D. Childs, 535; Cramer B. Potter, 383, and George W. Fitch, 268. E. H. Lewis, Charles R. Carter and Virginia Burnside were elected to the commission. Mayor Mitchell got in trouble as soon as he took office. The commissioners refused to confirm his appointments and he filed a mandamus suit to compel them. The worst fight centered over the appointment of Dr. W. E. A. Wyman to the position of city health officer held by Dr. W. J. Tanner. The controversy ended with a fight in the City Hall when Dr. Tanner took issue with remarks made by the mayor. The mayor suffered painful injuries. Dr. Tanner handed in his resignation and Dr. Wyman took office without any more opposition. Dr. Tanner was arrested, but released without payment of a fine.

On June 18, 1920, bond issues totaling $448,000 were ratified, including $105,000 for the city gas plant, $125,000 for the city water plant, $50,000 for municipal railways, $125,000 for sewers, $8,000 for lights in waterfront park, $35,000 for fire department equipment, $20,000 for white way lighting and $20,000 for street paving. A proposed issue of $112,000 for construction of streets, drives and boulevards in Waterfront Park was defeated, 142 to 206.

A. F. Thomasson was re-elected to the commission again at the election on April 5, 1921. Other commissioners elected were E. G. Cunningham, John J. Woodside and O. R. Albright. The losing candidates were E. A. Hinds, A. T. Anderson, Walter P. Fuller and Joseph A. Sharp.

Bond issues totaling $260,000 were approved by the voters on May 1, 1921. Of the total, $65,000 was the extension of municipal railways, $175,000 for the extension of the municipal gas plant and $20,000 for improvement of city buildings, including alterations to the city hall.

The opposition against Mayor Mitchell, which had been growing for some time, resulted in a movement to recall him from office in the fall of 1921. The direct cause

The Soreno, St. Petersburg's first million-dollar hotel, completed in 1923

of the recall was a so-called "booze party" in the city hall. Petitions charging drunkenness were circulated by Thornton Parker and the required number of signatures being obtained, the commissioners called a recall election for November 15, 1921. The vote was 1,374 to 1,033 in favor of the recall. Five candidates besides Mr. Mitchell entered the race for the office and in order to prevent a splitting of the vote among Mr. Mitchell's opponents, a white primary was called for December 5, 1921, the candidates agreeing to abide by the decision and all withdraw except the one getting the largest number of votes. The result of the primary was: F. F. Pulver, 1,035 first choice votes; S. D. Harris, 831; Dr. George W. Fitch, 303; Dr. E. C. Beach, 246, and C. M. Blanc, 150. At the regular election, held on December 24, 1921, Mr. Pulver polled 2,168 white votes and 4 negro votes, and Mr. Mitchell 1,109 white and 303 negro. Mr. Pulver, with a majority of 760, was declared elected.

Mayor Pulver was re-elected on April 4, 1922. The vote was as follows: F. F. Pulver, 1,578 white, 15 negro; George W. Fitch, 985 white, 24 negro; Noel A. Mitchell, 267 white, 331 negro. Mrs. Virginia Burnside and Charles R. Carter were re-elected to the commission and R. R. Pearce was chosen to succeed E. H. Lewis.

A bond issue of $365,000 was approved on July 1, 1922, which included $50,000 for Bayboro Harbor, $15,000 for a sewage disposal plant and $300,000 for a municipal power plant. Another bond issue, of $1,037,000, was approved in December, 1922. It provided $125,000 for an incinerator, $463,000 for drainage, $79,000 for bridges, walls, etc., $15,000 to purchase land at Crescent Lake Park, $20,000 for city warehouse, $160,000 for city water-works, $50,000 for municipal gas plant, $30,000 for municipal street railways, $75,000 for City Hospital, $10,000 for Mercy Hospital, $8,000 for fire station and $2,000 for installation of toilets at Williams Park.

A movement to recall the mayor was launched late in 1922 by E. J. Foster, editor of the *Pinellas Post*, and J. M. Atkins, financial secretary of the carpenters' union. Foster and Atkins were backed by some of the church people of the city who believed the mayor was not enforcing the prohibition laws properly. Petitions were circulated and the required number of signatures obtained, and the commissioners ordered a recall election to be held. The matter was carried to the courts, however, and the petitions were thrown out because the affidavits accompanying them did not show that the mayor had done anything for which he could be removed from office.

Foster and Atkins then started circulating new petitions, charging that the mayor had used "abusive and profane" language when addressing them and that he had distributed "Bolshevik" circulars purporting to have come from the Foster faction. An election was called for June 5. The recall of the mayor was advocated strongly by the *St. Petersburg Independent*.

Again the matter was taken to the courts, a writ of injunction being sought by seventeen citizens in an attempt to prevent the disgrace which would result to the city from an attempt to recall the second mayor in succession. After hearing arguments which lasted all day, Judge M. A. McMullen of the Circuit Court denied the writ and ordered the election to be held, on June 5, 1923. Mayor Pulver's friends rallied to his support and voted, 1,249 to 963, to keep him in office.

E. G. Cunningham, O. R. Albright, Paul R. Boardman and John J. Woodside were re-elected to the commission at the election held April 3, 1923. The defeated candidates were Roy L. Dew, B. A. Lawrence, Jr., David R. Grace, Bainbridge Hayward, S. R. McIntosh, P. K. Smiley, O. B. Welsh, Ray Kimball, George Burnett, A. B. Gerner, Walter S. Ross.

A new city charter was adopted on August 14, 1923, by a vote of 431 to 356. Only about 17 per cent of the qualified voters of the city were sufficiently interested to cast their ballots. The new charter provided for the establishment of eleven departments and divisions as follows: Department of finance, department of public utilities, department of public works, division of health, division of police, division of fire, division of law, division of taxes, board of public parks, library and city advertising board, hospital board. It also curtailed the powers of the mayor and provided that in the future the commissioner receiving the highest number of votes should hold that office. Lew B. Brown was chairman of the board which drafted the charter and A. P. Avery was vice-chairman.*

―――
*See Events of the Years, Page 45.

VII

PINELLAS COUNTY

THE rapid development of Pinellas County during the past decade has been due, in some measure, at least, to the fact that it was divided in 1911 from Hillsborough County, "the grand old county of Florida."

Freedom from Hillsborough was obtained only after a long and bitter fight, during which the Tampa political machine brought every pressure to bear to keep the county intact. This, despite the fact that the advocates of division had all the arguments on their side and sought only justice.

The chief grievance of the divisionists was that Hillsborough spent practically all the tax money for the Tampa section of the county. Nothing was spent on the peninsula for the construction of roads or bridges, even though there was an acute need for an adequate highway system. Hillsborough even haggled about providing money for the schools. The school appropriations, especially for the growing city of St. Petersburg, always were inadequate, even for ordinary running expenses. When the construction of new school buildings was suggested, the Hillsborough commissioners disregarded the peninsula entirely.

The reason for this discrimination against the peninsula was that the county commissioners were dependent upon the Tampa vote for their political existence. As a result, what the Tampa section wanted, it got, and the requests of the West Coast section were sidestepped.

Another argument of the St. Petersburg divisionists was that it was difficult for St. Petersburg people to reach Tampa, the county seat. The trip had to be made by boat and the boat schedules were such that it was not always possible to return the same day. To reach Tampa by land was out of the question. Going by train required a full day and necessitated two changes. The condition of the roads made it almost impossible to drive over, even after automobiles came in use.

The county division fight really began way back in 1887. W. A. Belcher, of Bayview, then representative from the West Coast, introduced and passed in the House a bill dividing Hillsborough, but Judge Joseph B. Wall, of Tampa, then state senator, promptly killed the bill after it reached the Senate.

After this early attempt, which undoubtedly was premature, little was heard about county division until 1906, when the issue bobbed up again stronger than ever. The cause of the divisionists was advocated and led from the beginning by W. L. Straub, editor of the *St. Petersburg Times*, and the victory which was finally won was due largely to his perseverance.

In 1907, Senator James E. Crane assured the divisionists that if the people of the West Coast wanted a separate county they could have it, and if petitioned by them to do so, he would permit such a bill to pass the Senate. In commenting on this phase of the division fight, the *Times* stated: 'The justice of the case was so apparent that he did not, any more than we, think of serious opposition. W. W. K. Decker, of Tarpon Springs, introduced the bill in the House during the session of 1907, but there was opposition, all right enough. As the bill progressed in the House, the heat in Tampa increased—and it became an awful time. It was something fierce. But Mr. Decker and the Pinellas backers won in the House and when the bill reached the Senate floor, poor Mr. Crane was up against it in all directions. A veil may be drawn here. Strenuous things transpired; the pressure from Tampa was terriffic; and—the bill never came back from the Senate committee."

The divisionists were not discouraged by this defeat. Instead, they began making plans for the next campaign. The "insiders" realized that strategy was needed to elect a senator who would be supported by the Tampa "anti's" and yet would be friendly to the cause. They found such a man in Don C. McMullen. In his campaign speeches, McMullen came out flatfooted and said he would not favor county division at the 1909 session of the Legislature. He discreetly kept quiet about what he would do at the 1911 session. The anti-divisionists accepted his words at their face value and did not oppose him. The "insiders" realized that if McMullen were elected, the county would not be divided in 1909, but that it surely would be in 1911. So they supported him and urged others to support him on the plea that he would give Pinellas a square deal. Naturally, they could not divulge the plan or McMullen's chances of being elected would be killed.

Two other candidates for senator appeared. Robert McNamee, of Tampa, was opposed to division. F. A. Wood, of St. Petersburg, led the movement for a divided county. In the first primary, on May 19, Wood polled a large majority of the votes in the St. Petersburg district, getting 310 to McMullen's 39 and McNamee's 46. He was snowed under throughout the county, however, and McMullen and McNamee went into the second primaries on June 16. The "insiders" threw their support to McMullen and he won out, 2,848 to 2,552.

John S. Taylor, of Largo, a division leader, was elected representative from this section at the same time. He was "playing the game" with McMullen and pledged himself not to work for division in 1909. Notwithstanding Taylor's pledge and the knowledge that McMullen would oppose it, some of the Pinellas boosters decided it best not to risk two years of delay and sent up the second Pinellas bill just the same. Taylor did not approve the step but kept hands off, and the boosters got it through the House on May 1, 1909. But McMullen insisted upon his promise of no bill for that session and opposed it when it reached the Senate. His opposition was fatal, inasmuch as the unwritten laws of "senatorial courtesy" provided that no bill of such nature should be passed without the approval of the senator from the county affected.

The third campaign was opened with a meeting at Clearwater, Monday, December 12, 1910. Tarpon Springs, Clearwater, Largo, Seminole and St. Petersburg were represented. S. S. Coachman, of Clearwater, was elected chairman and Charles H.

Evans, also of Clearwater, secretary. It was shown that $150,000 had been given to the county by Pinellas for good roads but that no good roads had been built. The divisionists propounded the question: "Is there any honest reason why the people of Pinellas Peninsula should not levy, collect and expend their own taxes?"

Numerous facts were presented to show why Pinellas should be separated from the old county. It was shown that it had 17 per cent of the population, 20 per cent of the voters, paid 23 per cent of the county taxes, and was taxed $6.34 per head as compared with $4.37 for the rest of the county. The 1910 census showed that the peninsula had 13,193 inhabitants and would stand twenty-third in the list of Florida counties so far as population was concerned.

A large delegation was present at the next meeting, held in Clearwater on January 17, 1911. John S. Taylor, of Largo, was elected permanent chairman and Charles H. Evans, editor of the Clearwater News, secretary. Those who represented St. Petersburg were S. D. Harris, W. L. Straub, A. Arnold, C. B. McClung, R. Veillard, W. E. Heathcote, George W. Meares, D. P. Johnson, F. W. Ramm and T. J. Northrup. W. L. Straub, J. J. Mendenhall, of Clearwater, and L. S. Johnson, of Largo, were named to serve on a committee of resolutions. It was agreed that when the county was divided, Clearwater was to be made the temporary county seat.

A campaign committee was named at the next meeting, held in Clearwater Tuesday, February 14, 1911. Members of the committee named were: John S. Taylor, Largo; Charles H. Evans, Clearwater; S. D. Harris, St. Petersburg; W. W. R. Decker, Tarpon Springs; DeLisle Hagadorn, Ozono; George W. Campbell, Green Springs, and John A. Campbell, Seminole. The bill, as drafted by the delegates, provided that, if passed by the Legislature and ratified by two-thirds of the voters of the peninsula, the county would be divided on October 1, 1911. The election was to be held September 5.

John S. Taylor and S. D. Harris went to Tallahassee on April 11 to start the fight. And a fight it proved to be. The Tampa political machine realized the seriousness of the situation and used all their influence to down the divisionists. The Tampa newspapers published vitriolic editorials by the score, denouncing Pinellas County and everyone in it. The St. Petersburg newspapers retaliated with more editorials, which almost burned the paper upon which they were printed.

In a sense, the fight was won for Pinellas County almost before it began. For a year previous to the session, Editor Straub, of the *Times*, had sent every issue of his propaganda-laden newspaper to every member of the Legislature, something the Tampa newspapers had neglected to do and, as a result, a majority of the legislators were almost as strong Pinellas boosters as Editor Straub himself.

Despite the fact that the Tampa newspapers, the Tampa Board of Trade, the Tampa politicians and a few backsliders on the peninsula brought out their heavy artillery against the bill, it was reported favorably by the House committee on April 20, passed by the House, 28 to 18, on May 5, and passed by the Senate, 20 to 9, on May 18. The anti-divisionists fought every step, but when Senator McMullen kept his promise and favored the bill in the Senate, their last hope was lost.

Assuming that Governor Gilchrist would sign the bill, which he did on May 23, the Pinellas boosters held a big celebration at Clearwater Monday night, May 22. Two coaches of enthusiastic boosters went from St. Petersburg, and big delegations were on hand from other towns on the peninsula.

The Pinellas County Club was organized Thursday, June 20, 1911, "to make a thorough campaign for political independence" to be attained by the referendum petition on November 14. John S. Taylor, of Largo, was elected president; A. C. Turner, of Clearwater, vice-president, and C. H. Evans, of Clearwater, secretary and treasurer. A branch of the club was formed in St. Petersburg on July 11 with S. D. Harris as president, C. W. Weicking, vice-president, C. E. Chambers, secretary, and J. Frank Harrison, treasurer.

Pinellas County became a fact on Tuesday, November 14, when the division bill was ratified by a vote of 1,379 to 505. The vote by localities was: St. Petersburg, 232 yes, 37 no; Seminole, 46, 0; Largo, 138, 25; Clearwater, 232, 37; Ozono, 52, 46; Dunedin, 22, 56; Green Springs, 21, 71; Tarpon Springs, 44, 204; Bay View, 6, 15. It was the biggest vote ever polled in the history of the county. All evening the streets of St. Petersburg were filled with a cheering, joyful crowd, celebrating the greatest victory that the peninsula had ever achieved.

The Tampa crowd made one more attempt to keep the peninsula for Hillsborough. The anti-divisionists attempted to prove that the bill was illegal but, on December 8, 1911, the State Supreme Court declared it constitutional and the County of Pinellas was separated permanently from Hillsborough.

The first election for the new county was held on December 15 and the following officers were elected: County commissioners, F. A. Wood, St. Petersburg; S. S. Coachman, Clearwater; O. T. Raisback, St. Petersburg; L. D. Vinson, Tarpon Springs, and J. T. Lowe, Ozono. School board, W. A. Allen, Clearwater; A. F. Bartlett, St. Petersburg; A. P. Beckett, Tarpon Springs. Superintendent of schools, Dixie M. Hollins, Clearwater. Clerk Circuit Court, C. W. Weicking, St. Petersburg. Sheriff, Marvel M. Whitehurst, Ozono. County judge, Leroy Bradon, Clearwater. Tax assessor, T. J. Northrup, St. Petersburg. Tax collector, E. B. McMullen, Largo. County treasurer, A. C. Turner, Clearwater. Superintendent of registrations, Albert S. Mearese, Anono. County surveyor, W. A. Rosseau, Dunedin.

Peace and harmony did not prevail after Pinellas County was formed. St. Petersburg accused Clearwater of "playing politics" and endeavoring to obtain complete control of the new county. The Clearwater politicians so maneuvered things that three men were elected as commissioners from the upper end of the county who would do as they said. As a result, the two St. Petersburg commissioners were outvoted on every important issue which conflicted in any way with the desires of the Clearwater "gang."

The opposition became apparent when the St. Petersburg commissioners began pushing for good roads. Inasmuch as the proposed program called for many miles of roads south of Clearwater, the three commissioners from the upper end of the county opposed it, as long as they could. Finally, however, they called for an election on June 4, 1912, on a $300,000 bond issue. It was defeated by the upper end of the county, 489 to 505. Incensed by this disregard of their needs, the residents of the lower end of the peninsula put up such a strong fight that the commissioners called for another election on December 3, 1912, on a $375,000 issue. It was carried almost unanimously in southern Pinellas and a heavy vote in the upper end against the issue was overcome. A system of marl roads was built through the county with the money.

A strong feeling of resentment against Clearwater and the Clearwater politicians developed in St. Petersburg as a result of evident discrimination against the lower end of the peninsula, and this resentment culminated in a movement to prevent Clearwater from being made the county seat.

The county commissioners on April 3, 1912, voted to levy a 5-mill county tax to build a courthouse and jail at Clearwater. St. Petersburg immediately arose in arms and secured an injunction from the State Supreme Court against the levy. The three up-county commissioners went ahead, regardless, bargained for a lot, and erected a building costing $3,750. The county treasurer, who was not a Clearwater man, refused to pay for the building, saying he had no funds for that purpose. There the matter rested for a while.

During 1913 and 1914 the county seat controversy became heated. A "County Club" was organized in St. Petersburg and petitions were circulated asking the com-

The Sunset Hotel at Pasadena-on-the-Gulf

missioners to call an election and allow the voters to determine where they wanted the county seat located. More than eight hundred signatures were secured, but the commissioners failed to act. A mandamus suit to compel them to do so was instituted. While the matter was still pending in the courts, Noel A. Mitchell on February 5, 1913, offered to give an entire block in his Court House subdivision, on West Central, to the county for a courthouse site.

After years of wrangling, the commissioners finally called an election for February 3, 1916, upon the question of bonding the county for $160,000 for a courthouse and jail at Clearwater. St. Petersburg voted 3 to 1 against it, but its opposition was not sufficient to overcome the support of the upper end of the county. The issue passed, 485 to 439. Still the controversy continued. It was not ended until March 10, 1917, when the State Supreme Court decreed that the county seat could not be taken from Clearwater until twenty years from the time Pinellas had become a county.

While the arguments about the location of the county seat were going on, the good roads boosters of the county got together and pushed through an improvement program. The marl roads, built in 1913, were better than the peninsula had ever had before and they served the purpose for a while. They rapidly deteriorated, however, and in a short time it was seen that better roads would have to be constructed. An election was called for in August, 1915, for a $715,000 bond issue to build seventy-three miles of brick roads. It passed, 808 to 629. On September 17, 1917, it was invalidated by Judge O. K. Reaves for a number of technical errors in the ordinance and another election was called for November 16. Again the issue passed, this time 827 to 754. It was contested and taken to the State Supreme Court, which validated it on February 1, 1916, permitting the work to proceed. The highway system, providing a network of nine-foot brick roads, was completed on November 15 of the same year.

A movement was started in 1916 to prohibit cattle raisers of Pinellas County from allowing their cattle to roam at large. It was argued that the cattle did considerable damage to truck farms and citrus groves, and were a menace on the highways at night. The movement gained headway, despite the determined opposition of the cattle men and their friends, and on October 23, 1917, a "no-fence" law was passed, 477 to 979. A cattle fence across the county was completed on October 19, 1918. This should have ended the trouble about the roaming cattle, but it did not. The law has never been adequately enforced. Even during 1923 two fatal accidents occurred in the county as a result of automobiles running into cows on the highways.

The nine-foot brick road built in 1916 served the purpose for several years, but when the traffic began to increase it was seen they were too narrow. Moreover, the brick had been laid directly upon a sand base which inevitably resulted in a rough surface. The need for a better highway system became apparent and on August 15, 1922, the voters were called upon to approve or reject a bond issue for $2,695,000. There were a number of features about the road-building program which were objectionable to the voters in the southern end of the peninsula and it was defeated, 1,234 to 1,657. On June 5, 1923, another election was called on a modified program and it was passed, 8 to 1.*

---
*See Streets and Roads.

VIII

CHAMBER OF COMMERCE
(INCLUDING BOARD OF TRADE)

Towns have been known to grow into cities without having Chambers of Commerce to push them along. But if it had not been for St. Petersburg's Chamber of Commerce, it is very doubtful whether St. Petersburg ever would have become the city it is today. Unquestionably, it has aided materially in making St. Petersburg bigger, better, more prosperous and more attractive. Composed of the city's most progressive men, and playing no part in politics, it has been able to point the way toward civic progress.

There was a time, of course, when the Chamber of Commerce was not the powerful body it is today. There was a time when it struggled along ineffectually, hampered by a lack of funds. But it was the failures of the early days which spurred the members on to further efforts.

The first Chamber of Commerce was formed in 1899, with a dozen members. Col. L. Y. Jenness, manager of the St. Petersburg Land & Improvement Company, was the first president. There were no dues, and the chamber accomplished nothing. It was more of a social organization than anything else. It struggled along for several years, with an occasional meeting.

That this early organization was ineffectual is indicated by an editorial in the *St. Petersburg Times* of April 19, 1902. Referring to a revival of activities in the Tampa Board of Trade, the editorial said: "St. Petersburg needs such a revival and needs it badly. We do not believe our Chamber of Commerce is dead, but it is so near to it that a stranger could hardly tell the difference. . . . . St. Petersburg is probably the least advertised town on earth that possesses and claims the attributes of a health or pleasure resort."

The Chamber of Commerce was reorganized at a mass-meeting held Monday night, June 2, 1902. A. P. Avery was elected president and J. W. Wright, secretary. Plans were discussed for boosting the city.

For a while, this reorganized chamber strove nobly to carry out its plans. On Monday, July 21, 1902, the members pledged themselves to pay $125 to pay for the publishing of 10,000 booklets to advertise the city. The following members were named to serve on the booklet committee: L. Y. Jenness, Arthur Norwood, C. A. Gladden, A. P. Weller, W. A. Holshouser, David Murray, J. C. Williams, Jr., and H. McQuiston. The F. A. Davis Publishing Company, of Philadelphia, agreed to print the booklets at cost and to furnish the cuts. The cost exceeded the original estimate by $25. When the booklets arrived several months later they were distributed to residents of the city for enclosure in letters to friends in the North. Records of the F. A. Davis Publishing Company show that, even though the booklets were done at cost, they were not paid for until several years afterwards.

At the annual meeting of the Chamber of Commerce held June 1, 1903, W. A. Holshouser was elected president and R. H. Thomas, secretary. The members recommended that the city should appropriate $500 for municipal advertising. The city fathers carefully considered the petition at the next meeting, on July 2, and then proceeded to vote it down, $500 being too large an amount in those days to spend "frivolously."

After this disheartening blow, the chamber again became almost inactive. The *Times* remarked on February 5, 1905: "If St. Petersburg only had a Chamber of Commerce or some such body—and the lack of one is a disgrace to the city—what a lot it could accomplish for the general upbuilding of the city at this stage." As if in echo to this editorial, a group of business men met in Mayor R. H. Thomas' office on February 14, 1905, and organized the Board of Trade.

Officers of the Board of Trade were elected as follows: F. A. Wood, president; A. F. Bartlett, vice-president; R. H. Thomas, secretary; J. F. Ridlon, assistant secretary, and J. Frank Harrison, treasurer. The following were named to serve on the board of directors: F. A. Wood, A. F. Bartlett, R. H. Thomas, J. Frank Harrison, Roy S. Hanna, Charles Weinman, David Moffett, A. P. Avery and Arthur Norwood. The executive committee was named as follows: Dr. F. C. Ahlers, J. Frank Harrison, W. A. Sims, C. B. Gillette, C. Perry Snell, J. L. Houle, David Moffett, George Edwards, Arthur Norwood, W. L. Straub, R. L. Raymond, L. C. Hefner, George Thomas, A. P. Avery and C. L. Howard. At a meeting held on March 16, Ed. T. Lewis and F. A. Davis were added to the board of directors and Dr. A. B. Davis, son of F. A. Davis, was elected assistant secretary.

Despite its auspicious beginning, the Board of Trade did not make much progress during the first year of its existence. One or two meetings were held, and then interest slackened. In the issue of February 17, 1906, the *Times* stated: "There is now considerable talk of reorganizing the Board of Trade, having a new deal, getting some new blood into it, and we understand that even 'the push' of the present body admit that it is dead, and that they are tired and disposed to quit."

On March 15, 1906, at a meeting in the office of Dr. A. B. Davis, the board came to life again, and elected new officers as follows: Judge J. D. Bell, president; C. A. Harvey, first vice-president; Roy S. Hanna, second vice-president; T. A. Chancellor, treasurer; Dr. A. B. Davis, secretary, and Albert H. Roberts, assistant secretary. Members of the executive committee were: W. A. Holshouser, R. L. Raymond, George Thomas, R. F. Taggart, B. C. Williams, A. J. Nye, Arthur Norwood and M. L. Stoner.

The election of new officers apparently injected new life into the organization. In less than a month the members decided to launch a campaign to raise $2,000 by popular subscription. Previous to this, in February, the board spent $35—all the money it could scrape together—to buy advertising space in newspapers throughout the state to contradict reports that there was an epidemic of smallpox in St. Petersburg. The $35 was spent so judiciously and brought such results that the people learned for the first time the value of advertising. The campaign for the $2,000 advertising fund was the result. The advertising committee was named as follows: Dr. A. B. Davis, Noel A. Mitchell, A. Williams Fisher, W. B. Powell and C. A. Harvey.

In less than a month the fund was oversubscribed. The list of subscribers, as published in the *St. Petersburg Independent,* issue of April 28, 1906, was as follows: $100 each—National Bank (Central National), First National Bank, Bay Shore Land Company, A. C. Pheil, James S. Norton, Joseph S. Sibley; $50 each—Harvey Real Estate Company, C. H. Lutz & Son, Florida West Coast Company, St. Petersburg Hardware Company, Wm. A. Holshouser, R. H. Thomas Realty Company, Smith & Northrup, Avery Real Estate Company, E. B. Rowland, Arthur Norwood, A. T. Blocker, Dent & English, Times Publishing Company, St. Petersburg Independent, Foley & Fisher, Sun Commercial Printing Company, Weller Hardware Company, P. B. Stoner & Son, Eureka Stone & Paving Company, Colonial Hotel, Huntington Hotel; $25 each—D. W. Budd & Company, Sims Brothers, L. C. Hefner, Dr. W. F. Wilcox, Dr. Thomas P. Welch, Dr. John D. Peabody, S. D. Harris, Ralph Veillard, E. C. McPherson, Dr. H. A. Murphy, Andrew Jackson, H. P. Bussey, Eddins & Roberts, West Coast Plumbing Company, George Edwards & Son, McLain Lumber Company, J. L. Klutts, E. L. Waggoner, Dr. J. L. Taylor, W. E. Heathcote, A. F. Bartlett, Annie Wood, Chautauqua Hotel; $20 each—Cyrus W. Butler; $15 each—C. J. Sims, C. L. Howard; $10 each—W. J. Slemmer, C. D. Hammond, W. A. Kerr and Wickersham & Rosselle. It might be said that this list comprised practically all of the real boosters of St. Petersburg in 1906—the boosters who were willing to back up their boosting with real money.

St. Petersburg in 1904 from the Tomlinson Tower, Fourth street and Second avenue south

The board took its first definite step toward the acquirement and beautification of the water front in 1906. The water front committee, composed of C. Perry Snell, A. F. Bartlett and Roy S. Hanna, secured options of two and one-half blocks fronting on the water and asked the authorization of the city council to purchase them and hold as trustees until such time as the city wanted to take them over. This authorization was given on April 24 and the council also requested the committee to secure options on as much of the remaining water front as possible.

Noel A. Mitchell was elected president of the Board of Trade at the annual meeting held Tuesday, March 18, 1907. Other officers elected were: Roy S. Hanna, first vice-president; A. F. Bartlett, second vice-president; Dr. A. B. Davis, secretary; T. K. Wilson, treasurer. Members of the executive board named were: A. P. Avery, A. Williams Fisher, J. G. Foley, A. F. Freeman, J. Frank Harrison, L. C. Hefner, W. A. Holshouser, A. Norwood, C. Perry Snell, R. F. Taggart, J. D. Bell, C. A. Harvey, T. A. Chancellor, S. D. Harris, H. A. Kellum and Rufus D. Jackson.

Dr. A. B. Davis, in his annual report, told of the many achievements of the board during the past year, heading the list with the $2,000 advertising drive. He mentioned that a committee had been appointed to investigate the possibility of persuading the Tampa Northern Railway to run its line into St. Petersburg. He said that the prospect of this being done was "fair." However, the railroad never came.

Roy S. Hanna was elected president of the Board of Trade for 1908. Other officers elected were: A. F. Bartlett, first vice-president; S. D. Harris, second vice-president; W. B. Powell, secretary, and T. A. Chancellor, treasurer. With these officials, the board continued to do good work for the city. Ten thousand copies of Dr. H. C. Van Bibber's report on the proposed "Health City" were printed and turned over to residents and tourists for distribution. One hundred thousand post cards showing St. Petersburg scenes also were printed. Most of them were distributed in the candy packages which were manufactured and sold by Noel A. Mitchell at his summer home at Sarvin Park, Conn. On March 18, 1908, when the officers were elected for the year, seventy-five members went to Pass-a-Grille for the annual outing.

It was during 1908 that the Board of Trade again began boosting for the water front. A committee, composed of A. F. Bartlett, Arthur Norwood, W. H. English, J. P. Titcomb and Captain F. E. Von Leue, investigated and reported that: "The general appearance of decay and neglect between the two docks—old boats, rotten piers, all sorts of riff-raff, and especially where the outgoing tide leaves large stretches of sand covered with a variety of animal and vegetable matter in all stages of decay —does not well comport with a live, progressive city such as St. Petersburg aspires and claims to be." The committee urged the board to take some action which would spur the city officials to do something with the water front lots held by the trustees, and also to acquire the remainder of the necessary property.

At a meeting held January 21, 1909, the board unanimously agreed to consider the advisability of recommending the city commission form of government. A committee, composed of A. F. Bartlett, W. R. Howard, Conradi and J. D. Bell, were appointed to see what could be done. At this same meeting W. B. Powell resigned as secretary, Noel A. Mitchell being appointed to succeed him.

In March, 1909, the board decided to reorganize and incorporate under the name of the St. Petersburg Chamber of Commerce, upon the recommendation of a special committee composed of L. C. Hefner, A. F. Bartlett and W. R. Howard. W. L. Straub, Dr. A. B. Davis and W. R. Howard were named as a committee on constitution and by-laws. It was decided to fix the annual dues at $10. T. J. Northrup, Noel A. Mitchell and A. P. Avery were appointed to serve on a membership committee. At another meeting, on March 30, the members decided to retain the old name but to go through with the incorporation, placing the organization on a businesslike basis. Officers elected were: A. F. Bartlett, president; S. D. Harris, first vice-president; W. L. Straub, second vice-president; board of governors—three-year term: L. C. Hefner, Lew B. Brown, R. Veillard, Roy S. Hanna; two-year term: Arthur Norwood, Noel A. Mitchell, Dr. H. A. Murphy, W. G. Howard; one-year term: T. A. Chancellor, T. J. Northrup, J. D. Bell and A. W. Fisher.

The board recommended at a meeting on April 13, 1909, that the city charter be changed to allow the initiative and referendum, give council authority to submit a $20,000 bond issue for a public library, and to levy a tax of not less than one mill or more than two to maintain the library and for general promotion purposes. It was not until years later that these recommendations were followed out. J. Frank Harrison was appointed secretary during the summer of 1909.

At the annual meeting of the board on February 15, 1901, A. P. Avery was elected president; W. R. Howard, first vice-president; S. D. Harris, second vice-president; C. E. Chambers to succeed Mr. Howard as governor, and T. A. Chancellor, T. J.

Looking east on Central from Fourth street. Photo taken in 1898

Northrup, Charles Braaf and A. F. Bartlett as new governors. J. Frank Harrison was reelected secretary by the board of governors on March 1. Mrs. Annie McRae was acting secretary during most of the following year.

Five thousand folders, describing the advantages of St. Petersburg as a summer resort, were ordered by the board on May 17, 1910. They were to be supplied by the F. A. Davis Publishing Company, of Philadelphia, in thirty days. This marked the beginning of the summer boosting movement.

S. D. Harris was elected president of the board on February 21, 1911. Noel A. Mitchell was elected first vice-president; C. E. Bonnell, second vice-president. New members of the board of governors elected were: John N. Brown, A. F. Thomasson, A. C. Odom, Jr., and H. A. Farmer. A ground floor room in the Roser building on Central avenue was leased by the board in November, 1911, for its headquarters. In the fall, 100,000 envelopes on which were printed St. Petersburg scenes were ordered and given to business firms for general distribution. A mounted tarpon was prepared for a window display and sent to a Northern city. It was passed from city to city before its days of usefulness was over.

Lew B. Brown was elected president of the board on February 20, 1912. Other officers elected were: Noel A. Mitchell, first vice-president; C. M. Roser, second vice-president. Governors named were: S. D. Harris, R. Veillard, R. S. Hanna and Arthur Norwood. Edmund C. Wimer was elected secretary a week later. Under the leadership of Mr. Brown, a vigorous campaign was conducted during the summer. At the beginning of the campaign, the 390 members were divided into two groups, the Blues and Reds. J. Bruce Smith was appointed leader of the Blues and Arthur Johnson leader of the Reds. The two teams combed the city for members, and a spirited rivalry developed. Parades were held, and each team did its utmost to attract attention. When the campaign ended it was found that the Blues had brought in 358 members and the Reds 260. As the membership fee was five dollars, the board received over $3,000 from the campaign. At the wind-up, a barbecue was held in Williams Park, the Reds, as losers, being compelled to serve the Blues and all the rest of the town. As a result of the campaign, the membership list was boosted to 1,008, larger than ever before and larger than it was again for several years after.

Arthur L. Johnson, chairman of the advertising committee, and Secretary Wimer announced plans in January for the first mid-winter carnival to be held from March 17 to 22. All arrangements were carefully worked out and the carnival proved to be a success in every particular, inducing hundreds of tourists to stay later than they ever had before.

Registration of tourists by the board was started during 1912, twenty-four leather-bound books being secured for the winter visitors to register their names and addresses. Previous to this, an attempt had been made by several stores and hotels to secure tourist registrations, but satisfactory results were never secured. The board's registration books proved so popular with the tourists that they were continued from then on.

At a meeting on February 14, 1913, the board voted to extent the city limits. A committee was appointed to make tentative plans, the members named being Roy S.

Hanna, A. F. Bartlett, A. C. Odom, Jr., C. Perry Snell and C. M. Roser. St. Petersburg, as it then was, contained two square miles. The plan, as finally approved, contained ten square miles, including the Bayboro and North Shore developments and a strip a mile wide out West Central to Boca Ceiga Bay. It was presented to the State Legislature and passed the House May 16, 1913, and the Senate a few days later.

One of the features of the board's activities during Mr. Brown's presidency was the New Year's dinner for tourists. The committee in charge was composed of A. R. Dunlap, Lew B. Brown, W. L. Straub, Mrs. Dusenbury and Mrs. L. C. Hefner. During the reception, 390 visitors registered from Ohio, 340 from Indiana, 275 from Illinois, 274 from Michigan, 250 from Massachusetts, 215 from Pennsylvania and 65 from Canada.

W. L. Straub was elected president on February 18, 1913. Other officers elected were Arthur L. Johnson, first vice-president; J. Bruce Smith, second vice-president; board of governors—A. F. Bartlett, Lew B. Brown, Joseph W. Taylor, A. W. Fisher and, to fill the unexpired term of Mr. Straub, T. A. Chancellor.

At a meeting on March 12, 1913, the board decided to ask the Atlantic Coast Line for a new depot, "one that would be a credit to the city," and appointed S. D. Harris,

Suwannee Hotel, completed in 1923, as seen from the top of the Pheil Building

E. B. Willson and A. R. Welsh on a committee to see the railroad officials. The new depot was secured during 1914.

Edmund C. Wimer resigned as secretary on May 5, 1915, his resignation to take effect on September 1. L. A. Whitney, formerly secretary of the Brownsville, Texas, Chamber of Commerce, was appointed secretary to succeed him on June 2. He served the organization faithfully and efficiently for seven years, resigning on September 1, 1920, to become secretary of the Fort Myers Chamber of Commerce.

The first big order for St. Petersburg folders was placed in September, 1913, by the board. Fifty thousand copies were ordered from the Matthews-Northrup Company, of Buffalo, at a cost of $4,000. The folders contained sixteen pages, with eighty-six views of St. Petersburg, including a large panorama view of the entire city. A year later a 50,000 reprint of the same folder was ordered. The contrast between these orders and the $125 order for folders in 1902 indicates how St. Petersburg had learned to appreciate the value of advertising on a large scale.

The Board of Trade was instrumental in securing the first band to play for the tourists during the winter season. During 1913, they made arrangements with the city commission whereby the city would pay $700 and the board $500 to engage a band to give three concerts a week from December 15, 1913, to March 15, 1914. A local band was engaged.

Charles R. Hall was elected president on February 17, 1914. Other officers elected were: Arthur L. Johnson, first vice-president; V. N. Ridgeley, second vice-president; governors—W. L. Straub, T. A. Chancellor, C. M. Roser, J. N. Brown. Edmund C. Wimer was elected to fill the unexpired term of Charles R. Hall. During 1914, the city commissioin turned over to the board $4,500 for city advertising and entertainment of conventions, as provided in the new city charter.

Arthur Norwood was elected president at the annual meeting February 16, 1915. Other officers chosen were: J. W. Coburn, first vice-president; George B. Hayward, second vice-president; board of governors—Roy S. Hanna, A. R. Welsh, J. Frank Harrison and G. Z. Roland. J. P. Lynch was elected to fill the unexpired term of Mr. Coburn.

Although the war disrupted the activities of the board to some extent, it continued to operate. Paul R. Boardman was elected president in February, 1916; Mr. Coburn, first vice-president, and Fred Lowe, second vice-president. The four retiring governors were retained for another year, Arthur Norwood being chosen to succeed Mr. Boardman.

On July 19, 1916, the board of governors awarded a contract to the Redfield-Kendricks-Odell Company, of New York, for 100,000 advertising folders, thirty-six pages, to cost $3,950.

J. W. Coburn was elected president in February, 1917. He resigned April 23 and was succeeded by the first vice-president, Fred T. Lowe. Charles R. Carter was elected president on March 5, 1918. Other officers were: Arthur L. Johnson, first vice-president; A. W. Fisher, second vice-president; governors—J. Frank Harrison, Roy S. Hanna, E. B. Willson and C. C. Carr. L. C. Brown was elected to succeed R. T. Thorn as director.

Mr. Carter was re-elected president in March, 1919. L. C. Brown was elected first vice-president and A. F. Bartlett second vice-president. Governors elected were: T. A. Chancellor, H. R. Frazee, W. McKee Kelley, E. C. Reed, and F. C. Carley to succeed Paul Boardman. Mr. Carter resigned shortly afterwards and Bradford A. Lawrence was elected to succeed him in the fall of 1919.

At the next election, the "old-timers," who had been at the helm for many years, turned over the reins to the "Young Turks." Several "old-timers" were retained on the board of directors to act as advisers. W. L. Watson was elected president and L. C. Brown vice-president. The directors named were: E. C. Reed, T. A. Chancellor, John N. Brown, J. G. Rutland, Henry Harris, C. C. Carr, Herman A. Dann, W. T. Tillinghast, Al. Gandy, B. A. Lawrence, Jr., C. R. Carter, R. H. Sumner, Noel A. Mitchell, H. L. Ermatinger and A. F. Bartlett. By formal action of the board of directors, the Board of Trade became the Chamber of Commerce on June 29, 1920. Upon the resignation of Mr. Whitney as secretary, Mr. Lawrence was appointed to succeed him on August 9, 1920, at a salary of $3,000 a year.

B. A. Lawrence, Jr., was appointed executive vice-president in May, 1922, and served until May 14, 1923, when Leo L. Eddy, who had been acting secretary for some time previous, was given executive secretarial powers.

L. C. Brown served the chamber as president during 1921; Herman A. Dann, 1922; J. W. Coburn, 1923, and B. A. Lawrence, Jr., 1924.

John L. Lodwick was employed by the Board of Trade during the winter of 1918-1919 to serve as publicity director and has held that office both for the Chamber of Commerce and city ever since. As a result of his efforts, hundreds of thousands of dollars' worth of free publicity has been secured for St. Petersburg in Northern newspapers.

During the past five years the Chamber of Commerce has conducted advertising campaigns on a large scale, with the result that St. Petersburg has attracted each winter a larger number of tourists. Large sums of money have been secured from the tax levy for library and advertising purposes. During the first year after the tax levy had been increased to two and one-half mills, the city budget for this purpose was $37,787. This was for the fiscal year ending June 30, 1922. For the fiscal year ending June 30, 1923, the city budget was $48,945, and for the year ending June 30, 1924, $61,600. In addition to the money obtained from the city for advertising purposes, the chamber has received large amounts by voluntary subscription. In 1922, the volunteer budget totalled $31,200; in 1923, $33,846, and in 1924, $65,000.

IX

FISHING AND BOATING

"THE pier at St. Petersburg presents a gay and animated spectacle when lined by fishers of all ages and both sexes, absorbed in casting or drawing in, or intent upon watching their lines. Numerous fish pails are quickly filled. Fish weighing twenty pounds or more are frequently caught from this wharf, and sometimes a huge tarpon is hooked. The principal catches consist of Spanish mackerel, sea trout, sheepshead and channel bass.

"If the sportsmen wish something of an expedition there are many spots from which to choose. A short carriage ride across the peninsula transports a party to the western shore, which faces a narrow inlet of the Gulf of Mexico, known as Boca Ceiga Bay. In this reach of salt water, and particularly in the neighborhood of Pass-a-Grille, the tarpon is abundant. The tarpon requires a vigorous arm, as it is as large and heavy as a man. Sea fish which may be caught here by less hardy and experienced sportsmen are the mackerel, grouper, blue-fish and red snapper. Other monsters of the deep which are killed in the vicinity of Pinellas Peninsula are jewfish and sharks, which turn the scales at hundreds of pounds. Turtles, oysters, clams and other edible species of shellfish are also plentiful."

The above quotation from an article of the August, 1897, issue of the *Medical Bulletin,* published in Philadelphia, indicates that fishing was one of the greatest attractions of St. Petersburg in the old days. The fish were plentiful, and the anglers could always be sure of good catches and good sport. It was nothing unusual for fishermen to get several hundred mackerel or trout in a few hours.

Probably the first club for anglers and boatmen was the one formed by Capt. W. Budd and some of his friends in 1905. A small building was built on piles at Pinellas Point at what was known as Budd's Beach. Frequent trips were made to the clubhouse and Captain Budd became famous as a maker of clam chowder. It was the duty of the other members to dig the clams and catch the fish for the dinners.

A more pretentious clubhouse was built at Pinellas Point by a club of five members in 1907. The members were T. E. Willson, E. H. Meyers, Ed. T. Lewis, J. G. Lewis and J. W. Key. B. C. Williams, who built the clubhouse, was made honorary member. The building contained a large dining hall, kitchen, pantry and six bedrooms, and was surrounded by a large porch. The name of "Pinellas Boating and Fishing Club" was adopted by the members. On January 26, 1908, the society held its first motor boat regatta. Nineteen power boats circled about E. H. Tomlinson's houseboat, Kootenay, and bore away for the point. About sixty assembled at the clubhouse and had a dinner prepared under the direction of Barney Williams. The centerpiece was a dish of clam chowder and it was said that not even Captain Budd, the chowder specialist, could have made a better dish.

Both these early clubhouses were wrecked by heavy storms, and now little trace of them remains.

Tarpon Club

The Tarpon Club of St. Petersburg was organized at a meeting of anglers held Monday night, November 10, 1907, at the home of Roy S. Hanna. Officers were elected as follows: George E. Downey, president; W. H. English, vice-president; W. L. Straub, secretary and treasurer. Directors named were: Roy S. Hanna, George Boyer, R. D. Jackson, Ed. T. Lewis and W. L. Straub. The object of the club, as decided at the meeting, was "to encourage the use of rod and reel in fishing, promote social intercourse among its members, aid in securing the protection of game fishes, elevate the sport to the highest standards, and to do all the things proper and necessary to attain these objects."

Membership in the club was limited to persons who had caught a tarpon in accordance with the club's rules regarding lines, rods, etc., and the officers were to be determined by the weight of fish caught during the season, the angler catching the heaviest fish to become president, the second heaviest, vice-president, and so on.

The club formally opened its first season on Friday, May 16, 1908, by taking charge of the Hotel Bonhomie, at Pass-a-Grille, which had been offered by the owner, George Lizotte, as the club's headquarters. The roll of honor, made up of those who had caught tarpon, included W. L. Straub, C. Perry Snell, W. H. English, S. Lewis King, Ed. T. Lewis, R. D. Jackson, George Boyer, D. McLewis, Thomas E. Lucas, W. F. Stovall, I. S. Giddens, Judge George E. Downey and L. C. Schwerdtfeger.

Those who caught tarpon during the first season after the club was organized and became eligible for membership were: J. H. Bonacker, I. S. Giddens, Thomas E. Lucas, Orville Rigby, T. B. Snyder, W. F. Stovall, of Tampa; Judge George E. Downey, Aurora, Ind.; J. H. Hardwick, Cleveland, Tenn.; L. C. Schwerdtfeger, Lincoln, Ill.; Dr. G. W. Wagoner, Johnstown, Pa.; John S. Unger, Munhall, Pa.; A. P. Avery, George Boyer, D. W. Budd, Mrs. D. W. Budd, J. Frank Chase, Dr. W. T. Davis, W. H. English, Roy S. Hanna, R. D. Jackson, Mrs. R. D. Jackson, Dr. L. H. Jones, S. Lewis King, D. M. Lewis, Ed. T. Lewis, W. J. Longman, R. E. Ludwig, George Presstman, C. Perry Snell, M. L. Stoner, W. L. Straub, Charles S. Turner, Owen G. Whitcomb, T. K. Willson, St. Petersburg.

Presidents of the club since its organization have been: 1908, George E. Downey; 1909, S. Lewis King; 1910, George Presstman; 1911, David W. Budd; 1912, Theodore Curry; 1913, David W. Budd; 1914, David W. Budd; 1915, M. Keith Neville; 1916, M. Keith Neville; 1917, David W. Budd; 1918, F. T. Lowe; 1919, David W. Budd; 1920, J. J. Duffy; 1922, Robt. B. Lassing; 1923, Cot McCall.

W. L. Straub served as secretary of the club until February 28, 1916, when he resigned because his private affairs made it no longer possible for him to take care of the secretarial duties. T. W. Weston was appointed to succeed him. Sherman Rowles became secretary in 1920. W. L. Straub again took the office in 1923.

During the first years of the club's existence, prizes were offered only for tarpon catches. Later, however, prizes were awarded on nearly all the game fish caught in the fresh and salt waters of this vicinity. Membership in the club has climbed steadily and it now is one of the strongest organizations of anglers in the South.

Cot McCall, of St. Petersburg, has the distinction of having caught the largest tarpon, according to the rules, in the history of the club. During the summer of 1922 he brought in a fish weighing 167 pounds, for which he won the presidency of the club in 1923. Previous to that the record for the largest fish had been held by M. Keith Neville, of North Platte, Neb., who caught a tarpon on May 31, 1915, which weighed 152 pounds.

St. Petersburg Yacht Club

The St. Petersburg Yacht Club was organized Friday night, October 29, 1909, at a meeting in the store of the Marine Supply Company. Dr. M. H. Axline was elected commodore; W. R. Jones, vice-commodore; W. L. Straub, secretary; Tracy Lewis, treasurer, and George Presstman, measurer. Directors named were: Dr. M. H. Axline, W. L. Straub, Tracy Lewis, Ed. T. Lewis, Walter Robertson Howard, George Weller and W. H. English.

The objects of the club, as set forth in the articles of incorporation, were "to promote, encourage and protect the interests of boating and boatsmen in and about the city of St. Petersburg." Reasons why it was formed were given in the November 2,

St. Petersburg's Yacht Club and Yacht Basin

1909, issue of the *St. Petersburg Times,* which stated: "While a boat club has long been needed and talked of, the particular thing that finally precipitated the movement was the constantly increasing need among boat people of protection for their property. Depredations among boats and boat fixtures had become almost intolerable, and led to the first meeting, from which the club has sprung. A clubhouse, regattas and other things for the betterment of the club members and St. Petersburg are contemplated and will follow as soon as the city shall improve the water front and they will be practicable."

On December 26, 1910, the club members went to Blind Pass for an outing. Twenty boats carried the members and their guests, one hundred in all. A shore dinner, arranged by Commodore Axline, was enjoyed at the pass, and a few contests were held in the afternoon. The first regular cruise of the club was held on Sunday and Monday, March 6 and 7, 1910. Eleven boats made the trip to Bradentown and return.

The lack of a yacht basin discouraged activities in boating and the club was more or less inactive until 1916, when the water front developments were well under way. To A. T. Roberts, a newspaper man who had been city editor of the *St. Petersburg Times* and was then publicity manager for the St. Petersburg Investment Company and its allied companies, are due the credit and honor, and the appreciation of the city, for having initiated the revival in interest. Mr. Roberts submitted to both local newspapers definite plans for an organization and obtained the support of both. The result was a call for a meeting of water front boosters issued by him and Lew B. Brown, the meeting being held at the Board of Trade rooms in what is now the Y. W. C. A. building on the evening of May 30, 1916. Seven boosters attended, namely: A. T. Roberts, Lew B. Brown, W. L. Straub, Ed. T. Lewis, C. W. Springstead, Arthur L. Johnson and Frank C. Carley. Mr. Brown was elected chairman and Mr. Roberts secretary.

These seven members unanimously decided that the time had come to make the long-discussed yacht club a fact, and they proceeded to get busy. A building to cost about $15,000 was determined upon and a finance committee was chosen, consisting of George S. Gandy, Sr., Ed. T. Lewis, C. W. Springstead, H. Walter Fuller, Frank C. Carley, Charles R. Hall and A. T. Roberts, Chairman Brown being also a member. In response to previous newspaper publicity, Architects H. H. Dupont and George W. Stewart had prepared building plans for submission to the committee. It was decided to invite membership at $25 each until one hundred should be obtained, when a permanent organization would be made. Full and continued newspaper publicity under the charge of Secretary Roberts started the membership in a stream; one hundred was soon reached, and then one hundred and fifty. At a meeting held on June 19 the membership list was gone over and found satisfactory, and an organization meeting was called for June 23.

On this date, June 23, the St. Petersburg Yacht Club was reborn, with the following duly elected officers: Frank C. Carley, commodore; A. G. Butler, Middletown, Conn., vice-commodore; D. W. Budd, rear commodore; A. T. Roberts, secretary; John D. Harris, treasurer. The directors named were: Lew B. Brown, Ed. T. Lewis, W. L.

Straub, A. L. Johnson, George S. Gandy, Sr., T. A. Chancellor, C. M. Roser, Roy S. Hanna, Dr. W. M. Davis, H. Walter Fuller, J. G. Foley, Robert Carroll, and C. W. Greene, of Tampa. Committees were appointed to take care of all preliminary work.

On July 12, the site committee's recommendation of the location at the foot of Central avenue was accepted and the city asked for a lease, and the building plans submitted by Architect George W. Stewart were accepted. The city granted the lease on the water front lot on August 26, making it for thirty years, the legal limit, with an option for thirty years more. The building contract was awarded to J. Frank Chase on November 29, and the actual work was started early in December.

Until the necessary bonds could be issued and sold, the construction of the building was financed by the pioneer St. Petersburg method of obtaining public funds by borrowing from the local banks on personal notes. The task of getting these notes and the money was placed with a committee consisting of Ed. T. Lewis and C. W. Springstead, and the following are the men who loaned their personal credit for the building of the clubhouse: W. F. Smith, J. Bruce Smith, Max A. H. Fitz, Robert T. Thorn, W. L. Straub, James Norton, A. T. Blocker, Frank Barber, Dr. F. W. Wilcox, D. W. Budd, Thornton Parker, Citizens Ice and Cold Storage Company, C. W. Springstead, Lew B. Brown, J. Frank Harrison, C. C. Carr, Cramer B. Potter, C. M. Roser, W. S. Branning, Tracy Lewis, R. L. Powell, L. C. Brown, L. H. Strum, R. E. Ludwig, H. R. Frazee, E. P. Harrison, John D. Harris, Paul R. Boardman, George Bardeen, C. H. Neimyer, H. Walter Fuller, George S. Gandy, Jr., Walter P. Fuller, Arthur L. Johnson, S. D. Harris, R. H. Thomas, Willson-Chase Company, Brown Brothers, W. J. Overman, Frank C. Carley, Ed. T. Lewis, H. W. Hibbs, D. E. Beach, Dent & English Co., C. Perry Snell, L. D. Childs, J. W. Sheppard, J. G. Foley, Edward Durant, W. B. Pope, T. J. Northrup, A. Norwood and C. M. Griswold.

All officers were re-elected in 1917 for a full term and on June 11, 1917, the executive committee to take charge of the management of the newly completed building was named as follows: Lew B. Brown, chairman and supervisor of accounts; H. R. Frazee, supervisor of house and grounds; Frank C. Carley, house service; Ed. T. Lewis, water front, and C. W. Springstead, membership.

The clubhouse was formally opened on June 15, 1917, at which occasion Commodore Carley presented the club with a beautiful silver "Commodore's Cup," on which were to appear from time to time the names of the club's commodores.

On August 9 a bond issue of $20,000 was authorized and steps taken for their issue and sale.

It soon became evident that a larger building must be provided and on April 22, 1921, at the annual meeting, the members voted unanimously that this be done; but because of various delays aand difficulties the work was not actually taken up until April 14, 1922, when a $50,000 bond issue was authorized for the purpose. Plans for the new building were prepared by the first architect, George W. Stewart, assisted by Architect Henry L. Taylor, were accepted, and the construction contract was awarded to Franklin J. Mason, Inc. Before the work was completed it was found necessary to increase the issue of bonds from $50,000 to $60,000. The completed clubhouse was formally opened to the membership on December 21, 1922.

George S. Gandy, Sr., was elected commodore in the spring of 1919 and re-elected in 1920; Lew B. Brown, 1921; A. W. Fisher, 1922, and A. P. Avery, 1923. The present officers besides Mr. Avery are: A. L. Johnson, vice-commodore; Al Gandy, rear commodore; John J. Woodside, secretary, and Max A. H. Fitz, treasurer.

X

SCHOOLS

FROM a one-roomed building in 1888, accommodating a teacher and twenty-nine pupils, to school plants valued at approximately $800,000, with eighty-six teachers and 3,200 pupils in 1923, is a remarkable achievement in thirty-five years' time. This, however, is the record made by St. Petersburg in the development of its public schools.

The first school session held in St. Petersburg was in a little wooden building, erected by the people of the city under the direction of the trustees of the Congregational Church and was presided over by the first teacher, Miss Mamie Gilkeson, who resigned at the end of two months' service, and was succeeded by Miss Olive Wickham. The building was located between Ninth and Tenth streets near the present Central avenue. Twenty-nine pupils were enrolled in the first class. This was in the latter part of 1888, after an appropriation for a four months' school had been obtained from the county board. On December 8, 1888, E. R. Ward, J. C. Williams and David Williams were appointed as trustees.

For the second term of the little school, during the winter of 1889 and 1890, Jacob Keagy was appointed teacher and David Moffett supervisor. Enrollment for this term reached thirty-two, and during the six months' terms the average daily attendance was twenty-six.

Mr. Keagy was re-appointed for the next term, which was extended to seven months, during which time the average daily attendance was thirty-one and the enrollment forty. Mrs. Keagy assisted her husband with the work of teaching the children during these two terms and for the following term of 1891 and 1892. Mr. Keagy was made principal and Mrs. Keagy assistant.

The increase in attendance made it necessary to secure larger quarters and a three-room building at Eighth street and Railroad avenue was secured. Work in this building was not satisfactory because of its unsuitable location. Writing of this time, Mr. Keagy said: "Confusion created by the distracting noises of trains, lumber cars and novelty works, so near the school room, renders teaching almost an impossibility—the only other trouble being the continual dropping in of new pupils." The enrollment for the term of 1891 and 1892 was seventy-four and lasted seven months.

The school continued to grow and the next year it was necessary to engage another teacher. The faculty consisted of Olin King, of Georgia, as principal; E. C. McPherson in charge of intermediate grades, and Mrs. E. J. Orr in charge of the primary department. A building at the corner of Fifth street and Central avenue was rented by the town council for use as a school building. It was later moved to the corner of First street and Central avenue and changed to the Clarendon Hotel, which was destroyed by fire in 1899.

In an account of that term, Mr. King said: "The municipal authorities defrayed the general expenses of the school—rent of houses, etc.—thereby rendering a valuable aid to patrons and dispensing with much annoyance that has hitherto attended the management of the school. The supervisor, David Moffett, has visited the respective rooms of the school once a month during the eight months' session."

On July 18, 1893, the first bond issue for St. Petersburg schools was approved 39 to 1. It was for $7,000. One-half of the bonds were taken by Col. L. Y. Jenness, manager of the St. Petersburg Land & Improvement Company. The rest of the issue was taken by other residents. The school erected with this money was the wooden frame building standing today on the corner of Fifth street and Second avenue north. It was then known as the Graded School. It included a library and assembly hall and seven classrooms. It seemed that at last ample room was provided for the children of St. Petersburg, as the registration at that time had not reached the hundred mark. The building was comfortably and durably furnished at a cost of a thousand dollars and for that time the accommodations were not excelled by cities whose population reached several thousand.

Because of a delay in the delivery of the furniture, the school term was shortened to five months, and during the period of waiting several families engaged Mrs. Keagy to teach their children and about thirty pupils were enrolled in this private school. Mrs. Keagy continued her school until 1896, when she again returned to public school instruction.

The first school was divided into eight grades, and permission was granted by the board to teach "some of the higher branches—algebra, physical geography, rhetoric, etc." The teachers in the new building were Olin King, Mrs. Charles Weihman, Miss Susie Abercrombie and Mrs. H. Bomford. David Moffett was again supervisor.

During the Summer of 1895, St. Petersburg was selected as the location for the County Normal. The session was eight weeks and was in charge of County Superintendent L. W. Buchholz, David Williams and Miss Mary Sydney Johnston. H. L. Whitney was elected principal for the next term of the public school at a mass meeting held in July, 1895, in the assembly hall. His appointment later was ratified by the county board. The same assistants as the year before were engaged, with the addition of Miss Maud Chase, who was appointed as assistant to the principal.

On February 22, 1896, the first Washington's Birthday celebration was held by the school children. The celebration was made possible by the generosity of E. H. Tomlinson, whose name was inseparably associated for many years thereafter with the progress of the school. Mr. Tomlinson presented the school with 250 silk and bunting flags and contributed in other ways to make the celebration a success. It was held annually until 1914 and became one of the big features of St. Petersburg's winter season. All the school children took part in a street parade through the business section and after the parade each year there were exercises in the Opera House or auditorium. Motion pictures were taken of the 1912 celebration and distributed all over the country. The school board discontinued the celebrations in 1914 because they were taking too much of the pupils' time.

During the term of 1895 and 1896 the school library was placed upon a substantial basis. A set of encyclopedias, containing twenty-six volumes, was presented by Miss Alice Barnard, for many years principal of schools in Chicago. Joseph Merry also gave a four-volume set of Gibbons' History of Rome. Others also contributed generously and from the proceeds of several school entertainments a dictionary was bought, and the reading room of the school was furnished.

All ready for the Washington's Birthday Celebration of 1899

For the term of 1896 and 1897 Mr. Whitney was re-appointed principal, with the following teachers as assistants: Miss Margaret Grady, Miss Laura Switzer, Mrs. Emily Keagy and Miss Maud Chase. For the term of '97 and '98 the faculty consisted of J. T. Lowe, principal; Miss Grady, E. C. McPherson, Mrs. M. S. Underwood and Mrs. Keagy. It was in this year that the school orchestra was organized, made possible by liberal gifts of money from E. H. Tomlinson and his father, Peter Tomlinson. The orchestra was first made up of three members, but later twenty-two musicians, chosen from all grades of the schools, joined the organization. Several entertainments given by the orchestra so increased the funds that at the end of the year equipment was valued at five hundred dollars, and the orchestra became a popular and profitable school institution.

In June, 1899, the people of St. Petersburg voted to make the St. Petersburg school district a special tax district, thus providing for a local board of three trustees and for the levy of a three-mill tax, which made it possible to maintain the school for a term of eight months.

The State Normal for South Florida, supported by the Peabody fund, was located in St. Petersburg the following summer. The teachers were Professor L. W. Buchholz, David Williams and Miss Greene, of Palatka.

E. C. McPherson resigned a short time before the close of the 1899-1900 term and Henry Damm was appointed to fill his place. A few weeks after the school opened, increased enrollment made necessary the appointment of a new primary teacher, and Miss S. A. Adams, of Warrensburg, Mont., a specialist in primary work, was engaged to fill the position.

Early in 1900 the School Cadet Company was organized and equipped through the financial assistance of E. H. Tomlinson. It was under the direction of Joseph E. Guisinger, of Warrensburg, Mont. The company of forty boys was presented with blue and tan khaki uniforms, cadet guns, a full complement of officers' swords and a regulation United States Army flag. During this term, the school also received $250 from Mr. Tomlinson with which to buy books. A library of more than 100 books was given to the school at this time by G. W. Southwell, former rector of St. Peter's Episcopal Church in this city. The books were part of the library of his daughter, Miss Emily Southwell, and were presented at her death.

Until 1899 the graded school was the only department of the school. In that year the principal was granted permission to conduct classes of first year high school work. At the beginning of the term of 1900-1901 the St. Petersburg High School was established by the county board and offered a three years' course in mathematics, science, history, English and Latin. Two teachers were added to the faculty, G. W. Chambers, assistant principal, and Mrs. Grant J. Aikin, (formerly Miss Maud Chase) as teacher of the second grade.

It was during this year that a lot adjoining the school grounds was purchased and a two-story brick building erected to provide rooms where manual training, physical culture and military science could be taught. The building was equipped for a regular manual training course and physical education course at a cost of $10,000. The never-failing generosity of E. H. Tomlinson and Peter Tomlinson made the introduction of these courses possible.

On the first floor of the new building was the principal's office and the workroom. This room was fitted with seats, desks and blackboards for class work, twenty-seven adjustable work benches, each having a full set of tools; a kerosene engine, shafting and belting to operate a saw; a planer, a grindstone, a jigsaw and a lathe. The second floor was occupied by a large hall for physical training purposes, gymnasium and cadet drills. The new school was opened on December 29, 1901, and was known as Manual Training Day. The town was filled with visitors for the formal opening, including 200 teachers from various parts of the state. The speakers of the day were Superintendent Hayes, of the State Normal at DeFuniak; Dr. Forbes, of Stetson University; Professor B. C. Graham, of Tampa, and Professor L. W. Buchholz, county superintendent. In the afternoon a reception was given in the manual training hall and drill exhibitions were given by the cadets.

During this term manual training was introduced into all the grades, paper folding and cutting in the primary grades, relief maps and sewing in the sixth and seventh grades, and after-school classes for teachers and advanced pupils in manual training. The fife and drum corps also came into existence at this time. A building for the corps was built by E. H. Tomlinson on Fourth street south on the north side of the railroad. The building later was purchased by the city and now is being used as a city hall.

Raising the flag at the Washington's Birthday Celebration in 1904

During the session of the Legislature of 1901, a number of St. Petersburg citizens requested T. F. McCall to go to Tallahassee and assist the Hillsborough County senator and representatives in pressing the claims for state aid for the schools. He took with him photographs and information regarding the work done in the schools, a letter from Mr. Tomlinson containing pledges regarding the use of the buildings erected by him, and letters endorsing his mission from many leading citizens of Tampa. The bill to assist in maintaining a normal and industrial department in the St. Petersburg schools was introduced by J. W. Williamson, of Clearwater, and became effective May 31, 1901. In this way, an appropriation of $5,000 a year for two years was secured from the state, and a state normal school was established. It was known as the St. Petersburg Normal and Industrial School and because of it three new positions were created—principal of the Normal and two assistants.

On August 27, 1901, the town approved a $11,000 bond issue for the schools for the purpose of purchasing a site and erecting the Normal and High School buildings. Lots were purchased from Col. L. Y. Jenness, west of the graded school, and a fine brick building was erected in the spring of 1902.

The Manual Training Annex on Fourth street south, built by Mr. Tomlinson, was completed late in 1901. It seated 5,000 persons and a pipe organ costing $2,000 was installed.

During the term of 1901-1902 a domestic science department was added to the school and work in this department was made part of the regular school course.

During the session of 1902-1903 a printing press and complete printing outfit was added to the equipment of the manual training department, and an eight-oared barge was presented to the physical training school. A thousand dollars' worth of scientific apparatus was also purchased for the school laboratory. Many of these gifts were made by E. H. Tomlinson. In 1904 a thousand dollars was spent in the purchase of books for the library, and more than 500 pupils were enrolled. The faculty for this year consisted of seventeen teachers.

The year 1905 found the St. Petersburg school plants valued at about $40,000—consisting of four school buildings. The schools received an annual income of $1,000 from the special tax district fund, $5,000 from the county school fund and $7,500 from the state appropriation for the normal and industrial departments, making an income of $13,500 from all sources.

The kindergarten department began as a private enterprise, established through the financial assistance of A. F. Bartlett, Roy S. Hanna and C. Durant, who recognized that there should be some place where children just under school age could be educated. Since 1904, the kindergarten has been part of the public school system.

The schools continued to grow; each year more pupils were admitted, until in 1906 the system included twenty-five teachers and 750 pupils. In 1907, all departments of the schools were free to residents on the lower end of the peninsula, except individual instruction in music, for which a small fee was charged.

In 1907, what was known as the Buckman bill changed the state subsidiary schools into one big school for girls at Tallahassee and another big school at Gainesville for boys. As a result, $7,500 from the state was lost in one year, but by rigid economy and contributions, things were kept going, and the schools continued to grow.

On Thursday, October 25, 1906, the city council authorized a bond issue for $63,000, which provided $16,000 for a new high school building and $5,000 for the public schools. This bond issue resulted in a controversy which lasted several years, and at times became very bitter. In 1907, the Supreme Court of the state decreed that the issue was illegal. Immediately thereafter, the council called for an election on a $80,000 bond issue, $25,000 of which was for the high school building. When the election was held, all the items in the bond issue were defeated, the vote on the high school issue being 76 for and 179 against it. On February 23, 1909, the council called for an election on a $30,000 bond issue for schools and a $45,000 bond issue for other improvements. Both issues were approved by substantial majorities, the school issue going over 180 to 39.

A site at the head of Second avenue north was chosen for the new building and a contract was let to W. C. Henry for the erection of a building to cost $28,000. A number of citizens of St. Petersburg were opposed to this site, inasmuch as it meant the closing of Second avenue, and they contested the bond issue. The State Legislature authorized the use of the site but the Supreme Court decided that the bond issue was invalid because cities in Florida could not issue bonds for school purposes since the schools were a county charge.

The building had progressed to such an extent by this time that it was impracticable to stop, and the question of providing money to complete it became all important. The county had spent no money on the building and it belonged entirely to the city of St. Petersburg. The city sold it to E. P. Harrison, John D. Peabody and A. F. Bartlett, who gave their notes for $10,000 each. Nine other indorsers were secured on each note and the money was obtained from the banks. Not until the county was divided were these notes taken up and the school turned over to the county.

The Glenoak School, the school for negro children, was built during 1914 with the proceeds of bond issues approved by the voters in the special school district. The Roser Park and North Side Schools were built during 1916. On June 8, 1915, an election was held on the question of issuing bonds to build a new high school, but it was defeated, 136 to 144. Early in 1917, however, a $175,000 bond issue was approved for the school and the contract was let. As a result of the increase in the cost of building materials at that period, the high school could not be completed for the $175,000 bond issue and nearly $100,000 more had to be voted during the next two years. The Junior High School, now under construction, is expected to cost $350,000. The enrollment in the junior and senior high schools at the beginning of the 1923-24 term was 1,175—200 more than last year.

Central avenue in 1924—looking west from between Third and Fourth streets

XI

REAL ESTATE

ALL the land within the town limits of St. Petersburg, as first platted, was owned by General John C. Williams, who had purchased it from W. F. Sperling and the state in 1876. In addition to the townsite, General Williams owned about 1,100 acres directly adjoining, making his total holdings in this section about 1,600 acres. According to the best information available, the general paid Sperling $3,000 for 640 acres and buildings, and paid the state one dollar an acre for the remainder. His total investment in lands did not exceed $5,000, and the site of St. Petersburg did not cost him more than $2,500.

On January 29, 1887, General Williams agreed to deed over one-half of the townsite to the Orange Belt Railway, provided the company would build a railroad through his property to the bay and construct a pier out to twelve feet of water. The town was surveyed and platted by A. L. Hunt, chief engineer of the Orange Belt. The railroad reached the edge of St. Petersburg on April 30, 1888. The first plat of the town was recorded by Peter A. Demens, president of the Orange Belt, on August 11, 1888. It was not until February 28, 1889, however, that the property was divided according to the agreement. Every alternate block was given to the railroad, or, rather, to the Orange Belt Investment Company, the holding company of the railroad. At the same time, the general gave to the investment company his one-half interest in the Detroit hotel, which he had helped to finance.

Practically the only sale of lots during the first few years was made by General Williams. The first lot in the original townsite was sold to Hector McLeod on August 9, 1888, and the second to J. C. Williams, Jr., on August 11. J. C. Williams, Jr., bought the southwest corner of Central and Second street for $700. A revised plat of St. Petersburg was made by General Williams during the summer of 1890 in order to make a few changes of minor importance. It was recorded on August 18, 1890, as "The Revised Map of St. Petersburg." The property holders who signed the agreement permitting the new plat to be made were J. C. Williams, Jr., D. D. Klinger, Mary T. Howard, E. Powell, J. R. Barclift, J. Douglas Jagger, A. P. K. Safford, A. Maltry, Theodore S. Maltry, E. Ward, Sr., and the trustees of the Congregational Church.

The holdings of the Orange Belt Investment Company in St. Petersburg were sold to the St. Petersburg Land & Improvement Company on October 6, 1890, after the Armour-Drexel-Clark-Stotesbury syndicate had taken over the railroad. Col. L. Y.

Jenness, who had come with the railroad, managed the St. Petersburg office. Prior to its sale, the Orange Belt Investment Company built the depot, a two-story office building and the Detroit hotel.

Practically all the advertising which St. Petersburg got during the nineties was paid for by the St. Petersburg Land & Improvement Company. Folders describing the lands for sale and the attractions of the newly-founded city were distributed far and wide, and many newcomers came here as a result. The company also aided in establishing a cigar factory, a wholesale supply house and a pavilion for the use of the public. It donated lots for churches, public buildings and for the first ice company. The company also bought one-half of the town's first bond issue of $7,000 for schools.

General Williams died on April 25, 1892, and in his will he gave all his property to Sarah Williams, his wife. Later, however, a settlement was made out of court and the property was divided between his wife and children. It was appraised at $160,000.

The St. Petersburg Land & Development Company continued to sell its holdings until December 15, 1906, when it sold the Detroit hotel, an office building at Third and Central, the water front lots where the old electric light plant stood, seventy-five city lots, and seventy-five acres adjoining the city to C. Perry Snell, Albert Hoxie and J. C. Hamlett. The hotel was soon sold again for $25,000.

Curiously enough, the first addition to St. Petersburg was made before the St. Petersburg plat was recorded. Jacob Baum's grove, west of Williams' property, was platted and recorded as the "Ward & Baum Addition of St. Petersburg" on April 4, 1888, nearly a month before the railroad came in. For a while, this addition, which included the Ninth street section, was the bonton district of St. Petersburg. It spurted ahead of the lower part of town, many of the best homes being located here. After a while, however, when "downtown" got started, the glory of Ninth street faded. Manufacturies began locating there and many cheap homes were built for the workmen. Negroes also began coming in. Property values remained low and many years passed before the Ninth street section came into its own again.

A number of stories are heard regarding the negro settlement around Ninth street. One of the stories is that the settlement resulted from "Cooper's Quarters," a group of ten or twelve negro shacks built by L. B. Cooper late in the nineties on Ninth street between the railroad and Second avenue south. Cooper, it is said, understood the negro's habits and knew that they liked to live close together. So he built the shacks accordingly, with a court in the center where the negresses could wash their clothes. "Cooper's Quarters" were soon filled and it wasn't long before other negroes came to live in that locality.

As the Ninth street section dropped behind in popular favor, the downtown section forged ahead. And the best homes were built either on Central avenue or north of Central. The section south of Central proved unpopular for a number of years. There were many reasons for this. In the first place, the drainage on the south side was poor and the topography of the land was such that there were many swamps—and many mosquitoes. New residents sought the high land north of Central. Moreover, they wanted to get as close to the school house as possible, and the first school house was located at Fifth street and Second avenue north. Still another disadvantage of the south side was the railroad tracks.

As a result of all these things, the north side jumped ahead of the south side and stayed ahead for at least two decades. Later on, after its first spurt, the north side got water. sewers and hard-surfaced streets before similar improvements were made south of the railroad, and these improvements naturally proved a big inducement to new residents.

Early in the nineties General Williams recorded a plat called Williamsville, in the Booker Creek district south of the town. Apparently no sales were made from this plat and C. A. Harvey and his associates afterward platted the same land.

Looking east on Central from Third street in 1898

The demand for property during the early years of the city's existence was very limited. A few hundred dollars in cash would buy almost any lot that a prospective purchaser coveted. There was so much land and so few persons who wanted to buy that values naturally remained low. The first increases occurred along lower Central and on the north side, but even in these choice sections lots were ridiculously cheap. Innumerable stories are heard about persons who bought for little or nothing and were made rich by the increase in values which has occurred since.

During 1912, real estate boomed in St. Petersburg. Values soared rapidly, in many cases doubling during the course of a few months. It was during 1912 that West Central lands were put on the market, and the advertising of these developments stimulated the real estate market in all parts of the city. Charles R. Hall, who had bought a large tract from the Florida West Coast Company, opened the first subdivision and sold the first lots on March 13. The prices ranged from $100 to $1,500, corners on Central being the highest priced. At the start of the sale, Mr. Hall allowed 50 per cent discount on the above prices, the discount being scaled down as the sale progressed.

The Florida West Coast Company, before opening its first subdivision, conducted a state-wide advertising campaign, attracting wide attention. Page ads. were carried in all of the largest newspapers of the state and double-page ads. in the St. Petersburg newspapers. When the sale opened, everybody in Florida, it is believed, knew of West Central and its wonderful possibilities for development.

Lots in the subdivision were sold at auction and on the first day of the sale 84 were disposed of for $34,820. On the second day, 78 lots were sold for $26,975. Before the sale ended, 441 lots went under the hammer, and the company received $115,999. Never before had there been such a market for lots in or near St. Petersburg. Everyone, it seemed, tourists and home folks included, went "lot crazy" and they snapped up everything that resembled a bargain.

An indication of the rise in values during 1912 is given by the record of the sales of the lot at the southeast corner of Fifth and Central, now occupied by the First National Bank. The city sold this lot during the summer of 1911 to the Knights of Pythias for $7,000. Early in 1912, the Knights of Pythias sold it to George Hatch, a tourist from Massachusetts, for $10,000. On March 12, 1912, Mr. Hatch sold to D. D. Dodge, of Rhode Island, for $12,500, and less than a week later, on March 18, Mr. Dodge sold to the Home Mechanics' Security Company for $15,500. The curious part about the whole thing was that each time the lot was sold there were many persons in the city who openly asserted that the price was outlandishly high and the purchaser would regret the transaction.

Other large deals were made during the first half of 1912. J. W. Sylvester sold a 40-acre tract, on March 12, at the corner of Ninth street and Johns Pass road for $12,000 to a group of Ohio capitalists. Mr. Sylvester had owned the property twenty-five years and had paid originally $100 for the entire tract. A few days later J. G. Lewis sold a 20-acre grove between Fourth and Fifth streets north and between Nineteenth and Twenty-second avenues for $20,000 to a group of local men. The price of $1,000 an acre for undeveloped land was considered by some as out of all reason.

Mrs. May Purnell, a proprietor of the Floronton Hotel, purchased the home of J. T. Yonce, at the southwest corner of Sixth and Central, for $15,000 cash. Yonce bought the lot in 1896 for $400, but Mrs. Purnell said she was confident the increase during the next decade would appear as great. Land in this locality at present is selling for at least $2,000 a front foot.

Beach drive property also was booming during this period. During the week of March 16 Mrs. Sadie Key announced that she had sold a lot on Ninth avenue near Beach drive for $2,500, and another at Beach drive and Twelfth avenue for $5,000— $66 a front foot. These were unprecedented prices and occasioned wide comment.

Real estate continued active during 1913 and 1914, numerous large deals being transacted. During this period there also was a pronounced interest in Gulf Beach properties. In January, 1913, the Gulf Beach Resort Company, with a capital of

$50,000, started a hotel on Treasure Island, south of Johns Pass, which had been subdivided in 1912 by George Roberts, pioneer settler of the island. Late in the same year Noel A. Mitchell started to develop Mitchell's Beach, north of Johns Pass. A hotel and bathhouse were erected, an electric light system installed, an artesian well sunk and cement sidewalks laid. Many lots were sold. The development later, however, proved a failure.

The outbreak of the World War in 1914 had an adverse effect upon real estate values in St. Petersburg. In some parts of St. Petersburg prices dropped, indicating that the boom of 1912 had resulted in inflated values. Those who had bought on a "shoestring" were caught, and likewise some of the large developers. Before the war ended, the Florida West Coast Company and allied companies went into the hands of receivers. St. Petersburg did not suffer from the war as much as many cities, but the effect of it was felt keenly.

During the past four years realty values in St. Petersburg have climbed steadily, but with none of the sensational, unsound increases of the 1912 boom.

North Shore

St. Petersburg can well boast of its North Shore. Without a doubt, it is one of the most attractive residential districts in all Florida. Millions of dollars have been invested there in homes. Northward the city has grown, and the growth has barely begun. For a while it halted at the edge of Coffee Pot Bayou, but now it has reached around and beyond.

North Shore section as seen from an airplane in 1924

North Shore and C. Perry Snell are indelibly linked together. It was Mr. Snell who recognized the development possibilities of this section and it was Mr. Snell who made it what it is today. While others scoffed at this land so near the water's edge, Mr. Snell figured out a way of lifting it above the water level and turning it into a beauty spot.

Mr. Snell's North Shore activities started back in 1904 and 1905, when he organized the Bay Shore Land Company, with F. A. Wood, A. E. Hoxie and A. C. Clewis. The Bay Shore and Bay Front subdivisions were the result. Both were located on Tampa Bay, extending from Fifth to Thirteenth avenues north.

These subdivisions served merely as a starter. Late in 1906, Mr. Snell joined with J. C. Hamlett and formed the partnership of Snell & Hamlett, purchasing the holdings of the St. Petersburg Land & Improvement Company. A. E. Hoxie also took part in the deal. In February, 1910, Snell & Hamlett purchased six hundred acres of land from the Tison-Turner-Flannery interests of Savannah, Ga. This tract lay between First street and Tampa Bay, starting at Thirteenth avenue north and extending along Tampa Bay across Coffee Pot Bayou and northward along First street to Johns Pass road.

Several smaller tracts were purchased from other holders, and about four hundred acres were secured a few years later from Erastus and Alice Barnard. On the Erastus Barnard tract, just east of the present State Masonic Home, was one of the oldest orange groves in this section, being more than forty years old. The old house is still standing and the grove is still bearing. All of this acreage, starting at Fifth avenue north and First street, was a wild, rugged palmetto land, being used for a cow pasture, with many ponds, bayhead and one or two small creeks running through it.

In 1911, the first real development work on North Shore was started. In that year Snell & Hamlett spent over $300,000. They built a trolley line connecting with the city line to the present terminus at Coffee Pot Bayou. Over two miles of seawall were built along Tampa Bay and the bayou. These improvements continued for several years and included roads, sanitary sewer system, water and gas mains, until an expenditure of over one million dollars was made.

Following the purchase by Mr. Snell of Mr. Hamlett's interest in all of Snell & Hamlett's holdings, he continued to add to his holdings and at present he owns all of the lands around Coffee Pot Bayou, extending to the south and westerly shores of Smack's Bayou. About twenty of the artistic homes seen in North Shore were erected by Snell & Hamlett, including the two homes at the entrance of Coffee Pot Bayou used for their residences for several years.

Among Mr. Snell's present plans for development in his North Shore section is a three-mile boulevard around the shore line of Coffee Pot Bayou; a new section of North Shore development to be known as Granada Terrace. It is to be a highly restricted, exclusive section for Spanish and Italian stucco homes. Not only the type of the house, but the exterior, the color scheme and the landscaping of the grounds will be controlled in the restrictions. Another development now in the process of execution is the "Bright Waters" section, the peninsula across from the Coffee Pot entrance running around Tampa Bay and including Bright Waters Bayou.

Bayboro

Until the Bayboro Investment Company was organized, St. Petersburg's possibilities for growth to the southward were abruptly and absolutely cut off by a wide swamp through which Salt and Booker Creek found their way to the bay; beyond the swamp was a magnificent stretch of high ground, but its development also was barred by the impassable swamp separating it from St. Petersburg.

Along in 1904, C. A. Harvey, then a beginner in the real estate business, conceived the idea of redeeming all this waste territory, and not only removing this obstacle to the city's growth, but of converting it into an instrument of still greater progress. His plans included the dredging out of a harbor and the filling in of the low lands.*

Mr. Harvey's means were limited, but his energy and confidence were not. He first interested Dr. H. A. Murphy and together they bought, early in 1905, thirty acres of this waste land; then he and A. F. Freeman bought seventy-five acres more, Harvey later buying out Mr. Freeman. On June 26, 1905, the Bayboro Investment Company was organized, which continued buying all the territory east of Fourth street, south of the city to about Nineteenth avenue. This included all of the swamp

---
*See Life of C. A. Harvey.

Looking south on Fourth street from top of Pheil building in 1924—Bayboro Harbor is seen in background

lands and most of the highlands beyond, about 180 acres in all. With the made lands, the company's holdings totaled about 250 acres. The original officers of the company were C. L. Howard, president; Dr. H. A. Murphy, vice-president; R. H. Thomas, secretary; T. K. Wilson, treasurer, and C. A. Harvey, manager. Others who were identified with the company in its early days were F. A. Wood, H. C. Dent, H. A. Kellam, A. Welton and Mr. and Mrs. W. S. Heathcote. Dredging was started by the company soon after its organization.

On July 15, 1910, the company reported that it had dredged a channel to the bay, had made a basin 450 feet wide and 1,460 feet long, with a mean depth of 14 feet. It also reported that it had sold $160,000 worth of lots and had spent $150,000 on improvements.

The trolley line to Bayboro was built by the company and turned over to the St. Petersburg & Gulf Electric Railway Company for operation. The first car went over the line on Thursday, January 5, 1911. Officials and stockholders of the Bayboro Investment Company were on board. A paved street to Bayboro was completed in 1914.

The plans of the company depended, to a great extent, upon the acceptance by the city of Bayboro as its commercial harbor. And to get the harbor, it was essential that the city get government aid. However, it was not until the spring of 1912 that the government appropriated $32,000 for dredging a channel and building a stone jetty, and it was not until the summer of 1914 that work was actually started. Before the government agreed to assist, the city had to pledge itself to acquire 600 feet of frontage along the harbor, dredge out the inside of the basin to a depth of 12 feet, keep it dredged out, provide rail connections with the harbor and build one pier. All these things were not done until the summer of 1923.*

Despite the delay in the completion of the Bayboro harbor project, the Bayboro section has developed rapidly during the past five years, since the end of the war. Numerous industrial concerns have been located at Bayboro and many attractive homes have been built in the residential district beyond. South Beach drive is considered one of the most exclusive parts of the city. C. A. Harvey died on January 18, 1914, but his heirs still control large sections of land in Bayboro.

Central Avenue and Pasadena

Since the beginning of St. Petersburg, Central avenue has been the city's main business thoroughfare. Today it extends seven miles from Tampa Bay to Boca Ceiga Bay straight across the peninsula, and it is being built up rapidly from end to end. Ten years ago the business section ended at Fifth street; now it has leaped beyond and gone past Ninth street, there being many business places even west of Booker Creek, at one time considered the extreme limit for development.

In the early days, property values along Central naturally were very low. The first sale recorded was for the southwest corner of Central and Second street, sold by General Williams to his son, John C. Williams, Jr., August 11, 1888, for $700. Even $700 was high for lots on Central in 1888 and for a number of years afterward.

---
*See Water Front Development.

Many lots between Second and Fifth streets sold for from $500 to $1,000. Today all the land in this section is worth more than $2,000 a front foot.

In 1895, Capt. J. A. Armistead offered his opera house for sale for $6,000, building and all. It was located on the south side of Central between Second and Third streets. In 1902, the West Coast Bank bought the southeast corner of Central and Second for $1,500 from the defunct St. Petersburg State Bank. In 1903, George B. Haines bought the southwest corner of Fourth and Central, where the Central National Bank building stands today, for $2,300. The building which stood on this site, once used by the State Bank, was thrown in for good measure. In 1906, Messrs. Snell, Hoxie and Hamlett bought the Detroit hotel from the St. Petersburg Land & Improvement Company and sold it in less than a year for $25,000. Today the lot alone is easily worth $500,000.

Property west of Fifth street on Central was cheaper during the early days. It was a residential district and any number of lots could be purchased for $700 each. It was not until 1912 that the business section leaped the Fifth street barrier and resulted in material increases in values. At present, no property east of Ninth street can be purchased at less than $1,500 a front foot.

Central avenue was not opened up clear through from First street to Ninth until 1894. At Third street there was a swale which extended across the avenue and made it impossible for teams to get through. Moreover, the avenue had not been opened up through Ward & Baum's addition, and the road jogged over toward the railroad

The Wood building on the north side of Central between Third and Fourth streets, erected by F. A. Wood in 1901—the second brick building in St. Petersburg

track a little west of Sixth street. The Third street swale was filled in and graded late in 1894, when the councilmen gave their notes to have the work done. About the same time the avenue was opened up through Ward & Baum's addition, council making an appropriation for pulling out the stumps of the old orange trees. But the avenue through the addition was only 50 feet wide, the developers having been unable to foresee the need of a wide business street. It was not widened to 100 feet and straightened until 1909, when a bond issue of $8,000 was approved to buy the necessary land. Even then, there was considerable opposition to the widening, many believing that a wide thoroughfare would never be needed above Sixth and that the $8,000 would be wasted. Had it not been for A. C. Pheil, who fought persistently for the project, it is doubtful whether it would have been completed until years later, when the cost would have been many times greater. An idea of the general feeling toward the project is given by the following editorial in the Times in the issue of October 20, 1906: "The widening of Central has been before the people and the council for years. It has never been popular. It is an improvement that would be of little practical benefit to the city at large. But it has been conceded by most people only as a friendly consideration to local interests there. The city is pledged to the work and must carry it out."

The extension of Central avenue west of Ninth street to Boca Ceiga Bay came as a direct result of the efforts of H. Walter Fuller and his associates. Mr. Fuller was the manager of the St. Petersburg Investment Company and its allied companies, organized for the development of St. Petersburg by F. A. Davis, of Philadelphia.

Mr. Fuller conceived the idea of extending Central shortly after he became connected with the Davis companies. He believed that westward was the logical direction for St. Petersburg to grow, and that the growth would be slow in coming without a bay-to-bay avenue. He tried to interest the people of St. Petersburg in the West Central project, but without success. The only backing he could get was from the Philadelphia backers of the F. A. Davis companies—the men who had more faith in St. Petersburg than the greatest local boosters. The Johns Pass Realty Company was organized for the purpose of acquiring the necessary lands.

During the period from 1909 to 1912, many large tracts were bought up by the company. One tract of 15,000 acres was purchased from W. W. Whitehurst, brother of the sheriff of Hillsborough County. The price averaged less than $5 an acre. Later, 3,200 acres were purchased from Hamilton Disston, who owned 4,000,000 acres in Florida, for $16,200. The Jungle, comprising 160 acres, was purchased from John Miller and William B. Henderson, of Tampa, for $2,500. The land had been secured by Miller and Henderson in payment of a $46 grocery bill from an old Spaniard who had homesteaded it before the Civil War.

By the end of 1911, the Johns Pass Realty Company had acquired all the lands needed up to Sixteenth street. Between Ninth and Sixteenth the land was divided into small holdings and the owners, foreseeing development, demanded high prices. The Central Land & Title Company was organized by Mr. Fuller and E. V. Pechin to buy it in. Within a few months, a half-mile strip in the coveted zone was purchased from fifty different persons at a cost of $175,000, more than all the rest put together.

Early in 1912, Charles R. Hall bought 80 acres in the West Central district from the Johns Pass Realty Company for $200 an acre. He started the sale of lots on March 12. His subdivision included three blocks from Twenty-fifth to Twenty-eighth streets. Another subdivision closer to town was sold at auction on March 18, 19 and 20 by the Florida West Coast Company, another subsidiary of the St. Petersburg Investment Company. Before the sale ended, 441 lots were sold for $115,999.

More West Central subdivisions were put on the market during the next few months by the Florida West Coast Company, Charles R. Hall, C. M. Roser, Noel A. Mitchell and the Central Avenue Heights Company, composed of G. W. Foster, R. H. Sumner, A. S. Paine and E. H. Hines. The demand for lots continued brisk until the outbreak of the World War and several thousand were sold.

Many inducements were used by these developers to sell the lots. The Florida West Coast Company, for instance, sold on one-third down payments, the balance to be paid in two years, one-quarter every six months. The company guaranteed that unless the sidewalks were down within six months after date of purchase, the other

A scene at the Jungle—one of the largest real estate developments in St. Petersburg in 1924

payments would be cancelled. Similarly, it guaranteed to have Central avenue opened from bay to bay in twelve months and the street-car line through in eighteen months. All these promises were kept. The car line reached Disston avenue on April 2, 1913, and Davista on April 29.

Paving Central avenue with brick was urged by Mr. Hall and Mr. Mitchell while the subdivision sales were in full swing. They wanted the best—nothing else would satisfy them. After the street-car line was in they worked harder than ever. Many said they were foolish—that it would be criminal to spend all that money on a road "through a wilderness." But they kept at it, and circulated petitions until enough signatures were secured. Financing the project by the city was made possible by the annexation into the city of a strip one mile wide on each side of Central. Inasmuch as the section was inside the city limits, the city could issue bonds to pay for the work and the lot owners were able to stretch their payments over five years. Lot owners on Central avenue paid 60 per cent of the cost, on First avenue 25 per cent, and on Second avenue 15 per cent. The contract for the paving was let late in 1914 and the work was completed less than a year later.

Davista was put on the market by the Florida West Coast Company about the same time the first subdivisions were opened on Central. The St. Petersburg Country Club was founded there as part of the Davista development program. Many miles of streets were paved, sewers and water pipes laid and shrubbery planted. Nearly fifty homes were built.

The progress of Davista and the West Central district was halted by the war. In 1916, the F. A. Davis companies went into the hands of a receiver.

Pasadena-on-the-Gulf is a direct outgrowth of Davista, which was purchased on April 12, 1922, through the Fuller Realty Company by Jack Taylor and Fred G. Aulsbrook, of New York, and Innes Henry, of Boston, who formed Pasadena Estates, Inc.

During the past year the company has spent more than a half-million dollars in the development of Pasadena, making it one of the beauty spots of Florida. Thou-

The gates of Pasadena-on-the-Gulf in 1924

sands of palm trees and shrubs have been planted in beautifying the parks and boulevards. Miles of paved streets and sidewalks have been completed. In addition, it has provided gas, a school and a block of community stores, including the Mocking Bird Tea Room. Several hundred thousand dollars' worth of lots were sold during the first year and more than a score of Spanish-type stucco houses were built.

Roser Park

Roser Park, one of St. Petersburg's completed developments, is noted for being one of the most attractive residential districts in Florida. It was started in the fall of 1911, when C. M. Roser purchased the C. D. Hammond home, with ten acres of grove, for $12,000, and five acres more from J. P. Lynch and Alexander Lynn. During 1912, he added to his holdings by purchasing all the abutting properties possible from various parties. In 1913, he bought from W. O. Budd a five-acre block running from Eighth to Ninth streets from the alley between Eighth and Ninth avenues to Booker Creek. One-third of this block was creek or gully and the rest of it was hillside. The price for the five acres was $25,000.

At the time these purchases were made there were no brick houses on the south side and Roser Park was not in the city limits. The possibilities for a high-class development seemed limited, but Mr. Roser persevered. His first step was the paving of Sixth street south, connecting Roser Park with Central avenue. Mr. Roser

The Mocking Bird Tea Room at Pasadena-on-the-Gulf in 1924

personally hired the Georgia Engineering Company to do the work and made the payment direct, co-operating with the city commissioners in hastening the project. The pavement was completed during 1914.

During the next two years approximately sixty homes were built in the subdivision. The war then stopped further progress, but later, in 1921, about twenty more homes were added.

A scene of semi-tropical beauty in Roser Park

About four acres of the thirty in the subdivision were turned over to the city as a city park, being named Roser Park. The winding creek, with the hills and tropical vegetation, have made this one of the beauty spots of St. Petersburg. Five lots off the east end of the subdivision were sold to the city at a very low price for a school, now called Roser Park school. Mr. and Mrs. Roser built the present nurses' home, furnished it, and gave it to the nurses as a permanent home. The old white hospital, which stood on the premises of the nurses' home, was moved over to the negro quarters and converted into a negro hospital.

Lakewood Estates

Lakewood Estates, beginning two and one-half miles south of the postoffice, embraces a large portion of Big and Little Bayous, overlooks Lake Maggiore, and has more than a mile of water frontage on Boca Ceiga Bay. It includes altogether 2,500 acres of land and extends across Point Pinellas. The development was started because of the belief of Charles R. Hall and his associates that this section of Pinellas Peninsula was favored with more natural advantages than any other part of the state and that a mistake had been made in locating St. Petersburg in its present location. They decided to correct the mistake by converting Point Pinellas into one of St. Petersburg's most charming and up-to-the-minute residential sections.

Since 1917 Mr. Hall and his associates have been taking steps to insure the fulfillment of their plans by acquiring such tracts as they deemed necessary, including the control of the Bayou Bonita section, the Lake Maggiore section, and the Bay Vista section, all of which were being developed by others companies but which now have been merged into the Victory Land Company, thereby insuring a uniform character of development and improvements.

At the present time, the Victory Land Company is developing the entire properties so acquired and which are known as Lakewood Estates. Over a million dollars already has been expended in the development work. Sanitary sewage disposal plants have been built and are now in operation, miles of streets are being paved, sidewalks and cement curbing are being constructed, and extensive parks are being laid out and planted. Water pumping stations have been built and mains have been laid. Electricity and telephone service have been provided.

The Bayou Bonito Club house on the shore of Little Bayou is the social headquarters for the residents of Lakewood Estates. Plans are now being prepared for a new clubhouse of Spanish and Moorish type to be built during 1924. The golf course, which will spread out like the wings of a butterfly over large tracts of land, is being

Bayou Bonita Clubhouse on the Lakewood Estates in 1924

completed under the direction of Herbert Strong. A feature of the estates is its driveways, which are so constructed that they parallel every fairway, making it possible for the gallery to follow every play made on the entire eighteen holes, either afoot or by motor car.

XII

GREEN BENCHES

THE famous green benches of St. Petersburg, found everywhere along the business streets and in the parks, came into existence as a result of a kindly impulse—the desire to be hospitable. St. Petersburg was inviting folks to visit her during the winter months, and it seemed fitting that she should provide seats for her guests. And so the green bench came to be.

Back in 1908, Fourth street and Central avenue was considered far uptown. Folks gathered at Second and Third streets, but it was hard to get them as far west as Fourth street and, granted they walked this far, no amount of persuasion or advertising could make them cross the street to where Mitchell's block—now the Snell Arcade—then stood. This augured ill for the real-estate business of Noel A. Mitchell, "the Sand Man," owner of the block, and he set about solving the problem.

Mr. Mitchell noticed that folks often entered his office for the sole purpose of sitting down. Weary with walking, they often asked permission to rest in the chairs against the walls. This gave Mr. Mitchell an idea. He ordered fifty benches made, painted them a bright orange, decorated them with advertising, and placed them outside his offices, on Fourth street and Central avenue, one Saturday night. Then he waited results.

The results were not long in coming. It seemed as if all St. Petersburg had been waiting for the advent of the benches. Every hour of the day, almost, they were filled to overflowing, and sometimes there were crowds standing waiting for a bench to become empty. Folks called it "Mitchell's prayer meeting." Fourth street began to be the most popular corner in the city. Crowds gathered on the benches to chat, bask in the sunshine or wait for friends. They were willing to walk two or three extra blocks for the opportunity of sitting down, and business began to flow to the real-estate office.

The interest of other merchants was aroused, and they thought it well to offer their customers or patrons a similar convenience. Mr. Mitchell was unable to keep up with the popularity of his orange benches. As fast as he had them made, folks wanted to borrow them. These, like the first, were painted a vivid orange, and across their backs in black letters were painted these words: "Mitchell, the Sand Man. The Honest Real Estate Dealer. He Never Sleeps." This, as Mr. Mitchell explained, demanded a bench with a back of generous proportions, to accommodate the advertisement, so folks were doubly assured of comfort.

These additional orange benches were scattered about the town, and gradually others saw the benefits Mr. Mitchell was deriving from the advertising thus secured. They began to make benches of their own. A heterogeneous collection appeared on the city streets—benches of all sizes, shapes and colors. They were plentifully sprinkled with advertising, but the weary tourist was exceedingly thankful to rest his back against the black letters proclaiming the merits of anything—pills or developments—so long as the bench was provided.

As one may imagine, the appearance of the city was not improved from an aesthetic standpoint by this odd assortment of benches, hospitable thought they might have been. During the administration of Mayor Al. F. Lang, steps were taken to standardize them. An ordinance was passed that nearly tolled the death knell of the green bench, so unpopular did it prove with the owners of the benches already on the streets. The ordinance demanded that all benches be of a standard size and color, and that after a certain date, all other benches which did not conform to the regulations would have to be taken off the streets.

A storm of protest arose from those who believed this to be an infringement of their rights. The benches were their property, they argued, and it seemed only fair that they should make them any size or paint them any color that they wished. It meant an expenditure of money, too, to have their benches cut down to standard size and repainted, and many preferred taking their benches home and chopping them up for firewood to obeying the ordinance. Mr. Mitchell suggested that the expense for this change fall on the city, but his suggestion was not carried out.

Many of the larger benches disappeared, but gradually merchants adjusted themselves to the change and came to see the necessity for such an ordinance. Benches were made thereafter of the size prescribed and painted green. So the green bench came into existence, the green bench whose ancestor had been the brilliant orange seat placed that Saturday night at the corner of Fourth and Central.

The green bench has become a distinctive part of St. Petersburg and it would be hard to think of Central avenue without them. Certain it is that hundreds of tourists and home folks would be at a loss without the good old benches to sink onto when waiting for trolleys, or chatting with friends, or when worn out with shopping. It bespeaks the hospitality of the city in an unmistakable manner, and assures the visitor that St. Petersburg is mindful of his comfort and his pleasure.

XIII

POSTOFFICE

THE first postoffice in St. Petersburg was established in 1888 in Ward's general store on Ninth street, E. R. Ward having been appointed as postmaster. The first letter containing St. Petersburg, Florida, in the address was received by Ed. T. Lewis. Up until that time Pinellas and Bonifacia were the only settlements on the peninsula which were recognized by the postoffice department.

Mr. Ward was succeeded in October, 1891, by D. W. Meeker, who moved the office to a building on the north side of Central avenue between Fourth and Fifth streets. Dr. George Kennedy was appointed to succeed Mr. Meeker late in 1895 and moved the postoffice to a small shack on Central on the site of the present Willson-Chase building. Dr. Kennedy held the office only three months, being followed by W. A. Sloan. The site of the postoffice was not changed until about two years later, when it was moved by Mr. Sloan to the south side of Central between Third and Fourth streets.

Central avenue as it looked in 1902

Roy S. Hanna was appointed to succeed W. A. Sloan in 1900. A short time later the postoffice was made third class and Mr. Hanna was allowed to hire one clerk at $25 a month and the salary of postmaster was advanced to $1,000. The office was moved to Colonel Livingston's building on the north side of Central between Third and Fourth streets, where it was kept for about three years.

The business of the office grew with the growth of the city and in 1905 Mr. Hanna called a number of the citizens together and told them he would have to have a larger office than he could rent with the money allowed him by the postoffice department. E. H. Tomlinson offered to erect a building at the northeast corner of Central and Fourth and to rent it to the government for five years at fifty dollars a month. His offer was accepted and the building was occupied February 16, 1907.

At Mr. Hanna's suggestion, the front was left out of the building and box holders could get their mail day or night. This was an unheard-of innovation and someone reported it to the authorities at Washington, resulting in the ultimatum that no rent would be allowed for the building until a front was put in. Mr. Hanna was satisfied that his plan was the best for a town like St. Petersburg and no change was made. A few months later a postmasters' convention was held in St. Petersburg and five government officials, including the fourth postmaster general, attended. The officials inspected the open office and gave it their endorsement as being adapted to the needs of

The St. Petersburg Open-Air Post Office, completed in 1917

a city like St. Petersburg. It was not long afterwards that the checks began coming in again to pay for the rent.

Free postal delivery for St. Petersburg was secured by Mr. Hanna as a result of a trip to Washington in October, 1906. The free delivery began in June, 1907.

With the rapid growth of St. Petersburg, it was not long before the Tomlinson building was outgrown. It was necessary for persons to form a line on Fourth street and receive their mail through the windows of the building. Despite the cramped quarters, however, it was not until February 24, 1915, that the office was moved to the City Hall Building, where the entire lower floor was occupied. At that time it was the largest postoffice in Florida.

The movement to secure a government building for St. Petersburg was launched in 1907, when Mr. Hanna and the Board of Trade urged the Postoffice Department to take action. An appropriation of $7,500 was included in the public buildings bill passed by Congress during the early summer of 1908 to buy a site for the postoffice. Negotiations for the site were started at once and on March 8, 1909, it was announced that the three lots on the corner of First avenue north and Fourth street, owned by the Congregational Church, had been purchased. The selection of this site aroused considerable criticism, many believing that the building should not be crowded in on one corner of a block and that enough ground should be obtained to allow for future expansion.

An appropriation of $55,000 was authorized by Congress in the summer of 1910. This did not satisfy the Board of Trade, the members contending that St. Petersburg deserved a better building than could be erected for this amount. Every effort was made to secure a larger amount and finally, in February, 1915, Congress provided $102,500 for the building and $5,000 additional for the site. On January 26, 1916, the contract was let for the present building to M. C. Holliday, of Greensboro, N. C., for $89,717. The postoffice architects said this building would be large enough to take care of the business of a city of one hundred thousand. It was outgrown, however, within a few years after completion.

Work on the new postoffice was started on March 2, 1916. Postmaster Hanna turned over the first shovelful of earth before a crowd of a thousand persons. Music, prayer, and speeches by city officials made up the program. In July of the same year, W. L. Straub was appointed to succeed Mr. Hanna as postmaster. The corner stone of the postoffice was laid with full Masonic ceremonies on October 12, 1916. The speakers were Mayor Al Lang, Mr. Hanna and Mr. Straub. The building was dedicated on Thursday, September 27, 1917.

Mr. Straub served as postmaster until the spring of 1923, when Mr. Hanna was again appointed.

XIV

CITY LIBRARY

THE first attempt to furnish free reading matter to the people of St. Petersburg was made by members of the Christian Endeavor Society of the Congregational Church in 1899, at a time when Miss Beulah Chase was president. The society managed to secure the interest of the young people of the other churches and a small room was opened in the old Durant block, at Fourth street and Central avenue. Magazines and a few books were on hand for those who cared to read them. The room was kept open for many months, a number of young people volunteering to serve as librarian. Interest finally waned, however, the room was vacated, and the furniture and library were stored.

The failure of this effort did not deter the library advocates from trying again. A mass meeting was called early in July, 1905, for consideration of a library plan, and a committee of eight was appointed to secure members and contributions. The committee made its report at another mass meeting, held later in the month at the school house. Arthur Norwood was chairman and Miss Pauline Barr, a well-remembered kindergarten teacher, was secretary pro tem. Eloquent speeches were made by R. H. Thomas and Roy S. Hanna, and a permanent organization was formed with 122 members under the name of the St. Petersburg Reading Room and Library Association. The first officers elected were Judge J. D. Bell, president; J. A. Sims, vice-president; Mrs. Annie McRae, secretary, and Mrs. Fred M. Allen, treasurer. Mr. Hanna was appointed as a committee of one "to hunt up lost materials of a past library." He fulfilled his trust and at the next meeting reported that he had recovered twelve chairs and two tables.

A constitution and by-laws were adopted at a meeting in the school house on August 28, 1905. The objects of the association were stated to be: "To establish and maintain a reading room and library for citizens and visitors, with special reference to provide good reading, literature and books for young men, with such games as shall be approved by the board of directors." Of directors, there were plenty—the officers of the association, the mayor, clerk and treasurer of the city and the members of the school board. The scale of month's dues was very elastic—some paid only 10 cents; others paid as much as 50. Later, it was found that games and amusements and reading did not mix well—in the same room, and the "appurtenances" finally had to be banished.

On September 4, 1905, the association decided to lease a room in the Bussey building, on the south side of Central between Third and Fourth. The room was kept open by twelve ladies in the afternoons and twelve men at night, each serving once every two weeks without pay.

During 1906, Albert H. Roberts kept the records of the association for the secretary, Mrs. Annie McRae, who was sick much of the year. Old members recall that Mr. Roberts lost the records and that when Mrs. McRae reproached him regularly, he would always assure her that he was working on a new trail that would lead to the missing papers—but they never were found. Mrs. Bellona Havens was engaged as librarian during 1906. She took the work mostly for the love of it, as she was paid very little.

Walter Platt, who served as president of the association in 1907, aided materially in improving the library. When he moved from the city before the expiration of his term the records showed that the association owed him more than eighty dollars, which he had advanced to fit up the reading room and for current expenses. He was never paid in full, although part of the money was raised at a "tacky party" attended by many of the society people, who were dressed in fantastic and ridiculous costumes.

A. F. Bartlett acted as president for the remainder of the term. During his administration the library was moved to the Strowger block, at Fourth and Central, and negotiations were begun for the Tabard Inn Library. After the library was received the books were placed in a revolving case which will always be remembered by old members because of a pernicious habit of wailing like a lost soul whenever touched.

Judge J. D. Bell was re-elected president in the fall of 1907. The records show that Miss Margaret Jenkins was tendered a "vote of thanks for her very faithful services as treasurer" during the preceding year. Miss Jenkins, in fact, served as treasurer during almost the entire life of the association, despite the arduous duties connected with the collection of the membership dues.

Mrs. Minnie Sorrels was appointed librarian in April, 1908. Shortly afterwards, a committee was appointed to file an application for a Carnegie library, but little was done to secure a donation at that time. T. J. Northrup was elected president in September, 1908. A short time later it was found necessary to vacate the room in the Strowger block and, inasmuch as no other room within the means of the association could be secured, it was found necessary to store the books and furniture for a time.

Although the library had been closed the association kept intact, and at the last meeting in 1908 Miss Margaret Jenkins was appointed librarian, a position she held until 1915. For a long time she served for a very small salary and, in order for her to get any money at all, she had to go out and collect it in monthly dues.

The reading room was re-opened in a room in the Mitchell block, at Fourth and Central, in 1909. It remained there until the new Carnegie library was completed. There was never another election of officers, Mr. Northrup being the last president. The directors met occasionally with the librarian, however, and advised about such matters as seemed necessary until late in 1910, when the library became a municipal institution with its expenses paid, or partly paid, by the city. The new city charter, which became effective July 1, 1913, provided that the library and city advertising funds should be handled by a Library and Municipal Advertising Commission. When the new city commissioners took office they appointed W. L. Straub president of this commission, Arthur L. Johnson, vice-president, and Mrs. Annie McRae, secretary.

As stated before, the movement to secure a Carnegie library for St. Petersburg was launched in 1908. The matter hung fire, however, for a number of years. In 1912, R. Veillard, a councilman at the time, entered negotiations with the Carnegie Corporation, and it was learned that the city could secure a donation of $12,500 if the city desired to accept it. This sum was considered insufficient and nothing more was done until late in 1913, when the Library and Municipal Advertising Commission took up the matter. Every effort was made to secure an increased donation, but no success was obtained until W. L. Straub, armed with a mass of letters and Sunshine City literature, went to New York and saw officers of the corporation. The strength of his arguments is indicated by the fact that the corporation agreed to increase the appropriation $5,000, making $17,500 in all.

While work on the plans was going ahead, the city fathers argued about the most desirable site for the library. They were unable or unwilling to provide a lot for the building other than land already in its possession and, consequently, the only available sites were on Mirror Lake and on the water front. The Mirror Lake site was selected as being the more central and more suitable in other ways. The contract

The Public Library of St. Petersburg, completed in 1915

for the building was let to W. C. Henry, who started work in October, 1914. The cornerstone was laid on December 19, 1914, with full Masonic ceremonies, in charge of Deputy Grand Master J. E. Crane, of Tampa. Governor Park Trammel was the principal speaker. Others who spoke were Dr. J. P. Hoyt, W. L. Straub, Major J. G. Bradshaw and Dr. George N. Sleight, then superintendent of schools.

The library building was completed on September 11, 1915, and on October 1, Miss Emma Moore Williams was appointed librarian and Miss Margaret H. Jenkins assistant librarian. The books were moved to the new building and on December 1, 1915, it was opened to the public. At that time the library had 2,600 volumes.

For several years Miss Williams and Miss Jenkins took care of all the work, but in time it became too much for them, and in 1917 Miss Mary Bright was appointed second assistant librarian. At the present time, in 1924, two other assistants are employed regularly and several others during the most busy periods. The library now has 12,000 volumes and approximately 6,000 borrowers. During the winter, as many as 10,000 books are circulated each month. Although the library is badly cramped for space, it is serving well the needs of the residents and winter visitors.

XV

HOSPITALS

ST. PETERSBURG'S first hospital was made possible by a small group of men who realized that a hospital of some sort was imperative. In 1906, Dr. J. D. Peabody purchased a lot on Second street north, near First avenue, with the intention of erecting an office and small private hospital. A. P. Avery became interested and offered financial assistance with the result that a building large enough to accommodate fifteen beds was erected. The St. Petersburg Sanitarium was formed and incorporated under the state laws. Donations amounting to about $2,000 were given by the citizens for furnishing the hospital, E. H. Tomlinson giving $1,000 for equipping the operating room.

After the hospital was completed, Dr. Peabody organized the most prominent practitioners of the city as an operating body. In March, 1907, officers were elected as follows: Dr. Peabody, president; Dr. Thomas P. Welsh, vice-president; Dr. F. W. Wilcox, secretary, and A. P. Avery, treasurer and business manager. The board of directors was composed of Drs. Peabody, Welch, Wilcox, J. D. Taylor, J. A. Childs and H. A. Murphy.

The hospital continued to operate as a private enterprise until April 28, 1911. It had never been a paying proposition, but during the four years it had received many patients and had been of great value to the city. In September, 1911, the building was sold to the Elks for a clubhouse and so used until the Elks took over their new building late in 1923.

A movement to establish a public hospital was started by some of the citizens, led by Rev. J. W. Harris, in 1909. E. H. Tomlinson gave $250 to be applied toward the purchase of a site and a half block at Seventh street and Sixth avenue south was purchased. Early in 1910, the city purchased the other half of the block, which contained a five-room cottage suitable for use as an emergency hospital. It was opened for public inspection on July 28, 1910, a reception being given by the Woman's Auxiliary. The first patients were received in August. All of the equipment of the St. Petersburg Sanitarium was given to the city institution when it started. The new hospital was called the Good Samaritan.

Shortly after the new hospital was opened it was seen that it was inadequate for the needs of the city and steps were taken by the Woman's Auxiliary to promote a larger undertaking, with the result that in 1913 the Augusta Memorial Hospital was established on the same property, being built under the direct supervision of J. A. Potter, one of the city councilmen. Later, owing to unsatisfactory financial arrangements regarding charity work, the name was withdrawn and the institution was called the City Hospital, retaining that appellation until 1923, when it was changed to the Mound Park Hospital.

Dr. Frank W. Wilcox was the first chief of staff of the Augusta Memorial and retained that office until his death in 1918. Every physician of the city was a member of the staff. Of this first staff only three remain at present: Dr. Wm. M. Davis, Dr. Harry C. Welch and Dr. John D. Peabody.

On the site occupied by the first city hospital, the Good Samaritan, there stands now the Roser Home for Nurses, the original cottage having been removed to Fourth avenue south and Twelfth street, remodeled and fitted for a colored hospital. This small building has been replaced by a modern, well-equipped institution at Ninth avenue south and Twenty-second street, known as the Mercy Hospital, under the care of the regular hospital board and regular service by the staff.

So rapid has been the growth of the city that the hospital facilities proved to be inadequate several years ago. Dr. Leroy Wylie perceived this and established and built at his own expense the Faith Hospital at Seventh avenue north and Twelfth street. It was opened in 1922. This hospital is modern in every respect, is a class-A institution as to equipment and management and, although a private institution, is open to any reputable practitioner in the city.

In 1923, after long continued solicitation by the profession and others interested in the work, the city commissioners authorized an election for a bond issue for $145,000 to erect an addition to the City Hospital. Before this came to vote it was cut by parties not in favor of the hospital project to $75,000. This issue carried and the money is now being spent in the erection of the east wing of the Mound Park Hospital.

XVI

PUBLIC UTILITIES

UP UNTIL about twenty years ago, the residents of St. Petersburg depended upon rain barrels and cisterns for their water supply. A number of efforts were made to obtain a water-works system, but nothing resulted. On May 8, 1896, the town council granted a franchise to the West Coast Development Company to furnish water to the town and agreed to contract for eighteen hydrants at $50 per hydrant. This company furnished electric lights and power, but the water franchise was never exercised.

During the Spanish-American War, the War Department sought for a supply of pure water for the troops which were stationed at Tampa, the Tampa water supply being inadequate and brackish. Tests were made of the water in Reservoir Lake (now called Mirror Lake) and it was shown that the water was of excellent quality. Permission was secured from the town council to run a pipe from the lake to the end of the railroad pier, and the water was taken on boats to Tampa. It also was used on the transports running from Tampa to Cuba.

On March 8, 1899, an election was called on a $5,000 bond issue to obtain a waterworks. The issue was approved, 17 to 5, but the election was later declared illegal. Another election was called on May 23, 1899, this time for a $10,000 issue. It passed, 31 to 9. Several years elapsed, however, before a pump was installed and pipes were laid. The first pipes were laid along Central avenue. Later they were extended to some of the more important residential sections.

Reservoir Lake continued to be the sole source of the city's water supply for a number of years. During the winter of 1905-06, however, the water level in the lake began to drop as a result of the increased water consumption and it was apparent that another source of supply would have to be found. The city council on November 28, 1906, employed W. W. Jacobs to dig a well. A short time before this an artesian well had been drilled in the Bayboro subdivision near Fourteenth avenue south and Bay street. The water was not especially good, but it was believed that a better vein might be encountered. The agreement with Mr. Jacobs called for a ten-inch well, to be drilled for $3 a foot.

A natural reservoir of water twenty feet deep was struck 450 feet below the surface. The supply was apparently inexhaustible and at first it was believed that the water contained no minerals and was as good in every way as that of Reservoir Lake.

The city rejoiced, but the rejoicing did not continue long. The housewives soon learned that the water was hard and when the well was used, during the next winter, there was a great deal of criticism. To stop the torrent of protests, the city found it necessary to fall back on the lake water late in the summer of the next year. It was then that steps were taken to acquire the last of the privately owned property around the lake.

Most of the land around the lake had been owned by B. C. Williams, Jacob Baum and Davin Moffett. The city had to buy the water from these owners of the riparian rights. Mr. Williams agreed, before 1908, to sell his portion to the city for $3,500, and the offer was accepted. The remainder was secured by improving and paving the street around the lake where it bordered on the owners' property.

Despite the fact that the water in the first well was hard, the city council contracted to have additional wells dug, on the principle that hard water is decidedly better than no water at all. In 1908 a second well was put down to a depth of 170 feet and a fine vein was found that rose to within eight feet of the surface. In May, 1909, a third well was sunk a depth of 138 feet. The water from both these wells, while hard, did not contain the percentage of minerals that was contained in the 450-foot reservoir of the first well. Moreover, it had been learned that a better grade of water could be obtained from well No. 1 by shutting off the lower vein and tapping a vein which had been encountered at the 150-foot level.

A test of the wells made in July, 1910, showed that 447 gallons were being pumped per minute from well No. 1, just north of the plant, and 360 gallons per minute from well No. 2, west of the plant. Satisfied with the tests made of these two wells, the councilmen decided that a test of well No. 3 was not necessary.

Three additional twelve-inch wells have been sunk at Mirror Lake since 1910. The pumping station is now equipped with the latest type of electrical well pumps which pump 4,000 gallons per minute.

Extensive tests made since the installation of the electric pumps have shown that the limit of the underground water reservoir at Mirror Lake has been reached and plans now are being made by R. E. Ludwig, director of public utilities, for opening up a new water supply on the eleven-acre tract owned by the city on Ninth avenue north, between Eighteenth and Nineteenth streets, where the railroad car barns and the electric power plant have been built. The engineers have established the fact that the underground water strata of Mirror Lake extend in a northwesterly direction, passing under the city tract. Consequently, the same quality of water is expected. The plans provide for the establishment of a sub-water station and for the sinking of a system of sixteen-inch wells. Ultimately this will be made the main pumping station, to be connected with the Mirror Lake station by large mains.

The growth of the water-works is indicated by the fact that on December 31, 1923 there were 6,503 water meters in service, as compared with 2,533 on December 31, 1918. The revenue for the fiscal year ending June 30, 1918, was $34,443.54, and for the fiscal year ending June 30, 1923, $80,598.80. This increase in revenue seems even larger when it is considered that the rate was reduced from 20 to 18 cents during the year of 1922-23.

Gas

The subject of providing gas for St. Petersburg occupied the attention of the city fathers for many years before anything definite resulted. The council granted a franchise to the Lewis-Slemmer-Howard Company in 1907, to extend for twenty years, but something happened to stop the legislation. Perhaps it was the threat made by F. A. Davis to fight the franchise in the courts on the ground that he had "exclusive rights to furnish lights for the city." The newspapers carried numerous stories to the effect that the company had purchased a site and started construction of the plant, but the project finally was dropped.

During the next five years the gas question bobbed up repeatedly, but it was not until 1913 that the city council went so far as to pass on a franchise. Late in February the council granted a thirty-year franchise to the McClure Company of Peoria, Ill., providing a maximum rate of $1.45 a thousand cubic feet. Mayor A. C. Pheil, a strong advocate of municipal ownership, vetoed the ordinance, but on March 6 the council passed it over his veto. However, the company did not proceed to build the plant, presumably owing to he fact that there was some doubt as to the legality of the franchise without a referendum vote. The company officials endeavored to get the franchise validated by the 1913 legislature, but failed, and thereafter stopped work on the plant altogether, thereby forfeiting the franchise.

Arguments presented by Mayor Pheil for municipal ownership of a gas plant finally began to have an effect and when the new city commission took office one of their first acts was to hire an expert to draw plans and specifications for a gas plant for franchise seekers to bid upon, with the understanding that if they did not bid low enough, the city would provide a municipal plant. C. D. Hammond, one of the commissioners, was an ardent advocate of a municipal plant and he aided materially in the consummation of the project.

A referendum election was called by the commission for December 3, 1913, to decide whether the city should grant a franchise to private individuals or build and operate its own plant. The citizens voted, 256 to 32, for municipal ownership. Immediately thereafter the commission called an election for March 3, 1914, on a $148,000 bond issue to purchase a site, build a plant, and lay mains. The bond issue carried, 140 to 60. Later it was learned that the election was illegal, as the ordinance had not been published as required by law. Another election was called for May 12, and again the issue was approved, this time 156 to 27. The city commission decided to build the plant at Seventh avenue and First street south, but so much opposition was aroused by the property owners in that locality that the commissioners decided to get away from the water front and build the plant in Twelfth street between Third and Fourth avenues south. The construction of the plant was started late in July and on December 1 the gas was turned on. Several days before this, on Thanksgiving Day, the work had advanced far enough to supply gas for the home of J. G. Bradshaw, commissioner of public affairs.

The gas plant has been enlarged considerably since 1914 in order to keep pace with the rapid growth of the city, and more modern equipment has been installed. The increase in gas consumption in the city can best be indicated by a few statistics. During the fiscal year ending June 30, 1916, 18,608,143 cubic feet of gas were made; during the year 1922-23, the production totaled 154,992,950 cubic feet. On December 31, 1915, there were 1,095 meters in service; on December 31, 1923, 9,446. In order to provide for the construction of the gas plant and the system of mains, $475,000 worth of bonds have been issued by the city. In addition, approximately $75,000 has been taken from the revenues for extensions of branch mains.

Municipal Trolley Line

Since the purchase of the trolley line from the St. Petersburg & Gulf Electric Railway Company, bonds totaling $220,000 have been issued by the city for rolling stock extensions, and improvements. This sum includes $75,000 worth of bonds issued at the time the lines were acquired. The First avenue and Ninth street loops were completed during 1922 at a cost of $65,000.

During the fiscal year ending June 30, 1919—the last year the trolley lines were operated by the St. Petersburg & Gulf Electric Railway Company, 1,383,741 passengers were carried and the revenues totaled $63,585.05. During the fiscal year ending June 30, 1923, 3,623,276 passengers were carried and the revenues totaled $179,114.46. On January 1, 1924, the municipal street railway system had approximately one hundred employes.

Municipal Power Plant

The municipal power plant at Ninth avenue and Eighteenth street north was built at a cost to the city of $311,000. It was completed on July 27, 1923, and now supplies power for the trolley lines, car barns, gas plant and City Hall. Power also will be furnished for the water plant and street lighting system upon the expiration of contracts with the Pinellas County Power Company. An effort was made by the city to sell surplus power to private consumers late in 1923, but the Pinellas County Power Company contended that it was protected from such competition by its franchise, took the matter to the courts, and the city was enjoined from entering the commercial field.

XVII

STREETS AND ROADS

AT THE TIME of the founding of St. Petersburg there were only three roads on the lower end of Pinellas Peninsula, and not one of the three was anything to brag about. The oldest road was the one cutting across the peninsula from Big Bayou to Disston City, near the present site of Gulfport. This road, now called Lakeview avenue, was not much more than a trail through the woods in the early days and in places it was almost impassable. The other two roads were no better. They ran north and south, and are now known as Disston avenue and Ninth street. They were made by the settlers "on the ridges," who planted citrus groves and had to haul their fruit to Pinellas or Disston City to be shipped.

The development of the highways system on the peninsula was delayed for many years because the peninsula was a part of Hillsborough county. The Hillsborough politicians proceeded on the theory that the peninsula should be given as little as possible, inasmuch as the peninsula's votes were of small consequence in the elections. When money was available for road building, practically all of it was spent in the Tampa district. An imitation road was built between Tampa and Clearwater, and Tarpon Springs, but the lower end of the peninsula got nothing except a few short stretches of marl roads which were almost useless, inasmuch as they started nowhere and ended nowhere.

The road improvements made during the Hillsborough control can be described very briefly. In November, 1903, the commissioners responded to insistent demands with a promise to hard-surface two and one-half miles from the city limits south on Ninth street to Lakeview avenue and west on Lakeview avenue toward Disston City. The work was started in December of the same year, but it was done very poorly and the road soon went to pieces. Several years later the county hard surfaced short stretches on Ninth street north and Fourth street north, outside the city limits, and also hard surfaced Johns Pass road, between Fourth and Ninth. On February 2, 1910, the commissioners let the contract for the construction of Seminole bridge, to cost $10,000, after $2,500 had been raised by popular subscription. The bridge was completed in August, 1911, and on September 12 one-third of it collapsed, due to faulty construction. It was not repaired until several years later, and then the work was done by Pinellas county, the peninsula having been separated from Hillsborough in the meanwhile.

As a result of the lack of worthwhile improvements, the people of the lower end of the peninsula found it almost impossible to drive to Tampa, either with teams or automobiles. They had to follow a trail which zigzagged around swamps and swales and through the pine lands. In places the sand was deep; in other places the wheels sank hub-deep in muck. During the rainy season the trail was often impassable for months at a time. In January, 1907, a party of motorists, including Dr. and Mrs. A. B. Davis, Mr. and Mrs. Noel A. Mitchell and James McCord, left Tampa for St. Petersburg. They were three and one-half days on the road. They had to go many miles out of their way to avoid a broken down bridge and had to make another detour to avoid a forest fire. They were stuck in the sand innumerable times. When they arrived in Clearwater they learned that gasoline was not for sale there, and they had to walk several miles before they could secure a supply.

Automobile owners of St. Petersburg organized an embryo auto club in 1909 and launched a campaign for better roads. However, due to the indifference of the Hillsborough politicians, they met with little success, even though they were moderate in their requests. They wanted a rock road from St. Petersburg to Clearwater and Tarpon Springs by way of Seminole and Largo; another rock road from Clearwater to Tampa by way of Green Springs, and a pine-straw road from St. Petersburg to Green Springs connecting with the Clearwater-Tampa road. They got nothing.

A pathfinders' trip to Brooksville was made on Sunday, November 14, 1910. The motorcade left at 6:30 in the morning and returned late in the afternoon. The roads from St. Petersburg to Tarpon Springs were described as "awful" and beyond Tarpon Springs "fair." Those who made the trip were Mr. and Mrs. Ed. T. Lewis, Mr. and Mrs. Tracy Lewis, George Presstman, Dudley Haddock, Mr. and Mrs. F. A. Wood, Mr. and Mrs. Horace Williams, Mr. and Mrs. Walter Miller, H. R. Binnie, C. H. Evans, Will Ramm, Mr. and Mrs. W. H. English, and Mrs. W. A. Holshouser.

Although Pinellas Peninsula did not have any good roads for motorists to practice on, it was a St. Petersburg man who won the first prize in the Tampa to Jacksonville endurance run which started from Tampa on November 23, 1910, held under the auspices of the Tampa Automobile Club. Horace Williams came in first and won the *Tampa Times* trophy and a five-acre tract in Zephyrville Colony, near Tampa. Ed. T. Lewis, also of St. Petersburg, came in a few seconds behind Perry G. Wall, of Tampa, who won second place.

On a wager made with David W. Budd, George B. Haines drove to Tampa on June 12, 1912, with three passengers, in five hours and fifty-nine minutes, thereby establishing a record for motoring during the rainy season. Mr. Budd contended that an automobile could not get through because of the heavy rains. Mr. Haines said he could get through in six hours, and a bet resulted. Driving a Haynes car, Mr. Haines left St. Petersburg at 11 in the morning, went over Cross Bayou on the railroad trestle and reached Largo at 3:40. The ten miles to Dunedin was made in fifteen minutes, and the party arrived at the courthouse in Tampa one minute within the time limit.

The failure of Hillsborough county to build roads on the peninsula was one of the main reasons why Pinellas county was formed. And yet, even after the new county came into existence, on November 14, 1911, the good roads boosters had difficulty in getting through a good roads program, due to opposition from the upper end of the peninsula. An election on a $300,000 bond issue was held on June 4, 1912, and defeated by a vote of 489 to 505. The good roads boosters kept up their fight, however, and on December 3, 1912, a bond issue of $375,000 was approved by a small majority.

A system of marl roads was built through the county when the bonds were sold. For a while the roads gave good service, but in time the rains played havoc with the marl surfacing, and the roads became almost as bad as they were before. A demand was made for brick roads, and although the brick advocates were strenuously opposed by a faction which considered brick roads too expensive, an election was called in August, 1915, on a $715,000 bond issue to build 73 miles of brick roads. It passed, 808 to 629, but was invalidated on September 17 for a number of technical errors in the ordinance. Another election was called for November 16, and again the issue passed, this time 827 to 754. The highway system, providing a network of nine-foot brick roads, was completed by November 15, 1916.

A few years after the system was completed it was seen that a mistake had been made in making the roads only nine feet wide. The shoulders could not be kept in good condition, even though repairs were made constantly. And the traffic was becoming so heavy that roads wide enough for two cars to pass were essential. A movement was started for wider and better roads, and an election finally was called on August 15, 1922, on a bond issue for $2,695,000. It was defeated by overwhelming opposition in St. Petersburg, led by the *St. Petersburg Independent*, which contended that the

Central avenue in 1892, before street improvements were started

road program as planned would benefit the upper end of the peninsula, and the commissioners who owned land along proposed laterals, far more than it would the St. Petersburg section, which would have to bear a major part of the tax burden. The vote on the issue was 1,234 to 1,657.

Following the defeat of this issue, the county commissioners worked out another program, with the assistance of good roads boosters in St. Petersburg. It provided for better built trunk lines than the first program and eliminated non-essential laterals which only benefited localities and individuals. The *St. Petersburg Independent* and *Times* gave the issue their full support, as did the newspapers in other cities of the peninsula, and it was approved by a six to one majority when voted on June 5, 1923. The issue of $2,597,000 for roads passed, 2,686 to 423, and the $266,000 issue for bridges, 2,708 to 403. The contracts for the roads were let on November 30, 1923, to the Peninsular Construction Company of Tampa.

Street Improvements

Comparatively little progress was made toward improving the streets of St. Petersburg prior to 1900. Central avenue was opened up and graded from First street to Ninth street in 1894 and surfaced with pebble phosphate in 1897. The famous "race track" was built about the same time: a pebble phosphate-shell road which made a loop through the business district and around the north side of Mirror Lake. Some work also was done toward improving the sidewalk crossings over the streets. This comprised about all the improvements.

The need for better streets was apparent and on July 2, 1903, the city council authorized a $10,000 bond issue for the paving of Central avenue "and also such residential streets as could be paved with the money remaining." After authorizing the issue, the council delayed in selling the bonds and starting work, due to controversies regarding which section of Central should be paved. The ordinance stipulated that it should be paved from Second to Fifth streets. Mayor R. H. Thomas contended that the pavement should be laid only between Third and Fifth, so there would be some money left for residential streets.

After considerable haggling, the ordinance was changed as a compromise to provide for paving from Second to Fourth and the contract was awarded in July, 1904, to Henry & Wishard, the city to pay $1.75½ per square yard for paving with brick and 55 cents a lineal foot for curbing. Work was started by the contractors, but in August several property owners along Central secured an injunction to prevent the city from assessing them for the cost of paving the street intersections. On September 2, the council repealed the first paving ordinance and passed another ordinance providing for paving from Third to Fifth streets. In December, before the stretch of paving was completed, another ordinance was passed to include the block from Second to Third. As a result of the delay, the city had to pay 7 cents a yard more for the paving than provided in the original contract.

Another $10,000 bond issue for streets was approved by the voters on July 18, 1905, and immediately a heated controversy started over whether brick or stone and marl should be used. Numerous petitions were circulated by the rival factions and at times the fight became quite bitter. Finally, however, the council decided to pave the business streets with brick and the residential streets with stone or marl, as follows: Brick, Central from First to Second and from Fifth to Sixth; short stretches on Second and Third streets south from Central to the depot. Stone or marl: Ninth street, from the south to the north city limits; First street, Central to Fourth avenue north; Fifth avenue north, from Second to Ninth sreets; Fourth avenue north, from the bay to Ninth street; Central avenue, from Sixth to Ninth street. Contracts for the paving were let to H. Walter Fuller, of Bradentown, on January 24, 1906, at the following rates: Marl, 52 cents per yard; brick, $1.67 per square yard; curbing, 45 cents per foot. Mr. Fuller was allowed four months for the brick and nine months for the marl.

The movement to widen Central avenue to Ninth street through Ward & Baum's addition was launched in 1906, but the work was not completed until 1909, due to opposition and to the invalidation of a bond issue in which an appropriation of $8,000 was included for buying the necessary land.*

On July 28, 1908, a $5,000 bond issue for crossings and hard roads was approved. 161 to 31. As the need for better crossings was acute, most of the money was used for that purpose. On March 23, 1909, an appropriation of $1,200 was included in a $45,000 bond issue for completing the work of hard surfacing Fourth avenue north from Fifth to Ninth streets, provided for in the 1905 bond issue but not completed.

*See City Government.

Central avenue, looking east from Fourth street in 1908—shortly after the avenue was paved

The marl streets, which had been built in 1906 rapidly went to pieces; the brick held up well. As a result, the controversy over which material to use died a natural death, and the number of brick advocates constantly increased. The value of paved streets was apparent, and it was not long before property owners in all parts of the city began clamoring for improvements. The result of all this was shown on July 19, 1909, when a $100,000 bond issue carrying $67,500 for paving was approved by a vote of nearly four to one. That date—July 19, 1909—really marks the beginning of St. Petersburg's good road work. From that time on, hardly a bond issue was presented to the voters which did not carry a large amount for improved streets.

On June 13, 1911, $35,000 was voted for streets, 131 to 41; on April 26, 1912, $65,000, 433 to 51; on August 24, 1913, $20,500, 174 to 34. After 1913, when the new city charter became effective, it was no longer necessary to vote on bonds for paving, the city commission being given the authority to issue paving certificates to cover the cost of paving any street where a majority of the property oyners approved the project. The only exception to this was in case where the city owned abutting property and had to pay its share of the cost.

During the war there was very little work done on the streets. Since the war, however, the number of street improvements has increased each year, culminating in the 1923 program, providing for thirty-one miles of brick and asphalt block streets to approximately $1,500,000.

Gandy Bridge

St. Petersburg and Pinellas county are separated from the mainland of Florida by Tampa Bay. The shortest route around the edge of the bay, from St. Petersburg to Tampa, is forty-three miles. However, by cutting across Old Tampa Bay, the upper arm of Tampa Bay, a short-cut route of only nineteen miles is made possible.

The idea of this short-cut route was conceived by George S. Gandy shortly after his first visit to St. Petersburg in 1902. He figured that Old Tampa Bay could be spanned with a bridge or causeway, and he made up his mind that unless someone got ahead of him, he would put through the project himself, just as soon as this section of the state had developed sufficiently to provide enough traffic to insure large earnings.

Thirteen years later, in 1915, Mr. Gandy decided that the time had come to begin the project. Gangs of surveyors were engaged to determine the shortest line averaging the shallowest depth between the two shores, and during the two years following many surveys were made and the necessary rights of way obtained in Pinellas and Hillsborough counties. In 1917 application was made to the War Department at Washington for a grant to cross the navigable waters to be spanned. For nine months the matter was in the hands of the department, due to opposition by parties who represented rival interests, but Mr. Gandy fought for the project until the grant was made, on February 11, 1918.

A number of bills, permitting construction work and granting a 400-foot right of way for all time across the bay, were pushed through the Florida legislature during the session of 1917.

Early in 1918, Mr. Gandy was ready to proceed with his construction plans, but the United States was at war and it was impossible to secure materials for construction. After the armistice, materials were so high in price that another delay was considered advisable. Following the period of expansion came the financial depression, when it was impossible to finance any new project, but in the fall of 1922, twenty years after the plan had been conceived and seven years after the surveys were made, the financing was arranged and construction started.

Within six months from the offering of the stock the entire issue had been subscribed and the money provided. Thus the plan that had taken twenty years to bring to fruition was accomplished, for it then became a question only of time before the greatest toll bridge of its kind in the world would be completed. The financial program involved the sale of 200,000 shares of 8% cumulative preferred stock, par value $10, callable at $11, also the issuance of 250,000 shares of no par value common

The Mason Hotel, completed early in 1924 at a cost of approximately $1,500,000

stock. This stock was sold in units made up of three shares of preferred and one of common. No bonds were issued.

The total length of the bridge and causeways is approximately five and three-quarter miles. Of this distance, approximately three and one-quarter miles is a sand-filled causeway, forty feet wide at the top, with a slope more gradual than the natural slope of the beaches and islands in this vicinity. The dredging of about three million cubic yards of sand was necessary for the causeways. The remaining distance of two and one-half miles is spanned by a reinforced concrete bridge twenty-four feet wide.

The first dredge, the "Tuscawilla," went to work on the west fill on September 24, 1922; the second dredge, the "Florida," on November 22, 1922, and the third dredge, the "Reliable," on March 28, 1923. The casting of the concrete pilings, necessary for the bridge, was started on May 15, 1923. The construction camp at Ganbridge, on the east end of the bridge, was completed on June 1, 1923, as was all preliminary work. Both causeways, and a large section of the bridge proper, were completed by December 1, 1923. All piling had been cast and all materials necessary had been purchased by that date, guaranteeing almost positively the completion of the project by the spring of 1924.

Anticipating the enormous flow of traffic which would pass over the bridge upon completion, Pinellas and Hillsborough counties made provision for building as fine a system of connecting highways as can be found approaching any bridge in the country. Construction work on Fourth street north, the road leading from St. Petersburg, was started on December 14, 1923; the contract provided that it be completed within six months. Work on other feeders was started shortly afterwards.

When the completion of Gandy Bridge became assured, the value of property along the roads leading to the bridge increased phenomenally, and a number of new subdivisions were put on the market, presaging the rapid development of that section of the peninsula.

Pass-a-Grille (McAdoo) Bridge

The Pass-a-Grille toll bridge, connecting St. Petersburg with the beaches of Long Key, was built by W. J. McAdoo, owner of more than 500 acres of land on the key. The contract for the bridge was let in June, 1918, to E. W. Parker, who built the Municipal Pier. The bridge was opened on February 4, 1919. Fire Chief J. T. McNulty was the first to pay toll, driving over with Lee Carey, of Davista. On May 11, 1920, the bridge was purchased by Frank Fortune Pulver. Several days later the Pass-a-Grille Bridge Company was formed, capitalized at $35,000. Officers of the company were Frank F. Pulver, president; J. J. Duffy, vice-president; A. F. Thomasson, treasurer, and G. W. Griffiths, secretary. Others interested in the company were H. R. McChesney, C. Perry Snell and Warren Webster.

XVIII

FESTIVALS AND CELEBRATIONS

FOR A NUMBER of years, the annual Washington's Birthday celebration presented by the school children was the greatest feature of the winter season in St. Petersburg. The first celebration was held on February 22, 1896, and consisted of a parade and exercises in the Opera House. It proved such an attraction, and drew so many persons to St. Petersburg, that it was repeated each year thereafter until 1914, when the school board ruled against it, on the ground that the preparations for the event were taking too much of the children's time. In 1912, moving pictures were taken of the celebration and shown all over the country. The celebrations, which were made possible through the generosity of E. H. Tomlinson, helped in no small way to spread St. Petersburg's fame.

In the fall of 1900 a Mid-Winter Fair Association was formed, 106 individuals subscribing ten dollars each to finance it. During the next winter a very successful exhibition was held in the Strowger building, at Fourth and Central. The fair remained open for a month, interest being stimulated by literary and entertainment programs. It proved a success in every particular and little difficulty was encountered in raising funds to erect a building for annual exhibitions. A lot on Second avenue north near Second street, where the Christian Science Church now stands, was purchased and a building was put up, called "The Auditorium."

The Auditorium also was used for a Chautauqua Assembly that was financed in the fall of 1903 by the citizens. A guarantee fund of $1,500 was required. At the first meeting W. A. Sims, Isaac Doolittle, A. Norwood and C. W. Butler each subscribed one hundred dollars. The balance was soon raised and on January 30, 1904, a program was announced to follow the Mid-Winter Fair. When the assembly closed on March 1 it was announced that all bills were paid from the receipts and no money would be required from the guarantors. In July of the same year an organization was formed to have charge of future assemblies. E. H. Meyers was elected president; A. F. Bartlett, vice-president; J. F. Rider, secretary, and Arthur Norwood, treasurer. The Chautauqua was an annual affair until 1912, when interest lessened and it was discontinued. The Mid-Winter Fairs had been dropped several years before, due to difficulty in securing attractive exhibits. The auditorium property was sold to the Christian Science Church and in settlement each subscriber received $26 for each $10 subscribed.

During the winter of 1913, the St. Petersburg Fair and Tourist Week was held, from March 17 to 22 inclusive. Booths were erected along Central avenue under the direction of Albert Johnson, and decorated by the merchants as they saw fit. Games were played in the mornings, parades were held in the afternoons and entertainments and firework displays were provided for the evenings. The program served to attract tourists here from other cities of the state and also to hold the St. Petersburg tourists a few weeks longer than usual.

In the following year a DeSoto celebration was held, which opened on Tuesday, March 24, and lasted four days. A parade was held on Tuesday, the landing of DeSoto on Wednesday, a floral parade of decorated autos and a baby show on Thursday, and a costume ball, fireworks and a "hoodlum night" on Friday. The celebration was directed by Frank Oates Rose, of Chicago. Noel A. Mitchell, assisted by H. D. Britton, made the arrangements. The chief characters in the pageant were Ralph C. Prather, DeSoto; J. R. Willits, King of Spain; Miss Eunice Wamsley, Queen of Spain; C. O. Bird, Chief Hirrihigua, and George Presstman, Juan Ortiz.

The summer of 1914 was featured by a "Society Circus," staged by L. A. Whitney and held in the auditorium. It began on July 4 and was continued on the two following days. A. W. Fisher, as Cyril, the Clown, was the feature artist on the program. Other acts were R. H. McWhinney, balancing; Eunice Wamsley, equestrian exhibition; Clarence Ridgeley, the rustic from Anna Maria; Hal Billeter, slack-wire artist; Fred Pellerin, Otis Beard and Loris Beard, trapeze acrobats, and Harry Mitchell, song and dance artist. J. G. Foley was ringmaster.

The first Festival of the States was held March 25-28, 1917, with Albert Johnson in charge. Miss Ida Batt was elected queen and Bub James, king. The king and queen were crowned before a large crowd at Second avenue and Third street north. Features of the festival were the parade of the states, band concert on Central, confetti battle on Tuesday and the Grand Royal Parade and costume ball on Wednesday.

Several years elapsed before the next mid-winter festival, held March 27-31, 1922, with Al. F. Lang in charge. Features of the celebration were the "Chimes of Normandy," played at the La Plaza Theatre, the Festival of the States parade, the Dance of the Sun Worshippers and the regatta and bathing-suit parade at the water front.

John Lodwick, city director of publicity, was in charge of the 1923 Festival of the States, which started on Monday and continued through the week, the celebration on the last two days being combined with a Rotarian conference held in St. Petersburg. The comic opera, "H. M. S. Pinafore," was given at the Plaza Theatre on Monday and Tuesday nights. Tournaments were held in all outdoor sports on the same days. The Festival of the States parade was held on Wednesday and in the evening a special concert was given in Williams Park by the Royal Scotch Highlanders Band, followed by a festival ball at the Gold Dragon and Green Lantern. A regatta at the Yacht Basin in the afternoon and a fireworks display on the North Mole in the evening featured the program on Thursday. The program on Friday and Saturday was in charge of the local Rotarians.

XIX

GOLF CLUBS

THE MOVEMENT to get the first golf course for St. Petersburg was publicly launched at a meeting of the Board of Trade on April 26, 1906. Noel A. Mitchell declared that St. Petersburg was losing many tourist golf players because the city had no course upon which they could play. He said that he had pledges for $2,500 worth of stock and that more could be secured. The members of the Board of Trade voted unanimously in favor of organizing a club and a committee was appointed to secure subscriptions. Members of the committee were Dr. A. B. Davis, J. G. Foley and W. L. Straub.

The stock subscribers met with the Board of Trade committee on May 17, 1906, and perfected a preliminary organization. Officers were elected as follows: Noel A. Mitchell, president; W. H. English, vice-president; A. B. Davis, secretary, and T. K. Wilson, treasurer. Directors named were: W. E. Heathcote, C. A. Harvey, C. A. Smith, Jr., C. W. Barker, A. F. Bartlett, J. G. Foley, David W. Budd, T. A. Chancellor, W. L. Straub, A. F. Freeman, F. E. Cole, S. E. Denny, Roy S. Hanna, R. W. Thomas, W. H. Adams, V. N. Ridgeley, and W. J. Longman.

At a meeting on May 23, the officials decided to locate the club at Disston City, agreeing to accept an offer of the Florida West Coast Company for 120 acres of land from the trolley line west to Boca Ceiga Bay, with the understanding that the club would purchase it at the end of five years for $45 an acre. Later, however, the officers reconsidered the proposition and decided that the land was priced too high. An offer made by the developers of Bayboro for land near Bayboro Harbor—then being dredged out—was acted upon favorably and steps were taken to have the course laid out at the company's expense.

Rapid progress was made on the course and in November a committee composed of C. W. Baxter, C. A. Smith, Jr., and W. H. English was appointed to take necessary steps to erect a clubhouse. The contract for the clubhouse was awarded in December, and J. H. Mullan, a professional golfer of Boston, was engaged to be instructor and have charge of the grounds. The club was opened in February, 1907.

Despite its auspicious beginning, the club was never a success. Members found it difficult to get to the clubhouse from the city on account of the deep sand. The players had either to walk or go two miles by boat, so they did not play. The professional finally became so lonesome that he gave his clubs to C. A. Harvey and left. The golf course grew up in weeds, the clubhouse became decrepit, and that was the end of the club.

St. Petersburg Country Club

Initial plans for the Country Club were made at a meeting on February 9, 1914, in the rooms of the St. Petersburg Club on First avenue north. One hundred attended. Charles R. Hall, chairman, announced that the Johns Pass Realty Company had agreed to donate 150 acres or more to provide grounds for a first-class course. Those present at the meeting expressed a strong sentiment in favor of accepting the offer, and the company engaged J. Franklin Meehan, golf expert of Philadelphia, to come here and plan the course.

Further details of the plan were made public at a second meeting on February 26, 1915, held at the Spa. It was announced that the Johns Pass Realty Company would deed outright to the club 160 acres for golf course and 160 building lots adjoining the course; $60,000 worth of bonds were to be issued, and 120 of the lots would be deeded in fee simple to the subscribers of the 120 bonds of $500 denomination each, one lot with each bond, the remaining sixty lots to be retained by the club to sell as it saw fit for the redemption of the $60,000. The realty company was to take a second mortgage of $60,000 on the golf course as the purchase price for the 160 lots. Of the $60,000 to be raised by subscription, $10,000 was to be spent on the clubhouse and $50,000 on the course.

The movement to secure a golf course and clubhouse met with a favorable reception and in less than a month the needed amount was subscribed. The subscribers were: Charles R. Hall, C. M. Roser, H. Walter Fuller, J. F. McBean, George S. Gandy, H. K. Heritage, A. F. Thomasson, Albert F. Lang, H. M. Pancoast, E. V. Pechin, G. W. Cooper, R. C. Benner, Walter P. Wilkins, Jacob S. Disston, William L. Murphy, Joseph Murphy, Henry W. Dupont, Paul Poynter, T. A. Chancellor, B. G. Steele, D. W. Budd, G. W. Foster, Wm. C. McClure, Roy S. Hanna, Lew B. Brown, J. Franklin Meehan, E. E. Madeira, T. J. Northrup, A. P. Avery, F. A. Wood, Dr. W. K. Bradfield, F. P. Lowe, Noel A. Mitchell, G. B. Haines, G. B. Hayward, Mrs. C. N. Crawford, Lilia Dusenbury, R. H. Thomas, A. Norwood, Wm. M. Davis, F. W. Wilcox, C. W. Wiecking, May F. Purnell, Emilie E. C. Rowland, Charles D. Hulbert, St. Petersburg Hardware Company, Southern Concrete and Construction Company, Willson-Chase Company, Dent & English Company, West Coast Abstract and Mortgage Company, R. J. Cole, J. N. Bethell, Ansonia Hotel, E. H. Tomlinson, Manhattan Market, S. D. Harris, St. Petersburg Novelty Works, A. E. Hoxie, George O. Osborne, Mrs. Mary E. Whiteley, H. B. Smitz.

At a meeting of the stockholders in June, Al. F. Lang was elected president; H. Walter Fuller, vice-president; H. M. Pancoast, secretary, and J. D. Harris, treasurer. Directors named were: A. P. Avery, A. F. Thomasson, Charles R. Hall, T. A. Chancellor, David W. Budd, and E. E. Madeira.

The course was laid out by A. W. Tillinghast, one of the most capable golf engineers in the country, and work progressed rapidly during the summer, every effort being made to have one nine-hole course completed by winter. The clubhouse was started on November 20, 1915.

The course was formally opened on January 1, 1916. The first game was played by Al. F. Lang and Dr. W. K. Bradfield against Judge William Dishman and Dr. Elton Wilcox, Mr. Lang and Dr. Bradfield winning, one up. Two hundred spectators watched the match. The clubhouse was formally opened March 10, 1916. Members of the reception committee were Mesdames Al. F. Lang, A. P. Avery, D. W. Budd, H. Walter Fuller, Charles R. Hall, John D. Harris, H. M. Pancoast, and A. F. Thomasson.

The second nine-hole course was opened January 15, 1916. The eighteen-hole course thus provided is 6,082 yards in length, par 72. C. J. Smith, golf professional at the Palma Ceia course in Tampa, arrived on May 2, 1917, to take charge of the club.

The St. Petersburg Country Club was purchased by the Allen-Fuller Company in January, 1924, and the announcement was made that thereafter it would be known as the Jungle Club.

Coffee Pot Course

Soon after the St. Petersburg Country Club course was opened, the game became so popular that another course was needed. It was about this time that C. Perry Snell started work on the Coffee Pot course, north of Coffee Pot Bayou. Actual work was started on May 3, 1919. The first-nine course was opened January 19, 1920.

The Coffee Pot course has the distinction of being probably the only one-man course in the country. Mr. Snell financed the whole thing as part of his North Shore development program. The course has been supported by the tourist and business men golfers and has been successful from the start.

The piece of land upon which the course is located is almost an island, being surrounded by Coffee Pot and Smacks bayous and Tampa Bay. At one place it is only a stone's throw from the waters of Smacks Bayou to the bay. It is so situated that it commands a breeze at all times. The soil is black and the land is of a flat, low nature which tends to hold the moisture and produce good greens and fairways and yet is near the water where it drains readily and quickly.

Players on the course have the privilege of using the attractive clubhouse of Japanese architecture. This clubhouse, with the Japanese garden adjoining, is one of the show places of St. Petersburg. It was built during 1919 and later enlarged.

Two nine-hole courses have been added since 1919 and at present work is progressing on another nine which when completed will give Coffffee Pot two eighteen-hole courses. The first eighteen-hole course is 6,108 yards in length and the second, when completed, will be 6,087. The links are so laid out and constructed that they call into play every club in an expert golfer's kit. The course is open to the public and there are daily, weekly and monthly season rates. The clubhouse is in charge of a competent caterer.

XX

PROHIBITION

ST. PETERSBURG was agitated by the prohibition controversy even before the town was incorporated, and the question of whether saloons should be allowed was an issue in the first election, held February 29, 1892. David Moffett was the candidate for mayor on the Anti-Saloon ticket, while General John C. Williams headed the open saloon faction. Moffett received 21 votes and General Williams 10. Even though the "drys" outnumbered the "wets" more than two to one, saloons were permitted to operate in the new town, the license fee being fixed at $100.

No determined effort to abolish the saloons in St. Petersburg was made during the next two decades. However, the prohibitionists lost no opportunity of stressing the benefits which would result if they were closed. For a number of years the W. C. T. U. published a column of prohibition propaganda in each issue of the *St. Petersburg Times*. Despite their work, the two saloons of the town continued to do enough business to keep open.

From 1910 on, the prohibitionists continued to gain strength in Pinellas County. Petitions requesting the county commissioners to call for a vote upon county prohibition were circulated, and enough signatures finally were secured. The election was called for July 2, 1913. The vote was 778 for prohibition and 668 against. St. Petersburg split even on the question, 359 votes being cast on both sides. During the day the W. C. T. U. served lemonade at the voting booths.

Although it was generally understood that the saloons would be allowed to remain open until their licenses expired on October 1, 1913, despite the result of the election, they were ordered closed by the sheriff, by order of the county commissioners, on Saturday night, July 5.

The "wets," stunned by the result of the election, took the matter to the courts, demanding a new election on the grounds that notice of the election had not been published as required in the newspapers. The Circuit Court decided against them, but when they carried their case to the district Supreme Court, in Tampa, Judge J. M. Robles, on October 13, 1913, set aside the election and the county was again wet.

The "drys" immediately circulated new petitions demanding another election, but when the names were counted, the county commissioners determined that they were insufficient. A few days later the city commissioners announced that the saloons could open again upon payment of the new license fee of $2,500. Moreover, the city commissioners stated that there would not be a limit to the number of saloons—as many could open as would pay the required fee.

As a result of all this, a mandamus suit was instituted against the county commissioners by the "drys" to call another election. They contended that there had been a sufficient number of signatures on the petitions which brought about the first election, and that these same petitions should be used in calling for another election, particularly since one of the county officers was to blame for having failed to advertise the election as required by law. After much wrangling in the courts, another election was called for February 3, 1914.

The saloonists, in the meantime, tried to open up again but they encountered a stone wall when they tried to secure licenses from the county tax collector, E. B. McMullen. He refused to grant the licenses on the ground that the applications were not accompanied by petitions signed by half of the registered voters in the precincts where the saloons were to be opened. The "wets" started to go to the courts to force him to grant the licenses, but decided to wait until after the election.

Both the wets and the drys rallied their forces for the election and almost filled the newspapers with their advertisements, presenting the arguments for and against prohibition. At times the contest became very bitter and allegations of crookedness were made by both sides. When the votes were counted it was found that the wets had won out, 902 to 798. St. Petersburg had gone on record for the saloons, 477 to 336. The saloons were opened again in St. Petersburg on March 4, 1914, and while there were only two before, now there were three.

Looking north on Second street from the Detroit Hotel in 1905

During the next year the prohibitionists continued to advocate their cause but without making appreciable inroads into the ranks of the "wets," particularly in the county. But out in the state at large they were continually gaining ground, and in the 1915 session of the State Legislature they forced through the famous Davis Package Law. This law, briefly, stipulated that the saloons could not be opened before 7 a. m. or remain open after 6 p. m.; that they would have to be closed on Sundays and holidays, and that nothing could be drunk on the premises. Intoxicating liquors could be sold, but not in quantities smaller than one pint. The wets would have to carry away the liquor to drink elsewhere. This became effective on October 1, 1915, and the saloons in St. Petersburg, as elsewhere throughout the state, were required to live up to it.

Spasmodic efforts to make the city completely dry were made during the following year but without results. However, the problem was in a way solving itself. The Davis Package Law made it impossible for saloons to be the gathering places, the neighborhood meeting places, which they were previously. By the time the United States entered the World War in April, 1917, only one of the three saloons remained open, and it was doing only a languishing business. During the summer of 1917 it too closed its doors, due to a lack of trade. Whether this lack of trade was due to a general reform on the part of the "wets" of St. Petersburg or to the fact that bottled goods could be bought cheaper in Clearwater and Tampa, is not clear. At all events, the saloon, or rather the "package house," closed and that was the end of the "saloon evil" in St. Petersburg.

A busy day on Central avenue in 1908

Prior to the closing of the last "package house" the "dry" organization made a determined effort to hold another election and make Pinellas bone dry. At a meeting on June 25, 1917, S. D. Harris was elected chairman of the campaign committee; A. C. Odom, Jr., vice-chairman; J. M. Endicott, secretary, and J. P. Lynch, treasurer. Petitions were circulated and the county commissioners called for an election on July 28. It was called off at the last moment, just before the polls opened, by a supersedeas granted by the State Supreme Court.

On November 5, 1918, the prohibition amendment to the State Constitution was ratified throughout the state by a big majoriy. Pinellas County voted dry, 557 to 146, the small vote indicating the lack of interest at that time in the issue. On November 27, 1918, the state ratified the prohibition amendment to the Federal Constitution. And that ended, once and for all, the long battle. After that, no liquor was sold in St. Petersburg except by the bootleggers.

XXI

BANKS OF ST. PETERSBURG

St. Petersburg State Bank

ST. PETERSBURG'S first bank, called the St. Petersburg State Bank, was organized January 20, 1893, with John A. Bishop as president; Col. L. Y. Jenness, vice-president, and H. A. Baker, cashier. Mr. Bishop was a phosphate operator and Col. Jenness was the manager of the Orange Belt Investment Company.

The State Bank occupied a little frame building on the southwest corner of Fourth and Central, where the Central National Baank now stands. It never did a flourishing business. During the first years of its existence, St. Petersburg was small and poor, and there was not a great need for a bank. Later on, after the town had started to grow, many persons began to mistrust the bank. They refused to deal with it, preferring to do their business with the banks in Tampa, Jacksonville or cities up North. In that they were wise, for on August 9, 1902, the bank failed to open. It had become involved in the affairs of a phosphate company in Pasco county, and when the phosphate company collapsed, the bank collapsed with it.

At the time the bank failed, the deposits of St. Petersburg people amounted to approximately $51,000, representing a large part of St. Petersburg's wealth. And when the bank failed to open, St. Petersburg was stunned. There was talk of a lynching. Mass meetings were held; a shotgun patrol was organized; the bank vaults were guarded. It turned out, however, that this last was unnecessary. When the president returned from Tampa, where he had been when the collapse came, it was learned that the bank vaults were empty.

John Trice, president of the Citizens Bank of Tampa, was named receiver and a fight was started to get back the depositors' money. For years the case was juggled around in the courts. To make a long story short, it was not until 1914 that the depositors received their last payments. And all the payments did not amount to more than twenty-five per cent of their deposits.

First National Bank

Following the collapse of the State Bank, the need for another, stronger bank became apparent, and on October 3, 1902, the West Coast Bank of Florida was organized with $25,000 capital. John Trice, president of the State Bank, was elected president.

Local men took $8,000 worth of the stock. A lot on the southeast corner of Second and Central, owned by the State Bank, was purchased and a three-story brick building was erected. The bank was opened February 9, 1903, and the deposits on the first day amounted to $23,600. John M. Clark, Jr., of Tupelo, Miss., a nephew of Mr. Trice, was made cashier. The members of the board of directors were: Mr. Trice, Mr. Clark, C. W. Springstead, J. C. Williams, DeLisle Hagadorn and Thomas P. Welch. Other stockholders besides the directors were J. S. Norton and A. P. Avery.

Upon the resignation of Mr. Clark as cashier about a year later, on March 30, 1904, T. A. Chancellor, assistant cashier of the Citizens Bank & Trust Company, of Tampa, was appointed to succeed him. Mr. Chancellor has served the bank ever since, as cashier until January 4, 1911, and thereafter as president. On January 18, 1905, J. S. Norton and Col. J. L. Young were added to the board of directors.

On July 5, 1905, The West Coast Bank changed its name to the First National Bank, following application made to the comptroller of the currency. The books of the bank were examined by a bank examiner on July 4.

The capital stock of the First National has been increased three times: On January 7, 1914, from $25,000 to $50,000; on June 12, 1917, from $50,000 to $100,000, and on July 10, 1920, from $100,000 to $200,000. These increases were made by the addition of $75,000 in new stock and the remainder in stock dividends.

The deposits of the bank have shown a steady increase. On December 31, 1903, they totaled $109,000; on December 31, 1912, $619,000; on December 31, 1922, $3,704,000, and on December 31, 1923, $5,984,001. The resources of the bank have increased in similar proportion. On February 9, 1903, they amounted to $48,707.33; on December 31, 1903, $136,707.33; on December 31, 1912, $726,593.77; on December 31, 1922, $4,361,209, and on December 31, 1923, $6,852,556.

On July 10, 1920, the First National Bank bought the Florida Bank & Trust Company, which had opened October 15, 1913, with A. C. Odom, Jr., president; Arthur Norwood, vice president; H. D. Edwards, cashier, and E. C. Wimer, secretary. The First National paid the $50,000 capitalization of the Florida and a premium. At the same time, the Home Security building at Fifth and Central was purchased for $300,000 by a holding company of First National stockholders. It is this building, enlarged in 1922, which is now occupied by the First National.

Officers of the First National on January 1, 1924, were: T. A. Chancellor, president; Max A. H. Fitz, cashier; C. W. Springstead, vice-president; R. J. McCutcheon, Jr., assistant cashier, and A. F. Miller, Jr., assistant cashier.

Central National Bank

Plans for a second bank in St. Petersburg were discussed at a meeting held March 21, 1905, and at the next meeting, on April 16, 1905, the plans were completed. Officers were elected as follows: F. A. Wood, president; A. F. Bartlett, vice-president; Roy S. Hanna, secretary. Members of the board of directors were: A. F. Bartlett, Roy S. Hanna, F. A. Wood, Ed. T. Lewis, Cyrus W. Butler, R. H. Thomas, C. L. Howard, J. R. Williams and Andrew Jackson.

The stockholders were: C. L. Howard, A. M. Lowe, W. E. Heathcote, C. H. Lee, J. R. Williams, A. Welton, E. H. Tomlinson, Mrs. C. E. Ferrand, V. N. Ridgeley, M. G. Gray, Ed. T. Lewis, John Young, R. H. Thomas, F. A. Wood, A. F. Bartlett, Cyrus W. Butler, E. H. Myers, E. T. Davis, H. M. Dopp, Roy S. Hanna, J. M. McClung, C. Durant, J. B. Bradner, R. Veillard, Noel A. Mitchell, C. Perry Snell, T. K. Wilson, F. A. Davis, R. L. Raymond, H. W. Sever, A. Norwood, A. T. Blocker, A. M. O'Quinn, L. G. Sartorious, J. T. Lowe, James E. Wilson, H. M. Ulmer and A. J. Nye.

It was decided at first to call the new bank the First National, but it was learned that the West Coast Bank already had applied for the name, so the stockholders agreed on the National Bank of St. Petersburg. The Southwest corner of Central and Fourth was selected as the site for the bank building and the lot was bought from George B. Haines for $5,000. Mr. Haines had bought this lot, with a building on it, for $2,300 in 1903, from the State Bank. The National started work on its building at once and on July 1, 1905, the bank was opened, with T. K. Wilson as cashier and A. M. Lowe assistant cashier.

In the spring of 1909, A. F. Thomasson was appointed cashier to succeed Mr. Wilson, and on January 11, 1910, he and L. B. Skinner were added to the board of directors. Shortly afterwards the name of the bank was changed to the Central National.

The Fountain of Youth at the foot of Third avenue south

The Central National's new building at Fourth and Central was started in the summer of 1911, and on April 26, 1912, the bank moved in. Another floor was added to the building during the summer of 1922 at a cost of approximately $100,000. Extensive alterations, providing almost double the amount of space and allowing an entirely new arrangement inside the building, were started during the summer of 1923.

A. F. Thomasson was elected vice-president of the bank on January 14, 1923. Charles M. Gray, who was assistant cashier, was named to succeed Mr. Thomasson as cashier. Harry C. Dent, F. E. Cole, Charles McNabb and C. M. Roser were added to the board of directors. On January 12, 1915, Mr. Thomasson was elected president to succeed F. A. Wood, who retired from active management. Other officers elected were: Roy S. Hanna, vice-president; C. M. Gray, cashier; H. T. Davis and W. L. Watson, assistant cashiers. Mr. Watson was appointed cashier in 1918.

Officers of the Central National on December 31, 1923, were: A. F. Thomasson, president; Roy S. Hanna, vice-president; W. L. Watson, cashier; H. D. Smith, assistant cashier; C. L. Armstrong, assistant cashier; Floyd A. Thomasson, assistant cashier. Directors were: J. F. Alexander, Bayard S. Cook, G. W. Cooper, Herman A. Dann, Wm. M. Davis, H. C. Dent, Roy S. Hanna, Frank J. Jonsberg, H. D. Smith, A. F. Thomasson, J. L. Watson, W. L. Watson, A. Welton. The resources of the bank on December 31, 1923, totaled $5,656,683.44. The deposits were $5,019,117.50, an increase of $2,068,329.15 during the year preceding.

American Bank & Trust Company

The American Bank & Trust Company, St. Petersburg's third bank, was organized Tuesday, February 15, 1910, with a capital stock of $50,000. A. P. Avery was chosen president; Col. Walter Robertson Howard, vice-president, and A. C. Odom, Jr., cashier. The directors named were Samuel Vickery, J. A. Potter, A. P. Avery, A. C. Odom, Jr., and W. R. Howard.

At first the name of the Pinellas Bank & Trust Company was chosen for the new bank, but later, before it opened, the name of American State Bank was selected. On May 25, 1912, a trust department was added, the name changed to the American Bank & Trust Company, and the capital stock increased from $50,000 to $100,000, the increase being made up of $25,000 stock dividend and $25,000 new stock, leaving a surplus of $25,000 at this time. On March 6, 1913, the capital was increased to $200,000. On December 31, 1923, the surplus and undivided profits amounted to $139,701.95; the resources totaled $3,851,729.55, and the deposits $3,500,027.60, an increase of $1,526,205.01 during the preceding year.

The American Bank & Trust Company was the pioneer in the trust business in St. Petersburg. The department was opened in charge of Attorney Wm. G. King and later was placed in charge of O. G. Hiestand. A complete set of trust books and records were installed in the department which acts as executor, administrator, guardian, trustee, receiver or assignee. In 1921 the trust department began to take

HISTORY OF ST. PETERSBURG 177

trustee mortgages and to sell first mortgage bonds. From that date up to December 31, 1923, it had sold nearly a million and a half of these bonds.

Officers of the bank at present are A. P. Avery, president; Wm. G. King, vice-president; O. G. Hiestand, second vice-president; D. E. Beach, cashier; J. A. Stringer, assistant cashier; C. E. Brickett, assistant cashier, and C. S. Hinds, assistant cashier. Directors of the bank are A. P. Avery, Wm. G. King, D. E. Beach, O. G. Hiestand, J. J. Duffy, J. N. Thorn, J. H. Brunjes, Wm. Muir, James Cribbett, Archie Aitchison, George O. Osborne, George W. Fitch, W. P. Powell, H. R. Frazee and George A. McCrea.

Ninth Street Bank & Trust Company

The Ninth Street Bank & Trust Company is the youngest bank in St. Petersburg, but since its organization it has shown a remarkable growth. It was organized on December 22, 1921, the original officers being J. N. Brown, president; E. G. Cunningham, vice-president; P. V. Cunningham, cashier; William Crawford, assistant cashier, and W. T. Baynard, secretary. Later, upon the resignation of P. V. Cunningham, Mr. Crawford became cashier.

Originally the capital stock of the bank was $50,000. This was increased on December 22, 1922, to $100,000. Shortly after its organization the bank occupied its new building at the northeast corner of Ninth and Central, where it is still located.

The St. Petersburg High School, completed in 1919

Officers of the bank on December 31, 1923, were John N. Brown, president; E. G. Cunningham, vice-president; William Crawford, cashier; J. H. Maddox, assistant cashier; W. Furlow, assistant cashier. The directors were F. F. Balch, W. T. Baynard, B. T. Boone, J. N. Brown, J. S. Cobble, William Crawford, E. G. Cunningham, C. R. Dulin, A. F. Paul, George W. Fitch and R. H. Sumner. The resources on December 31, 1923, totaled $1,711,516.15 and the deposits $1,566,052.61, an increase of $1,098,491.95 during the preceding year.

XXII

PUBLICATIONS

ST. PETERSBURG'S first newspaper was established by Young A. Lee, a young man from New Orleans, who came to Florida in 1888 and settled at Charlotte Harbor, a small settlement on Charlotte Harbor Bay, near Punta Gorda. Charlotte Harbor at that time was enjoying a real-estate boom, due to the coming of the railroad, and Mr. Lee started a small monthly paper called *Our Florida Home* to help the boom along. However, the paper did not pay and in October, 1890, he came to St. Petersburg and decided to publish here. The first issue appeared on December 21, 1890, under the name *South Florida Home*.

Mr. Lee published the paper as a weekly until March, 1893, when he changed it to a monthly and reduced the size of the page giving it the appearance of a magazine. His subscription price was at first one dollar, but later he reduced it to fifty cents. He obtained a large list of advertisers scattered all over the country and at one time printed six thousand copies. Ill health made it necessary for Mr. Lee to suspend publication in 1896. He moved out of the city to Glen Oak and for a time was engaged in the real estate business. He died May 10, 1902. A file of the papers was preserved by his widow, now Mrs. W. W. Burchfield.

The *West Hillsborough Times*, the predecessor of the *St. Petersburg Times*, was established in 1884 by Dr. T. J. Edgar and M. Joel McMullen, who obtained a Washington press and a few cases of type and began the publication of a weekly in Dunedin. The first issue appeared in September, 1884. In December of the same year A. C. Turner bought the paper and moved it to Clearwater, and employed Rev. Cooley S. Reynolds as editor and chief compositor, with two of Turner's boys—David, thirteen, and Henry, eleven—as apprentices. After about eighteen months Mr. Turner took charge of his paper as editor and, with the assistance of his two boys, continued its publication until the fall of 1892, when it was sold to Rev. R. J. Morgan, who moved the paper and plant to St. Petersburg, changing the name after a few months to the *St. Petersburg Times*.

Mr. Morgan sold the *Times* a few years later to J. Ira Gore, of Cedar Keys, and then established the *Sub-Peninsula Sun*, which was published until about 1905. Mr. Gore continued to publish the *Times* until his death in 1900. In 1901 it was purchased from J. Ira Gore, Jr., by W. L. Straub, A. P. Avery and A. H. Lindelie. Shortly after, Mr. Straub became the sole owner. In 1907, the *Times* became a semi-weekly, and on January 12, 1912, the first daily appeared. In the same year the Times Publishing Company was incorporated, with Paul Poynter, of Sullivan, Ind., as president; W. L. Straub, vice-president and editor, and C. C. Carr, secretary and treasurer.

Mr. Straub continued to serve as editor of the *Times* until July, 1916, when he accepted the appointment of postmaster of St. Petersburg. He was succeeded by E. E. Naugle, formerly managing editor of the *Jacksonville Metropolis*. In the spring of 1923, Mr. Carr left the company to establish the C. C. Carr Advertising Agency, and was succeeded by D. B. Lindsay, of Fayetteville, S. C. A short time later Mr. Naugle resigned to join the St. Petersburg Land & Development Company and Mr. Straub again took the editorship.

The Sub-Peninsula Sun was started during the summer of 1902 by Ira P. Gore, Jr. It was a small weekly which never proved profitable. Mr. Gore sold out in October, 1904, to C. B. Gillette, who in turn sold to the Times Corporation on September 29, 1906, and the publication of the paper was discontinued.

The Independent, the afternoon newspaper of St. Petersburg, was established as a weekly by Willis B. Powell, of Bunker Hill, Ill., in 1906. Mr. Powell was assisted financially in starting the paper by R. H. Thomas, F. A. Wood, and Noel A. Mitchell. The first paper appeared on March 3, 1906. As the *Sub-Peninsula Sun* was still in existence, this gave the city of three thousand inhabitants three weekly newspapers. In 1907, Mr. Powell began publishing the *Independent* daily, except Sundays. He had

A view of the seawall built at the Jungle as part of the development program

a hard fight for existence, as indicated in an editorial in October, 1907, in which he stated: "Things haven't run smoothly every minute but, like a prize fighter, every time I get biffed I come up smiling. I am smiling now in my newly painted office. It isn't mine yet. It belongs to the St. Petersburg Building & Loan Association. I have paid $80 on it. The rest is to be paid in installments. * * * I want you to subscribe for my evening paper and pay me $2.50 in advance for it for six months, for I need the money."

Lew B. Brown, editor and publisher of the *Harrodsburg (Ky.) Democrat,* purchased it December 15, 1908. On September 1, 1910, the *Independent* made a unique offer, promising to distribute its entire circulation free of charge on every day the sun did not shine upon its office up until the time of going to press. Up to January 1, 1924, the paper had been given away seventy-one times, an average of about six days each year. The *Independent,* through this novel scheme, undoubtedly has aided greatly in advertising the city.

The Tourist News, a magazine for the tourist visitors of St. Petersburg, was established on September 1, 1920. The first issue of the magazine, printed in Tampa, appeared on December 4, 1920. On June 1, 1921, the company was reorganized and a plant installed at 176 Central avenue to print the magazine and do commercial

Onlookers at the boat races during the 1923 Festival of the States celebration

printing. In the summer of 1923 a modern building containing 10,000 feet of floor space was erected on Eighteenth street and Second avenue south, adjoining the Seaboard Air Line tracks.

Officers of the Tourist News Publishing Company at present are: J. Harold Sommers, president; W. Roy Cashwell, vice-president; R. B. Lassing, secretary, and M. L. Plaskett, treasurer. Mr. Sommers is editor of the *Tourist News* and Karl H. Grismer is managing editor. The *Tourist News* is published monthly during the summer months and weekly from November 1 to May 1.

The Pinellas County Real Estate Journal and Industrial Record, a monthly magazine, was started by the Tourist News Publishing Company in the spring of 1924.

The Pinellas Post, a weekly labor paper, was established in the fall of 1921, the first issue appearing on November 6. The paper is edited by E. J. Foster and is published in its own plant, owned by the *Pinellas Post, Inc.*, of which E. J. Foster is president; L. H. Whitney, vice-president and secretary, and Judge E. F. Wilson, trustee. *The Pinellas Post* has the endorsement of the Building Trades Council and the Central Labor Union.

XXIII

BASEBALL

AS A TRAINING CAMP for major league baseball teams St. Petersburg has gained national publicity. The movement to get a team here was launched in the summer of 1913. A number of baseball fans formed the St. Petersburg Baseball Association, capitalized at $10,000, the money to be obtained by popular subscription. J. W. Taylor was elected temporary chairman; E. C. Wimer, temporary secretary, and E. H. Ladd, treasurer. On August 15, 1913, the company changed its name to the St. Petersburg Major League & Amusement Company and decided to increase the capitalization to $50,000. P. W. Coe was elected president; Paul R. Boardman, vice-president; E. C. Wimer, secretary, and D. E. Beach, treasurer. The directors named

The Baseball Park at the Water Front, completed in 1922

were P. W. Coe, D. E. Beach, E. C. Wimer, Paul R. Boardman, E. H. Ladd, V. N. Ridgeley and A. C. Odom, Jr.

Although all the plans of this company did not materialize, an arrangement was made whereby the St. Louis Browns would train in St. Petersburg during the spring of 1914, St. Petersburg to provide the diamond and pay transportation expenses of forty men to and from St. Petersburg and pay all their expenses while here. A site for the park at the head of Coffee Pot Bayou was leased from Snell & Hamlett for three years and work began at once in clearing the ground of palmettoes and trees.

The Browns arrived on February 16, 1914, and on February 27 the first baseball game between two major league teams was played in St. Petersburg, between the Browns and the Chicago Cubs. The Cubs won 3 to 2. Four thousand baseball fans, from all parts of the county, attended.

The receipts during the first season amounted to approximately $10,500 while the expenses totaled $11,500, leaving the baseball company with a deficit of about $1,000.

Through the efforts of Al. F. Lang, the Philadelphia National League team was brought to St. Petersburg for the spring training of 1915. The players arrived on March 1, 1915, and had such good training that they went back North and won fourteen out of the first fifteen games played. They were never headed throughout the summer and won the world's championship. The officials of the club were so well pleased with St. Petersburg as a training camp that they agreed to come back again the following spring. When the players arrived, on March 6, 1916, they were greeted at the depot by a crowd of two thousand fans.

The Phillies returned again in the spring of 1917 and the spring of 1918. The Indianapolis American Association team came in 1921 and trained at a park provided at Seventh avenue south. The Boston Braves came in 1922, 1923 and 1924. A movement was started in the winter of 1923-24 to secure an American League team to train in St. Petersburg, as well as the Boston Braves.

In 1921, a plot of ground at the foot of First avenue south, facing the water front, was secured from the Park Board on a 99-year lease for a ball park. A grandstand was erected and the playing field prepared in time for the training of the Boston Braves in the spring of 1922. The ball park now is one of the best in the entire South.

Although St. Petersburg had an independent ball club of its own for many years, it was not until the summer of 1914 that it joined a league. With Tampa, Lakeland and Fort Mead it formed the Florida League and played scheduled games for the remainder of that season. League baseball did not prove profitable and after a short existence the club was disbanded.

St. Petersburg entered the Florida State League in 1920 and played during the first summer at the park on Seventh avenue south. Since then the "Saints" have played at the water front. During the summer of 1922 the "Saints" won the state championship. In 1923 they finished at the bottom of the league. Al Lang was elected president of the Florida State League in 1922 and re-elected in 1923 and 1924. J. Harold Sommers was president of the St. Petersburg club in 1923 and 1924, succeeding Bob Carroll.

XXIV

SOCIETIES AND CLUBS

Park Improvement Association

THE WOMEN of St. Petersburg have at all times taken a leading part in the development of the city. Back in 1888, when St. Petersburg was just coming into existence, they held picnics and entertainments, sold ice cream and lemonade to raise money to build a wooden sidewalk along Central avenue, starting at Ninth street. Money was scarce in those days, and several years passed before the walk could be extended down to Second street. But the women kept behind the project until it was completed.

On July 4, 1889, when the first big excursion was run into St. Petersburg, the same women who had built the sidewalk banded together and arranged for a big celebration, serving dinner in a big warehouse across from the depot on Second street, where the Blocker Transfer Company later was located. From their homes the women brought huge baskets of food and wash boilers of coffee, and when the crowded train came in, meals were served to the excursionists. Mrs. Meeker and Miss Jessie Welton were cashiers. They collected $108 and the money later was used to build the wooden sidewalk.

A few years later the women again strove for developments and this time they concentrated their efforts on Williams Park, then called City Park. An organization was effected, officers chosen, and the Park Improvement Association was born. The officers were Mrs. George L. King, president; Mrs. George Anderson, vice-president; Mrs. Jeannette Baum, treasurer and secretary. The members were Mrs. Elizabeth Ferdon, Mrs. A. Welton, Mrs. Sarah Armistead, Mrs. C. Durant, Mrs. Branch, Mrs. Allen, Mrs. G. B. Haines, Mrs. Burchfield, Mrs. Meadow, Mrs. McPherson and Mrs. Norwood. The younger members were Pearl and Fay Moffett, Mrs. Will McPherson, Edna Badolet, May King and Grace Baum.

Actual work of improving the park was started on "Park Day," held after an official proclamation had been issued by Mayor David Murray late in 1893. On this day the park was formally taken over by the town. Coffee, cake and ice cream were served by the women and the women and the men together started the work of laying walks and clearing out the undergrowth.

Although the men helped on Park Day, their interest in the work soon died down, and the women found it necessary to do all the work themselves. They completed the walks, built a fence to keep out the wandering cows and hogs, and, in about 1895, raised sufficient money to erect a bandstand. Their work was greatly retarded by boys who persisted in breaking up the benches, tearing down the bandstand and filling up the pump with sand. The men would do nothing to stop the depredations of the boys and finally the women became discouraged and the Park Association was discontinued.

Woman's Town Improvement Association

Early in May, 1901, the Woman's Town Improvement Association—popularly known as the W. T. I. A.—was organized with twenty-eight charter members. As the name implies, the association was organized for the purpose of beautifying the town, making it a better place in which to live. Mrs. A. P. Weller, wife of the manager of the St. Petersburg Electric Light & Power Company, was elected president; Mrs. W. L. Straub, first vice-president; Mrs. F. E. Cole, second vice-president; Miss A. A. Michael, secretary, and Mrs. G. B. Harris, treasurer.

The charter members of the association were Mrs. Frank E. Cole, Mrs. Charles A. Wymer, Mrs. Frank Harrison, Mrs. P. B. Stoner, Mrs. Charles A. Root, Mrs. Mamie Henry, Mrs. Amos Avery, Mrs. J. Frank Chase, Miss Lena M. Chase, Mrs. Windsor Smith, Mrs. James P. Hoyt, Mrs. C. N. Crawford, Mrs. R. H. Springstead, Mrs. C. M. Williams, Mrs. W. E. Allison, Mrs. A. P. Weller, Mrs. Grady, Mrs. C. C. Wilder, Mrs. Shellenberger, Mrs. W. L. Ainslee, Mrs. W. L. Straub, Mrs. F. A. Wood, Mrs. G. B. Haines, Mrs. S. S. Stults, Miss Ellen Davis, Miss A. A. Michael, Mrs. P. A. Goff and Mrs. Fisher.

The association started in immediately raising funds for beautification work. Monthly meetings were held and at each meeting plans were made for bringing a few more dollars into the treasury. A refreshment sale on July 4, 1901, netted $57.60. This fund was increased by contributions solicited by the members. In November, the association asked the citizens to donate trees, shrubs and century plants, and at the same time the members announced that the first Wednesday in December of each year would be arbor day for the park. Many trees and plants were received and planted on that day in 1901 and for a number of years thereafter.

Water was needed in the park to keep the young trees and plants from dying, so the association obtained enough money to bring in a water pipe. That done, the members turned their attention to the need for walks. Shell walks were laid diagonally through the park early in 1902, and in the same year the association had the old wooden fence torn down. The hogs and cattle had been banished from the town by that time, and the unsightly fence was no longer needed.

Additional money to carry on the work was raised by the association during the winter months by having booths at the mid-winter fairs where the members sold various articles. And on October 30, 1902, the women arranged a ball game between the "fats" and leans," which netted $45. It is a matter of record that the ball game broke up over a dispute with the umpire, but that did not stop the association from keeping the receipts.

Six-foot walks were built on three sides of the park in the spring of 1903, costing $562, of which the women had raised all but $112. An entertainment held during the winter had brought in $204.

In July, 1904, the association lost one of its most active workers when Mrs. Weller had to leave with her husband, who had to leave this climate. Mr. Weller died a few years later in Denver, Colo. Before Mrs. Weller left, the association presented her with a diamond broach, in recognition of her services as president of the society since its beginning.

Mrs. W. L. Straub was elected president to succeed Mrs. Weller. Other officers in 1904 were Mrs. R. H. Thomas, vice-president; Miss A. B. Michael, secretary, and Mrs. George B. Haines, treasurer. In 1905, Mrs. F. A. Wood was elected president; Mrs. W. L. Ainslee, first vice-president; Mrs. C. W. Springstead, second vice-president; Mrs. W. H. English, secretary; Mrs. T. A. Chancellor, treasurer, and Mrs. A. T. Blocker, treasurer of the poor sick fund.

The association continued to do good work for the city for several years. The work of beautifying the park slackened only when the city could afford to take over the burden. The park was turned over to the city in 1910. By this time the park had been graded, palmettoes grubbed, plants and trees planted, concrete walks laid and a fountain built.

Early in 1909, the association started a movement to get a building of its own, and on March 3, 1909, a tag day was held which brought in about $400. At a meeting on August 6, 1909, the members decided upon the location of the building and made a payment on the lot. A loan was secured from one of the banks, making it possible to go ahead with the construction. Several delays occurred, however, and it was not until 1913 that it was ready for use. The Board of Trade had quarters in it for several years.

Mrs. Herman Merrell, who had been president for four years, declined re-election in 1916 and Mrs. John Newkumitt was elected to succeed her. After a lengthy dis-

The St. Petersburg Cash Store in 1897, now the Harrison-Powell Company

cussion, the members decided to sell the building, inasmuch as there was much less need of the personal work that the members had performed in years passed and interest in the association had largely ceased. The members had looked for the co-operation of women's clubs and other civic organizations when they took over the building, but this was not forthcoming, as the clubs were unwilling to pay for the use of the rooms and the association was unable to pay off its indebtedness as they had expected to be able to do from rentals.

The 8 per cent interest on the $9,000 mortgage used up about all of the association's income. The building was at that time valued at $20,000. The Young Women's Christian Association was then looking for a place to locate. The idea occurred to members of the W. T. I. A. to turn over their building to this organization. Consequently, they gave their interest in it as a gift to the Y. W. C. A., on condition that the organization would assume the mortgage, and the building has been occupied by the Y. W. C. A. ever since.

Presidents of the W. T. I. A. since its inception are as follows: Mrs. A. P. Weller, 1901-04; Mrs. W. L. Straub, 1904; Mrs. F. A. Wood, 1905; Miss Ellen Davis, 1906-07; Mrs. T. A. Chancellor, 1908; Mrs. C. C. Wilder, 1909; Miss Ellen Davis, 1910-11; Mrs. F. E. Cole, 1912-13; Mrs. Herman Merrell, 1914-15; Mrs. John Newkumitt, 1916; Mrs. T. A. Chancellor, 1917; Mrs. Herman Merrell, 1918-1924.

The present officers of the W. T. I. A. are: president, Mrs. Herman Merrell; first vice-president, Miss Jessie T. Morgan; second vice-president, Mrs. W. T. Eaton; reporting secretary, Mrs. George H. West; treasurer, Mrs. John Newkumitt.

The association is actively interested at present in the beautification of streets and homes, and has been exerting itself to interest citizens in the beautifying of the city by the planting of shrubs and flowers. Each year a flower show is held by the members, and twice a year a flower and shrub exchange is put on, in May and October. The association is also actively interested in every civic movement which is uplifting and contributes annually to such movements as the social service organizations, the Christmas Sunshine Club, the Needlework Guild, which gave last year forty-two garments to the needy, the Travelers' Aid and others. The organization, as a member of the State and National Federation of Women's Clubs, also interests itself in matters before the Legislature which have to do with improvement and uplift.

Woman's Club of St. Petersburg

The Woman's Club of St. Petersburg was organized on February 7, 1913, with fourteen charter members: Mrs. C. A. Easterley, Mrs. Horace Hill, Mrs. Norris Levis, Mrs. N. Brandenburn, Mrs. Henry F. Combs, Mrs. Gilbert Frederick, Mrs. Eugene Massey, Mrs. J. E. Oates, Mrs. F. H. Kirker, Mrs. A. E. Holmes, Mrs. F. V. Kessler, Mrs. G. W. Lord, Mrs. J. W. Sealey, and Mrs. W. S. Blackburn. Mrs. Easterley, who took a leading part in the organization of the club, was elected first president. Other officers elected were: Mrs. Horace Hill, first vice-president, and Mrs. Norris Levis, recording secretary and treasurer.

The object of the organization, as stated in the by-laws, "shall be mutual helpfulness and united effort for the highest development of humanity."

Mrs. Easterley served as president from 1913 to 1920, when she was succeeded by Mrs. Charles H. Hawley. Mrs. Hawley served as president during 1920 and was reelected in 1921. She was succeeded in 1922 by Mrs. Wm. J. Carpenter. The officers for the year of 1923 were: Mrs. H. R. Sackett, president; Mrs. C. H. Hawley, first vice-president; Miss Mary L. Simon, second vice-president; Mrs. J. C. Blocker, corresponding secretary; Mrs. A. P. Cudaback, recording secretary; Mrs. C. A. Williams, treasurer; Mrs. Betty Foley, custodian, and Mrs. Sarah Bigelow, auditor. The directors in 1923 were: Mrs. C. A. Easterley, Mrs. John L. Burnside, Miss Louise King, Mrs. W. M. Brownback, Mrs. Roland Hill, and Mrs. Willard E. Dow. Chairmen of the various departments were: Mrs. Nat B. Brophy, applied education; Mrs. D. C. John, applied sociology; Mrs. Andrew Johnston, citizenship; Miss Elizabeth Bigelow, fine art; Mrs. Katherine B. Tippetts, legislation.

Ten regular meetings of the club are held each season in the Congregational Sunday School building. Study classes are held under the auspices of the club almost daily. Those in charge of the classes for the season of 1923-24 were: Capt. John C. Leonard, current events; Mrs. M. T. Webster, current literature; Mrs. Arthur G. Lewis, modern literature; Mrs. A. K. Sargent, travel study class; Mrs. Carl A. Williams, nature study; Mrs. H. B. Weaver, ancient civilization; Prof. S. H. Clark, spiritual element in Shakespere (private); Mrs. Willard E. Dow, parliamentary law (private); Madame Clauson, Spanish (private).

The club at present is making a specialty of training the juniors in club work. The junior organization, under the chairmanship of Mrs. J. Harmon Greene, has 60 members with an auxiliary of 700.

The Woman's Club, which is affiliated with the General Federation of Woman's Clubs, and also with the county and state organization, ranks fourth in size in Florida, having approximately 375 members.

Carreno Club

The Carreno Club of St. Petersburg was organized February 6, 1913, with ten charter members, who were: Mrs. E. A. Jefferies, Mrs. B. Hume, Mrs. Sidway, Miss Winifred Bidell, Mrs. Augusta Germain, Mrs. A. T. Blocker, Mrs. Alice Buhner, Mrs. L. D. Childs, Mrs. L. C. Patterson, and Mrs. J. B. Robinson. The first officers elected were: Mrs. Sidway, president; Miss Winifred Bidell, vice-president; Mrs. Grace B. Hume, secretary. The object of the club, as stated in the constitution, "shall be the musical, literary and social culture of its members."

Presidents of the club since its organization have been: Mrs. Sidway, 1913; Miss Winifred Bidell, 1913; Mrs. E. A. Jefferies, 1914, 1915, 1916; Mrs. F. A. Wood, 1917; Mrs. Frank Chase, 1917-18; Mrs. A. F. Thomasson, 1919; Mrs. W. G. Brownlee, 1920-23; Mrs. A. D. Glascock, 1923-24.

The present officers of the club besides Mrs. Glascock are: Mrs. Roland Wilkinson, first vice-president; Mrs. Jessie S. Pamplin, second vice-president; Mrs. James

Hames, third vice-president; Mrs. William Graeske, secretary; Miss Ida Trimble, corresponding secretary; Mrs. F. A. Wood, treasurer; Mrs. Jesse Thomas, press secretary; Mrs. C. E. Kemp, librarian.

Meetings are held on the first and third Wednesdays of each month from October to June at the Congregational Church. The club now has 110 active and 200 associate members. The club was federated in 1917. The Junior Carreno Club, established in 1920, has sixty members, all under eighteen years of age. The first vice-president of the Carreno Club serves as president of this organization.

Memorial Historical Society

In July, 1920, Mrs. W. T. Eaton published a call for a meeting of those interested in forming a historical society. Thirty-five persons attended the meeting held July 20 in the City Hall. It was decided to organize immediately, and the following officers were elected: Mrs. W. T. Eaton, president; Capt. George M. Lynch, first vice-president; Miss Jessie Morgan, second vice-president; Mrs. H. B. Smitz, secretary, and Mrs. Annie McRae, treasurer.

Steps were taken a short time later to incorporate the society. The application for a charter was signed by the officers as given above, and it was obtained December 27, 1920. By that time 140 persons had joined the society.

The objects of the society, as given in the charter, are: "To discover, secure and preserve data and articles relating to all matters of historical interest, particularly of the state of Florida, and to maintain a museum art gallery and library and cultivate and diffuse knowledge of the subjects aforesaid. To procure by lease or purchase suitable buildings, which shall include a room for the Daughters of the American Revolution, to be maintained by them, and to do any and all things consistent with the objects herein expressed."

At some date prior to January 1, 1922, R. W. Main, of St. Petersburg, had secured a lease on a site on the North Mole for an aquarium and museum and had erected the building now occupied by the society. At the date given, he made a sale of the building to the society for $6,500, taking notes for all but $500. Some remodeling was done and the city gave a ninety-nine-year lease of the property, conditioned upon its being properly maintained by the association.

A fine collection of memorial and historical articles is already in the building and its growth will soon call for an addition. No charge is made for admission, but many visitors make small contributions to the fund necessary to meet expenses.

The present officers of the society are: President, Mrs. W. T. Eaton, who has held the office since the organization; first vice-president, Jonathan P. Smith; second vice-president, Mrs. Herman Merrill; recording secretary, Mrs. H. B. Smitz; corresponding secretary, Mrs. Mary Apple; treasurer, T. A. Chancellor, and curator, Mrs. Frances Lambert.

Audubon Society

The Audubon Society of St. Petersburg was organized at a meeting held November 25, 1909, in the Belmont Hotel, called by Mrs. Katherine P. Tippetts. Those present besides Mrs. Tippetts were Dr. John E. Ennis, Mrs. N. A. Fullerton, Mr. and Mrs. S. E. Barton, Mr. and Mrs. W. R. Trowbridge, E. S. Upham and Miss Jessie Morrell. Officers were elected as follows: Mrs. Tippetts, president; Dr. Ennis, first vice-president; Mrs. Barton, secretary, and Mrs. Trowbridge, treasurer. Mrs. Tippetts has served as the president of the society ever since. Those who have served as first vice-president include Dr. Ennis, Lew B. Brown and Miss Beulah Chase.

To begin with, the local club concerned itself primarily with educational work in the schools, teaching the children to preserve bird life. It helped materially in getting the State Legislature to approve the bill for state-wide protection for the robin, passed May 29, 1913.

The next step of the club was to promote a city ordinance compelling the licensing and tagging of cats, the licenses to cost one dollar a year. All cats without tags were to be done away with, on the grounds that they killed birds and were disease-carriers. All sorts of fun was poked at the new ordinance and many of the residents rose up in wrath. The ordinance finally was tabled and is still in the discard. This is one of the very few times when the society failed to accomplish what it advocated.

In January, 1915, the club helped to organize and finance the St. Petersburg Humane Society, of which Dr. James Hoyt was elected first president. After a brief existence, the society expired and was never re-organized.

Through the efforts of the St. Petersburg Audubon Society and societies in other near-by cities, a chain of bird sanctuaries have been established through Pinellas County. A great stimulus to the society's work in this regard was furnished when Roy S. Hanna gave Mud Key, opposite the hotel at Pass-a-Grille, as a bird reservation. Previous to this, in March, 1906, Bird Key was set aside as a government reservation to be designated as the Indian Key Bird Reservation. In order to make this reservation possible, Mr. Hanna gave up certain rights he had to the key.

St. Petersburg probably has the Audubon Society to thank for the fact that all its pelicans have not been exterminated. During the World War, in 1917, the fishermen of Pinellas County wanted the pelicans taken off the protected list on the alleged grounds that they ate young fish and thereby diminished the supply. Members of the Audubon Society secured proof, however, that the pelican does not eat edible fish and Mrs. Tippets put up such a strong plea for the birds at a meeting at Ormond Beach that the proposal was dropped.

Some of the society's best work has resulted through its efforts in establishing Junior Audubon work in the schools, teaching the children the value of birds; also, through its efforts to secure the enactment of legislation protecting bird life in the state. At the session of the State Legislature in 1923 a bill was passed providing for the compulsory study of the value of birds in all schools of the state.

The Audubon Society at present has about 100 members. The officers are Mrs. Tippetts, president; Miss Beulah Chase, first vice-president; Mrs. H. C. Case, second vice-president; Mrs. Harriet K. Sparks, secretary, and Mrs. S. W. Foster, treasurer.

St. Petersburg Art Club

The beginning of the Art Club of St. Petersburg, which has meant much in the development of a cultural atmosphere in this city, was the outgrowth of the founding ten years ago of the Florida Art School by the late J. Liberty Tadd, head of the Industrial Arts School of Philadelphia, and a national figure in art education.

On the death of Dr. Tadd the work of the art school was assumed and is still carried on by his wife and daughter. With the thought of fostering the ideals of her husband, as well as to stimulate a wider appreciation of cultural things, Mrs. Tadd, principal of the art school, called a meeting of a group of people whom she believed would be interested in the formation of an art club. Out of that meeting, held at the Huntington Hotel in the fall of 1919, was formed the Art Club of St. Petersburg. The first officers elected were George F. Bartlett, Racine, Wis., president; Mrs. A. F. Thomasson, first vice-presdent; George M. Lynch, second vice-president; Mrs. L. J. Gunn, third vice-president; Mrs. F. W. Kingsley, secretary; Mrs. R. J. Dew, treasurer; directors, F. J. Harper, Mrs. Alice Buhner, Mrs. C. Countryman, Mrs. Perry Snell, Dr. George Baumgras, Grafton Dorsey.

Since its beginning the Art Club of St. Petersburg has held a series of ten exhibitions each season. The distinguishing feature of these displays has been the high standard of art insisted on as a requisite to showing under the auspices of the club. Through the personal acquaintance of Mrs. Tadd and her daughter, Mrs. Edith Tadd Little, with artists and art organizations of the North, it was possible to obtain cooperation of an invaluable kind in maintaining this standard. George Inness, Jr., was one of the first exhibitors before the new art club. From his studio at Tarpon Springs he sent a collection of four landscapes to be shown here. Since then, Mr. Innes has loaned a collection of his paintings each year to be exhibited under the auspices of the art club.

Another notable exhibition that first season of 1919-20 was a collection of etchings by Joseph Pennell, the only one of the kind that had ever been shown in the South up to that time.

There have been many important and notable exhibitions since then. When the exhibition of war paintings, made especially for the government by Captain Harding, was sent on tour through the country, St. Petersburg was the second place chosen for their showing, Philadelphia being the first. The Art Club of St. Petersburg was the first organization of the South to receive a display of original illustrations from the Curtis Publishing Company, of Philadelphia. The famous "Immigration Paintings" by Susan Ricker Knox, which were used to focus attention of Congress on the conditions that prevailed at Ellis Island at the time, were shown by the Art Club a year ago. Twice the club has been honored by the distinguished artist, Frank W. Benson, of Boston, a member of that unique group known as the "Ten Painters of America."

Not the least interesting of the exhibitions is the one held at the close of each year representing the work of the students of the Florida Art School. During this exhibition is awarded the gold medal given each year by C. Lee Cook, of Louisville, Ky., for the most meritorious original work done during the preceding year by any student of the school. In addition to this award, other prizes are given by local patrons of the Art Club for the encouragement of work among the art students.

The club has been especially committed to a policy of encouraging a better appreciation of art among the children of the city. Not only are the semi-monthly exhibitions thrown open to the free access of the public, but the school children are brought in classes to view the pictures on display. Informative talks on art and its value as an aid to the highest development of the child mind are given during the attendance of the pupils.

Since its organization three persons have served as president. Following Mr. Bartlett, Lew B. Brown served two terms. He was succeeded by Frank F. Jonsberg. The present officers are Frank F. Jonsberg, president; Frederick Williamson, vice-president; Max A. H. Fitz, treasurer; Miss Sarah Orvis, corresponding secretary; Mrs. Jane C. Owen, recording secretary; directors, Lew B. Brown, C. C. Carr, W. H. Franklin, Frank F. Pulver, Mrs. J. Liberty Tadd, Mrs. K. B. Tippetts, E. B. Black.

The finances of the club are derived from the membership dues, and by voluntary public subscription. No appropriation has ever been made by the city or other organization for the maintenance of the club and its activities. The meetings and the exhibitions of the club are held in the Florida Art School. The building, with its wide porches fronting on Tampa Bay, offers an ideal place for the work of the art school and for the activities, both social and artistic of the art club. The building has the only art gallery south of Atlanta. Besides the exhibitions of the art club, the Art School maintains a permanent display all the year round.

Rotary Club

The Rotary Club of St. Petersburg was founded in 1920, with nineteen charter members, including W. L. Straub, A. F. Thomasson, T. A. Chancellor, A. P. Avery, C. C. Carr, L. B. Brown, Robert Markland, A. L. Johnson, J. G. Foley, Jack York, Leonard Whitney, Al Lang, G. B. Shepard, Robert Walden, Roy Sellers, Howard Frazee, George Gandy, Byrd Latham and B. A. Lawrence.

The first president was W. L. Straub, who served until 1922. He was followed by A. F. Thomasson, and in 1923 C. C. Carr became president of the club. Herman Dann served as president during the season of 1924.

Besides Mr. Straub, the original officers of the club included A. L. Thomasson, vice-president; G. B. Shepard, secretary-treasurer, and J. G. Foley, sergeant-at-arms.

The officers of the club for 1924 are Herman Dann, president; Dr. William Davis, vice-president; Robert Walden, secretary; L. C. Shepard, treasurer, and Jack Dyer, sergeant-at-arms. The directors for 1924 are H. A. Dann, C. C. Carr, G. B. Shepard, Dr. William Davis, Bayard S. Cook, L. C. Shepard, Ed. T. Lewis, Robert Walden and T. P. Lane.

Present members of the club are J. Lee Barnes, Paul B. Barnes, Donald E. Beach, Charles C. Carr, Charles R. Carter, T. A. Chancellor, Bayard S. Cook, Herman A.

Dann, Herbert T. Davis, Dr. William M. Davis, H. C. Dent, Roy L. Dew, Robert L. Ely, Max A. H. Fitz, James G. Foley, George S. Gandy, Joe W. Gerow, Roy S. Hanna, John D. Harris, S. D. Harris, Bainbridge Hayward, Arthur L. Johnson, Sam Jones, Dr. O. M. Knox, Freeman P. Lane, Albert F. Lang, Coleman H. Lassing, Robert B. Lassing, Byrd M. Latham, B. A. Lawrence, C. C. Laughner, Ed. T. Lewis, Leon Lewis, John Lodwick, George M. Lynch, Robert I. Markland, Franklin J. Mason, William J. Melvin, Will Muir, Dr. Ralph Murphy, Edward E. Naugle, Edward T. Poulson, Frank F. Pulver, F. N. Robinson, Sherman Rowles, Jefferson Rutland, James A. Scanlan, Say F. Scott, Roy V. Sellers, Guy B. Shepard, L. C. Shepard, Wilbur F. Smith, J. Harold Sommers, W. L. Straub, A. F. Thomasson, Walter Tillinghast, Robert R. Walden, William Watson, Dr. Charles Williams, Dr. A. S. York, E. B. Willson, E. G. Dyer, D. B. Lindsey, C. M. Buckley, Ralph Devoe, Frank Jonesburg, Dr. T. C. Holmes, Jack Taylor, John Lee and John Boice.

The slogan of Rotary is "He profits most who serves best." Its mission is to teach the gospel of correct business, embodied in the club's code of ethics.

Civitan Club

The Civitan Club was founded in November, 1921, as a branch of the International Civitan Clubs. The first officers elected were: Bob C. Smalley, president; John B. Sims, vice-president; O. O. Feaster, vice-president; William Crawford, secretary; Karl B. O'Quinn, treasurer. The motto of the club is "Builders of Good Citizenship," and its mission is the "civic upbuilding of the community." The club meets every Wednesday noon in the Episcopal Parish House.

Officers of the club in 1924 were: Rev. D. S. Pooser, president; E. H. Dunn, vice-president; Edward M. Fisher, secretary, and Karl B. O'Quinn, treasurer. The members of the club in 1924 were: Carlton Beard, R. G. Blanc, B. B. Blackburn, Hugh Bradley, Jim Bailey, Otto Bocher, R. B. Burr, C. A. Campbell, J. T. Campbell, H. M. Carpenter, Harry W. Childs, Walter H. Childs, D. B. Cunningham, W. M. Carluett, Paul W. Cutler, M. M. Deiderick, Nick Dennis, Fred Dillman, C. R. Dulin, Edgar H. Dunn, Edward M. Fisher, Oscar Gilbart, J. B. Girardeau, G. M. Gordon, Cliff Goodman, J. W. Hassler, H. C. Hansbrough, S. G. Johnson, B. B. Kelleher, Ernest Kitchen, R. I. Leavengood, Long, S. R. McIntosh, Albert Miller, R. E. Milliken, J. E. Morrison, A. E. Newman, Jack O'Brien, Karl B. O'Quinn, Rev. D. S. Pooser, S. B. Predmore, J. E. Preston, Paul Reese, W. Roush, John S. Rhodes, John B. Sims, Bob C. Smalley, M. A. Spooner, H. H. Stern, Louis E. Stoughton, Robert Sinclair, C. W. Talbot, Joe N. Touart, R. W. Thompson, Dr. H. W. Wade, Walter E. Wakeman, H. D. Wallin, H. D. Walker, G. W. Wylie, L. A. Wylie, H. H. Williams, and T. G. Young.

Pinellas County Medical Society

Several attempts were made to organize a county medical society immediately after Pinellas county was born, but little enthusiasm was shown outside of St. Petersburg. However, the movement gradually gained strength and on October 4, 1913,

Dr. John D. Peabody, of St. Petersburg, invited every doctor in good standing in the county to meet at a dinner to be given by him at the Detroit Hotel on the evening of October 7 for the purpose of organization. Those who attended the dinner were Dr. L. B. Dickerson, of Clearwater; Dr. Davidson, Largo, and Drs. Frank Wilcox, M. H. Axline, Hugh Murphy, Wm. M. Davis, Joseph T. Hume and John D. Peabody, of St. Petersburg. Drs. Albaugh and Douglas, of Springs, were prevented from coming, but were in favor of the organization.

After the dinner, those present met in business session and organized under the laws of the American Medical Association, becoming a component part of the Florida Medical Society. Thus the baby county of the state placed in existence the baby medical society. The officers elected at this meeting were distributed through the county towns as follows: Dr. L. B. Dickerson, Clearwater, president; Dr. A. T. Albaugh, Tarpon Springs, first vice-president; Dr. Davidson, Largo, second vice-president, and Dr. Wm. M. Davis, St. Petersburg, secretary and treasurer.

The society has functioned ever since this meeting and has kept the plane of the medical practice at the highest level. From the ten original members it has grown to a body of about fifty men and women and takes an active part in all matters pertaining to the betterment of public health.

Those who have served as presidents of the society are: 1914, Dr. L. B. Dickerson, Clearwater; 1915, Dr. A. P. Albaugh, Tarpon Springs; 1916, Dr. F. W. Wilcox, St. Petersburg; 1917, Dr. H. C. Welch, St. Petersburg; 1918, Dr. R. H. Knowlton, St. Petersburg; 1919, Dr. A. J. Wood, St. Petersburg; 1920, Dr. W. M. Davis, St. Petersburg; 1921, Dr. J. M. Peabody, St. Petersburg; 1922, Dr. L. Lambdin, St. Petersburg; 1923, Dr. R. D. Murphy, St. Petersburg, and 1924, Dr. O. M. Knox, St. Petersburg.

Tourist Societies

The tourist societies of St. Petersburg, made up of tourists from various localities in the United States, undoubtedly have aided materially in making St. Petersburg one of the most famous resort cities of the world. The societies provide an ideal means for the tourists to mingle together and become acquainted. Entertainments are held at regular intervals. The membership fee charged is so low that everyone can join.

To Illinois goes the honor of being the first state represented in the city with a going organization. Captain J. F. Chase, Rev. J. P. Hoyt and M. Arter called the first meeting of Illinois tourists on January 1, 1902, and officers were elected, Mr. Arter begin chosen first president.

The Illinois society held meetings regularly from then on and attracted so much favorable attention that other states were encouraged to form similar organizations. The New England States were the next to organize, Rev. J. P. Hoyt calling the New Englanders together just two weeks after the Illinois society was formed.

The order in which other societies organized was as follows: Michigan, March 7, 1907; Wisconsin, 1908; New York-New Jersey, February 13, 1909; Pennsylvania, 1913; Canada, February 24, 1913; Ohio, January 13, 1914; Indiana, 1914; Iowa, January 3, 1917; Southland, January, 1909, and Maine, 1920. This list does not include all of the societies. Some disorganized to be organized again later on. Many states organized and then merged with other societies. During the Winter of 1923-24, practically every section of the country was represented by a society in St. Petersburg and the total membership exceeded 12,000.

In 1914, there were ten large societies in the city and the need was seen for one central organization, composed of representatives from each of the societies. Mr. Arter, the first president of the Illinois society, conceived the idea of a Presidents' Union and a meeting was held on February 2, 1914, at which time the union was organized.

The following were the initial members of the union: M. Arter, president Illinois society; Mat Savage, president Pennsylvania society; D. L. Crandall, president New England society; Dr. R. McGurk, president Michigan society; H. C. Thurmond, president West Virginia society; W. W. Welch, president Ohio society; William Lindsay, president Wisconsin society; J. E. Brown, president Canadian society; J. M. Johnson, president Indiana society; Dr. C. M. Slack, president New York-New Jersey society.

Meetings are held by all of the societies at regular intervals and interesting programs are given by skilled entertainers. In addition to the indoor meetings, each society has one or more outdoor events during the season—a clam bake, a picnic or an excursion over Tampa Bay. Many of the societies meet in the City Hall, either in the auditorium or Presidents' Union room; others meet in the churches. Plans have been discussed for several years for a tourists' Concordium, to be built on the water front, but nothing definite has resulted.

The members of the societies do not confine their boosting to the time while they are in St. Petersburg. They carry it with them when they return to their Northern homes, and they tell their friends what a fine place St. Petersburg is during the winter months. Hundreds of first-time tourists come to St. Petersburg each fall for no other reason than that they have heard so much about the city from the tourist society boosters that they have become determined to visit the city and see for themselves what it actually is.

XXV

PARKS

Williams Park

WILLIAMS PARK was not so named in the original city plat. For many years it was called just "City Park." Later, when other parks were established by the city, and a more distinctive name was needed, "Williams Park" was chosen in honor of General John C. Williams, founder of St. Petersburg. In a way, "Demens Park" would have been just as appropriate, inasmuch as it was Peter A. Demens who recorded the first town plat. However, the name Williams Park was selected and it came into general use about 1908.

In the early days of St. Petersburg, Williams Park was just a piece of oak and pine woods, not particularly attractive. Along the northern side there was a natural ditch which carried off the overflow waters from Mirror Lake. About the only use made of the park at that time was as a site for picnic parties. Some time late in the '90s the women of the town raised money to build a fence around the park to keep out the wandering cows. They also erected a bandstand and made many other improvements.*

In 1902 members of the Woman's Town Improvement Association, organized in 1901 for the purpose of aiding in beautifying the town, had the fence around the park removed, and in the next year a challenge was issued that marked the first real movement toward beautifying the spot. On September 5, 1903, W. L. Ainslee issued this challenge: "I hereby challenge any man of my age, on the top side of God's green footstool, to pull more weeds than I do in the city park on Tuesday, September 8, between sunrise and sunset." Roy S. Hanna answered the challenge in this manner: "Believing that I can pull more weeds than W. L. Ainslee, and wishing to prove how little he knows about such things, I hereby accept his challenge, provided he will furnish two able assistants and five ladies of the Woman's Town Improvement Association as judges."

On the day set, both men arrived at the park, and at a given time, started work. They grubbed palmettoes and pulled weeds all day long, under a hot sun. Mr. Hanna won, and was awarded a boquet of flowers by the ladies. About a third of the park was cleared of undergrowth. Stimulated by this good example, other men of the city aided in the work or contributed small sums to have others do it. Before the end of the year the park was cleared.

Shell walks were laid in the park in June, 1901, but it was not until 1903, that six-foot asphalt walks were laid around the park, at a cost of $562. The shell walks

---
*See Park Improvement Association.

had been paid for largely by Burton S. Coe and J. C. Williams, who gave $112. Money for the asphalt walks was raised, small amounts at a time, by the W. T. I. A.

In 1906 the Library Association asked permission to erect a building in the park, and the council granted the request. Members of the W. T. I. A. objected so strongly, however, that the project was abandoned. Up to this time the association had spent approximately $2,000 on the beautification work in the park and consequently was given a voice in its usage. Trees, shrubs, flowers and grass had been planted by these zealous workers and a fountain had been erected in the center of the park. Interest in the work slackened during the next few years, however, and when the upkeep of the park was turned over to the city by the association in 1910, palmettoes and weeds had again taken possession of the property.

The first park commissioner was appointed by the council in 1911 and in February, 1912, $252 was spent in improvements, consisting mainly of green benches for the accommodation of visitors. A short time later cement walks were built through the park at a cost of about $3,000. The old bandstand for band concerts was used until early in 1920, when the new bandstand was built by the city at a cost of $10,000.

The Royal Scotch Highlanders Band was engaged by the city to play ten weeks during the winter of 1917-18. The first concert was given on January 13, 1918. The Highlanders won the approval of the tourists from the beginning, and when their engagement ended, money was provided for them to stay two weeks longer. Also, they were persuaded to come back again the following winter to play for fourteen

Williams Park in 1897

weeks, for $9,360. The cost for the 1917-18 engagement had been $6,500. The contract with the Highlanders was renewed for the 1919-20 season, but in the following year Weber's Band of Cincinnati was engaged. This band did not prove as popular as the Highlanders, so arrangements were made to bring the latter back for the next season. The Highlanders now have made St. Petersburg their headquarters.

In 1921, Mr. and Mrs. James H. Paine, of Cleveland, Ohio, expressed their interest in the Sunshine City by providing for the erection of a drinking fountain in the center of the park, and endowing it so that it is supplied with ice winter and summer. A memorial also was erected at the Fourth street entrance to the park in 1921 by the St. Petersburg War Mothers. The monument contains a bronze tablet bearing the names of St. Petersburg youths who gave their lives in the World War.

Shortly after the city took over the upkeep of the park it began to be the center of the activities of the various pleasure clubs. The horseshoe players, members of the Sunshine Pleasure Club, invaded it first in 1913, and lanes were provided for their use. Then came the roque players, and the players of chess, checkers and dominoes. At first, there was room in the park for the members of all these clubs, as well as for the band concerts. Thousands congregated there during the winter months, and Williams Park became famed throughout the country.

As the membership in the various clubs increased, however, it became evident that additional playgrounds would have to be provided elsewhere to prevent congestion. The work was hastened by an injunction against the city obtained by the Williams heirs in the spring of 1922, preventing the city from allowing any club to have exclusive rights over any portion of the park. The Williams heirs contended, and were supported by the court, that the park had been given to the city with the understanding that it would be open "to the public" at all times, and that no individuals, or groups of individuals, should have special privileges. As a result of this injunction, the headquarters of the pleasure clubs were moved in the fall of 1923. The roque courts and some of the horseshoe lanes were left in the park for anyone who desired to play on them.

Water Front Park

Water Front Park, extending from Bayboro Harbor to Fifth avenue north, was included in St. Petersburg's water-front development, the land being acquired from the private owners through negotiations which lasted for years. Improvement work was started in 1910 and is still being carried on. The major part of the park board's budget has been spent during the past two years in beautifying the property, with the result that Water Front Park rapidly is becoming one of the most beautiful parks in the entire country.

In 1922, after it became necessary to remove the pleasure clubs from Williams Park, the park board began making provision for the clubs at the water front. A grand stand and clubhouse were erected for the Sunshine Pleasure Club, made up of horseshoe and quoit players, and lanes were built. Many roque courts also were constructed. In 1923, a clubhouse was built for the Checker, Chess and Domino Club and a clock golf course was completed in front of the Soreno Hotel. A number of tennis courts also have been provided.

Other Parks

The original plat of St. Petersburg included about two-thirds of Mirror Lake, then called Reservoir Lake. It was of quite different shape than at present, portions of it having been dredged out and others filled in during 1913. A large part of the adjoining land was owned by B. C. Williams, who offered to sell it to the city in 1903 for $3,500. The offer was accepted by the city council and the land acquired. On March 23, 1909, $15,000 was voted to buy additional land around the lake and in 1910 this city-owned property was declared a public park.

The water which drained into the lake during the rainy season often caused it to overflow its boundaries and in 1912 an eighteen-inch drain was laid to Tampa Bay, lowering the level of the lake four feet. However, the drain was not large enough to carry off a rainfall of sixteen inches which fell on August 8 and 9, 1915. The lake overflowed again, and the library building, then under construction, stood upon an island. At the lower end of Fifth avenue north a gully was cut nearly 200 feet long and from eight to nine feet deep.

At a concert given by the Royal Scotch Highlanders Band in Williams Park in 1924

The pavement around the lake was completed during the summer of 1914, the work having been started on June 26. During the years since then many improvements have been made in the park and it is now one of the beauty spots in the city. The St. Petersburg Lawn Bowling Club has its headquarters on the north side of the lake with an attractive clubhouse and a number of rinks. Tennis and roque courts also have been provided by the city in the park.

Shell Mound Park, at Sixth street and Sixth avenue south, was purchased by the city in 1909 for $1,500. This park contains one of the few remaining shell mounds within the city limits. Originally there were seven mounds in the vicinity, but the other six were leveled when the shells were hauled away for use of streets and sidewalks.

In 1911, General Koster offered the land around Round Lake to the city for $600. The land was purchased and later converted into Round Lake Park. A well was sunk to keep the water in the lake at an even level, serving to fill up the lake in the dry season and lower it in the wet season.

A block in Hall's No. 3 Subdivision, at Second avenue north and Thirty-ninth street, was given to the city for park purposes by Charles M. Hall in 1913. Up to January 1, 1924, the city park board had been unable to find funds to start improvements on this property, known as Seminole Park.

Sunset Park, at the western end of Central avenue on Boca Ceiga Bay, was given to the city by the St. Petersburg Investment Company in 1913. The work of beautifying the park was started in 1923, the expense being borne by the park board and Pasadena Estates, Inc.

Fifty-six acres around Crescent Lake were acquired by the city for park purposes from C. Perry Snell in 1919, $30,000 being paid for the tract. Little was done toward beautifying this park until 1923 when a drainage system was started, making further improvements possible. A city nursery has been established on the south shore of the lake under the personal supervision of W. F. Smith, chairman of the park board. Plants and palms now in this nursery are valued at more than $20,000.

In 1922, land east of Beach drive on the south side was dedicated to the city for park purposes by Judge J. M. Lassing and others.

Other parks owned by the city are the following: Roser Park, east of Eighth street along Booker Creek; Wood Park, between Eighth and Ninth street along Booker Creek; Haines Park, small plots east and north of the Atlantic Coast Line depot; Beach Drive Park, a small plot seventy-five feet wide between Beach drive and the Bay at Seventh avenue north.

XXVI

POPULATION

THE federal census of 1890, made two years after St. Petersburg was founded, showed a population of 273. So far as is known, no attempt was made to determine again the exact number of residents until the federal census of 1900, which credited St. Petersburg with a population of 1,575. This increase of nearly 600 per cent indicated that St. Petersburg was forging ahead at a rapid gait, and the census figures were received with considerable satisfaction on the part of the local boosters.

In 1904, the *Times* Publishing Company compiled the first directory of St. Petersburg and it showed there were 2,227 men, women and children in the city. Despite the fact that this indicated a material gain over the census figure of 1900, it did not please everyone. F. A. Davis, head of the St. Petersburg Investment Company and allied enterprises, wrote from Philadelphia that the *Times* must have made some mistake.

"If the figures given by the directory are complete," wrote Mr. Davis, "I owe a pretty strong apology to a good many people. . . . .Are you quite certain that there is not a mistake, and that the first figure should not have been a '3' rather than a '2', or is it not possible that a few streets or blocks are left out, or that the colored population was overlooked? There surely must be a far greater population in St. Petersburg. . . . ."

Although the *Times* would have been very willing to admit it had underestimated the population, the editor was forced to say that "every nose" had been counted, and that the directory was accurate. "We would all be pleased if the city were larger," the editor stated, "but it is not. The figure of 2,227 is right."

The *Times* directory of 1907 fixed the population at 3,233, a gain of 45 per cent during the preceding three years. The directory of 1908 showed the population to be 4,071, and the 1909 directory, 4,626. In the year following, another federal census was made, and the population of St. Petersburg was announced as 4,127. The report resulted in considerable criticism from the St. Petersburg boosters who believed the city was much larger. They asserted that the census was incomplete, and their arguments were strengthened by the 1910 directory made by the *Times,* giving the population as 5,162. Whether the census was wrong, or the directory, is no longer a matter of considerable moment.

The Board of Trade in 1913 estimated the population to be 10,782; the city directory of 1916 placed it at 13,812, and the 1918 directory at 17,530. As might have been expected, these estimates were too high, as shown by the 1920 federal census, which gave St. Petersburg's population as 14,237.

Since 1920, St. Petersburg has seen its period of greatest growth and has expanded in every direction. The most conservative place the population at about 25,000 at the present time (1924), and many say it exceeds that figure.

XXVII

CHURCHES

Episcopalian Churches

(ST. BARTHOLOMEW'S, HOLY SPIRIT, ST. PETER'S)

THE EPISCOPALIANS have the honor of having established the first church on Pinellas Point. The organization was completed at a meeting held at the home of Robert Staunton on April 20, 1887, and arrangements were made to erect a church, St. Bartholomew's, on Lakeview avenue. Land was donated by Susan C. and Dr. John B. Abercrombie and construction was started during the following summer. The founders of the church were H. Beck, Mrs. Jacob Baum, W. J. Godden, H. W. Gilbart, Mrs. Wm. B. Mirandi, Mrs. C. Jones Parry, R. W. Staunton, H. H. P. Seabrook, Josephus Singlehurst and G. White. The church was completed late in 1887. The first officers were Rev. Gilbert Holt White, rector; Robert Staunton, senior warden; Herbert Beck, junior warden, and W. J. Godden, treasurer. Church records show that $246 for the church was raised in America, $383 in England, and $44 at a bazaar held by the church members.

Services were held in St. Bartholomew's Church until 1895 when the property was turned over to the trustees of St. Peter's Church in St. Petersburg. Thereafter the church grounds were used for burial purposes, the ground being consecrated by Bishop Weed.

The first Episcopalian church in St. Petersburg was established soon after St. Petersburg came into existence. A lot at Eleventh street and Second avenue north was given by Jacob Baum and a small building erected. It was completed late in 1889 and regular services established by Rev. Gilbert Holt White, then rector at St. Bartholomew's. This arrangement continued during the pastorate of Rev. White and also that of his successor, Rev. Henry H. Ten Brock, who was in charge of both missions about two years.

In December, 1893, Rev. G. W. Southwell came to Florida from Syracuse, N. Y., to spend the winter, and by request of Bishop Gray, took charge of the work in St. Petersburg. About this time the Holy Spirit Church was moved to Fourth street and Second avenue north to a site which had been purchased from and partly donated by the St. Petersburg Land & Improvement Company. In March, 1894, it was thought best to organize the work in St. Petersburg with a mission separate from St. Bartholomew's, and the necessary economical steps having been taken, an organization was effected under the name of St. Peter's Church. The bishop appointed the officers of the vestry as follows: Rev. George W. Southwell, pastor; Robert W. Staunton, senior warden; Jacob Baum, junior warden; David Murray, secretary, and Herbert Beck, trustee.

Rev. Southwell left St. Petersburg following the death of his daughter in April, 1898, and he was succeeded in the winter of the same year by Rev. F. C. Eldred, who served only a few months. He was followed by Rev. T. J. Purdue. During his pastorate, the present St. Peter's Church was built by E. H. Tomlinson, who bore all the expense. It was completed early in 1899. Mr. Tomlinson also built the rectory.

Rev. Purdue was succeeded by Rev. C. M. Gray, who served faithfully from January 1, 1901, to the time of his death on April 1, 1911. Rev. E. E. Madeira, who had been helping Rev. Gray for a short time, was appointed to take his place as rector. He served for more than six years. The church organ, one of the finest in the South, was installed in the church during his service. Subscriptions for the organ, which cost $11,000, were taken by Rev. Madeira and H. W. Gilbart. Rev. Madeira retired late in the summer of 1917 and he was followed by Rev. W. W. Williams, the present rector, who held his first services on All-Saints Day, November 1, 1917.

Congregational Church

Within less than half a year after the first train pulled into St. Petersburg, the first church was organized—in a railroad car near the depot on Ninth street. The organization was started on October 7, 1888, and completed on December 8 by Rev. A. H. Missildine, representing the Congregational Home Missionary Society. Rev. D. G. Watt, of England, then preaching in the vicinity, was the moderator. There were twenty-five charter members, of whom only two are now living, Mr. and Mrs. E. C. McPherson.

Although the church was called the First Congregational, the Presbyterians of the town united with the Congregationalists to make it possible. The services were held in a small building, used also for a school, and afterward for a parsonage, between Ninth and Tenth streets, near the present Central avenue. The building was inadequate and efforts were made immediately to secure better quarters. A lot at the corner of Fourth street and First avenue north, where the postoffice now stands, was donated to the congregation by General John C. Williams and a church was built costing $2,260, of which $1,000 was donated by Mrs. H. Q. Armour, who with friends also gave the furniture. The church was opened for worship on March 23, 1889, and dedicated January 13, 1890.

In 1901, the Presbyterians withdrew to organize a church of their own under the leadership of Rev. I. A. Auld. The pastors who had served the church up to this time were as follows: Rev. D. G. Watt, 1888-89; Rev. R. J. Morgan, 1889-91; Rev. G. W. Hardaway, 1891-94; Rev. F. D. Jackson, 1894-96; Rev. I. W. Auld, 1897-1900.

The Congregationalists continued their worship under the pastorates of Rev. J. P. Hoyt, 1901-10; Rev. Newman Matthews, 1911-12; Rev. D. Y. Moor, 1912-13; Rev. C. E. Harrington, 1913-18, and Rev. Kerrison Juniper, 1918 to the present time.

The lot upon which the old church stood was sold to the United States government on March 11, 1909, for $7,500, for use as the postoffice site. The edifice was sold to the Advent Church and moved to the corner of Sixth street and Fifth avenue south, where it now stands.

Lots on the corner of Fourth street and Third avenue north were purchased and a new church, costing about $26,000, was erected. The parsonage, erected in 1902, also was moved to this location. The new church was open for worship April 7, 1912, and then again after alterations on October 3, 1913.

The following facts in connection with the history of the First Congregational Church are of interest: At the first annual meeting, on January 12, 1889, after all bills were paid, there was $1,000 in the treasury; now it owns a property valued at about $150,000. The church voted to incorporate on November 4, 1901. The church assumed self-support in 1903. The organ was installed in 1903. The gallery was built in 1920. The church was enlarged in 1922. The new Sunday-school building was erected in 1923.

At the present time the First Congregational Church has 350 members on the active roll. The church officers at present are: pastor-emeritus, Rev. Jas. P. Hoyt; pastor, Rev. Kerrison Juniper; deacons, J. D. Bell, Wm. Lindsay, E. E. Smallman, E. C. McPherson, Harry E. McCardell, T. J. Northrup, R. L. Stiles and H. R. Sackett; trustees, Charles A. Bullard, Arthur L. Johnson, D. A. Lewis, Arthur W. Johnson and Roy LaBrant; treasurer, R. L. Stiles; clerk, E. H. Long.

First Avenue Methodist Episcopal Church

In 1890, Rev. H. J. Walker, presiding elder, was attracted to St. Petersburg as a suitable place in which to organize a Methodist Episcopal Church. General John C. Williams offered a site for a church building and on December 15, 1890, a corporate body of trustees was formed. The St. John's River Conference of the Methodist Episcopal Church met in January, 1891, and the presiding bishop appointed Rev. George E. Skaft to organize, if possible, a church in St. Petersburg in connection with his work in Tarpon Springs.

An organization was effected February 17, 1891, under the name First Methodist Church. Twenty members were enrolled and arrangements were made to hold services every alternate Sunday in the school house. On May 10, 1891, a Sunday school was organized. At this time a deed for a lot for a church building at Central avenue and First street was given by General Williams. The close of the first year showed a good membership and a good Sunday school.

George E. Skafte was reappointed pastor in 1892, in which year the first church edifice was built on a lot 60 by 100 feet. The building was 24 by 38 feet and was planned to be a part of a larger edifice in the future. This church, valued at $500, was a large undertaking for so few members. A Ladies' Aid Society and Epworth League were organized shortly after the new church was opened, and both have done efficient work ever since.

The second church building was a small frame structure which stood on the corner of Central avenue and Fifth street, now occupied by the La Plaza Theatre.

Rev. A. E. Drew was serving his second or third year at Tarpon Springs at the time. He visited St. Petersburg, canvassed the situation, and thought he had the vision of a new and flourishing church. He induced the presiding elder, Rev. L. S. Rader, to sanction his removal from Tarpon Springs and appointment to St. Petersburg. He removed at once and with great enthusiasm began work for a new church. The result was the building of the shell dash church which stood on the corner of First avenue and Fifth street north. The church was completed at a cost of about $10,000, occupied in the Winter of 1905-06, and dedicated January 20, 1906. The name of the church was changed to the First Avenue Methodist.

The present main building, at First avenue and Fifth street north, was built in 1913, and, soon after, the annex or Sunday-school building was erected; but with all this additional room and added facilities, it became necessary to build again and, in 1921, the business men's Bible class erected the third annex at a cost of $6,000.

The church has had a very wonderful growth during the past dozen years and is now very prosperous—a strong force for righteousness in the city. Since its beginning the church has had twelve different pastors, but has come into its greater prominence and success under the pastorates of A. E. Drew, Addyman Smith, S. A. Keene, R. A. Carmine and the present pastor, Rev. E. Ellsworth Reynolds. At present, the church has a membership of about 700.

First Baptist Church

The First Baptist Church of St. Petersburg was organized in 1892 with Rev. Mr. King as pastor. For a time, services were held in a small building on Eighth street north, near Central avenue. This building also was used for public school purposes. Later, the services were moved to a two-story building, known as Cooper's Hall, which had been erected on Central avenue where the American Bank & Trust Company building now stands. Rev. Mr. Edwards, of San Antonio, Fla., occupied the pulpit at that time.

Rev. Mr. Walters became pastor of the church in August, 1893, and served the congregation faithfully for three years. The work at that time received some financial aid from the Florida Baptist State Board. During Rev. Walters' pastorate, a lot was purchased on Second street north, near Central avenue, on which a small building was erected. The congregation worshipped in the First Methodist Church while the new church was being built. In 1896, the building was moved from Second street to the southeast corner of Sixth street and Central avenue, where the church continued to worship until 1912, when that location was sold to H. T. Smallwood. The reason the church gave for moving from the old location was that it "wanted to get uptown."

The present location, on Fourth street opposite the park, was purchased in the spring of 1911 from Mr. Barnes for $6,500. During the same year the church was moved to the new location.

Rev. M. A. Clouts was called to the pastorate in 1897 and ministered the congregation until March, 1900. He proved a true and faithful worker. Rev. D. M. Dungen was then called and served the church one year. Rev. J. W. Harris was the stated supply for the church from January 1, 1901, to October 10, 1902. Later, Dr. Harris organized the Grace Baptist Church. The next pastor was Rev. W. F. Thompson, who served the church from November, 1902, to June, 1905. Rev. S. G. Mullins was then called and began his work as pastor on October 1, 1905, and remained with the church until November 1, 1908. During his pastorate, the church building, then at Sixth and Central, was enlarged and repaired, and much progress was made in the general work of the church.

Rev. J. E. Oates, then pastor at DeLand, Fla., was called to the church as pastor on April 1, 1909, and continued to serve until July 1, 1914. It was during his pastorate that the present location was acquired and the church erected. The old building was moved to the rear of the new church and used for Sunday-school classes.

Rev. W. C. Taylor rendered faithful services as pastor of the church from August, 1914, to August 1, 1917, and the church made splendid progress. Following Rev. Taylor's pastorate, Rev. Edward T. Poulson, then doing notable work in Orlando, Fla., was urgently requested to accept the pastorate of the church. Thoroughly convinced that there was a great future for St. Petersburg, and hence, a great opportunity for the Baptist Church, Dr. Poulson accepted the call and began his pastorate on January 1, 1918. During the following six years, the church grew from a small village church to a city church with large proportions, whose membership was close to 700 and whose annual budget exceeded $30,000. In 1918, the church property was valued at $32,000; in 1924, a conservative valuation is $325,000. The new edifice, of classic design, has two large auditoriums and many Sunday-school rooms, with a total seating capacity of about 3,000. The new building cost the congregation $150,000 and was completed during 1923. The church, in addition to its other extensive work, has established and maintained two flourishing mission stations in rapidly growing sections of the city. The church has one of the largest constituencies of young people in the city, including two Boy Scout organizations numbering about one hundred members.

Catholic Church

When the territory which is now covered by St. Petersburg and adjacent towns was known simply as Point Pinellas, the Jesuits of Tampa were the first priests to officiate at religious worship for the Catholics. Mass was first celebrated at Point Pinellas, in the San Jose Hotel, by Rev. Father Wideman, in September, 1892. Because of the small congregation, which numbered about twenty, the priests attended but once a year for three years.

From the year 1895, visits to the Point were more frequent. The visits were made by Father Le Blanc, who, in 1901, went to Key West. He was succeeded by Fathers O'Sullivan and Barry. In 1906, Father Barry searched for a site on which to build a church. A lot was purchased on Sixth street south between Fifth and Sixth avenues. In the meantime, while money was being collected to build a new church, Father Brislan, who succeeded Father Barry, celebrated Mass in the Fair Building, on February 8, 1908. He had a congregation of seventy persons, many of whom were tourists.

The new church was built soon after 1908. The priests from Tampa made regular visits to officiate at Mass. The congregation having become large enough to warrant a new church and a location nearer town, two lots on the corner of Fourth street south and Third avenue were given by Mr. Barrett, of Philadelphia. In 1911, Father Fox arranged and prepared to use the new site for the purpose intended. The corner stone of the building on this site was laid in 1913. The sermon on that occasion was preached by Father Finnegan, of Tampa. On October 26, 1923, Mass was celebrated in the new church for the first time, the Rex Theatre having been used for that purpose until then.

The church building at Fourth street and Third avenue south has served the needs of the congregation since 1913. On account of the increasing number of Catholics in St. Petersburg, especially in winter, the Jesuits of Tampa came over every Saturday so as to be ready for Sunday morning.

The parish was well organized in 1914 and 1915 when Father Wallace was appointed to look after its needs. Under his rectorship the church was renovated by some needed repairs. Through his diligence a house was bought next to the church to be used as a rectory and dwelling-place for the priests. In 1917, when this building was purchased, the parish had increased by hundreds of newcomers. So much progress had been made that Archbishop Curley, who was then bishop of this diocese, came frequently to encourage the people of the young parish.

About March 17, 1919, a change in rectors took place. Father Wallace was succeeded by Fathers Newlan, Waggemans, Cronin, Carbajal and Clarkson until December, 1920, when Archbishop Curley assigned a secular priest to the rectorship of the parish and the Jesuits were relieved, by agreement, of its care. The first secular priest appointed was Father J. J. O'Riordan, who holds charge of the parish at the present time. The congregation has enlarged to such an extent that instead of two Masses being celebrated, four were found to be necessary to give all a chance of attending to their obligations. The population of the parish during the summer of 1920 numbered 300 and during the following winter, from December to April, an average of 1,500 attended the church each Sunday.

An assistant, Father O'Keeffe, was appointed in December, 1921, to help with the work of the parish during the months while the tourists were in town. In September, 1922, Father Elslander succeeded him as assistant and he still continues in that capacity.

Owing to the growth of St. Petersburg, it was necessary to lay plans for the growth of the parish. To that end, properties were purchased during the summer of 1922 in three different parts of the city—north, south and west. It is hoped that two parishes will be firmly established, the second on the north-side site selected to accommodate the growing population of that district.

First Methodist Church

The First Methodist Church of St. Petersburg was organized in 1889 by Rev. J. M. Diffenworth, and the charter members were Mrs. Florida Curry, W. F. Divine, Mrs. W. F. Divine, Mr. and Mrs. Meadows, Mrs. Nettie Carr and Mr. Ball.

The first church was built on Central avenue and Seventh street about 1892 by Rev. Ira S. Patterson. Later that lot was sold and another acquired at Third street and Second avenue north, where the present church was built in 1902. Various additions have been made since.

The pastors of the church have been, besides those named, A. S. Whedon, W. C. Norton, J. A. Howland, H. Dutill, E. J. Gates, Geo. W. Mitchell, N. H. Williams, B. Margeson, J. F. Bell, Olin Boggess, M. H. Norton, W. F. Dunkle, W. J. Carpenter and S. W. Walker.

Plans have been adopted to build a quarter-million-dollar church on the present site, which will be, when completed, not only one of the best work shops for the church in Florida, but one of the most complete plants in the United States. Every department of the Sunday school is provided with an auditorium, kitchen and class rooms. Seating capacity of the church will be about three thousand. The Sunday school capacity will be about twenty-five hundred.

The present church lot is 100 by 200 feet, and will be practically covered by the new church. Very soon all of the present buildings will be torn down and removed. The congregation expects to be in their new church in the early part of 1925.

First Presbyterian Church

Following evangelistic services conducted by Rev. J. M. Evans, of Kentucky, who had been engaged by the Presbytery of St. John's for such meetings, the First Presbyterian Church of St. Petersburg was organized in November, 1894. Rev. I. M. Auld was called from his work in Orange county to serve as pastor. Arrangements were made with the First Methodist Episcopal Church, then located at Seventh street and Central avenue, to use their building certain Sundays in the month. A little later, the Congregational Church, which was without a pastor, invited Rev. Auld to serve in that capacity. His Presbytery giving its permission, the Congregational Church furnished the building and the Presbyterians the preacher. Each church preserved its own individuality, getting some Home Mission help from their respective boards.

This arrangement continued satisfactorily for years until the Presbyterians, upon the recommendation of Presbytery, decided to build a home of their own. A few of the fifty members preferred to remain with the Congregational Church, but the majority went on with their plans for building, and called the Rev. W. W. Powell, of Oakland, Florida, to serve as pastor. Services were held for a time on alternate Sundays in the little building at Fifth street and Central avenue, then known as the Northern Methodist Church. Rev. Powell served the Presbytery at Clearwater twice a month, but after a short time resigned his pastorate there and devoted all his time to the work in St. Petersburg.

In 1899, the Ladies' Aid Society, which had been a very active factor in the work of the little church, purchased a lot at the corner of Third street and Fourth avenue north for $300. At that time there was very little development beyond Second avenue north and many persons joked about the Presbyterians having bought "out in the woods." However, the congregation went ahead and built an attractive little church, the building committee consisting of Rev. Powell, J. G. Bradshaw and J. C. Jenkins. In 1903, Rev. W. S. Milne, of Micanopy, Florida, came as pastor, and it was during his pastorate that the lot west of the church became its property through the gift of Mr. and Mrs. L. M. Dean. A manse was built about this time.

In December, 1908, Rev. J. F. McLean, of Lakeland, Florida, came to serve as pastor. While he was in St. Petersburg alterations were made to the church, enlarging the seating capacity. Rev. McLean was succeeded in November, 1912, by Dr. G. E. Moorehouse, who came here from Kansas. It was during his pastorate that the splendid brick edifice was erected. It was completed in December, 1913, and was at that time the largest church in the city. The pipe organ was installed shortly afterward, the cost being partly borne by Andrew Carnegie. St. Petersburg was making rapid strides in its growth about this time and the membership of the church increased rapidly.

Rev. W. J. Garrison, the present pastor, succeeded Dr. Moorehouse in January, 1917, coming here from Birmingham, Alabama. The church debt being arranged for, the building was dedicated and a large number of members were added. The Sunday-school building, the Davidson Memorial, was completed in January, 1922. Mrs. R. M. Davidson and her daughter contributed $20,000 toward the building in memory of the husband and father, who had made St. Petersburg his winter home for many years.

The church has now on its roll a membership of about 600. Many changes have taken place, members coming and going, but it has always contributed largely to benevolences and advancing the work of its own denomination. Three foreign missionaries are supported by the church and Sunday school. The Ladies' Auxiliary recently has taken a share in the support of a lady missionary in Brazil, besides which native workers and children are supported by classes and individuals. Home Mission work has not been neglected, and two lots have been purchased and extension work in another part of the city is being planned.

First Christian Church

The Christian Church was organized in St. Petersburg by Rev. A. Flower in January, 1900, with eighteen charter members. The charter members remaining in fellowship with the congregation at present are Mrs. Nevada Bramlitt, Mr. and Mrs. R. W. Miller and Mrs. Gertrude Starkey. The organization of the church was due indirectly to a revival held in 1899 by Rev. R. E. McCorkle.

Soon after the organization, a double lot was purchased at the southwest corner of Fifth street and First avenue north for $650. The church members were very much elated when they were offered $500 for the 50-foot corner fronting on Fifth street. Upon this inside lot a building was erected 24 by 40 feet. It was necessary, however, a few years later to make an addition to the building. In 1909, the present location at the corner of Second avenue and Fourth street south was purchased. The congregation had the usual struggle to maintain an existence, this condition being gradually relieved by revivals held by J. P. Rowlison, J. F. Montgomery and Sam J. White. It might be interesting to state that for weeks of evangelistic service these men, fired with a zeal for the cause of Christ, received by way of remuneration from $34 to $41.50.

The first regular pastor was Rev. J. F. Montgomery, who, the records tell us, "was paid $380, and the Ladies' Aid gave $100 for his annual house rent." Rev. W. A. Harp was the second minister and served the church one year. Chester Sprague was then employed, remaining two years, during which time the church made considerable progress. At the conclusion of his ministry, Rev. E. L. Frazier took charge of the work and was very successful in bringing to the community a comprehensive understanding. The present building was dedicated by George L. Sniveley in January, 1911. The resignation of Rev. Frazier took effect in July, 1911, and soon thereafter a part of the congregation formed what was known as Central Christian Church. This congregation employed Rev. J. S. Howe, and the church at Fourth street and Second avenue south employed J. E. Gorsuch, of Tennessee. The two congregations continued until July, 1913, at which time both congregations deemed it wise, in view of the fact that the Christian Church stands for unity in Christ, and in consideration of this fundamental of the Christian faith, the two churches united and, with Mr. Gorsuch as pastor, have worked harmoniously ever since.

In 1915, Mr. Gorsuch resigned, and Rev. Homer F. Cook was called to the pastorate. In 1917, owing to ill health, Rev. Cook tendered his resignation, and Rev. W. A. Harp was called again to become the minister of the church. Rev. Harp carried the work forward from 1917 to June, 1920, when he resigned, and Rev. D. S. Pooser was called and took up the work in September of that year. Since that time the church has purchased additional property, having paid this obligation entirely, and at present is free of all indebtedness.

The membership of the church has increased 150 per cent under the present leadership. The church stands as one of the popular institutions of St. Petersburg in that it radiates sympathy and helpfulness to all, irrespective of their religious complexion or affiliation. The congregation anticipates and is making preparation to build a modern workshop, as the present equipment is inadequate to present needs. The average attendance in the Bible school is around 50 per cent more than the enrolled membership of the church. One of the outstanding features is the pastor's men's Bible class, which has the distinction of having within its membership men of every religious belief and numbers who are not affiliated with any church. This class of men only meets at 9:30 Sundays in Odd Fellows' Hall.

Grace Baptist Church

The Grace Baptist Church was organized October 16, 1903, with Rev. J. W. Harris as pastor. The original members were Rev. and Mrs. J. W. Harris, Capt. and Mrs. Tuck, Mr. and Mrs. Lewis Hutchinson and daughter, Mr. Hutchinson, brother of Lewis Hutchinson; Mr. Park, wife and mother; J. H. Cashwell, Mrs. Susie Waters, Miss Eva Waters, Miss Ela Waters and Miss Effie Bangs. The lot cost $800 and the building $1,600, the first dollar of which was secured by Dr. Harris through the sale of the grove of Dr. Holland.

The present structure on Fourth street south, at the railroad tracks, was erected in 1909 at a cost of about $10,000.

The church has had two pastors, Rev. Harris, who served from 1903 to 1919, and Rev. W. H. Hubbard, whose pastorate began November 1, 1919.

Due to a lack of space in the present edifice, the winter congregations cannot be accommodated and a movement has been started to secure a new and larger building.

Conferences for the study of the Bible, ministering to the winter visitors, was inaugurated in the temple by Dr. Harris. From these conferences has grown the Florida Bible Institute, of which Dr. Hubbard is dean. This institute is furnishing courses in various branches of Bible study, church history and study of missions and methods in Christian service. Many of the world's most famous preachers and teachers have taught and preached in the Baptist Temple and are among the teachers in the institute. Twenty-six native workers have been placed in foreign fields.

At present, the Grace Baptist Church has 159 members, 103 of whom have been received under the present pastorage.

Trinity Evangelical Lutheran Church

The Trinity Evangelical Lutheran Church was organized by Rev. A. N. Warner, D. D., on March 26, 1911, with eighteen charter members. The first services were held in a room in Ramm's Garage. During the first year of its existence, the congregation purchased two lots, 80 by 100 feet, at Fifth street and Second avenue south, and a chapel was erected immediately. Rev. H. J. Mathias was the first regular pastor. He was succeeded by Rev. John Hall, who came to the city in 1913, and remained as pastor of Trinity until the fall of 1917, when he resigned to undertake work as chaplain in the United States Army. During his pastorate an eight-room parsonage was built.

Rev. W. E. Pugh began work as pastor of the church on July 1, 1918. Increasing membership and influence required larger quarters. The property was sold to the Young Men's Christian Association in March, 1921, and a site for a new church was purchased at Fifth street and Fourth avenue north. The present parsonage at 425 Fifth street north was purchased at the same time. A new church was started on the new site in January, 1922, and the building was completed early in 1924. The building committee consisted of the pastor, O. R. Albright, Jos. E. Mundorff, Otto F. Bocher, Victor A. Boeke and C. L. Sorrick. The general contractor was Victor A. Boeke. The Lutherans now have a property valued at $125,000.

First Church of Christ, Scientist

A Christian Science Society was organized in St. Petersburg at a meeting of about fifteen persons in 1900 in the old Strowger building on the southeast corner of Central avenue and Fourth street. Thereafter meetings were held regularly on Sundays and Wednesdays. In order to secure more commodious quarters, the society moved some time later to a building on the water front which was owned and offered to the society by the G. A. R. Shortly afterwards, a building was purchased on Third street south, now occupied by the Salvation Army. It was during this time that the organization fulfilled the requirements necessary to be known as a church, having more than sixteen members and an advertised practitioner. A charter was then secured and the organization became known as the First Church of Christ, Scientist.

In 1913, the church purchased the fair building in Second avenue north near Second street. At present, two services are being held there on Sundays to accommodate the congregations. A reading room is also maintained by the church for the public on the fifth floor of the Sumner building. Two lots have been secured at the corner of Third street and Fifth avenue north, where a new structure will be erected in the near future, again indicating the growth and progress of this movement.

XXVIII—WORLD WAR

ST PETERSBURG contributed nobly toward the winning of the World War. Hundreds of young men, the flower of the city, entered the service, and those forced to remain at home subordinated all other things to the main task of hastening victory. Every war loan was oversubscribed and every call made by the Red Cross was answered generously.

The first effect of the war upon St. Petersburg was the halting of work on paving contracts, due to difficulty encountered in disposing of the bonds. The city was unable to find a market for its certificates and on August 16, 1914, notified the contractors that the work would have to wait. Within a few months, however, it was seen that the war would not disturb the financial structure of the nation, the certificates were sold, and on October 13 the city commissioners ordered the paving to proceed.

Late in 1914 the war began to have an adverse effect upon business in St. Petersburg, particularly in real estate. Although as many tourists visited the city as in previous years, few cared to make large investments. The uncertainty of the times, and the knowledge that the United States would have to enter the war sooner or later, caused a lull which was all the more noticeable because of the boom of the two preceding years. Few lots were sold and developers who were heavily involved suffered seriously.

A short time after the declaration of war against Mexico, the St. Petersburg men in the National Guard of Florida were called into service. The members of the Hospital Corps of the Second Regiment left June 22, 1916, and after a short stay at the mobilization camp in Jacksonville, entrained for the border. The corps consisted of Major H. M. Axline, Sergt. M. J. Groves, Sergt. P. H. Graham; Einstein Booth, private first class; Carl A. Muller, Richard White, Hugh S. Hughes, Lucian Lepper, Clarence A. Altum, Robt. M. McMullen, Jerald Santas, Byron Reeves, John P. Sherman, Milton B. Fulcher, Rudolph Nelson, Richard Newsham, Ross Weaver, Dr. J. R. Hawkins, Roy McVey, privates. Sergeant Phillip Graham died at Laredo, Texas, March 13, 1917, from nephritis. The corps returned to St. Petersburg on March 18, 1917.

The tragedy of the World War was brought home to the people of St. Petersburg late in 1916 when word was received of the death of Tony Jannus, killed in the Russian Aero Service on October 12, 1916. Mr. Jannus had come to St. Petersburg with the Benoist Airboat Company in 1913 and was well known in the city. Roger Jannus, brother of Tony Jannus, was killed in France during the summer of 1918.

On June 5, 1917, 737 St. Petersburg men registered in the first draft; 291 did not claim any exemption. The Coast Artillery Company left for Fort Dade on September 12, 1917. Thereafter, hardly a month passed until the end of the war that more men did not leave to enter the service. Lawrence Melzer Tate, eighteen years old, the son of Mrs. Helen Keller, 935 Nebraska avenue, was the first St. Petersburg boy reported killed. He died when the steamer Lakemour was torpedoed by a submarine on April 11, 1918.

St. Petersburg's quota in the First Liberty Loan drive was $193,850; $194,150 was subscribed. The committee which conducted the campaign consisted of T. A. Chancellor, representing the banks; Arthur L. Johnson, the Merchants' Association; Mayor Al. F. Lang, the city, and Fred P. Lowe, the Board of Trade. In each succeeding loan campaign, St. Petersburg subscribed more than was asked for.

The St. Petersburg Chapter of the American Red Cross worked incessantly during the war period. The chapter was organized on April 5, 1917, at a meeting in the First Baptist Church called by Mrs. B. A. Greene, president of the Woman's Club. Mrs. John Burnside was appointed temporary chairman and Mrs. Sherman Rowles, secretary and treasurer. During the first week, 124 members were secured. On April 17, the first formal meeting was held at the home of Mrs. Edith Lincoln Pratt. Mrs. George N. Sleight was made temporary chairman. Chairmen of the various committees were Mrs. Lew B. Brown, Mrs. James Samson, Miss Lena Chase, Dr. James Samson, Mrs. Maud Aikin, Mrs. J. C. Blocker, Mrs. T. W. Blocker and Mrs. T. W. Weston. The first Red Cross drive on June 18 netted 1,026 members and $6,901.78. The charter was granted on June 12, 1917. R. H. Thomas was elected chairman; Mrs. John Woodside, vice-chairman; Mrs. Sherman Rowles, secretary, and Mrs. C. W. Springstead, treasurer. These officers, with the exception of O. G. Hiestand, who was elected treasurer to succeed Mrs. C. W. Springstead, served during the war.

St. Petersburg men who died in the service were: Officers: Clyde Crenshaw Caswell, first lieutenant, field artillery; James Abel Johnson, second lieutenant, infantry. Enlisted men: Lewis N. Brantley, George Donaldson Griffin, Edward Theodore Hall, George Harold Myers, James Clyde McCraven, Harry J. Newkumet, Wesley Noble, William Foster Newell, Seymour Andrew Prestwood, Stewart D. Ramsauer, Lawrence M. Tate, Paul Other Webb, Carey Herriott (colored), Charles Hargray, Jr. (colored).

WHO'S WHO
IN
ST. PETERSBURG

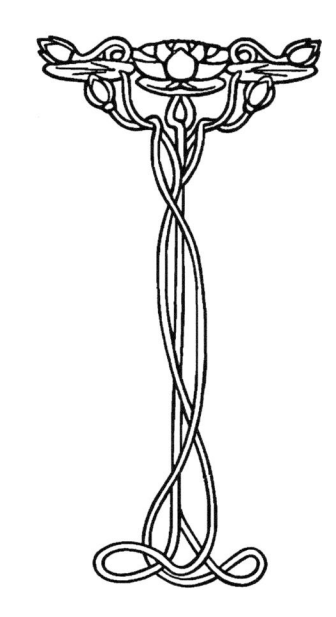

"History is the essence of innumerable biographies."
—*Thomas Carlyle.*

J. C. Williams

J. C. Williams

To John Constantine Williams St. Petersburg owes its existence. He came to Pinellas Point in 1875, bought many hundreds of acres, persuaded a railroad to extend its road to the peninsula, laid out the plans for a town, and St. Petersburg was born—"a town at the end of nowhere."

The story of the founder of St. Petersburg must begin with a story of his father, Major General John R. Williams, one of the pioneer residents of Detroit, Mich. In his youth, John R. Williams was a captain of artillery in the United States army, stationed at Detroit. In 1816 he resigned from the army because he disliked his superior officer, General Hull, and opened a general store. His customers were soldiers, hunters, and Indians; his goods were largely paid for in furs. Twice a year he received his goods from New York by way of Buffalo on a sailing vessel and twice a year he shipped his furs.

In 1824 Detroit became a city and Williams was elected as its first mayor. He was re-elected three times. He was the first president of the first bank in Michigan and was one of three to found the Detroit Free Press. From 1832 to 1852 he was major general of the state militia. His savings were invested in real estate and at his death in 1854 he was probably the wealthiest man in Michigan. In 1858 his property was divided among eight children, the share of each being appraised at $105,000.

John C. Williams was born January 25, 1817. When four months old he was christened in St. Anne's Catholic church. Little is known of his early years. He was never a soldier but was a member of the Brady Guards, a uniformed company of Detroit young men. His title of general was a complimentary one only, given to him after he settled in St. Petersburg. He was married in 1846 and ten children were born to the couple.

An obituary notice published in the South Florida Home at the time of his death stated that General Williams had "satisfactorily discharged the duties of the offices of city treasurer, supervisor of Greenfield, deputy register of deeds, and justice of the peace for several terms, in Detroit." While in Detroit he had an office in a building which he owned opposite the Detroit City Hall. He resided on an eighty-acre farm on Woodward avenue, four miles back from the river, which his father had leased to him when he married. When his father died he willed him this property which he immediately started to subdivide and sell. More than a hundred deeds made by him are recorded in Detroit.

General Williams came to Florida in 1875 for his health. He suffered from asthma and his physician ordered him to seek a milder climate. From Jacksonville he went up the St. Johns river and visited Lake Okeechobee, Key West, Punta Rassa, Tampa and Clearwater, but found no place that suited him. At Cedar Keys, while on his way home, he was told of Point Pinellas. Returning to Clearwater, he drove here, and was satisfied with what he found.

From then on, General Williams strove to develop this section. He bought about 1,700 acres and in 1879 he settled on the estate and attempted to farm. His venture turned out poorly and he returned north. On November 7, 1881, a divorce from his wife was granted him by Circuit Judge F. H. Chambers in Detroit. On July 29, 1882, he was married again to Mrs. Sarah Judge (nee Sarah Craven), of Canada.

After disposing of his property in Detroit he came back to Florida, building a home in Hyde Park in Tampa. On January 29, 1887, he signed an agreement with the Orange Belt Railway to build a road through his property on Pinellas Peninsula. The negotiations which resulted in the agreement were conducted largely by Mrs. Sarah Williams and Henry Sweetapple, treasurer of the railroad.

At the start of the yellow fever epidemic in Tampa in the fall of 1887, General Williams and his wife came to the peninsula and lived for a while at Big Bayou. Together they made plans for laying out the new town, which was surveyed early in 1888 by A. L. Hunt, chief engineer of the Orange Belt. In 1891 General Williams began the construction of his home at Fourth street and Fifth avenue south, which later was widely known as one of the show places of Florida. Thousands of dollars were spent for interior decorations. The work was completed shortly before his death. The home is now a part of the Manhattan Hotel.

During April, 1892, General Williams began to fail. Ten years before he had suffered a stroke of apoplexy from which he never had fully recovered. The South Florida Home, in telling of his death, said in the issue of April 29:

"A pall of sadness envelopes the town! Its father, its benefactor, its far-seeing originator and friend is no more! His familiar figure will no longer be seen at his place of business, where for years he has loved to spend a portion of each day. The familiar walks he so oft has trod will know him no more.

"St. Petersburg, his idol, which his means rescued from the tangled wilderness and swamps of a few years ago, and which today is the most prosperous little town in the southern portion of the state, owes much to him, who, with such wisdom, guided her earliest years. He had been complaining for some weeks, but a few weeks ago had about recovered, and the citizens hoped to see him at his business office, but a most serious complication seized hold of him, just as he seemed well enough to start out again, and although tender and skillful assistants sought to ward off the dread affliction, all help proved futile, and he rapidly grew worse until near the time of his death, when he fell into a peaceful slumber from which he never awoke. Up to the time of his death he was fully conscious, and although perfectly aware his end was near, he met it without a murmur or complaint."

The only public bequest made by General Williams was a lot for a fire house. He left practically all his property to his wife. Later, however, an arrangement was made out of court whereby the property was divided between his wife and his children by his first wife. The value of all his property was estimated to be between $125,000 and $150,000.

Those who knew General Williams tell of his kindly disposition and of his many charities. Scrupulously honest himself, he expected others to be honest in their dealings with him. He was somewhat autocratic in his ways and his orders had to be strictly obeyed. If they were, his employes found him to be a kind and liberal master.

Of his four sons, B. C. Williams and J. Mott Williams are now living in St. Petersburg. J. C. Williams, Jr., now resides in Tampa and John M. Williams is dead. Two daughters, Mrs. Mary Fisher and Mrs. H. N. Schirp, are living in St. Petersburg. Mrs. Cornelia Mott Morse, another daughter, lives in Sulphur Springs. A fourth daughter, Mrs. Josephine Bain, died some years ago.

Peter A. Demens

St. Petersburg was conceived by General John C. Williams; it was made possible and named by Peter A. Demens, the man who brought in the Orange Belt Railway. Without the railroad, St. Petersburg would be nothing more than it was fifty years ago—a thinly settled stretch of land on the shores of Tampa Bay; with the railroad, it grew to become one of the world's most famous resort cities. In planning the town, General Williams had everything to win and nothing to lose; in building the railroad, Demens took a chance on winning—and lost.

Demens might be described as a soldier of fortune, a born promoter. He was a man of remarkable talents and brilliant personality. He made friends quickly, and the friends trusted him. He had the vision necessary to launch "impossible" projects, and the determination necessary to put the project through. This was proved in the case of the Orange Belt Railway. A weaker man would have given it up long before it was completed; Demens finished the job even after he knew it would bring no financial gain. Fighting against heavy odds, he brought the railroad to St. Petersburg, and the town came into existence.

Demens—some say his correct name was Petrovitch A. Demenscheff—was born in Petrograd, Russia, in 1860. Descended from a noble Russian family with large estates in the government of Tver, he later became a Marshal of Nobility, and was on intimate terms with the most powerful men in the Russian empire at the time. He was first cousin of Prince Petroff and a captain in the Imperial Guard. In 1880 he left Russia, a political exile, and made his way to Florida, first locating at Longwood.

Within a short time he organized a

Peter A. Demens

lumber mill under the name of Demens, McClain & Cotter and built a sawmill at Longwood, about ten miles southwest of Sanford. To bring logs to the mill, a haphazard railroad was laid out into the woods. Demens bought out his partners in about 1883 and continued to operate the mill himself. Shortly afterwards he obtained a contract from the South Florida Railroad to build the station houses on the railroad's branch from Lakeland northward to Dade City. The contract proved profitable and Demens managed to save up several thousand dollars.

From 1886 to the summer of 1889 Demens devoted all his time to the financing and construction of the Orange Belt Railway.

After being forced to sell out his interest in the railway and Orange Belt Investment Company, Demens went to Asheville, N. C., where he bought a planing mill and operated it for three years. In 1892 he went to Los Angeles. His first venture there was a steam laundry. He knew nothing about the business, but he made it so successful that in three or four years he was able to sell out for $200,000. He invested a portion of this money in citrus groves near Alta Lomo, a town he founded about forty-five miles outside of Los Angeles, and he devoted most of his remaining life to orange culture and the marketing of fruit, becoming prominent in the California Citrus Exchange.

During the last fifteen years of his life, Demens paid little attention to business matters. He had a residence in Los Angeles but spent most of the time on his ranch at Alta Lomo. He wrote many articles on European affairs for the Los Angeles Times and went to Europe for the Associated Press to report on political conditions.

Though in close touch with the affairs of Russia and a constant contributor to the current literature of that country, he was not connected with its government until 1916, when in response to urgent request from Russian friends he went to New York and took charge of the tangled affairs of the Russian government's purchasing bureau, which had become disorganized through the swift changes in Europe. After several months of hard work, he returned to his southern California home.

Demens knew Prince Lvoff, Prof. Miliukoff and many of the men who formed the cabinet of the new republic. The latter turn of affairs, and the ultimate betrayal of Russia by traitors, was one of the big shocks that finally undermined his health. He gradually weakened and died on January 21, 1919, death being caused by a complication of diseases.

Demens was married in Russia and four children were born there: Claudia, Helen, Vadim and Inna. Valdimar and Eugene were born in Florida. Vera was born in Asheville, N. C. At the time of the father's death, two daughters and three sons were living. Mrs. Demens died shortly after the death of her husband.

After leaving Florida in 1889, Demens never returned to the state or to St. Petersburg. The heirs now own many valuable properties in California, including a ranch of 400 acres, 50 acres of which are set to 31-year-old Washington Navels. Miss Inna Demens is well known as an author, while the sons are engaged in business.

F. A. Davis

It has been said, and unquestionably the statement is founded on facts, that F. A. Davis put St. Petersburg ten years ahead in its development; that he gave it the things which made possible its future growth and put it ahead of other resort towns on the West Coast of Florida.

Mr. Davis began work for St. Petersburg when it was insignificant and unknown; when none of the streets were paved and when there were few houses and no brick buildings. It was a town at the end of a railroad, and that was all. And yet, despite the humble appearance of St. Petersburg, Mr. Davis saw in it great possibilities—he dreamed that it would become a great city. And because he dreamed, and worked to make his dreams come true, St. Petersburg was pushed forward on its march to prosperity.

Mr. Davis gave St. Petersburg its first electric light company, its first trolley line, its first real advertising. He was a visionary — he admitted it himself; in many ways he was impractical—his best friends say that about him. He foresaw

F. A. Davis

the progress of today, but he was fifteen years ahead of his time. Consequently, he lost money, and his companies failed, but St. Petersburg gained.

Frank Allston Davis was born on September 8, 1850, in Duxbury, Vt. His early boyhood was spent on the farm of his parents. He was educated in the country schools near Duxbury. During the winters of 1867 and 1868 he taught school at Peru, North Windham and Middletown, of Andover, Vt. In the spring of 1868 he moved to Asbury, N. J., where he taught two years. During the summer vacations he took up the selling of mowers and made such a success that he gave up teaching to devote all his time to the work. In 1872 he became interested in the publishing of county atlases and histories. In 1880 he settled in Philadelphia and engaged in the publishing of medical books and periodicals. His company became one of the best known of its kind in the world, its greatest work being Sajous' Analytical Cyclopædia of Practical Medicine.

During the winter of 1889-90 Mr. Davis became afflicted with a severe case of muscular rheumatism. In search of relief he went to Florida and in April, 1890, he went to Tarpon Springs, where he made a quick and complete recovery. While in Tarpon Springs Mr. Davis recognized the chances for development offered on the peninsula and decided to take a part in its advancement. He undertook the promotion of a sanitarium, advertising it through his medical publications. Mr. Davis succeeded in interesting a number of physicians throughout the country, but the project did not prove successful.

While in Tarpon Springs Mr. Davis made the acquaintance of Jacob Disston, who afterwards aided him financially in many of his projects. The first of these was the founding of an electric light plant at Tarpon Springs. Mr. Davis put in about $2,000 of his own money and Mr. Disston advanced several thousand more on a first mortgage. The light plant failed, principally because the people of Tarpon Springs would not give it any support. Mr. Davis finally became disgusted and turned toward St. Petersburg, which he had visited for the first time a few years before. In 1897 the plant was removed to St. Petersburg.

During the next few years Mr. Davis spent large sums of money in advertising St. Petersburg. Hardly an issue of his medical publications appeared without some reference to St. Petersburg or Pinellas Peninsula. He also published for some time the "Florida Magazine," devoted almost exclusively to St. Petersburg. The magazine represented a constant and heavy loss, but was believed justified by the interest it created.

In 1902 Mr. Davis began working to establish an electric railway from St. Petersburg to Disston City, on Boca Ceiga Bay. He enlisted the aid of his Philadelphia friends in putting over the project, and finally, in 1905, the line was completed. The line did not prove to be as profitable as Mr. Davis had figured it would be, and more than once it was on the verge of going into the hands of the receivers. It was kept alive only by the continued support of the stockholders, checks being sent from Philadelphia each week to cover the deficits.

During the next few years Mr. Davis' activities became more and more extended. Nearly a dozen new companies were formed as subsidiaries of the St. Petersburg Investment Company to handle developments in all sections of the lower end of the peninsula. One of the greatest achievements of these companies was the West Central development.

A project of the companies which resulted less satisfactorily was that of Pinellas Park. Thousands of acres in that section were purchased in 1909 and 1910 and a fortune was spent in draining the land, laying out small farms, and starting a town. Pinellas Park was advertised all over the country and for a short time it boomed. Later, however, the town went into a decline. Many of the settlers left, discouraged after the failure of their farming efforts.

The work of Mr. Davis in behalf of St. Petersburg was recognized by the Board of Trade at a meeting of the governors held on January 30, 1913, when they elected him the first honorary life member. The resolution, adopted by a unanimous vote, read: "Whereas, Mr. F. A. Davis, from pioneer time in St. Petersburg to the present, has been a loyal and untiring worker for the Board of Trade and for many a vital interest in St. Petersburg and vicinity, be it resolved * * * that in recognition of Mr. Davis' valuable service to the community as a citizen, investor, and promoter, and in appreciation of his helpful co-operation with us in our Board of Trade work and enterprises, we do hereby bestow upon him the greatest honor within our gift, by electing him an honorary member of our Board of Trade for life."

Mrs. Sarah Armistead

After the outbreak of the World War the financial condition of the various Davis enterprises became weakened. Worry over the fate of the companies gradually undermined Mr. Davis' health and he died on January 12, 1917. Late in the same year the Davis companies went into the hands of a receiver. Mr. Davis was survived by his widow and one son, Dr. A. B. Davis. Interment was made in West Laurel Hill Cemetery, Philadelphia.

Mrs. Sarah Armistead

Mrs. Sarah Armistead, "the mother of St. Petersburg," was born in London, Ontario, August 18, 1847, the daughter of James and Isabella (Stewart) Craven, the former a native of England and the latter of Scotland.

Mrs. Armistead was the eldest of a family of five children, and she was educated in the schools of London. When she was fifteen years old she became the wife of John R. Judge, and fourteen years later she was left a widow with two children: Robert C. M. Judge and John R. Judge.

While in Detroit, Mrs. Judge met General John C. Williams, to whom she was married on July 29, 1882. For four years after their marriage, General and Mrs. Williams lived in Detroit, and then went to Tampa, Fla., in December, 1886. In Tampa they erected the first fine residence to be built in Hyde Park.

General and Mrs. Williams came to St. Petersburg in 1887 because of a yellow fever epidemic in Tampa. For their trip they chartered the steam tug O. D. C., of Key West, which landed them at Disston City dock, from which they walked to George King's sawmill, where they hired a surrey and team and drove to Mrs. Sterling's boarding house at Pinellas. From there they walked to the Williams home—then a four-room shanty, boarded up and down, set in the midst of a forty-acre bearing grove.

In St. Petersburg Mrs. Williams interested herself in all public affairs, and took an active interest in the negotiations with Henry Sweetapple which resulted in bringing the Orange Belt Railroad to St. Petersburg.

Mrs. Williams tells the story of the naming of the town, giving as her version of it the story of drawing straws for the honor. General Williams, according to the story, wished to call the city Detroit, while Peter Demens wished to call it after his Russian home, so Mrs. Williams held broom straws for the gentlemen to draw, saying that he who chose the long straw might have the privilege of naming the town. Demens was the fortunate one, and called it St. Petersburg, whereupon General Williams named the first hotel Detroit.

General and Mrs. Williams built a beautiful residence in the new city, located where the Manhattan Hotel now stands. It was beautifully decorated with hand paintings, and is said to have set the standard for homes in the growing community.

On April 2, 1892, General Williams died, after a long illness. September 10, 1894, Mrs. Williams married Captain James Anderson Armistead, a Virginian.

Mrs. Armistead had studied dancing in her youth, and was in great demand at benefit performances in the interest of the city. In this and many other ways she assisted in raising money for charities. She was a member of the Congregational Church in Tampa and assisted in building the Congregational Church in St. Petersburg. She was a member of the Francis Scott Key Memorial Association, and for six years was an active member of the Woman's Christian Temperance Union of Tampa, and of the Independent Order of Good Templars.

During her residence in St. Petersburg Mrs. Armistead was also a member of the W. T. I. A. and the Eastern Star, as well as the Woman's League.

Mrs. Armistead died December 15, 1917, while on a visit to Detroit. She was buried beside General J. C. Williams in Elmwood Cemetery in Detroit.

Jacob S. Disston

Although Jacob S. Disston has never lived in St. Petersburg, he probably has done as much to help in the development of the city as most men who have lived here since St. Petersburg was founded. At several crucial periods in the life of the F. A. Davis enterprises, Mr. Disston backed them with his fortune, enabling them to continue. Without Mr. Disston, the Davis projects could not have been put through, and without the Davis projects, the development of the city unquestionably would have been retarded.

Jacob Disston was born in Philadelphia on August 4, 1862, the son of Henry and Mary (Steelman) Disston. The father was the founder of the firm Henry Disston & Sons, Inc., saw manufacturers. The son was educated in the Episcopal Academy of Philadelphia and in the University of Pennsylvania. In 1885, he came to Florida upon the advise of his physician and in response to the urging of his brother, Hamilton Disston, who had just purchased from the state four million acres of land at twenty-five cents an acre. From Tampa, where the railroad ended, he drove through the woods to Tarpon Springs where a hotel had just been finished by his brother's company.

One of the things which attracted him to Tarpon Springs was an article, "The Frostless Pinellas," written by Dr. Van Bibber, of Baltimore. A few weeks after he arrived on the peninsula a heavy frost occurred which caused great damage. Mr. Disston began to have grave doubts regarding the fitness of the title, but later he learned that frosts occurred very rarely and he liked the peninsula so well that he has been returning every year since.

During the next few winters Mr. Disston spent much of his time driving over the peninsula over the woods trails. He visited the site of St. Petersburg for the first time in 1887. At that time there were only a few scattered homes in this locality. He made his headquarters at Disston City at a hotel which had been erected in anticipation of the completion of a proposed railroad to that point. The railroad never came, and Disston City did not prosper.

Mr. Disston met Mr. Davis for the first time during the winter of 1890. Mr. Davis had come to Tarpon Springs for his health and upon recovery, began making plans to aid in the development of this section. He first attempted to establish a sanitarium at Tarpon Springs, but the project fell through, even though he obtained the assistance of many physicians throughout the country. Later, Mr. Davis started an electric light plant at Tarpon Springs. He was aided financially in this project by Mr. Disston. When it was learned that the plant would not pay in Tarpon Springs, Mr. Disston agreed to its removal to St. Petersburg.

Mr. Disston again assisted Mr. Davis when the trolley line was being projected. He furnished the money to help buy the rails and the line finally was built to Disston City. Mr. Davis had obtained other financial assistance on the strength of an option he held on 3,300 acres of land around Disston City at $5 an acre. In 1910, the Disston City Land Company, which owned the land, became tired of the delay in the exercise of the option and informed Mr. Davis that if he did not pay at once for the land, the option would be cancelled. Mr. Disston loaned him the money needed and the land was deeded to Jacob M. Vodges as trustee. Later, the money was paid back and the land was deeded back to the St. Petersburg Investment Company.

The loans made by Mr. Disston to the Davis companies continued to increase during the next few years. Finally, they reached the total of $250,000. Having such a large sum at stake, Mr. Disston requested that Mr. Vodges be made president of the St. Petersburg Investment Company. During Mr. Vodges's administration, Mr. Disston advanced a further sum of $100,000 to build the trolley line from Ninth street and Central avenue to Davista and later on advanced another $100,000 for the building of the new electric light plant.

When the war depression came on and the Davista companies went into the hands of the receiver, Mr. Disston waited for

Jacob Disston

over two years before foreclosing on his mortgage. At last he was forced to take this action as there did not appear to be any other course to pursue, all the creditors clamoring for their money. During the receivership, Mr. Disston advanced $10,000, so that employees of the company could be paid their wages, in default for nearly eight weeks. His total loans to the companies, before and during the receivership, aggregated between $500,000 and $750,000.

On April 7, 1919, Mr. Disston and Warren Webster and Horace F. Nixon, of Camden, N. J., members of the bondholders' protective committee, bought the trolley line at Clearwater at forced sale for $165,000. They held mortgages totaling $250,000. On August 30, of the same year, they sold it to the city for $175,000, losing $75,000 on the transaction.

Although Mr. Disston has disposed of most of his real estate holdings in this section, he still is greatly interested in the development of the city.

Mr. Disston has lived every winter for a number of years at Belleair. He is a heavy stockholder in the firm Henry Disston & Sons, Inc., is the president of the Tacony Trust Company, of Philadelphia; director of the Third National Bank, and Pelham Trust Company, of Philadelphia, and is a trustee of the Free Library of Philadelphia. He is a member of the Philadelphia Cricket Club, Manufacturers Club, Union League of Philadelphia, Sunny Brook Golf Club, and University Club. He is a member of the Episcopalian Church.

Mr. Disston was married in Philadelphia in 1883 to Miss Effie Fleming. They have eight children.

John A. Bethell

John A. Bethell, one of the first residents of Pinellas Point, was born in Key West, Fla., on July 21, 1834. From his boyhood he followed the water for a living, engaging in fishing, wrecking, coasting and piloting. In 1856 he located on Pinellas Point, embarking in the business of fishing for the Cuban market.

At the outbreak of the Civil War, Mr. Bethell left the point and joined the Confederate Army, Company K of the Seventh Florida Regiment. After the war he was married in Tampa to Miss Sarah C. Haagen.

In 1867 he returned to Pinellas Point, bought land, built a home and set out an orange grove. Later he entered the mercantile business at Pinellas and also became the agent for lumber schooners plying between this port and Pensacola. For fourteen years he served as postmaster of Pinellas and also was justice of the peace for three years.

John Bethell

In 1914 Mr. Bethell published his "History of Pinellas Peninsula," in which was given an invaluable record of the early settlers of this section of the state.

Mr. Bethell died on April 12, 1915. He was survived by seven children: Clifford O., William C., John A., Jr., Mrs. W. H. Jones, Cora G., Mrs. Alma Matterson, and Florence.

Horace Williams

Horace Williams was born in St. Petersburg on February 9, 1884, the son of J. C. Williams, Jr., and Nettie (Cox) Williams. J. C. Williams, Jr., was a son of General J. C. Williams, the founder of St. Petersburg, and came to the peninsula for the first time with his father in 1879, nine years before the railroad was completed. He was a member of the first town council and was prominently identified with the activities of the city for many years. He is now living in Tampa.

Mrs. Nettie Williams, the mother of Horace Williams, was a member of one of the pioneer families of the peninsula.

Horace Williams attended the public schools of St. Petersburg and later completed a business course in the University of Florida. Upon leaving school, Mr. Williams became bookkeeper of the Crystal Ice Works, owned by his father. When the N. C. Williams Company took over the plant in about 1909, Mr. Williams became manager, and retained that position when the company was reorganized as the Citizens Ice & Cold Storage Company in about 1912.

During the war, Mr. Williams served as captain of Company I, Fifty-sixth Infantry, Seventh Division, for twenty-one months, ten months of this period in France. He participated in the campaign of Saint Mihiel, and during the St. Mihiel drive was gassed and wounded in the leg.

After the war Mr. Williams came back to St. Petersburg and worked for six months with the company he had left to enter the service and then founded the Williams-Beers Ice Company, of which he is now president.

On May 1, 1907, Mr. Williams was married to Miss Ida Louise Weller, the daughter of A. P. and Isabelle Weller, the former the first manager of the St. Petersburg Electric Light Company, brought here from Tarpon Springs in 1897. Mr. and Mrs. Williams have one son, Horace Williams, Jr., now seven years old, who is attending the public school. Mr. Williams is a member of the American Legion, 40et8, B. B. O. E., the St. Petersburg Yacht Club, and the Kiwanis Club.

Jacob Baum

Nine years before the first train arrived in St. Petersburg, Mr. and Mrs. Jacob Baum came here from Pennsylvania, built a home and planted an orange grove. The family has lived here ever since.

Mr. Baum was born in Westmoreland County, Pennsylvania, on December 24, 1834. He was reared on his father's farm. On November 25, 1878, he was married in Kittaning, Pa., to Miss Jeannette Chandler, of Pugwash, Cumberland County, Nova Scotia. Mrs. Baum had received her education in the Nova Scotia public schools, at a convent on Prince Edward Island, and at the Pittsburgh Female College, of Pittsburgh, Pa.

Mr. and Mrs. Baum, shortly after their marriage, decided to go to Florida to start an orange grove. They were influenced in making their decision by Mrs. Baum's brother, A. B. Chandler, who had visited many parts of the state while working on a government coast survey boat. Of all the places he had seen, he liked Pinellas Peninsula the best. Upon his return home, he purchased from the state of Florida forty acres adjoining Mirror Lake, paying ninety cents an acre. Mr. Baum purchased eighty acres at the same price. Mr. Baum's land extended from the lake to what is now First avenue south, and from the alley between Sixth and Seventh streets to Fourteenth street.

The land purchased by Mr. Chandler and Mr. Baum was some of the most desirable in this locality. General J. C. Williams failed through an error either on his part or on the part of state officials to include it in his purchases from the state. When he learned that he did not own it, he tried immediately to get possesion and applied to the state for its purchase. Mr. Chandler and Mr. Baum,

Horace Williams

however, had got ahead of him and he could not secure it.

Upon arrival on the Point, Mr. and Mrs. Baum lived in an abandoned log cabin northwest of the lake until their own home, built from lumber they had brought from Tampa, was completed. They had three neighbors: H. A. Weir, who owned land west of the lake; Mr. Baum's brother, A. B. Chandler, who had preceded them in coming by a few months, and the Cox family, which owned a grove about a mile south of Booker Creek.

As soon as they were settled, Mr. Baum cleared the land and set out an orange grove. His trees were seedlings and of slow growth. The first good crop they bore was destroyed by the heavy freezes of 1894-95. The trees, however, were not injured and a number are still standing at First avenue north and Seventh street. No crop of any good value could be grown except sweet potatoes. Mr. Baum kept a horse and helped to clear land for other settlers.

The number of settlers in this locality gradually increased and in 1887, when it was apparent that the proposed railroad to Williams' property would be completed, the town-to-be experienced a small boom. One of the newcomers was E. R. Ward, who had a store at the village of Pinellas. He purchased a building at Ninth street and First avenue south from Mr. Baum and moved his store. The first post office was located in this building with Mr. Ward as postmaster.

Mr. Ward purchased five acres from Mr. Baum and the two joined in making the Ward and Baum plat, recorded April 4, 1888. The railroad reached the edge of the town on April 30 of that year. General Williams' map of St. Petersburg was not placed on record until August. By that time many lots in the Ward and Baum plot had been sold at prices ranging from $30 to $60 a lot. For a number of years the Ninth street section was the main part of town.

Mr. Baum died on October 8, 1894. In 1899, Mrs. Baum sold her old home and purchased two lots on First avenue north between Second and Third streets, paying $1,200 for the two. Here they built a rooming house of twenty-two rooms. For many years Mrs. Baum provided accommodations for winter visitors. Mrs. Baum sold the property in 1920.

For many years Mrs. Baum took an active part in the development of the city. She was one of the first members of the Park Improvement Association and served the organization as treasurer and secretary for a number of years. With the other women of the city she helped raise the money to build the first wooden sidewalk, from Ninth street to Second street on Central, and also the first band stand in the park.

Mr. and Mrs. Baum had one child, Grace C., who has the distinction of being the first child born within the present limits of St. Petersburg. On June 24, 1900, Grace Baum was married to Claude Sullivan Pepper, of Rising Sun, Ind., who had come here with his family in 1891. Mr. and Mrs. Pepper have one son, Joseph Basil Pepper.

David Moffett

David Moffett

David Moffett, St. Petersburg's first mayor, was born in Monroe County, Indiana, on April 20, 1842, the son of John and Letitia (Strong) Moffett, both natives of South Carolina. He was reared on his father's farm and became a tiller of the soil. During the winter months he attended the country schools.

In 1879, Mr. Moffett moved to Florida, first locating in Marion County. Not satisfied with the prospects of that section of the state, he came to Pinellas Peninsula late in 1881. At that time there were less than a score of families in this locality. He built his home at what is now Ninth street and Moffett avenue and engaged in orange culture and truck farming. He planted his first grove, containing thirty acres of trees, in the Ninth street ridge section, between Twenty-second and Twenty-sixth avenues. In 1890 he purchased the old Weir grove on the west side of Reservoir (Mirror) Lake. In the year following he sold his first grove to C. W. Springstead, who, many years later, converted it into the Springhill subdivision.

In 1892, Mr. Moffett was elected first mayor of St. Petersburg, running against General J. C. Williams. Mr. Moffett headed the Anti-Saloon ticket, while General Williams was the leader of what was generally understood as the Open Saloon faction. Mr. Moffett received twenty-one votes to the general's ten. In 1896 and 1897 he served on the town council. He also was supervisor of the schools for a number of years. Although Mr. Moffett had been raised a Presbyterian, he became a member of the Congregational Church in St. Petersburg and was chairman of the board of trustees until a year before his death. An ardent prohibitionist, he took an active part in all the prohibition movements in the county and city.

Mr. Moffett was twice married; in 1868 to Mattie L. Strong, of Tennessee, who died in May, 1889, and in September, 1890, to Janie Mitchell, of Alabama. He had four children: Fay, wife of W. J. McPherson; Reese, Pearl, and Wade. Mr. Moffett died on January 25, 1921.

H. W. Gilbart

Harold William Gilbart was born in 31 Carlton Hill, St. Johns Wood, London SW, on February 4, 1865, the son of Frederick Hughes and Mary Ann (Robinson) Gilbart. He was educated in a private school in Wandsworth, Surrey, and in St. Marks College, in Middlesex, from which he was graduated in the spring of 1882. After leaving college he was tutored by George Whiffen, trustee for his mother's estate, who wanted him to become a chartered accountant.

Mr. Gilbart had no liking for accounting or clerical work and after receiving his diploma in 1883, he decided to go to the United States. He knew exactly where he wanted to go, having made up his mind one night while looking at a map of the United States with his mother. His eye fell on Pinellas Peninsula, in Florida, and its location struck his fancy. On the map the peninsula looked very small and Mr. Gilbart was confident that he could build his future home anywhere upon it and see water on both sides.

Mr. Gilbart left England on November 5, 1883, but it was not until more than a year later before he arrived on the peninsula of his dreams. The delay was caused by the theft in Philadelphia of five of his trunks containing almost all of his money, approximately a thousand pounds. He had left the trunks at the depot and a short time later lost the checks. Some one found them, took them to the depot, and got the trunks. Several days elapsed before Mr. Gilbart discovered his loss and by then the trunks had disappeared. He took work in a Phila-

H. W. Gilbart

delphia hotel and worked his way up from bell boy to clerk. He never gave up the idea of going on to Pinellas Peninsula, however, and on November 5, 1884, a year after he left England, he took a boat from Philadelphia.

When Mr. Gilbart reached Florida his money was running low and he could not pay for his transportation beyond Fort Mason, on the St. Johns River. He was determined, however, to go on to Pinellas Peninsula, so he walked from Fort Mason to Tampa. Upon arriving there he had only forty-five cents in his pocket. He came across the bay in "Tiny" Williams' boat and made his way to the home of the Watt family, and from there to the home of W. J. Godden, on Tangerine avenue. To his surprise, Mr. Gilbart learned that he and Mr. Godden had been reared within three miles of each other in London and that Mr. Godden had had an office in the same building where he had learned to become a chartered accountant.

The two men became close friends and lived together for many years. In the beginning, neither had much money but they managed to make ends meet. Mr. Gilbart got his first job from Wm. B. Mirandi, agent for the Disston interests. He was paid fifty cents a day for ten hours' work. Later he purchased ten acres of land from the Disstons for $50— mostly on credit, and Mr. Godden purchased the same amount. On this land they raised stock and all the produce they needed.

Early in the '90s, the two men made an arrangement with Hamilton Disston whereby they were to be given forty acres of land for digging what is now the Green Ridge ditch to Salt Creek. They completed the job and selected forty acres adjoining the eighty acres they already owned. The land they received comprised practically all the land which had been drained and when Mr. Disston later came to view the drainage project, and saw that he had given away practically all he had gained, he considered it a great joke upon himself.

During the years which followed, Mr. Gilbart engaged in citrus fruit and pineapple culture. His home on Tangerine avenue became one of the show places of the peninsula. He put all the money he had into real estate—at one time he owned more than 500 acres. One of his early purchases was the eighty acres overlooking Lake Maggiore, for which he paid $25 an acre. He subdivided this into five-acre tracts and sold them; some of the five-acre tracts he again subdivided into one-acre tracts. The last two he sold netted him $4,500.

On May 15, 1895, Mr. Gilbart was married to Miss Emma L. Andrews, daughter of Milo and Emily Ann (Pengilly) Andrews, of Owen Sound, Ontario, Canada. The marriage ceremony was performed by Rev. G. W. Southwell in St. Bartholomew's Church on Lakeview avenue, the oldest church on Pinellas Point. Mr. and Mrs. Gilbart have five children, all boys: Oscar William, assistant secretary of the West Coast Title Company; Russell Hughes, one of the proprietors of the Franklin Service Agency; Kenneth, of the Fidelity Loan Company; Gordon Craig and Dudley Spencer, now in school.

Mr. Gilbart has been a silent partner in many commercial enterprises in St. Petersburg and is now president of the West Coast Title Company. He was one of the first members of the St. Petersburg lodge of the Woodmen of the World, and is a member of the St. Petersburg Yacht Club. He was one of the founders of St. Bartholomew's Church and is now a member of St. Peter's Church. Incidentally, Mr. Gilbart is perhaps the only living white man who has been initiated into the tribe of Seminole Indians, with whom he lived off and on for nearly eight years. He still visits them occasionally.

Arthur Norwood

Arthur Norwood was born in Margate, England, December 19, 1860, the son of Mr. and Mrs. Thomas Norwood. He was sent to school in London, and after leaving school received his business training in a men's furnishing store in the West End of that city. He came to Pinellas Peninsula in 1886 with his brother, Urban, and went to Disston City, where H. H. Richardson, an intimate friend, and a number of other Englishmen had settled.

Urban Norwood returned to England in October of the same year, but Arthur remained, building a shack to live in about a mile northeast of Disston City. The home was burned down shortly afterward, destroying all his possessions except the clothes he was wearing. About this time he was appointed teacher of the Disston City school, where he taught for three terms. During the first two years he received $25 a month, but during the last year his salary was raised to $30, a munificent sum in those days. In addition to his teaching, Mr. Norwood whitewashed the school building, dug a well, and built desks and blackboards "as contributions to the cause."

In the spring of 1889, after the end of the school term, Mr. Norwood bought out the stock of a small store in Disston City and moved it to St. Petersburg, about a year after the first train had entered the town. He established his first store at what is now about the corner of Central avenue and Ninth street. As the years passed, the lower part of St. Petersburg gradually outstripped the Ninth street section, and in 1897 Mr. Norwood moved his store to a building at Fourth and Central, keeping his grocery at Ninth street. The first telephone in St. Petersburg was put up between these two stores, the work being done by A. P. Weller, manager of the electric light company. Later Mr. Norwood sold the grocery store to John C. Blocker.

Mr. Norwood's last place of business was in the Jones block, on the north side of Central between Third and Fourth. He sold out about 1916 to T. J. Northrup, who later formed the Northrup-Rutland Company. Although it was his intention to retire from active business, he could not stand inactivity and later entered the tile business. He now is associated with the Pasadena Estates, Inc.

Mr. Norwood has been actively connected with the government of St. Petersburg since the town was incorporated in 1892. He was a member of the first town council, re-elected in 1894 for another term of two years, and recently completed another term of four years. He has been a member of the Board of Trade and the Chamber of Commerce from the time they were first formed. He was elected president of the Board of Trade in 1915. He is a member of the Knights of Pythias Lodge and the Christian Science Church.

Mr. Norwood was married to Miss Alice Creasy in Disston City in 1887, who had come from England a short time before. His wife died in May, 1912, and on August 30, 1913, Mr. Norwood was married again to Mrs. Emily H. (Lampe) Hedgeland, of Cleveland. Mr. Norwood has one daughter, Mrs. Hazel Pereira, who now lives in Oakland, California.

T. A. Whitted

T. A. Whitted was born on April 3, 1858, in Boone, Ia., the son of Elbridge and Caroline E. (Aldridge) Whitted. He was educated in the country schools and worked with his father on the farm until the family came to Florida in 1878. The father and sons drove through with a mule team, bringing the family possessions; the women folks came by train.

Arriving in Florida, the family located in Manatee. The father purchased land and started an orange grove. The son, T. A. Whitted, went to work in the saw mill of W. S. Warner. In 1884, he went to Disston City, now known as Gulfport, to take charge of the saw mill of George L. King, the pioneer mill man of Pinellas Point. During the next summer, while business in the mill was slack, Mr. Whitted helped the "mailman" in bringing the mail from Tampa to Big Bayou in a small sailboat.

Early in April, 1888, when the Orange Belt Railway was nearing the edge of St. Petersburg, Mr. King moved his saw mill to the new town, locating on Booker Creek at what is now Twelfth street. Mr. Whitted continued to operate the mill and

Arthur Norwood

T. A. Whitted

during the next few years planed and sawed all the lumber used in the first buildings of St. Petersburg.

In 1893, Mr. Whitted leased the mill from Mr. King and operated it for one year. Later, he became associated with A. C. Pheil in the St. Petersburg Novelty Works and has been associated with that company practically ever since.

Wr. Whitted served on the town council in 1894 and 1895. During this period the swale across Central avenue, near Third street, was filled in. With the other councilmen, Mr. Whitted signed a note in order that the town could get the money to have the work done. The first school house of St. Petersburg also was built in this period.

Mr. Whitted played the double bass viol in St. Petersburg's first orchestra, organized in 1891 by Professor Libby. Other members of this orchestra were Charlie Lee, Will Thornton, Milt Longstrath, Louis King, May King, John Goodnough and Tracy Lewis. When the orchestra disbanded in 1894, Mr. Whitted and A. C. Pheil organized the first St. Petersburg band. For some time the band practiced in the Whitted home at Eleventh street and Baum avenue, but the neighbors finally objected to the "noise." The band then moved to the end of the railroad pier and the music, wafting in over the waters, kept the whole town awake. After a while, however, the band began to play really good music and many concerts were given in Williams Park. A band stand, erected in about 1895, was paid for through the efforts of the women in selling refreshments at the entertainments.

Mr. Whitted was the treasurer of the Carpenters' Union for eighteen years. He is one of the charter members of the I. O. O. F., having joined when the local lodge was founded in 1892. He belongs to all branches of the order and represented the local lodge several times at the Grand Lodge. He has been a member of the Christian Church for many years and was a member of the building committee when the new church was built.

On April 19, 1887, Mr. Whitted was married on Long Key to Miss Julia Jennettie Phillips, daughter of Captain Zephaniah Phillips, pioneer settler of Long Key. Mr. and Mrs. Whitted had three sons: Clarence E. Whitted, now associated with Mrs. Whitted in the sale of real estate; George B. Whitted, now

Lieut. J. Albert Whitted

living in Hammond, Ind., and Albert Whitted.

Albert Whitted was born on February 14, 1893. He attended the public schools and high school of St. Petersburg. He taught the drum corps for several years while in school and for one year thereafter. Later, he established a motorcycle shop and sold the Indian motorcycles. On March 17, 1917, he enlisted from West Haven, Conn., in the aviation corps. He was one of the first 250 flyers of the United States Navy, his pilot's number being 179. He was commissioned a first lieutenant on September 25, 1918, and served as chief instructor of advanced flying at Pensacola. In February, 1919, he was in full charge of the naval manoevres at Guantanamo Bay, Cuba, being sent there from his station at Pensacola. He came here with his plane, the Bluebird, on December 9, 1919, to do commercial flying. During the next few years thousands of residents and tourists went up with him for flights. During the summer of 1921 he built the Falcon at Pensacola and brought it back to St. Petersburg in the following winter. On August 19, 1923, Lieut. Whitted was killed with four passengers when the propellor of the Falcon broke, while making a flight near Pensacola. His death was mourned by hundreds of his friends in St. Petersburg. Lieut. Whitted was survived by his widow, Mrs. Francis L. (Brent) Whitted, and two children, Catherine Eugene and Francis Louise, who are now living in Pensacola in the Brent home.

Ed. T. Lewis

Edson T. Lewis was born in New Milford, Pa., January 19, 1872, the son of Fred W. and Alice (Denison) Lewis. He attended the public schools of Owego, N. Y., until the family moved to St. Petersburg on March 7, 1888, before the Orange Belt Railway was completed to the edge of the town site. An acre of land was purchased near Ninth and Central from Jacob Baum for $50 and his father built a home, the first to be erected within the town limits.

Mr. Lewis first found employment in the saw mill of George L. King. Shortly afterwards he secured a position at Ward's General Store at Ninth street where he remained until October 3, 1888, when he left to become a clerk in the general store at Central avenue and Second street owned by J. C. Williams, Jr. At that time there was nothing in that section of the city except the depot, the Detroit Hotel, the Orange Belt Investment Company's office building, and a few ramshackle shacks. The section around Ninth street was considered the main part of town.

In 1892 Mr. Lewis left the Williams General Store to take active charge of a soft drinks store which he had formed in partnership with Edward Durant in 1891. He purchased the lot on the northeast corner of Central avenue and Third street in 1894, while the swale across the avenue was being filled in, and a short time later established the firm of Ed. T. Lewis, selling groceries and general merchandise. The business grew rapidly and many improvements were made to the store. It became one of the show places of the city and when F. A. Davis brought prospects to the city in an attempt to interest them in his various enterprises, he in-

Ed. T. Lewis

variably took them to the Lewis store to show them evidences of prosperity.

During the late '90s, Mr. Lewis acted as banker for many residents and tourists. Deposits made with him totaled at times as much as $160,000 and he had accounts with banks in Tampa, New York, and Des Moines, Ia. Later, in 1904, Mr. Lewis helped to establish the Central National Bank. His business connections have continued to increase during the past twenty years and at the present time, Mr. Lewis is interested in numerous companies both in St. Petersburg and Tampa.

Mr. Lewis was one of the leaders in the movement to establish brick as the standard paving material for St. Petersburg. He was a member of the city council during 1906 and 1907 at the time when the city was carrying out its first important good roads program. Many contended that the city should use marl, and when the council decided on brick, an injunction was sought in the courts by the marl advocates to restrain the council from proceeding. The brick advocates won, however, and the paving proceeded.

Mr. Lewis was identified for years with the movement for the municipal ownership and beautification of the waterfront. He was one of the eight waterfront boosters who were present at the meeting held the night of December 20, 1905, at the home of Col. J. M. Lewis when plans were decided upon to conduct an organized campaign. During the years which followed, Mr. Lewis' interest in the waterfront did not decrease and he helped materially in carrying the project through. Mr. Lewis also has been an advocate for public ownership of all public utilities and has aided in the establishment of the municipal gas plant, street railway system, and power plant. While a member of the city council he introduced the ordinance to widen Central avenue from Sixth street to Ninth and was appointed by the council to make settlements with the property owners.

Mr. Lewis has been a member of the Chamber of Commerce for many years and served for twelve years as chairman of the lighting committee. He is a member of the Mason fraternity and B. P. O. E., the St. Petersburg Country Club, the St. Petersburg Tarpon Club, St. Petersburg Yacht Club, and the Art Club. He is affiliated with the Congregational Church.

Mr. Lewis was married to Nellie Demarset in Englewood, N. J., on November 29, 1894. They have one son, Leon D. Lewis, who is now general manager and treasurer of the Citizens Ice Company.

Col. L. Y. Jenness

Lyndon Yates Jenness was born in Methuen, Mass., June 17, 1843. His parents were John and Salome (Wilson) Jenness, both natives of New England. He received his early education in his native state.

During the Civil War, Mr. Jenness served four years in the Federal army, which he entered as a musician. When he left service he was ranked as a lieutenant. The honorary title of "Colonel" was later bestowed on Mr. Jenness by his friends.

Mr. Jenness was severely wounded in the battle of Spottsylvania, and during the last three years of war took part in twenty-six different battles, serving with Company F, Thirty-second Massachusetts Regiment. At the conclusion of the war, Mr. Jenness completed a course in Comer's Commercial College, of Boston. Later, he entered the hotel business, and was engaged in this for several years in New York and Connecticut.

In 1879, Mr. Jenness came to Florida and took charge of the hotel at Key West, acting as proprietor. He was later in the hotel business at Cedar Key, Tarpon Springs and Brooksville. When the old Orange Belt Railroad was projected Mr. Jenness was made land commissioner for its promoters at St. Petersburg.

The property in St. Petersburg owned by the Orange Belt Investment Company was deeded to the St. Petersburg Land & Improvement Company shortly after the Orange Belt Railroad was acquired by a group of Philadelphia capitalists in 1889. Mr. Jenness was retained by the capitalists to serve as the manager of this land company. During the next fifteen years he took an important part in the development of St. Petersburg, and put through more real estate deals than any other man on the peninsula.

For several years Mr. Jenness was president of the St. Petersburg State Bank, and was one of the organizers and the first president of the first Chamber of Commerce in St. Petersburg, in 1898.

Mr. Jenness was actively engaged in the development of St. Petersburg up until December, 1906, when he retired, after disposing of his remaining holdings in the St. Petersburg Land and Improvement Company.

He was a Knight Templar, Knights of Pythias and past commander of the Kit Carson Post of the G. A. R.

Mr. Jenness was married April 13, 1869, to Annie M. Ozias, of Philadelphia, Pa. He died on May 9, 1914.

David Murray

David Murray was born in Dover, N. H., the son of George O. and Martha Ann (Stackpole) Murray. He was educated in the schools of Dover and the Institute of Technology in Boston. Shortly after leaving school he entered the employ of the Harrisburg Ice Machine Company, of Harrisburg, Pa., and in about 1888 was sent to Colombia, South America, where he supervised the work of building ice plants at Cartagena and Barranquilla.

Returning to the United States in 1889, Mr. Murray was married to Miss Sarah E. Robinson, in Birmingham, Ala., on July 6, 1890. Mrs. Murray's sister, Miss Mittie Robinson, is at present living at 324 Beach drive.

Mr. and Mrs. Murray came to St. Petersburg for the first time in 1890, Mr. Murray being sent here to put in the plant for the Crystal Ice Company, the first ice company of St. Petersburg. He continued with the company as manager for several years and then put in a plant for Barney and J. C. Williams. In 1902 he left to go into business for himself in California.

On April 28, 1893, Mr. Murray was elected mayor of St. Petersburg to fill out the term of Mayor Judge Wm. H. Benton, who died suddenly while on his way to Tampa. Soon after taking office he issued a proclamation setting aside a day as "Park Day." On the day set the City Park, now known as Williams Park, was surveyed and formally and legally accepted by the town officials. The work of beautifying the property also was started. The women served coffee and cake and supervised the work. Later walks were laid and a bandstand was built.

While mayor, Mr. Murray laid the cornerstone of the first public school building in St. Petersburg. Some time later he was one of the leaders in a movement to acquire the water-front property and dig a channel in from deep water to near the foot of Central avenue. The channel was dug, by volunteer labor, but nothing resulted at that time from the movement to buy the water front.

After going to California, Mr. Murray located in Hanford, where he has since been located. At present he owns three ice plants in that city and a large olive ranch.

Mr. Murray is a past member and still a member of the St. Petersburg Masonic lodge. He also is a charter member of the local lodge of the Knights of Pythias.

While in Florida Mr. Murray devoted much time to the natural history of the state and was recognized as one of the state's leading conchologists. He also made a list of all the medicinal plants which grow in Florida. For a time he was one of the field workers of the Smithsonian Institute.

Mr. and Mrs. Murray have two children living: George H. Murray, sales

David Murray

manager of the Sun-Maid Raisin Association, in Philadelphia, and Miss Emily Murray, a graduate of Stanford University and Columbia University.

Roy S. Hanna

Roy S. Hanna was born in Rochester, Ind., June 10, 1861, the son of Joseph and Philora (True) Hanna. The father was the proprietor of the famous Hanna Woolen Mills of that city. Shortly after the end of the Civil War, he went to Kankakee City, Ill., where he established other woolen mills and in 1874 he went to Marysville, Tenn., where he established the first woolen mill in the South.

Roy S. Hanna was educated in the public schools of Kankakee, Ind., and Marysville College, in Marysville, Tenn., from which he was graduated in 1882. After leaving college, Mr. Hanna taught school for two years in Williamsport, Ind., and then went into the law office of General Robert N. Hood in Knoxville, Tenn. In 1886, Mr. Hanna found it necessary to go to Florida on account of poor health and he located at Punta Gorda where he published a newspaper known as the Punta Gorda and Charlotte Harbor Beacon.

At that time the Florida Southern Railroad was extending its rails southward toward Punta Gorda, and the small town was experiencing a big land boom, the boosters prophesying that Punta Gorda soon would become one of the most important cities in Florida. The erection of a large hotel by the railroad and northern capitalists was expected to stimulate the growth, but few newcomers arrived. At the outbreak of the yellow fever epidemic in 1887, Mr. Hanna went back to Tennessee, remained there a few months and then returned to Punta Gorda to continue publishing the newspaper. While in Punta Gorda Mr. Hanna continued his study of law and in 1888 he was admitted to the Florida bar after taking examinations at Bartow, given by Circuit Judge Williams, later governor of the state.

In the fall of 1891, Mr. Hanna left Punta Gorda and came to St. Petersburg. A short time later he was appointed deputy collector and inspector of the Port of St. Petersburg, to serve under the United States Revenue Department. At that time many small boats from Cuba stopped at St. Petersburg and the duties of the deputy collector were exacting. Mr. Hanna held the office until 1900 when he resigned to become postmaster, succeeding W. A. Sloan. A. P. Avery was appointed to the office relinquished by Mr. Hanna.

A short time after Mr. Hanna became postmaster the St. Petersburg post office was made third class and business increased to such an extent that Mr. Hanna hired a clerk at $25 a month. The postmaster's salary was increased to $1,000 a year. The office grew with the city and in 1905 Mr. Hanna called a meeting of several citizens of St. Petersburg to discuss the need for larger quarters. As a result of this meeting a building was erected by E. H. Tomlinson at Fourth and Central and rented to the government at fifty dollars a month. The open post-office of St. Petersburg today is the result of a suggestion of Mr. Hanna that was put into effect in Mr. Tomlinson's building, that customers might get their mail day or night.

Roy S. Hanna

Free postal delivery for St. Petersburg was secured by Mr. Hanna as a result of a trip to Washington in October, 1906. It soon became necessary to remove to still larger quarters and after the postoffice had occupied the entire first floor of the City hall building for some time, Mr. Hanna and the board of trade urged the postoffice department to secure a government building. The movement was launched in 1907, and in the summer of 1910 an appropriation of $55,000 was made for the purpose.

Mr. Hanna and others made every effort to secure a larger amount of money and finally $102,500 was provided by Congress for the building and $5,000 additional for the site, and work on the new postoffice was started in March, 1916, when Mr. Hanna turned the first shovelsfull of dirt for the building.

Mr. Hanna was succeeded as postmaster by W. L. Straub in 1916, but was again appointed to the position in the spring of 1923.

At about the time he was first made postmaster in St. Petersburg, Mr. Hanna bought the south half mile of Long Key, where Pass-a-Grille is now located, from Dr. Gehring who had acquired it from Captain Z. Phillips, the father of Mrs. T. A. Whitted. The price was $1,000 and Mr. Hanna had great difficulty in raising the sum for the purchase. He secured the last $400 needed from a Mr. Morey of Tampa, on the stipulation that it be called Morey's beach. A short time later an attempt was made to auction off the lots on the island, Morey's Tampa agent taking charge of the arrangements. Nearly a thousand Spaniards and Cubans of Tampa took advantage of the offer to make the trip without charge. So many wanted to go that delays occurred in getting boats and the excursionists arrived at the island late in the afternoon. And when they finally landed, everyone made a break for the water to go in swimming. The auction sale was a complete failure. Later the owners divided the lots among themselves to dispose of as they saw fit.

Mr. Hanna has taken an active interest in all civic affairs ever since coming to St. Petersburg. For sixteen years he fought with a few other water-front boosters to secure the water front for St. Petersburg. He helped in the establishment of the schools and was one of the organizers and supporters of the Board of Trade. With others, he purchased property so that the Tampa & Gulf Coast Railroad could come into the city. He was a director of the Bayboro Company, the St. Petersburg & Gulf Electric Railway, and the St. Petersburg Transportation Company which operated steamers between St. Petersburg and Tampa. Mr. Hanna also was one of the organizers of the Central National Bank and has served as vice-president of the institution since the beginning.

Mr. Hanna was oppointed chairman of the Park Board immediately after the board had been established and served for six years. While he held that office Mirror Lake was beautified, the low lands along the edges being filled in and the center dredged out. Through his efforts, Round Lake was saved for the city although many persons wanted to fill it in. Mr. Hanna, with the assistance of Mrs. Katherine B. Tippetts, during this period prepared labels for hundreds of trees in the city, giving their scientific names.

In 1902, Mr. Hanna learned that the government wanted Bird Key, of which he was the owner, as a bird reservation. After correspondence with President Theodore Roosevelt, he turned over all his rights in the island.

Mr. Hanna was married on September 4, 1905, to Miss Jennie Ridgeley, of Chicago, the ceremony being performed in St. Petersburg.

Mr. Hanna is a member of the St. Petersburg Rotary Club and the Elks Lodge.

Capt. Zephaniah Phillips

Capt. Zephaniah Phillips, pioneer settler of Long Key, was born in Toronto, Canada, on March 2, 1837. When he was two years old the family came to the United States and located in Illinois. He received his education in the schools of Illinois and when fourteen years old began to learn the blacksmith's trade. He engaged in that work for several years and then went into business for himself.

At the beginning of the Civil War, he joined the First Cavalry of Illinois at Equality, Ill., and left there for camp on May 1, 1861. He was in the first battle at Lexington, Md., and there fought for three days without food, then being taken prisoner. Later he was released and he then enlisted in Company F, 120th Illinois Infantry, being commissioned as a lieutenant.

After the war Capt. Phillips started a grocery store at Harrisburg, Ill., where he married Mary E. Pierce of that city. He was the inventor of many patents, one of the most important being the Phillips Burglar Proof time safe, without combination or key hole in the door. This was the first safe of the kind ever invented.

Capt. Phillips came to Florida with his family for his health in 1882, first locating in Waldo. In March, 1884, he came to Pinellas through the influence of Col. B. F. Livingston and also to install the machinery of George L. King's saw mill. In September, 1884, he took his homestead on Long Key. Later he platted and named Pass-a-Grille, naming it after the pass that divides Long Key and Pine Key.

Capt. Phillips came to St. Petersburg with his family to live in 1891. He lived here until he died on January 21, 1903. He was survived by his widow and four children: Mrs. T. A. Whitted, Mrs. Anna Betts, Clarence E. Phillips, of Tampa, and Zephaniah Phillips, Jr.

Capt. Zephaniah Phillips

C. W. Springstead

C. W. Springstead was born at Fond du Lac, Wisconsin, July 11, 1858, the son of Warren W. and Mary (Cary) Springstead, natives of New York state, from whence they moved to Wisconsin in 1858. Mr. Springstead's father was a lumberman, farmer and merchant, and his activities took him into the frontier regions of Wisconsin, and amid such surroundings the son was reared.

He was the second child in a family of six, and was educated in the public schools of Wisconsin, where he remained until the age of twenty-two, when he came to Brooksville, Fla. His father died in Florida at the age of sixty-six; his mother died at the age of thirty-four.

Mr. Springstead remained in Brooksville for ten years, and was engaged there in the orange business, planting the trees and developing them to a crop-bearing age. In 1890, believing that the location and climatic advantages of the Pinellas Peninsula would prove an ideal field for extensive citrus growing, he moved to St. Petersburg.

Here he bought seventy-two acres of land on the ridge at Ninth streeet, about a mile from Central avenue, and his groves came to a bearing age at about the same time as the development of St. Petersburg reached his section. Joining with other property owners of the locality, Mr. Springstead led the movement to extend street car lines, electric light lines and gas mains. He subdivided his tract, improved it with hard-surfaced streets and put it on the market. This Spring Hill subdivision is now practically sold out and has become one of the most attractive residential districts of the city.

Mr. Springstead was one of the founders of the First National Bank and has been vice president of the institution of St. Petersburg since its inception. He also helped to organize the St. Petersburg Yacht Club and is one of its charter members. He is a member of the Masonic

C. W. Springstead

fraternity and has been connected with the Board of Trade and Chamber of Commerce for many years.

Mr. Springstead was married in 1888 to Mrs. Kate Williams, who was also a native of Wisconsin.

E. H. Tomlinson

Edwin H. Tomlinson was born in 1844 in Ne-squan-tuck-et, Conn., the son of Peter Tomlinson and Augusta Tomlinson, (nee Hyde). He was educated in the public schools of Connecticut, and at the age of eighteen was employed as a bank clerk at the salary of four dollars a month.

When the Civil War broke out, Mr. Tomlinson was preparing for college, but his studies were interrupted, and he went into the oil fields of Pennsylvania, where he remained for five years.

At the end of this period he went to Aiken, S. C., where he and two other men built the first tourist hotel in the south, at a time when Florida had not been heard of as a winter home for tourists.

From South Carolina, Mr. Tomlinson went to Santo Domingo, where he was part owner and operator of a large sugar plantation. While there he acted as United States consular agent for a period of three years at the port of San Pedro de Macoris.

From 1874 to 1897, Mr. Tomlinson was interested in mining in the Rocky Mountain regions of the United States, and filled several official positions with various mining concerns both here, in Alaska and in British Columbia. Some of the positions he occupied in the years that followed were president of the Last Chance Mining Company, of British Columbia, in 1894; vice-president of the Empire Gold Mining Company, of Arizona, and director of the Parrot Silver and Copper Company, of Butte, Montana, in 1895.

In 1897, Mr. Tomlinson retired from active business, after having visited practically every country of the world while on his various business trips.

On March 6, 1891, Mr. Tomlinson first visited St. Petersburg, of which he had heard while visiting his friend Mayor Sperry in Orlando Fla. Attracted by the fishing and cruising to be had in its waters he came to the city, which he has visited regularly every winter since.

Ever since his arrival Mr. Tomlinson has contributed most generously to the public welfare of St. Petersburg. He built the first manual training building in the city and turned it over, fully equipped, to training St. Petersburg boys and girls in manual training, domestic science, military tactics, and gymnastics, as well as kindergarten facilities for the younger children. The building is used today as the city hall, having been altered for the purpose.

In all his connections with the schools of the city Mr. Tomlinson showed the same generosity, the same helpful interest. He provided an organ for the manual training building, fully equipped a students' orchestra, and provided for the Washington's birthday celebrations of the city for many years.

Mr. Tomlinson also built the original electric pier, and the Fountain of Youth pier, and drove the artesian well now known as the Fountain of Youth. All his waterfront improvements are now the property of the city.

Mr. Tomlinson lived at first at the house still standing at Fourth street and

Second avenue, and many still remember the Marconi tower, 200 feet high, which he constructed there for experimental purposes for Marconi who was his friend. The plans of the inventor were altered, however, and the tower was later taken down by the subsequent purchaser of this property, Joseph C. Sibley.

Mr. Tomlinson also made a gift of St. Peter's Episcopal church and the rectory, all completely furnished, and the church equipped with an organ, to the parish.

Mr. Tomlinson also donated generously to the hospitals of St. Petersburg, to the Y. W. C. A., and contributed large sums to the local post of the American Legion and the Boy Scouts. In short, no worth while public institution in St. Petersburg has been without his financial aid, and in spite of it all he declares he has been a thousandfold repaid for his efforts by "the fun he got out of it."

Mr. Tomlinson has never been married. He is at present spending his winters in St. Petersburg and his summers in North Carolina, where he has constructed a dormitory for the girls of the Y. W. C. A. of Spartanburg, S. C., built on the model of the battleship Maine. Here he entertains hundreds of association girls and their secretaries every summer. He is engaged in oil business to "keep himself active and interested," in El Dorado Pool in Arkansas and Texas.

R. H. Thomas

Robert Henry Thomas was born February 22, 1861, in Woodford County, Ill., the son of D. E. Thomas and Minerva Jane (Barnes) Thomas.

He was educated in the Lacon schools in Manhall County, Ill., and as a young man engaged in the drug business there. Later he became the owner of a hotel, which he managed until December, 1900, when he came to live in St. Petersburg, as the result of a fishing trip to Florida which he made at the time.

In 1893, Mr. Thomas visited St. Petersburg with a party of friends from the north who were on a pleasure trip south, and was so impressed with the business possibilities in the town that he decided to make his home here later.

In 1900, in casting about for a business location he returned to St. Petersburg, and engaged in the real estate and insurance business. He bought a grove and pinery on Tangerine avenue and in 1901 built a home on Third avenue north. He still lives in the house on the premises.

In 1902, Mr. Thomas was elected mayor of St. Petersburg and was offered the nomination for a second time in 1903, but declined. However, he was re-elected in 1904, and served two years more.

Mr. Thomas was one of the organizers of the Central National Bank, and was one of the committee of three to procure first government aid for the Bayboro harbor project. He was active in all improvement movements of the time.

Mr. Thomas has continued to engage in real estate and the insurance business, and also is actively interested in the buying and selling of stocks and bonds. He is a director of the First National Bank, and is connected with several business corporations in St. Petersburg. He also served as secretary of the Chamber of Commerce in its early days.

During the World War, Mr. Thomas served as chairman of the St. Petersburg

E. H. Tomlinson

R. H. Thomas

Chapter, American Red Cross. When the war ended this organization had 4,500 members.

Mr. Thomas is a member of the Elks lodge, and the St. Petersburg Country and Yacht clubs.

On February 28, 1893, Mr. Thomas was married to Ada Taggart, in Lacon, Marshall County. Mr. and Mrs. Thomas have one daughter, Ida Lorena Thomas. Mrs. Thomas is an active worker in the W. T. I. A. and served in Red Cross work during the war.

Mrs. Annie McRae

Mrs. Annie McRae was born in Forsyth, Ga., the daughter of Thomas D. Pennington and Amanda (Alexander) Pennington. She came as a child to Florida with her parents, and was educated in the public schools of Orange County and under private tutors.

Her father in the early '90s came to St. Petersburg where he established the St. Petersburg Novelty Works, which he later sold to A. C. Pheil. In 1894, he came here to make his permanent home. He died in St. Petersburg on December 27, 1912, leaving two children besides Mrs. McRae—William J. Pennington and Miss Theodosia M. Pennington.

Mrs. McRae was married to J. H. D. McRae, a Methodist minister of the Florida conference, and they had one son, Thomas A. McRae, a graduate of St. Petersburg High School, a soldier of the World War and a government civil service employe in St. Petersburg.

At the death of her husband, Mrs. McRae was employed as a bookkeeper for the St. Petersburg Hardware Company, a position she occupied for eight years. Later she opened an office as public stenographer, notary public and commissioner of deeds.

During the many years she has lived in St. Petersburg Mrs. McRae has given freely of her time and interest to organizations promoting public welfare. She acted as secretary for the St. Petersburg Board of Trade, and wrote most of the advertising matter distributed by that organization to advertise the city.

For many years Mrs. McRae was secretary of the St. Petersburg Reading Room Association, and when this was later merged into the city's first library, she became a member of the first library board, under whose direction the present Carnegie Library was built. In 1913, she was appointed secretary of the Library and Advertising Board, serving two terms. She was also the first woman secretary of the local Democratic Club.

Mrs. McRae has also served as secretary of the League of Women Voters in St. Petersburg, the Memorial-Historical Society, and other social and civic organizations, and in 1921 she was appointed secretary of the City Planning Board.

James A. Armistead

James A. Armistead, four times mayor of St. Petersburg, was born in Lynchburg, Va., September 16, 1841, the son of Anderson H. Armistead, a tobacco manufacturer of Virginia, and Mrs. Elizabeth S. (Langhorne) Armistead, daughter of Colonel Maurice S. Langhorne, of Lynchburg. His mother died when he was two years old.

Mr. Armistead was educated in his native city, and in 1857 entered the Virginia Military Institute at Lexington, where he remained for nearly two years, leaving to join his father, who had gone to Baltimore in 1858. In Baltimore Mr. Armistead studied chemistry under Dr.

Pigot, a well-known analytical chemist, until 1861. In this year he entered the Confederate service, "running the blockade" at Baltimore and making his way to Richmond. There he joined the Thirty-ninth Virginia battalion of cavalry, which served as General Lee's bodyguard throughout the war. Mr. Armistead was sergeant-major of this command, and served with it until the surrender, being paroled at Lynchburg, May 26, 1865. During the last three years of the war he was with General Lee in all his campaigns in Virginia and Pennsylvania.

When the war ended Mr. Armistead engaged in merchandising at Gilmores Mills, Va., and in 1867 went to Lynchburg, where he conducted a grocery and commission business, which was destroyed by fire in 1871. He then purchased a stock farm near Abingdon, Va., on which he remained for seventeen years.

In 1885, because of his wife's poor health, Mr. Armistead moved to Florida, and located first in Brooksville, where he engaged in the hotel business. From Brooksville Mr. Armistead went to Bartow, where he was proprietor of a hotel until 1895, when he came to St. Petersburg and interested himself in real estate.

Mr. Armistead took an active interest in city affairs, and served four terms as mayor of the city, having been elected for the first term in 1896, and being re-elected in 1897, 1898 and 1900.

During his days at the institute, Mr. Armistead met Ollie L. Arnold, whom he married December 16, 1863, at Natural Bridge, Va. She died in 1893, leaving five sons and three daughters. September 10, 1894, he married Mrs. Sarah Williams, widow of General John C. Williams of St. Petersburg.

Mr. Armistead was a member of the Masonic Order, and during the Spanish-American War he served as captain of the local military company raised for home protection. Mr. Armistead died in Bartow, Fla., Aug. 10, 1907, while visiting his daughter, Mrs. Y. S. Dial. Interment was made in the family burial ground in Bartow.

Albert T. Blocker

Albert T. Blocker was born in Cumberland County, North Carolina, on September 27, 1872, the son of Charles H. Blocker and Sallie (Cromwell) Blocker. The family moved to Florida a short time later and Albert T. Blocker was educated in the grade schools of Dade City and attended the Florida State College, then located in Lake City.

After the freeze of 1895, Mr. Blocker came to St. Petersburg, looking for a business location. For the first two years he conducted a dairy business and later started a livery and transfer business. In 1904, while seeking a site for a new building, he was offered the two lots where the Poinsettia Hotel now stands for $1600. The owner tried to convince him that the lots would prove a good investment at that price but Mr. Blocker was skeptical. Moreover, he decided that if he had his place of business so far away from the depot and main business section, all his trade would go to his competitors. So he bought the property on Second street south opposite the A. C. L. depot, paying $3,500.

In 1913, Mr. Blocker sold his livery and transfer business to W. L. Spitler of

James A. Armistead

Albert T. Blocker

Tampa who still conducts it under the name of the Blocker Transfer Company. From 1913 to 1917, Mr. Blocker engaged in the real estate business. In 1914 he was elected county treasurer and in 1916 he was elected county assessor, which position he holds at the present time. He served as deputy sheriff from 1900 to 1912.

Mr. Blocker has taken an active part in the city government for many years. He was elected councilman in 1904 and served two years. In 1910 he was elected mayor and it was during his administration that a $100,000 bond issue was approved by the voters. This was the largest bond issue passed in the city up to that time and included $35,000 for the waterfront, $5,000 for street crossings, $5,000 for the waterworks, $15,000 for the improvement of Reservoir Park and Lake Park and $35,000 for street improvements. Mr. Blocker's experiences with the "Apple Man," who blockaded the main streets with his sales, will long be remembered by old residents.

In August, 1901, Mr. Blocker was married to Miss Hattie Mae Dean of St. Petersburg. Miss Dean was a native of Memphis, Tenn., and was living in Florida at the time of her marriage.

Mr. Blocker is a Knight of Pythias and also a charter member of the Elks Lodge, No. 1224, in which he has served as Exalted Ruler and District Deputy Grand Exalted Ruler. He also is a member of the St. Petersburg Yacht Club.

Abram C. Pheil

Abram C. Pheil was born in Williamsson, Pa., was reared and educated there and at the age of seventeen, in 1884, came to Florida and located in Citrus County. In 1894 he heard of the opportunities of the West Coast and came to St. Petersburg. He arrived here with very little money but with a determination to succeed. He secured a job in the sawmill of George L. King and worked for wages of about a dollar a day.

Mr. Pheil was married in St. Petersburg on December 6, 1896, to Miss Lottie Close, of Baltimore, Md.

Small as his wages were at the beginning, Mr. Pheil managed to save a little and buy a few lots, mostly on credit. He built houses on the lots and managed to sell at a profit. Before many years had passed, Mr. Pheil became sole owner of the sawmill and shortly after, he plunged, buying the St. Petersburg Novelty Works on credit. He never missed a payment. Thirteen years later he sold for $40,000.

Before Central avenue was paved with pebble phosphate in 1897, Mr. Pheil took it upon himself to start improvements. He hauled sawdust from his mill and distributed it over the deep sand, filling the ruts. The famous "sawdust trail" was the result. It extended from Seventh street to the water front. Mr. Pheil helped to organize the first brass band in St. Petersburg and he played a tuba in it for a number of years.

Mr. Pheil took an active interest in city government and was an ardent advocate of municipal ownership of all public utilities. He was elected a member of the city council in 1904 and was re-elected for another two-year term in 1906. During his second term, Mr. Pheil led the fight to widen and straighten Central avenue between Sixth and Ninth streets. He was elected mayor in 1912 and served until August, 1913, when the commissioners took office under the new charter.

Mr. Pheil set a new record for real estate transactions when he paid $2,250 for a lot on Central avenue between Fourth and Fifth streets with a frontage of sixty-seven feet. Many said that he was throwing his money away by paying such an "outlandish" price. With characteristic vision, Mr. Pheil began the construction of an eleven-story building next to the Central National Bank on Central. Work on the building was delayed a number of times, first by the war and then by difficulties in getting building materials. Mr. Pheil carried on the work on his own resources, paying for each lot of materials as he received it. Shortly before his death Mr. Pheil expressed the wish that he could live long enough to see the building completed, but the wish was not granted. He died on November 1, 1922, after a lingering illness. All the city mourned his death, particularly those he had helped by his many kind deeds. The city offices and many business houses closed in his honor during the funeral. The Knights of Pythias Lodge, of which he was a member, had charge of the funeral service. Rev. W. W. Williams read the service. Burial was made at the Bartholomew Cemetery.

Mr. Pheil was survived by his widow; three sons, Abram, Jr., Harvey and Clarence; one daughter, Bertha, and three brothers, William H. Pheil, of St. Petersburg; J. C. Pheil, of Inverness, Fla., and David Elmer Pheil, of Cordale, Ga.

The Pheil building, which stands as a monument to Mr. Pheil, was completed during the winter of 1923-24 and leased for hotel purposes.

W. E. Allison

William Elmore Allison was born January 12, 1868, in Troutmans, North Carolina, the son of William Lafayette and Asenath (Cavin) Allison.

His early education was received in the public schools of Troutmans, where he lived with his parents on a farm until he was twenty-one years of age, when he went to Leesburg, Fla., to learn cabinet-making and building construction. While in Leesburg he purchased an orange grove, which was destroyed in the freeze of 1895.

In 1895, Mr. Allison came to St. Petersburg, where he started in the building and contracting business. One of his last buildings was the American Bank and Trust Company in Central avenue. Mr. Allison was also engaged in St. Petersburg in a livery business, the real estate business and the hotel business, having built the Allison Hotel, of which he is at present the proprietor.

Mr. Allison is a member of the Masonic lodge, the Knights of Pythias, and served as a member of the city council for two terms.

In 1897 he married Miss May Belle Oliver of St. Petersburg. They have two sons, Elmore William Allison, twenty-four years old, and Charles Edward Allison, eighteen years old. The former is owner and manager of the Allison Auto Electrical Service Company, which he established in 1921, and the latter is a student.

A. C. Pheil

W. E. Allison

Mrs. Allison is active in club work, being treasurer of the Daughters of the American Revolution, state historian of the Daughters of American Colonists, is a past chief of the Pythian Sisters, is a member of the Eastern Star, the Woman's Club, the Carenno Club, the Woman's Town Improvement Association, and a member of the Daughters of the Confederacy.

James G. Bradshaw

James G. Bradshaw was born in Giles County, Tenn., September 12, 1853, the son of the Rev. James M. Bradshaw and Anna (Brown) Bradshaw.

When a small boy, Mr. Bradshaw moved to Chattanooga with his parents, and his youth was spent there and at Cleveland, Tenn. In 1870, the family located in Covington, Ga., where the father became president of the college of that city. Mr. Bradshaw was educated in the schools of Tennessee and Georgia, finishing at Emory College, Oxford.

In January, 1873, he came to Florida and experimented with raising long staple cotton in Orange County. His experiments proved unsuccessful, and he engaged in the orange grove business on a homestead about ten miles from Orlando.

Mr. Bradshaw remained there until 1884, when he abandoned the grove and started in the drug business at Apopka, where he continued until 1890, when he removed to Oakland, then the quarters of the Orange Belt Railroad. He conducted a drug store in this town, filling prescriptions for the railway hospital at that place, and when the road was absorbed by the Plant System Mr. Bradshaw moved to St. Petersburg and continued in the drug business in that city.

For two years Mr. Bradshaw was a member of the city council, and president of the council during the last year of his service in it. For four years he was a supervisor and trustee of the St. Petersburg public schools. On July 1, 1913, he was elected commissioner of public affairs, and during his term of office served the city as mayor. Mr. Bradshaw was commissioner and mayor until July 1, 1916, when the new city charter, providing a different form of government, went into effect.

Mr. Bradshaw was a member of the Knights of Pythias.

J. G. Bradshaw

On December 17, 1876, he was married to Miss Cora Prince, in Apopka. They have two daughters: Annie C. Bradshaw, now Mrs. E. J. Mansfield, Greenville, S. C., and May Bradshaw, now teaching in Central Primary School. Annie Bradshaw was the first graduate of the St. Petersburg High School.

Mr. Bradshaw died on December 23, 1917.

Captain J. F. Chase

Captain John F. Chase was born at Chelsea, Maine, in 1842, and received his early education in the public schools of his native town. At the outbreak of the Civil War he enlisted in the Third Maine Regiment, and later became cannoneer of the Fifth Maine Battery. During the entire period of his war service Captain Chase distinguished himself by acts of bravery, and for his heroic deeds in the battle of Chancellorsville, May 3, 1863, he was presented a medal by act of congress.

Captain Chase received forty-eight wounds at the battle of Gettysburg, July 2, 1863, by the bursting of a shell, which destroyed his right arm and blew out one of his eyes. For two days he lay on the battlefield, and when he was finally removed to the hospital, erysipelas had affected all his wounds. He was accordingly placed in a tent outside the hospital, hope for his recovery having been abandoned. Captain Chase, aided by his remarkable constitution, recovered, and upon regaining consciousness asked, "Did we win the battle?" A song was written around these words, and another song, "Chancellorsville and Its Artillery Hero," was also written in honor of Captain Chase.

After the war, when he had recovered sufficiently from his wounds to travel, Captain Chase went to Augusta, Me., where he invented several articles, including an air-cooling disc still for the purification of water, a revolving harrow, a machine for labeling cans, and an automatic mop wringer.

Captain Chase came to St. Petersburg in 1895.

In 1905 he established Veteran City, in co-operation with the Florida West Coast Company, one of the F. A. Davis organizations, and every effort was made to attract veterans from all over the United States. Veteran City gradually fell into a decline, however, and finally was given up altogether.

Captain Chase was actively identified with the movement which established a post of the G. A. R. in St. Petersburg. He was also a member of the Odd Fellows and Knights of Pythias. He was also one of the originators of the state societies, the first of which was the New England Society. He died on November 27, 1914.

Captain Chase had married Maria Merrill, who was born at Freeport, Me., and died in St. Petersburg in August, 1921. They were the parents of nine children. Of these the following are living: Lena M. and Beulah C. Chase, Mrs. Maud Aiken, J. Frank Chase, of Oklahoma, and Ralph M. Chase, also of Oklahoma.

In 1905 Miss Beulah Chase opened a small remnant store in a wooden building on Central avenue. In 1907, after the business had proved a success, Miss Lena Chase entered the firm with her sister, and the company became B. & L.

Chase. The enterprise continued to prosper, and in 1909 the company was incorporated as the Willson-Chase Company, with Miss Beulah Chase as president. In 1914 a five-story building, complete in every department, was erected by the company, and is still occupied today. Extensive improvements were made during the summer of 1922, at which time the company occupied the Haines building, nearly doubling its floor space. At present it is one of the leading department stores of the south.

Mrs. Maud Aiken was for many years connected with the St. Petersburg schools, and is at present the owner and principal of the Aiken Open-Air School.

Edgar Harrison

Edgar Harrison, twice mayor of St. Petersburg, was born in Morgantown, W. Va., on April 7, 1829. When he was eleven years old the family moved to Iowa City, Ia., then just a small hamlet. The family lived there for many years, and Edgar Harrison, when he became older, served as sheriff of the county and held other official positions.

In 1857, Mr. Harrison was married to Miss Eliza M. Patton, of Uniontown, Pa., whose people also were among the pioneers of Union City.

In 1870, the family moved to Paola, Kansas, and five years later came to Florida, settling in Paola, which was named by them in honor of their former home. Mr. Harrison invested a large part of his money in orange groves and, with his sons, started a general merchandise store under the name of Harrison & Sons. He also conducted the postoffice.

The freeze of 1894-95 dealt a serious blow to the family, completely destroying the groves and ruining the business of the store. Mr. Harrison's complete capital was wiped out. The family then moved to St. Petersburg, where the sons, J. F. Harrison and Edgar P. Harrison, went into business.

Mr. Harrison took an active part in St. Petersburg politics for a number of years. He was elected mayor in 1899 and again in 1901. He was a factor in the elections for many years later. On May 19, 1899, Mr. Harrison signed the famous ordinance which banished the wandering cows from St. Petersburg. The cattle barons predicted that this ordinance would have dire results—but St. Petersburg kept on growing.

Mrs. Harrison died in 1907. Mr. Harrison, now almost ninety-five years old, is living with his son, E. P. Harrison, at 202 Second street north.

Edgar Harrison

J. F. Harrison

J. Frank Harrison was born in Iowa City, Ia., on July 31, 1859, the son of Edgar and Eliza M. (Patton) Harrison.

When the family came to St. Petersburg in 1895, Mr. Harrison and his brother, E. P. Harrison, bought the stock of the W. A. Sloan general merchandise store and started in business in a small building on the southeast corner of Central Avenue and Third street. The building was only twenty-five feet wide and sixty feet deep, but it was plenty large enough to hold the stock which the Harrisons then had to sell.

Handicapped by having only a very small amount of capital, the Harrisons

J. F. Harrison

had a difficult struggle in keeping the store alive during those early years. However, each year the business showed an increase, and finally the old building was outgrown. A new building was erected on the same site, and in 1906 the old building was moved to the other side of the railroad and used as a warehouse. Many additions have been made to the store during the past decade in order to handle the increasing volume of business, which now exceeds a million dollars annually. Several changes have been made in the name of the concern, which now is known as the Harrison-Powell Company.

Mr. Harrison has always taken an active part in the affairs of the city and for many years was connected with the Board of Trade. He served as secretary in 1909 and 1910 and was a member of the board of governors for a number of years. Always he has devoted much of his time to advancing the interests of the city.

Mr. Harrison has been a director of the First National Bank since 1912. He is a member of the Knights of Pythias, the F. U. A. and the Woodmen of the World. He is also a member of the Presbyterian Church.

In 1878, Mr. Harrison was married to Miss Mattie H. Johnson, of Jacksonville, Fla. They have an adopted daughter, Margaret.

E. P. Harrison

E. P. Harrison was born in Iowa City, Ia., on December 29, 1860, the son of Edgar and Eliza M. (Patton) Harrison. He was educated by private tutor and in the high school of Steubenville, Ohio, from which he was graduated in 1882.

In 1895, when the family came to St. Petersburg, Mr. Harrison and his brother, J. F. Harrison, established the business which now is known as the Harrison-Powell Company.

Mr. Harrison was a member of the school board for many years and has been a contributing member of the Board of Trade and Chamber of Commerce since coming to the city. He is a member of the Woodmen of the World and Fraternal

E. P. Harrison

Union. He is also a member of the Presbyterian Church.

On August 15, 1894, Mr. Harrison was married to Miss Ada M. Shepherd, of Wellsburg, W. Va. They have two sons, J. Edgar, now with the Harrison-Powell Company, and C. Frank Harrison, who is attending Stetson University in Deland, Fla.

R. H. Sumner

R. H. Sumner was born at Crawley, England, thirty miles south of London, on April 21, 1879, son of William and Susan (Simmons) Sumner. In 1885 the family came to Florida, first locating at Eustis and moving to St. Petersburg in 1895. William Sumner, a contractor, engaged in business here for a number of years and has now retired.

Mr. Sumner, the oldest of nine children, six of whom are now living, was educated in the common schools. When about thirteen years old he began earning practically his own living. He learned the trade of painter and later established a paint and wall paper business in this city. He sold out in 1908 to devote his entire time to real estate business, handling his own properties.

During 1922 Mr. Sumner erected the first steel building in St. Petersburg at the southwest corner of Seventh and Central. When work on the building was started, many said that Mr. Sumner was making a mistake by investing so much money in a building so far out of the main business section. In less than two years, however, the business section has reached and passed Seventh street, and the Sumner building now is considered to be advantageously located. Mr. Sumner is the owner of Royal Palm Cemetery and also owns 100 acres of citrus groves in the county. He has built many of the best homes in the city.

Mr. Sumner was elected as county commissioner for District No. 1 in 1918 and has held the office since. He is a Democrat in politics. He is a director in the Ninth Street Bank and Trust Company and is chairman of the finance committee of the Episcopal Church.

Mr. Sumner married Bettie S. Blocker, daughter of Charles H. and Sallie A. Blocker, in 1900. They have two children, R. H., Jr., and Sallie Mae, now Mrs. E. B. Willson, Jr.

A. P. Avery

A. P. Avery was born in Franklin County, Ohio, and received his education in the public schools of that county.

On December 28, 1897, Mr. Avery came to St. Petersburg for a change of climate. Prior to that time he had been engaged in the real estate business. In 1900 he was appointed deputy collector of the port of St. Petersburg to succeed Roy S. Hanna, who then became postmaster. Later he became engaged in the banking business and subsequently became president of the American Bank & Trust Company.

Mr. Avery has taken a deep interest in the governmental affairs of St. Petersburg ever since coming here. He served on the town council in 1899 and 1900. In 1916, after the commission-mayor form of government went into effect, he was elected as a commissioner and he was re-

R. H. Sumner

A. P. Avery

elected for another two-year term in 1918.

Mr. Avery has been actively connected with the Board of Trade and Chamber of Commerce for many years. He served as president of the organization in 1902 and again in 1910. He also was a member of the board of governors for a number of years.

Mr. Avery is connected with the Avery & Roberts Marine Ways, the W. H. Streeter Cigar Company, the Guarantee Title & Trust Company, the Crystal Beach Company, and the Mountain Home Company of Hendersonville, N. C. He is a Mason, a member of the Elks' Lodge, and Knights of Pythias. He has been a continuous worker for St. Petersburg and its betterment every day he has lived in the city.

Mr. Avery's wife is Mathilda (Beach) Avery.

A. F. Bartlett

A. F. Bartlett was born in Southampton, Mass., March 5, 1853, a son of Samuel C. and Rhoda (Searles) Bartlett, who were also natives of Massachusetts. Three brothers of the Bartlett family became residents of New England during Colonial days and Josiah Bartlett, of New Hampshire, became one of the signers of the Declaration of Independence.

After attending the public schools, Mr. Bartlett pursued a preparatory course in the Phillips Academy at Andover, Mass., and later entered Yale, where he pursued a partial course and then completed his studies in Oberlin College, Ohio, from which he was graduated in the class of 1882. For two years he was in charge of a boarding school known as Stanford Seminary in New York, and following his graduation from Oberlin he accepted the superintendency of the city schools at Yankton, S. D., where he remained from 1882 until 1887. During the next three years he was professor of mathematics and sciences in Yankton College. For two years he was teacher in the preparatory department at Oberlin and he spent two years in studying educational systems in various cities. Later he took charge of the public schools at Lake Geneva, Wis.

While in South Dakota, Mr. Bartlett took a very active part in the prohibition campaign, taking charge of a special campaign paper in connection with his college work. The work was so strenuous that he was compelled to retire for two years.

Mr. Bartlett visited Florida for the first time during the summer of 1896, coming on a summer excursion which cost him $38 for the round trip. While in Tampa, Mr. Bartlett heard a little about St. Petersburg and remembered how a friend of his, in Lake Geneva, Wis., had boosted the town. He decided to take time to visit the peninsula and made the trip on a beautiful moonlight night. He stopped at the Clarendon Hotel, near the waterfront. The next day he was taken on a trip through the town and surrounding country by Col. L. Y. Jenness, manager of the St. Petersburg Land & Improvement Company. Col. Jenness showed him an orange grove with about forty acres of land on Ninth street, owned by George R. Johnson, a Civil War veteran, and tried to persuade him to buy. Mr. Bartlett took a few hours to think it over and then made the first payment on the property, to cost about $5,000. He then returned north.

Mrs. Bartlett came to St. Petersburg without her husband in the following winter. She liked the climate and when she went back north again, the family began making preparations to leave Wisconsin and make St. Petersburg their permanent home. He still lives on the same ground he first bought and it might be said that his home is one of the very few in St. Petersburg which has never been for sale.

Although Mr. Bartlett has never been actively engaged in teaching since coming to Florida, he has retained his interests in schools. He served for eight years on the local school board of St. Petersburg and three years on the county school board. He was one of the small group of men who were instrumental in starting the first kindergarten in the city.

Mr. Bartlett was one of the organizers of the Board of Trade and was president of the body at the time it was incorporated. He has held every office in the organization except secretary. When the control of the Chamber of Commerce was turned over to the young business men, Mr. Bartlett was still retained on the board of directors.

Mr. Bartlett has taken a leading part in the development of the waterfront and was one of the men who acquired the waterfront lots and held them in trust until the city could take them over. He also was one of the men who bought the land needed by the Tampa & Gulf Coast Railroad so that it could enter the city. He was first vice-president of the Central National Bank, which he helped to organize. He helped to organize different organizations for the protection and culture of orange groves and has been made a life member of the State Horticultural Society. During the war, he joined with Roy S. Hanna in the manufacture of citrus products for the government.

Mr. Bartlett was married to Miss Alice A. Ford, of New Haven, Conn., in 1876. They have three children: Ralph; Irene, the wife of John M. Park of Washington, D. C., and Ruth, wife of H. Charles Barnes.

W. C. Henry

Walter C. Henry was born in Irdell county, North Carolina, March 6, 1856, the son of William F. and Dovia (Cavin) Henry, both natives of North Carolina. The father, who was a cooper by trade, owned a farm, and it was there that Walter Henry spent a large part of his youth, receiving his education in a little log cabin school house.

Leaving the farm when he was twenty-one years old, Mr. Henry learned the carpenters' trade and in 1882 he came to Florida, locating in Leesburg, where he went into business as a contractor and as a wholesale dealer in lumber and building materials. Instead of getting paid in cash for many of the buildings he erected, he took second mortgages. When the big freeze of 1894-95 killed all the groves, property values dropped to almost nothing and the second mortgages were worthless. Mr. Henry lost all he had, and was compelled to start all over again, with wife and three children.

In the fall of 1896 he took his men and went to Tampa, intending to go into business there. He was advised, however, that there were more contractors then in Tampa than there were buildings to be built, and that they were taking contracts

W. C. Henry

at such low prices that they could hardly pay the wages of their men. Mr. Henry then came on to St. Petersburg, which he heard was growing steadily. He liked the town and decided to stay. Col. L. Y. Jenness, manager of the St. Petersburg Land & Development company, offered to sell him a lot at Fifth street and Central avenue, where the First National Bank now stands, for $400—with no down payment, provided he erected a building upon the lot at once and would pay $100 a year.

Mr. Henry started work at once, erecting a two-story building with his work shop on the lower floor and living rooms above. Within 6 years he sold it for $1,800, netting him a good profit. From then on, Mr. Henry engaged in a general contracting business.

Mr. Henry was elected to the town council in 1901 for a two year term. Before his term expired, a bond issue of $11,000 was appropriated for the construction of a new school. In order to bid for the contract, Mr. Henry resigned from the council. He was low bidder, and the contract was awarded to him, he to do the work for $10,200. This was the first building built especially for school purposes in the town.

In July, 1904, the first contract for brick paving was awarded to Mr. Henry, and his partner at the time, O. G. Wishard. They agreed to pave three blocks of Central for $1.75½ per square yard. The work was held up for some time by discussion over who should pay for the street intersections—the town or the property owners and a new contract was necessary. This time Mr. Henry agreed to do the work for $1.82½ per square yard. He paved Central from Second street to Fifth.

In 1909 Mr. Henry built the first high school in St. Petersburg, contracting to do the work for $32,000.

Mr. Henry was engaged in the contracting business until a few years ago when he retired to handle his own properties. His last contract was for the construction of the Public Library.

Mr. Henry is a member of the Elks and the Methodist Episcopal church. He also has been a contributing member of the Board of Trade and the Chamber of Commerce almost since their inception.

On February 16, 1888, Mr. Henry was married to Miss Mamie Dinkins, daughter of Mr. and Mrs. Mack Dinkins, in Fort Mill, S. C. They have four children: Love L., Mack L., Mrs. Bessie L. Bainard, and Walter L. All are living in St. Petersburg except Walter L. Henry who is now in Midland, Mich.

W. A. Holshouser

William Alexander Holshouser was born in Paris, Tenn., February 6, 1873, the son of William S. Holshouser and Cynthia Ann Roberta (Dickensen) Holshouser, the former a native of South Carolina and the latter of Alabama. The family came to Florida January 1, 1883, and settled in Orlando.

W. A. Holshouser was educated in the public schools of Orlando and studied one year at Rollins College. While a youth he engaged in the drug business and came to St. Petersburg in October, 1896, to take over the management of a drug store.

For twenty-one years Mr. Holshouser

W. A. Holshouser

conducted a drug store in St. Petersburg, and left this to engage in the real estate business. He is now the head of the Holshouser Realty Company, and is a director in the Guarantee Title and Abstract Company.

He is the Past Grand Patriarch of the Independent Order of Odd Fellows, and was Grand Treasurer of the order for four years. He is also a life member of the St. Petersburg Lodge 139 Masons, the Grotto and Egypt Temple of Tampa, Fla.

Mr. Holshouser has been treasurer of the city of St. Petersburg for two years and secretary of the local school board for three years. During the time he was on the school board he had active charge of the erection of the three ward schools in St. Petersburg and the negro school in Tenth street and Third avenue south.

Mr. Holshouser was one of the twelve original members of the Chamber of Commerce, which was organized in 1898, with Colonel L. Y. Jenness as president. In 1903 he served as president of the Chamber for one year. It was during this administration that the first booklets advertising St. Petersburg were printed.

Mr. Holshouser was married April 15, 1897, to Catora Reynolds in Orlando, Florida. They have one child, now living, Miss Elizabeth Holshouser, who is at present teaching in the Roser Park School in St. Petersburg. She is a graduate of Stetson University with the degree of A. B.

Mrs. Holshouser was co-manager of the drug store for eleven years and is now a member of the Holshouser Realty Company. She was one of the founders and charter members of the Eureka Chapter O. E. S., and Golden Rod Rebekah Lodge. She is also one of the founders of the W. T. I. A. and while chairman of the building committee had charge of the erection of the W. T. I. A. building, now occupied by the Y. M. C. A.

D. W. Budd

David Wilson Budd was born in Monticello, Fla., on December 4, 1883, the son of William and Julia A. (Fennell) Budd, the former of New Jersey and the latter of North Carolina. The family came to St. Petersburg in March, 1896, and David Budd completed his school work in the St. Petersburg public schools.

After leaving school Mr. Budd went to work in the drug store of J. G. Bradshaw, where he remained for two years. He then worked a few years for J. C. Williams, Jr., proprietor of the City Drug Store. In 1902 he passed the examinations of the State Board of Pharmacy and in February, 1903, he opened up the drug store of D. W. Budd & Co. A year later he bought out the interest of his partner, I. S. Levy, now head of the I. S. Levy Wholesale Drug Company of Tampa.

In 1910 Mr. Budd and James Autrey purchased from F. A. Wood the two-story brick building on the north side of Central between Third and Fourth streets, where his drug store is now located. At the same time Mr. Budd bought from Mr. Wood the forty-foot lot adjoining the brick building. On this lot there was a one-story frame building which Mr. Wood had built originally for a postoffice. For these properties, which had a combined frontage of 120 feet on Central, Mr. Budd paid $40,000. The deal was one of the largest made in St. Petersburg up to that time. Six months later Mr. Budd sold the forty-foot lot for $18,000.

Mr. Budd always has taken a keen interest in outdoor sports. He probably has caught more tarpon than any other angler of the country and was president of the Tarpon Club for many terms. In 1913 he won the state championship in clay pigeon shooting. He also has won many other honors in shooting contests.

Mr. Budd is a member of the St. Petersburg Country Club and St. Petersburg Yacht Club, and also is a member of the B. P. O. E., No. 1224. He has been a contributing member of the Chamber of Commerce for many years.

George Edwards

George Edwards was born in North Wales on June 8, 1853, the son of Edward and Mary (Morris) Edwards. He came to this country with his parents in April, 1859, the family settling in Fairhaven, Vt. The father, who was a musician, died in 1862 and the mother about a year later, leaving seven children.

George Edwards, then only nine years old, went to live with friends. He attended the common schools of Westminster, Mass., and the Worcester Academy at Worcester, Mass. In the summers between school terms he learned the painter's trade, and partially earned his own living from the time he was thirteen years old. He was married on November 27, 1876, in Springfield, Vt., to Miss Abbie J. Reed, of Sharon, N. H.

In 1882, Mrs. Edwards suffered from poor health, and the family physician ordered her to seek a milder climate. The family left Boston on Thanksgiving Day of the same year and came to Florida, first locating in Tangerine, Orange County. They remained there six months and then homesteaded in Hernando County, near Mannfield. In 1889, Mr. Edwards purchased forty acres within the town of Mannfield. While there he learned the blacksmith and wheelwright trade.

During the summer of 1897 Mr. Edwards resolved to move from Mannfield, principally because he wanted to bring up his children in a better environment and give them better school advantages. He left home in June and traveled to many sections of the state, arriving here in August. Of all the places he had seen, he liked St. Petersburg the best, and he decided to make this town his future home. Returning to Mannfield, he tried to sell his property. The freeze of 1894-95 had left that section of the state impoverished and he was able to get only $300 for the house and land, in which he had invested more than ten times that amount in cash.

Coming back to St. Petersburg, Mr. Edwards purchased a lot 40 by 100 feet on the south side of Central avenue, where the Pheil Theatre is now located, from Col. L. Y. Jenness of the St. Petersburg Land & Improvement Company. The lot, now worth more than $150,000, cost Mr. Edwards $450, and he was required to pay only $50 down—the balance when he could pay it. At the same time he also bought five acres on Ninth avenue north, just west of Ninth street, for $375, paying $15 down.

On his Central avenue lot, Mr. Edwards built a two-story building, with a carriage and blacksmith shop below and living rooms above. He remained in business there for ten years, when his health broke down and he was required to sell out. He built a home on his Ninth avenue land, moved there, and rented out his store to a grocery company. Mr. Edwards and his family have resided on Ninth avenue north ever since. He has spent much of his time in buying and selling properties and building homes for rent and sales.

Mr. Edwards was a member of the town council from 1898 to 1902. In 1903 he was elected mayor and it was during his administration that St. Petersburg became a city. While a member of the council, Mr. Edwards also served two terms on the school board. In 1912 he was elected a county commissioner from this district and he served for three terms, until 1918.

Mr. Edwards is a thirty-second degree Mason, and is a member of the Commandery, Shrine, and Knights of Pythias. He has been a member of the Chamber of Commerce since its organization.

Mr. and Mrs. Edwards have four children now living: Marcus G., assistant postmaster of St. Petersburg; Grace M., Mrs. Bernice Lord, of Plainfield, N. J., and Mrs. Irma Brown, of this city.

W. B. Powell

William P. Powell was born April 12, 1874, in Iowa City, Iowa, the son of George and Sarah M. (Patton) Powell, the former of Wilmington, Del., and the latter of Uniontown, Pa. The father had gone to Iowa before the coming of the railroads and was one of the pioneers of the state. The great-grandfather of William Powell, who was also the great-grandfather of J. Frank Harrison, established the second newspaper west of the Allegheny Mountains, the Genius of Liberty, in Uniontown, Pa., during the Revolutionary War period.

Mr. Powell attended the schools of Iowa City and was graduated from the high school in 1891. In the next fall he entered the State University of Iowa and was graduated with the degree of Bachelor of Science in Civil Engineering. During the next two years he worked as civil engineer on the Mexico, Curernavaca &

W. P. Powell

Pacific Railway, at Puente de Yxtla, Mexico; the Ferro-Carrill Electrico de Jalapa y Cordova, in Jalapa, Mexico, and the Michoacan & Pacific Railway at Tuxpan, Mexico.

In April, 1897, Mr. Powell came to Florida to visit the Harrisons and to see what damage had been done to his citrus grove in Orange County by the freezes during the preceding two winters. He found that all the trees had been killed, and the grove almost worthless. He liked this section of the state and he liked St. Petersburg, so he decided to become identified with it. J. Frank Harrison and Edgar Harrison were at that time owners of the St. Petersburg Cash Store and he became associated with them in enlarging it. The name of this company was later changed to the St. Petersburg Hardware Company, still later to the Harrison Hardware & Furniture Company, and, in the fall of 1923, to the Harrison-Powell Company.

Although financially interested in the above companies, Mr. Powell spent most of his time during the years which followed in Cedar Rapids, Iowa, coming to St. Petersburg occasionally during the winter months. During the greater part of this period he was manager of the Ætna Life Insurance Company for Northern and Eastern Iowa. He held this position until October 1, 1922, when he resigned to take active part in the business of the Harrison Hardware Company.

Mr. Powell is a director of the American Bank & Trust Company and is a member of the Elks and Masonic Lodge. He also is a member of the St. Petersburg Yacht Club, Kiwanis Club, and University Club. While in Cedar Rapids, Mr. Powell was vice-president and a director of the Cedar Rapids Chamber of Commerce.

On October 21, 1896, Mr. Powell was married to Miss Louise Alford in Waterloo, Iowa. They have two children, Mrs. John B. Wallace, now living in St. Petersburg, and Eleanor Powell, now attending Vassar College.

A. P. Weller

A. P. Weller was born in New Village, N. J., on July 8, 1856, the son of William and Sarah Weller. He was educated in the public schools of New Jersey and later learned to be a telegrapher, working in a telegraph office in Philadelphia. In 1895 he went to Tarpon Springs to take charge of an electric light plant which had been founded there by F. A. Davis and Jacob Disston. Mr. Davis was Mr. Weller's cousin.

The light plant failed to pay in Tarpon Springs and in 1897 it was moved to St. Petersburg under the direction of Mr. Weller, who continued to serve as manager. The plant was a makeshift affair, breaking down continually, and Mr. Weler's duties were very exacting. He worked night and day, and his health began to fail. In 1903, when work was started on the St. Petersburg and Gulf Electric Railway, another Davis enterprise, his work became even more strenuous. His physical condition steadily became worse. In the spring of 1904 he went to Colorado Springs, Col., where he died on January 24, 1905.

Mr. Weller was married on May 12, 1880, in Paterson, N. J., to Miss Isabelle Garrabrant. Mrs. Weller upon coming to St. Petersburg with her husband, took an active interest in the development of the town and was one of the founders, and first president, of the Women's Town Improvement Association. She died on April 13, 1905, in Paterson, N. J.

Mr. and Mrs. Weller were survived by a daughter, Ida Louise, who was educated in the schools of Tarpon Springs, St. Petersburg, and the Randolph-Macon College in Virginia. She was married on May 1, 1907, to Horace Williams, grandson of the founder of St. Petersburg. Mr. and Mrs. Williams have one son, Horace, Jr., now seven years old.

T. J. Northrup

Thomas J. Northrup was born in Lower Peach Tree, Ala., on May 28, 1862, the son of Thomas and Mary (Davis) Northrup, both natives of Alabama. Thomas was the elder of two sons. He was educated in the grade schools of Alabama and in 1880 he came to Florida, locating in DeLand. He remained there for two years, engaging in the fruit business.

T. J. Northrup

From DeLand Mr. Northrup went to Sumterville, in Sumter County, and bought an orange grove. During the next decade he spent his time developing this grove and engaging in the contracting business. In 1892 he went to Inverness and worked in a general store, learning the business. His grove at Sumterville, which he had kept, was completely destroyed by the freeze of 1894-95.

Dissatisfied with the prospects in Inverness, Mr. Northrup in 1898 visited a number of places in South Florida in search of a place in which to start business for himself. He came to St. Petersburg in August of that year and decided that the surroundings were ideal for a large city. With a capital of $600 he opened a small grocery store. His trade increased as the city grew and in 1916 he bought out the business of Arthur Norwood. At present Mr. Northrup is president of the Northrup-Rutland Company, one of the largest stores of its kind in St. Petersburg.

Shortly after St. Petersburg became a city in 1903 Mr. Northrup was appointed to fill a vacancy on the city council. In 1904 he was elected for a two-year term and during this period served as chairman of the council. He was elected mayor in 1906, defeating F. E. Cole and Edgar Harrison. He declined the nomination in 1908. In July, 1913, at the first election after the commission form of government went into effect, Mr. Northrup was elected commissioner of public works, receiving the highest number of votes cast. While holding this office Mr. Northrup helped the city acquire the water front, built the gas plant and first incinerator, and helped in the extension of West Central to Boca Ceiga Bay. Mr. Northrup also served as the first tax assessor of Pinellas County.

Mr. Northrup was married in February, 1895, to Miss Nettie Smith, a native of Georgia, whose family had come to Florida when she was a small child. She was the daughter of Sanford and Susan (Anderson) Smith. Mr. and Mrs. Northrup have four children: Robert, who is a partner of Mr. Northrup in his business; Benjamin, Marie and Marjorie. Benjamin and Marie are now in college and Marjorie is in high school.

Mr. Northrup is a charter member of the Chamber of Commerce and Kiwanis Club, and for many years was one of the governors of the Board of Trade. He and all the members of his family are members of the Congregational Church.

Henry W. Hibbs

Henry W. Hibbs was born in Newport, N. C., February 12, 1862, the son of Hawkins W. and Eunice Hibbs. He was educated in the public schools of North Carolina, and later engaged in the farming and trucking business.

In February, 1889, he came to St. Petersburg, attracted by the fact that the railroad had established a line in this city, and so made possible the shipping of fresh fish, with which the waters of the bay and gulf were literally alive.

Mr. Hibbs established in St. Petersburg one of its most important industries—the shipping of fresh fish to northern markets. He is president of the Hibbs Fish Company, president of the Citizens Ice & Cold Storage Company and a director of the First National Bank. He is also a mem-

Henry W. Hibbs

ber of the Masonic Lodge and a Knight of Pythias.

Mr. Hibbs was elected mayor of St. Petersburg in 1894-95, serving two one-year terms. It was during his administration that the first real public improvement began in St. Petersburg—the filling in of the swale that extended across Central avenue at Third street, the building of the first school, and the laying down of board and oyster walks. Hogs were also barred from the streets.

Mr. Hibbs was married in Newport, N. C., October 7, 1883, to Nannie S. Rowe, and they have six children: Charles B., Blanche, Walter, Olivia, Henry W. Jr., and Mabel. The sons are in business with their father.

W. L. Straub

William L. Straub was born at Dowagiac, Mich., on July 14, 1867, the son of Henry and Mary (Woosley) Straub. After receiving a common school education he went, at the age of sixteen, to that portion of Dakota Territory which then was endeavoring to become the state of North Dakota. In 1888 he became editor and owner of the Sargent County Rustler; from 1894 to 1895 he was editor and part owner of the Oakes (N. D.) Weekly Republican, and from 1895 to 1899 was managing editor of the Grand Forks (N. D.) Daily Herald.

Poor health made it necessary for Mr. Straub to seek a milder climate during the winter of 1898-99. He came to Florida and found his way to St. Petersburg. He was benefited greatly and returned north again in the spring, only to find a few months later that he was not strong enough to withstand the rigors of a North Dakota winter. So he came back to St. Petersburg—this time to stay. His attention naturally turned to newspaper work and in April, 1901, he joined with A. P. Avery and A. H. Lindelie in purchasing the St. Petersburg Times, owned by the widow of the late J. Ira Gore. In 1903 he bought out his partners. In February, 1912, he established the Daily Times, and in September of that year Paul Poynter and C. C. Carr became associated with him in the Times.

He was appointed postmaster of St. Petersburg on July 21, 1916, and was reappointed by President Wilson in December, 1920. His confirmation, with thousands of others, was blocked in the senate until the Harding administration came and he was succeeded May 31, 1922, by Roy S. Hanna. In the spring of 1923 he returned to the Times again as editor-in-chief.

During his long service as editor of the Times, Mr. Straub had many opportunities to aid in the development of St. Petersburg—and he sidestepped none of them. For many years he fought for the municipal ownership and beautification of the water front. He inaugurated and led the movement to create Pinellas County by separating Pinellas Peninsula from Hillsborough County. He aided in the establishment of St. Petersburg's system of parks. He has been identified with the Chamber of Commerce since the beginning and served as its president during 1913. He was instrumental in securing a larger donation from the Carnegie Corporation than had been offered, making possible the construction of the Public Library. The Pinellas County Board of Trade was organized through the efforts of Mr. Straub and he was elected as its first president. He took a leading part in the organization of the St. Petersburg Tarpon Club, St. Petersburg Yacht Club, and Rotary Club. He was chairman of the City Planning Board from the time it was created until the resumption of his work as editor-in-chief of the Times.

Mr. Straub is a prominent member of the Knights of Pythias and served the order for three terms as chancellor commander. He is also a member of the Elks.

Mr. Straub was married to Sarah A. Moore, daughter of Joel S. and Flora T. Moore, of Dowagiac, Mich., on November 21, 1891. They have one daughter, Blanche M., now Mrs. Jay B. Starkey, of St. Petersburg.

C. Perry Snell

C. Perry Snell was born in Bowling Green, Ky., June 5, 1869, the son of C. P. and Isabelle Snell. After being graduated from Ogden College in Bowling Green, Mr. Snell entered the retail drug business, in which he remained for seventeen years.

Mr. Snell visited St. Petersburg for the first time on his wedding trip in January, 1899, shortly after he had been married to Miss Lillian Allen, in Columbia, Tenn. Within two weeks after his arrival, Mr. Snell made his first investment in St. Petersburg property, purchasing the half block where the Colonial Hotel now stands. Part of this property was a swamp and had to be filled in. A little later, Mr. Snell acquired the other half of the block where the Soreno Hotel was erected in 1923.

It was not until 1904 that Mr. Snell realized his desire to have a home in St. Petersburg. The following item, which appeared in the issue of the St. Petersburg Times on February 20, 1904, welcomed the announcement that he was going to build: "C. Perry Snell, of Columbia, Tenn., who has spent several winters here after visiting California, Mexico and foreign countries of soft climate, has found St. Petersburg the best of all and has decided to establish his permanent residence here. Mr. Snell owns the north half of Block 23 . . . .

C. Perry Snell

and on the two lots at the corner of First street and Fourth avenue north will erect an elegant residence. Mr. and Mrs. Snell are of the most desirable people and will be welcomed to the community as permanent residents."

That was the bginning. Mr. Snell began the work of development which is still going on. In 1905, he organized the Bay Shore Land Company in company with F. A. Wood, A. E. Hoxie and A. C. Lewis, and the Bay Shore and Bay Front subdivisions were the result. Both are located on Tampa Bay and extend from Fifth to Thirteenth avenues north. Mr. Snell's next step was taken in December, 1906, with J. C. Hamlett, a capitalist of Crockett's Mills, Tenn., and A. E. Hoxie, of St. Petersburg. All the holdings of the St. Petersburg Land & Improvement Company were purchased, including the water-front lots where the old electric-light plant stood, several hundred city lots and several hundred acres surrounding St. Petersburg. These properties were put on the market and sold out. About the same time, Mr. Snell joined with Mr. Hamlett and formed the partnership of Snell & Hamlett.

Snell & Hamlett's next development was the old Hanley grove, located west of and including the west half of Mirror Lake. At that time St. Petersburg derived its water supply from this lake and for several years paid water rental to Snell & Hamlett. About this time another subdivision west of the lake, known as West Lake, was promoted by the firm. Another development was the Crescent Lake Addition, lying along Fourth street, starting at Thirteenth avenue north. Through Mr. Snell's offer to the Park Board, the city acquired fifty-six acres of this tract now known as Crescent Lake Park.

Early in 1910, Snell & Hamlett made several large purchases of land bordering on Tampa Bay and the real North Shore development began. On March 8, 1919, Mr. Snell announced that he had bought out Mr. Hamlett's interest in all of Snell & Hamlett's holdings, including the Post Office Arcade property. Shortly afterwards he announced plans for the Coffee Pot Golf Course. The courses were started on May 3, 1919, and opened on January 19, 1920.

Aside from his real-estate developments, Mr. Snell probably has done most for the city through his long continued boosting for the water front. Mr. Snell was named as a member of the executive committee of the Board of Trade following its reorganization in 1905 and has been associated with the Board of Trade and Chamber of Commerce ever since. He was associated with the company which bought the Pass-a-Grille bridge in May, 1920, from Frank F. Pulver, who had purchased it a few weeks before from W. J. McAdoo. He was one of the original stockholders of the Central National Bank.

Mr. Snell's favorite hobby is the collecting of miniature pictures; the exhibit he held during the winter of 1923 at the Florida Art School was the first exhibit of its kind in the state. Mr. and Mrs. Snell have been abroad six times and many of their miniatures have been collected while traveling through European countries.

In 1923, Mr. Snell donated $30,000 to enlarge Ogden College and also guaranteed the annual sum of $2,500 to provide a chair of philosophy.

James D. Bell

James D. Bell was born August 30, 1840, at Exeter, N. H. His parents were James Bell and Judith Bell (Judith Upham). He was educated at Phillips-Exeter Academy and Harvard Law School and was admitted to the New Hampshire Bar in November, 1865. He came South and made his home at Beaufort, S. C., where he practiced law for about six years. He served a term as county judge of Beaufort County, and was also a member of the Reconstruction Constitutional Convention.

He came to Hawthorne, Florida, about 1880, and bought an orange grove, remaining there some years.

After having lived in Florida some twenty years he came to St. Petersburg in 1900, where he has resided ever since. He had visited St. Petersburg previously, as well as other parts of Florida, and de-

James D. Bell

cided that it was the best and most promising town in the state. He bought an orange grove here and also engaged in the pineapple business, and afterwards resumed the practice of law, which he continued until about five years ago.

When the commission form of government was first inaugurated in St. Petersburg, Judge Bell served a term as municipal judge under the Bradshaw-Northrup-Hammond administration. He has always been forward in promoting civic projects; is a past president of the St. Petersburg Board of Trade (now Chamber of Commerce) and was president of the old St. Petersburg Reading Room and Library Association, the forerunner of the present Carnegie Library. He is chairman of the Board of Deacons of the Congregational Church, having been elected a member of the board for life.

In 1868 he married Mary A. Bugbee, of Lebanon, New Hampshire. Of this union, one son, Frank U. Bell, born in 1869, survives. He is a clothing manufacturer and lives in Lebanon, N. H. Mrs. Bell was one of the pioneer members of the W. T. I. A., and has been always an active and useful member of civic, social and church circles of St. Petersburg.

Bob C. Smalley

Bob C. Smalley was born in Hoopeston, Ill., April 29, 1896, the son of Robert C. and Sarah (Hickman) Smalley. The family came to St. Petersburg in 1900. After being graduated from the St. Petersburg High School, Bob Smalley attended one year at the University of Illinois and two years at the University of Florida in Gainesville.

Upon leaving college, Mr. Smalley became associated with C. Buck Turner and C. Perry Snell in building and developing work. He spent three years in this work and then established the Bob C. Smalley Company at 1180 Central avenue, distributors for Hupmobile and Rickenbacker cars. At present he is owner and manager of this company. He also is manager of the Smalley Investment Company in the new Soreno Hotel building, doing a general real estate business and mortgage loans, and is vice-president in the Soreno Hotel Corporation.

Mr. Smalley is a life member of the

Bob C. Smalley

Blue Lodge, Chapter, Knights Templar and Scottish Rite. He is also a Shriner and master of ceremonies of the Selama Grotto. He was the organizer of the Civitan Club and served it for two years as president. He is a member of the board of directors of the University Club, president of the Sigma Alpha Epsilon Alumni Chapter of St. Petersburg, and a member of the local post of the American Legion. He is a member of the Episcopal Church. He served for two years as a governor of the Chamber of Commerce and is now a member of the board of directors.

Mr. Smalley was married on January 1, 1921, to Miss Cornelia Ross Dulin. After the wedding ceremony, the couple started on their wedding trip by flying to Tampa in an airplane piloted by Lieut. Albert Whitted, accompanied by friends in two other airplanes. Mr. and Mrs. Smalley have a baby daughter, Cornelia Juanita. Mrs. Smalley was chairman of the woman's entertainment committee during the T. P. A. convention held in St. Petersburg late in 1923.

F. E. Cole.

F. E. Cole was born in Owego, N. Y., on March 19, 1858, the son of Merritt J. and Martha (Hines) Cole, both natives of New York State. He was educated in the district schools of Bradford County, Pennsylvania, and Sweensburg College, at Grand Rapids, Mich.

A short time after leaving school Mr. Cole went to Idaho and British Columbia, where he engaged in mining for a number of years. From there he went to Los Angeles, where he went into the grocery business and organized Station D of the postoffice, which he ran for three years. In about 1899 he went back to British Columbia to work in mines owned by a company of which E. H. Tomlinson was president.

In 1901 Mr. Cole was persuaded by Mr. Tomlinson to come to St. Petersburg. Upon arriving here he purchased a half block at Second avenue south and Fourth street, where the Elks' Home is now located. A large part of this land had been planted to pineapples. Mr. Cole paid $6,000 for the property, pineapples and all. He built his home on the one hundred feet facing Fourth street.

For a number of years Mr. Cole was engaged in raising pineapples, his pinery being one of the best on the peninsula. In 1907, however, he was forced to discontinue, prohibitive express rates making the industry unprofitable. The express company had made a rate of $1.50 a crate to northern markets when the industry was first started and promised better rates when the crop became greater. Instead of lowering the rates, however, the company constantly advanced them. In 1907 the growers received notice that the rate had been increased to $2.35. They refused to pay it and the industry was killed. At that time there were fifty-four acres in pineapples in this section of the peninsula and about 10,000 crates were being shipped out annually.

In 1908 Mr. Cole started the Ansonia Hotel in the two upper floors of the Tomlinson building, erected by E. H. Tomlinson during the preceding summer. Mr. Cole has operated the hotel ever since.

Mr. Cole has taken an active interest in the city government for many years.

F. E. Cole

He was appointed to the council early in 1903 to fill a vacancy caused by the resignation of one of the members, and was serving on the council at the time when St. Petersburg became a city. Mr. Cole was re-elected at the next election for a two-year term. In 1906 he was defeated by T. J. Northrup in a close race for mayor. In 1908 he was again elected to the council and served until 1910. Mr. Cole also served for two years as justice of the peace.

Mr. Cole aided in the financing of the Mid-Winter Fair Auditorium on Second avenue north, now occupied by the First Church of Christ, Scientist. He was manager of the building for five years, during which period it was used for the Chautauquas, fairs, and many other entertainments. It was the only building in St. Petersburg at the time in which a large number of persons could meet.

Besides operating the Ansonia Hotel, Mr. Cole served as a director of the Central National Bank for six years and the Bayboro Investment Company for seven years. He has been a member of the Board of Trade and Chamber of Commerce since coming to St. Petersburg and served four years as a member of the board of governors. He is now serving his third year as a member of the City Hospital Board.

Mr. Cole was married in Kootenai, Idaho, on April 16, 1888, to Miss Ella Shepard, daughter of Dr. and Mrs. G. B. Shepard, of Sheboygan Falls, Wis. Mrs. Cole took an active part in the work of the Woman's Town Improvement Association for a number of years and served one year as president. She is now the oldest living member of the association.

F. A. Wood

Frank A. Wood was born in Brownsville, Ontario, Canada, on March 31, 1861, the son of E. F. and Mary (Cosgrove) Wood, the former a native of Ireland and the latter of England. The mother died in 1862 and the father later married again and moved to Michigan, where he engaged in farming until his death.

Frank Wood was the youngest of a family of two sons and two daughters, and following the death of his mother he was adopted by the family of Charles Andrews and educated in the town of his birth. Later Mr. Wood attended the Normal School of Ottawa, Canada, and at the age of seventeen he began teaching. In the fall of 1881 he entered the Brantford Collegiate Institute in his native province, and following his graduation, he taught one year.

Later Mr. Wood went to the woods of Michigan, where he was engaged as a bookkeeper in the lumber mills until 1888, when he went to Seattle. There he was employed by the Bothell Lumber Company, where he remained until 1891. Thereafter, Mr. Wood spent a number of years in British Columbia, becoming part owner and manager of the Last Chance Mining Company. E. H. Tomlinson also was connected with this company and it was through Mr. Tomlinson's influence that Mr. Wood came for the first time to St. Petersburg, in 1901.

Mr. Wood liked St. Petersburg from the moment he first saw it and he thought so highly of its possibilities for future development that he immediately purchased a large lot on the north side of Central avenue, between Third and Fourth streets, and erected the Wood building, the second brick building to be erected in St. Petersburg.

Despite this early investment, Mr. Wood did not become a permanent resident of St. Petersburg until 1904, when he built his home, Brookside, on the south side of the city. In April, 1905, Mr. Wood organized the Central National Bank, of which he became president. He held this position until January 12, 1915, when he retired from active business and was succeeded as president by A. F. Thomasson.

Mr. Wood took an active part in the fight to separate Pinellas Peninsula from Hillsborough County. In the primary election held on May 19, 1908, he ran for the state legislature as the leader of the divisionists. He received an overwhelming majority of the votes on the peninsula, but the two other candidates led throughout the remainder of the county and entered the second primary.

Despite this defeat, Mr. Wood continued advocating a separate county and aided materially in the movement. When Pinellas County became a fact, Mr. Wood was elected as one of the first county commissioners. Later he served one term in the state legislature and was a candidate for governor.

Always a booster of St. Petersburg, Mr. Wood was a leader in many of the movements for the development of the city. He served as president of the Board of Trade in 1905 and was actively connected with the organization for many years. He also was one of the early supporters of the St. Petersburg Country Club and the St. Petersburg Yacht Club.

As one of the organizers of the Bayshore Development Company, Mr. Wood aided in starting the development of the North Shore section of St. Petersburg. He also was one of the early backers of the Bayboro Investment Company, which reclaimed hundreds of acres of land in the Bayboro district and created Bayboro Harbor. Mr. Wood also was one of the founders of the Tampa Bay Transportation Company in 1906. With W. E. Heathcote and W. R. Fuller, of Tampa, he went to New York and purchased the steamer Favorite.

On June 21, 1899, Mr. Wood was married to Miss Annie B. Shepard, of Sheboygan Falls, Wis., in Los Angeles, Cal. Mrs. Wood was active for many years in the work of the Woman's Town Improvement Association in beautifying St. Petersburg, serving one year as president of the organization. She also aided materially in musical work in St. Petersburg and has been a member of the Carenno Club, Echo Club, and Woman's Club. She is at present living in St. Petersburg.

Mr. Wood died on May 22, 1921, after a long illness.

John N. Brown

John N. Brown was born in Webster, Sumter County, Florida, on October 9, 1876, the son of J. L. and Minerva (Wells) Brown, the former a native of Alabama and the latter of North Carolina. The grandfather of John Brown, Nathan N. Brown, a Methodist minister, was the originator of the famous Parson Brown orange and had a large grove near Webster.

John Brown went to school in the Sumter County schools and later attended the Georgia Business College, in Senoia, Ga., near Atlanta, from which he was graduated in 1897. He then went to work for the Southern Express Company as express messenger through Florida, Georgia and Alabama, and in 1902 was appointed express agent in St. Petersburg. He held this position until May, 1911, when he resigned on account of poor health, caused by overwork.

Mr. Brown has taken an active interest in city and county government for a number of years. He was elected to the city council in 1910 and served two years. He was elected county tax assessor in 1912 and served two terms, until 1916. In that year he was elected clerk of the circuit court. He took office January 1, 1917, and has been re-elected three times. In 1924 he declined to run again for re-election and will leave the office on January 1, 1925.

Mr. Brown was one of the founders of the Ninth Street Bank & Trust Company and has served as its president since its organization. He also is the owner of the Suwannee Hotel, at First avenue north and Fifth street. The Suwannee, which has 118 rooms and is modern in every respect, was started in October, 1922, and completed by December 10, 1923, on which date it was formally opened to the public.

Mr. Brown is a Mason, being a member of the Chapter, Commandery, and Egypt Temple of Tampa. He is also a member of the Knights of Pythias and the Elks. He served as a member of the board of governors of the Board of Trade from 1910 to 1920, and was a member of the City Advertising and Library Board at the time the public library was built.

On April 3, 1894, Mr. Brown was married to Miss Sarah Celeste White, of St. Petersburg, formerly of Live Oak, Suwannee County, Florida. They have three children, one girl and two boys: Dorothy Elizabeth, 17; Paul Morton, 12 and John Mercer, 10. The children are now attending school in Clearwater where the family has lived since Mr. Brown was elected clerk of courts. Miss Dorothy Elizabeth Brown will be graduated from the Clearwater High School in the Spring of 1924.

Katherine Bell Tippetts

Mrs. Katherine B. Tippetts was born in Somerset county, Maryland, the daughter of Nathaniel Thomas Bell and Julia Frances (Hawkes) Bell. Her father was descended from the Maryland Planters, one of whom married Lady Rebecca Revelle of England. Her mother's ancestors were original settlers in Massachusetts, having come over in the Mayflower.

Mrs. Tippetts received her education largely in private schools for girls and with private teachers, and her training covered a large field. She became proficient in five languages and received a broad literary training.

Mrs. Tippetts married William H. Tippetts, of New York, who was special European correspondent to American newspapers, and held financial interests in several New York newspapers. Mrs. Tippetts and her husband made their headquarters in New York, but spent much of

Katherine Bell Tippetts

their time in foreign countries. In her travels Mrs. Tippetts came into contact with some of the literary lights of the world, and her inclinations led her to enter the literary field, and she contributed to some of the leading periodicals of the country. She has also written books under the pen name of Jerome Cable.

In 1902 Mrs. Tippetts came to Florida in the hope that her husband's failing health would be restored in the climate of St. Petersburg. After the death of her husband she assumed charge of his affairs and became owner of the Belmont Hotel, which she has managed ever since, as well as erecting office buildings, and interesting herself in other business activities.

While managing her business in St. Petersburg, Mrs. Tippetts educated her three sons and a daughter. Two of her sons graduated from Princeton University, and the eldest, William, also graduated from Harvard Law School and is now practicing law in New York City.

The second son, Charles, was a commanding officer in the army of occupation following the armistice in the World War. Ernest, the youngest son, who was in school at the time of the war, served in the student army of LaFayette College, and later entered the Georgia School of Technology. Her daughter, Frances, was graduated from the Woman's College of Tallahassee, Florida, and is now the wife of Dr. J. Kent Johnston of Tallahassee.

Mrs. Tippetts is one of the most active clubwomen in the state. She is president of the Florida Audubon Society, founder and president of the St. Petersburg Audubon Society, vice-president of the Florida Legislative Council, vice-president of the Florida Federation of Women's Clubs, and chairman of finance of the Young Women's Christian Association of St. Petersburg.

Mrs. Tippetts, recognizing the need for legislation to conserve the bird life in the state of Florida, was successful in causing St. Petersburg to be established as a bird sanctuary, and laws for the protection of bird life in the vicinity have resulted from her efforts. She is also past president of the Pinellas County Federation of Women's Clubs, and for nine years was a member of the city park board in St. Petersburg.

George S. Gandy

George S. Gandy

George S. Gandy was born in Tuckahoe, N. J., October 20, 1851, son of Lewis and Jane A. (Reeves) Gandy. After completing a grammar school course, Mr. Gandy started as an office boy in the firm of Henry Disston & Sons, saw manufacturers of Philadelphia. He remained with the firm for eleven years, working up to a position of responsibility.

In 1882 Mr. Gandy became secretary and treasurer of the Frankford and Southwark Railroad company, and later was made vice-president. He also was president of the Omnibus Company General and president of the Fairmont Park Transportation Company, and vice-president of the Electric Traction Co.. He was instrumental in building a number of trolley lines, including the Holmesburg and Tacony, and Doylston and Willow Grove roads, and the Fairmont Park road. He also was active in construction work, building the People's Theatre and Textile Hall, as well as more than two hundred residences.

Mr. Gandy first came to St. Petersburg in 1903 with F. A. Davis, publisher of Philadelphia, who was the founder of St. Petersburg's electric light plant and who was then trying to finance the trolley company. Mr. Davis succeeded in interesting him in the city, which then had less than 2,000 inhabitants, and for a number of years Mr. Gandy was associated with the various Davis companies serving as president of the St. Petersburg Investment Company, St. Petersburg & Gulf Railway Company, and St. Petersburg Electric Light & Power Company. Later he resigned from all the companies because he was not satisfied with the method of financing the various projects.

In 1912, Mr. Gandy purchased property at the corner of Central avenue and Fifth street and constructed the Plaza, theatre and office buildings. Many believed that Mr. Gandy would lose heavily on the undertaking and for a year or two the Plaza was referred to as "Gandy's

White Elephant". It turned out, however, to be an excellent investment and now is worth many times what Mr. Gandy paid for it.

Mr. Gandy conceived the idea of a bridge across Old Tampa Bay, providing a short cut route between St. Petersburg and Tampa, shortly after his first visit. He realized, however, that this section of the state had not developed far enough at that time to make such a bridge a paying proposition. He bided his time and in 1915 he began making the necessary surveys. The financing of the bridge was completed early in 1923 and the construction work was rushed.

Mr. Gandy is a former commodore of the Yacht Club of Sea Side Park, New Jersey; the Yachtsmen's Club of Philadelphia, and the St. Petersburg Yacht Club. He is a member of the Hamilton Lodge F. & A. M. No. 500, Freeman Chapter No. 243, and Mary Commandery, Lu Lu Temple of the Mystic Shrine at Philadelphia, Selama Grotto, Elks Lodge No. 1224, and Rotary Club.

In 1887 Mr. Gandy was married to Miss Clara Frances Miller in Christ's Church, Philadelphia. Their children are George S., Jr., Alfred L., Mrs. Clara Frances Wilkinson, Mrs. Ruth Sarven, and Marion. George S. Gandy, Jr., is secretary and treasurer of the Bay Construction Company and director of the Gandy Bridge Company. Alfred L. Gandy is secretary and treasurer of the Gandy Bridge Company and represents the Gandy Bridge Company on the construction work.

C. A. Harvey

C. A. Harvey was born June 16, 1868, in Jessup, Ga., the son of William Harvey and Nancy (Grandham) Harvey. He received his early education in the public schools of Jessup.

As a young man he engaged in the hotel business in Thomasville, Ga., and also was the owner of a sawmill there. When the prices of lumber decreased to a considerable extent he sold his mill and decided to move to Florida. In August, 1903, he came to St. Petersburg, where he decided to settle, being impressed with the possibilities for development he saw in the city.

Shortly after coming here, Mr. Harvey

C. A. Harvey

rented a small hotel and conducted it for the winter. In the winter following he became interested in real estate and went into business with E. B. Rowland, one of the few real estate men in the city at that time. In 1905 he became associated with F. A. Freeman in real estate, and about this time purchased from Mrs. Sara Armistead the tract of land later known as Bayboro Harbor and the Rouslynn subdivision.

This land was purchased with the idea of reclaiming all the swamp land through which Salt and Booker creeks found their way to the bay. Mr. Harvey's plans provided for dredging a harbor and filling in the low lands, thereby making accessible for development a fine high stretch of ground which lay to the south. Mr. Harvey's means were limited and it was necessary for him to interest others in the project. Only a few had any faith in the proposed development, but Mr. Harvey persevered until he secured enough support to purchase the necessary land and start work on the improvements.

As a result of Mr. Harvey's vision, St. Petersburg now has a commercial harbor, and the south shore section of the city, included in his development, has become one of St. Petersburg's most attractive residential sections.

Mr. Harvey was a member of the Elks' Lodge and the Modern Woodmen of the World. He also was a member of the Methodist Church.

On June 7, 1894, Mr. Harvey was married to Miss Lucille Edmondson on the Edmondson plantation in Brooks county. Mr. and Mrs. Harvey had three children: Charles L. Harvey, Mrs. Estelle Harvey Sullivan, and Miss Ruth Harvey. Mr. Harvey died on January 18, 1914, after a long illness. Interment was made in St. Petersburg.

Charles L. Harvey is engaged in the real estate business in St. Petersburg and in the promotion of subdivisions, as well as the general brokerage business. He is also a general contractor, and the owner of the Pass-a-Grille Casino. He is general manager of the Fidelity Development Company and the Bayboro Investment Company, and owner of the Acme Tile Manufacturing Company.

Charles L. Harvey spent three years in the Military Academy and later entered the Georgia Technical Institute, where he studied electrical engineering. At the outbreak of the war he entered the aviation service and served from 1917 to 1919. Upon his return home he entered the real estate business with H. Walter Fuller and Walter P. Fuller. Later he bought the outstanding stock of the Bayboro Investment Company and took over the management of the company. He also promoted several subdivisions in St. Petersburg—the latest of these being Floral Villa Estates.

Noel A. Mitchell

Noel A. Mitchell was born in Block Island, R. I., on January 9, 1874, the son of Edward and Mary Jane (Smith) Mitchell, both of Rhode Island and both descendents of families which came to this country in the days of Roger Williams.

After attending the grammar and high schools of Block Island, Mr. Mitchell went to work for the Wheeler-Wilson Sewing

Noel A. Mitchell

Machine Company in Providence, R. I. In the evenings he took a course in a business college.

In 1892, Mr. Mitchell went into the confectionery business and originated Mitchell's Original Atlantic City Salt Water Taffy. He introduced this taffy first at Atlantic City and later at other resorts on the Atlantic seaboard. The taffy proved popular and finally sold in all parts of the country.

Mr. Mitchell first came to Florida in 1898 to put his taffy on sale in Jacksonville and Atlantic City. During the next winter he helped to manage a hotel at Eugallie, Florida. One of his experiences that winter was a fishing trip to Jupiter Inlet with Joseph Jefferson, Senator Matt Quay and Grover Cleveland, three of the most noted men of the time.

During the next few years Mr. Mitchell managed the sale of his taffy and also ran amusement parks in Savin Rock, Conn., and Lighthouse Point, Conn., visited by as many as a hundred thousand persons a day.

Mr. Mitchell was married on October 15, 1901, to Miss Adelaide B. Mitchell, daughter of Mr. and Mrs. Jesse D. Mitchell, of New London, Conn. In the fall of 1903, Mrs. Mitchell saw a display of shells at a store in Block Island which attracted her interest. The woman who operated the store told her many of the shells had been gathered at the beaches near St. Petersburg, Fla. Mrs. Mitchell decided she would like to go to St. Petersburg during the next winter. Mr. Mitchell wanted to go to Daytona. To decide, they agreed to draw straws. Mr. Mitchell won—so they went to St. Petersburg.

Mr. and Mrs. Mitchell liked St. Petersburg from the first day they saw it, and they decided to build a home and come here each winter. A short time later he purchased the lot, 100 by 200, at the corner of Second avenue and Third street north, diagonally across from Williams Park. Mr. Mitchell paid $2,000 for the property and people told him he had paid $1,000 too much. Within the next year he built three houses on the lot, one being for his own home. The Mitchell apartment building, containing eighteen apartments, was built during the summer of 1920.

Ever since coming to St. Petersburg, Mr. Mitchell has neglected no opportunity to boost St. Petersburg and to advertise its attractions. He has been an active member of the Chamber of Commerce from its beginning and served one term as president. Later he served as secretary, and while holding that office spent much of his own money in advertising the city. He helped to finance the first golf course in St. Petersburg, built at Bayboro. He paid $1,000 to bring the Benoist Airboat Line to St. Petersburg. He paid the expense of the barbecue held in Williams Park at the celebration upon the completion of the Tampa & Gulf Coast Railroad. He had moving pictures taken of the Washington's Birthday celebration in 1912, at his own expense. The pictures were shown throughout the country. For a number of years Mr. Mitchell included a picture postal card of St. Petersburg in each package of his taffy sold in northern resorts. Millions of cards were distributed in that way.

Mr. Mitchell engaged in real estate business in St. Petersburg for a number of years, advertising himself as "Mitchell, the Sand Man." In 1907, he purchased the Durant block at Fourth and Central for $15,500 and opened a real estate office. During the next year he purchased some benches which he placed in front of his office—and so the famous green benches of St. Petersburg were originated. In 1914, Mr. Mitchell sold the Durant block for about $90,000.

During the real estate boom of 1912 and 1913, Mr. Mitchell conducted operations on a large scale. As an agent for Charles R. Hall, he made the first sale in the West Central section, selling a half block facing on Central avenue to A. F. Bartlett. In 1913, Mr. Mitchell opened the Court House subdivision and offered to give a block to the county, provided the county courthouse would be erected there. During 1913 and 1914, Mr. Mitchell spent a large sum in the development of Mitchell Beach. With other developers of St. Petersburg, Mr. Mitchell suffered a severe blow when the World War started and real estate sales dwindled to almost nothing.

Mr. Mitchell was elected mayor of St. Petersburg on April 6, 1920. He served until November 15, 1921. He was a candidate for re-election to the office at the primaries held March 4, 1924.

Mr. Mitchell is a thirty-second degree Mason and a Shriner, Egypt Temple of Tampa. He is also a life member of the Elks, Lodge No. 1224, and a member of the Loyal Order of Moose, and Woodmen of the World.

Mr. and Mrs. Mitchell have one daughter, Gladys Mitchell, who now is in her second year of high school.

T. A. Chancellor

T. A. Chancellor was born in Okolona, Mississippi, December 12, 1868, the son of John Sanford and Matilda (Gilliam) Chancellor, the former a native of Virginia and the latter of Alabama. He was the third son in a family of four children.

After attending the public schools in Okolona, Mr. Chancellor entered the University of Mississippi. At the end of his freshman year he went to work as a clerk in a general store of Okolona and later became a bookkeeper in a dry goods store in the same town. In 1888 he accepted a position as clerk and bookkeeper

T. A. Chancellor

in the Jacksonville freight office of the Florida Central & Pensacola Railroad Company, now the Seaboard Air Line Railroad. After the yellow fever became epidemic in Jacksonville later in the same year, Mr. Chancellor returned to his old home in Okolona where he was re-employed by the dry goods store.

In 1894, Mr. Chancellor went to Tampa to accept a position in the Exchange National Bank of Tampa, just organized after the failure of the Gulf National Bank in 1893. In the following year he was made teller and later was promoted to the position of assistant cashier. In 1904 Mr. Chancellor came to St. Petersburg and accepted the position of cashier of the West Coast Bank, which became the First National Bank in July, 1905. Later Mr. Chancellor was promoted to the presidency of this organization. Mr. Chancellor is also a director in the Citizens American Bank & Trust Company of Tampa, director in the West Coast Title Company of St. Petersburg, and a director in the Fidelity Loan & Saving Company.

Mr. Chancellor is interested in all local organizations and has held the following offices: Chairman of the City Library and Advertising Board; chairman of the local school board; vice-president of the Y. M. C. A., and vice-president and treasurer of the Chamber of Commerce. He is also a member of the Knights of Pythias, St. Petersburg Yacht Club, St. Petersburg Country Club, and St. Petersburg Rotary Club. He is a member of the first Baptist Church where he served as chairman of the board of trustees.

On October 23, 1901, Mr. Chancellor married Mary Trice, the daughter of Colonel John Trice of Tampa. They have one daughter, Mary, now twenty years old. Mrs. Chancellor has always been active in church work and civic development and served as president of the Woman's Town Improvement Association during the period when it was doing the greatest work for St. Petersburg. She was also a member of the City Park Board.

Chas. D. Hammond

Charles D. Hammond was born March 1, 1844, in Rushford, N. Y., the son of a Methodist preacher. He was educated in the public schools and began his life's work at the age of seventeen as a telegraph operator on the Erie Railroad. He held this position until 1872, excepting for one year's enlistment in the Civil War.

In 1872 he was employed by the New York and Oswego Midland Railroad as train dispatcher in Oswego, N. Y., and two years later was employed in the same capacity on the Delaware & Hudson Railroad, in Troy, N. Y. After one year's service he was appointed division superintendent and in 1886 he was appointed general superintendent, a position he held until his retirement in 1904.

Immediately after his retirement Mr. Hammond came to Florida for rest and recuperation. By accident he settled in St. Petersburg. Upon his arrival he bought a ten acre grove from T. F. McCall, just outside the city limits, and eight years later he sold this tract of land to C. M. Roser and it became part of the present Roser Park.

Charles D. Hammond

In 1913, Mr. Hammond was nominated for commissioner of public works when the three commissioner form of government was adopted in St. Petersburg. He served three years, when the form of government was again changed.

During Mr. Hammond's administration many improvements were accomplished in the city. The municipal gas plant was erected, twenty miles of brick pavement were laid, and West Central avenue from Ninth street to Davista—now Pasadena —was opened and paved. The first work of importance in connection with Bayboro harbor was also done at this time, the harbor being dredged to 10 feet of water and 300 feet of concrete dock constructed.

Mr. Hammond was a member and first master of the American Railway Guild. He is a Master Mason, a Royal Arch Mason, Knight Templar and Shriner.

On January 29, 1866, Mr. Hammond was married to Miss Eleonora Babcock in Friendship, N. Y. They had been married nearly fifty-seven years at the time of her death, which occurred Nov. 12, 1922. He is at present living a retired life in St. Petersburg.

S. D. Harris

Samuel David Harris was born in Sumter County, Fla., April 6, 1866, the son of Thomas H. and Permelia (Griffin) Harris. When he was very young the family moved to Pinellas Peninsula and settled on a farm near Clearwater; consequently, Mr. Harris has the distinction of being one of the oldest residents of this part of the state. He was educated in the common schools of this county, and when a young man went to sea.

In 1884, at twenty-eight years of age, he gave up the seaman's life and settled on the peninsula, becoming interested in the culture of citrus fruit. Later he owned and managed a number of groves. On November 9, 1887, at Benton, Columbia County, Florida, Mr. Harris was married to Miss Emma Cane, whose family was among the pioneers of North Florida. They had three sons. The first died in infancy. The two living are John D. and S. Henry Harris, lawyers in St. Petersburg.

In order to give his two sons better school advantages and also for business reasons, Mr. Harris moved to St. Petersburg during the summer of 1905 and established a general merchandise and feed store. Shortly afterwards he entered the undertaking business, in which he was engaged for thirteen years. Since then he has bought and sold real estate with success.

Mr. Harris, who belongs to the Democratic party, was elected to the State Legislature from this county in 1916 and served during the sessions of 1917, 1919 and 1921. As a county division advocate, he took a leading part in the movement to separate Pinellas Peninsula from Hillsborough County. Always actively interested in the affairs of St. Petersburg, he served on the board of governors of the Chamber of Commerce for several years and was elected president in 1911. While holding this office he was one of a committee of three to represent the city of St. Petersburg before the Board of Engineers in Washington, D. C. This committee was successful in securing the gov-

S. D. Harris

ernment aid which made Bayboro Harbor a possibility. Mr. Harris later served one term as vice-president of the Chamber of Commerce.

Mr. Harris served for several years on the board of trustees for the local schools and also on the City Hospital Board. He was chairman of these bodies during the terms of his membership. Mr. Harris is now president of the Board of Directors of the Young Men's Christian Association and has held the position from its beginning and, with others, was instrumental in making this organization possible for St. Petersburg.

Perhaps Mr. Harris has been most successful in the field of Christian education, having been superintendent of Sunday schools in the Methodist Church for many years. He also has performed good service for the city and state in working for legislation which made possible the present high standard of the public school system and the state institutions of higher learning. Mrs. Harris, who also served for many years as a Sunday School teacher, is recognized as being one of the most successful workers with young people in the state.

Mr. Harris is a Mason and is also a member of the I. O. O. F., Knights of Pythias, Woodmen of the World, and the St. Petersburg Country Club.

H. Walter Fuller

H. Walter Fuller was born in Atlanta in 1868, being one of four children. His father, Henry A. Fuller, was captain of cavalry in the Confederate Army for four years and as a result of the war the family lost a plantation of some twenty thousand acres in Northwestern Georgia and moved to Atlanta, where H. Walter Fuller's father, Henry A. Fuller, engaged in the wholesale mercantile business.

H. Walter Fuller, after having been an employee for two years in an Atlanta bank, at the age of eighteen, came to Tampa, Florida, in search of health and a career. He soon established a commission house business in citrus fruits, shipping at first to his father in Atlanta and later to Mobile, New Orleans and other points. He established a steamship line from Tampa to Mobile and New Orleans, with the steamship Cumberland, this line being eventually forced to discontinue because of railway competition. He later moved to Bradentown, while a cousin, W. R. Fuller, remained in Tampa, and his brother, C. P. Fuller, established the town of Ellenton on the Manatee River, while still a third brother moved to Milwaukee to eventually become head of the First National Bank and Trust Company of Milwaukee, with assets of over $50,000,000.

Bradentown consisted of a settlement of possibly twenty houses when Mr. Fuller moved there, which he soon incorporated into a village and later represented Manatee county, of which Bradentown was the county seat, first as representative and then as senator in the state legislature. Notable bills which he passed, which are still on the statute books, include the bill regulating net fishing and one under which drainage districts are created and established.

Mr. Fuller's business interests while at Bradentown included among other things truck farming, citrus grove development,

H. Walter Fuller

contracting, orange packing, mercantile business and real estate. In 1906 he bought a schooner which had been wrecked, converted it into a power boat and established a boat line on Tampa Bay, which eventually became the Favorite Line of steamers, owning five boats, including the Favorite and Pokanoket, which are now a part of the Wilson Line.

In 1907 the panic stopped all development and business in Bradentown and finding himself with forty or fifty pairs of mules, he became a successful bidder for the first hard roads in Pinellas county and moved to St. Petersburg, where he later became identified with the street car line and the St. Petersburg Investment Company. Under his management the car line grew from seven to twenty-three miles of trackage; the power plant was moved from the present site of the Yacht Club to its present location near Sixteenth street, which plant he built. In 1909 he commenced operations which in 1913 resulted in the opening of Central avenue from Ninth street to Boca Ceiga Bay.

Following the failure of the St. Petersburg Investment Company in 1918 because of war conditions he engaged in a general real estate business in Philadelphia and St. Petersburg. In the summer of 1922 he took over the development of Laurel Park in Hendersonville, N. C., which has since grown to a point which requires his entire time during the twelve months of the year.

Arthur L. Johnson

Arthur L. Johnson was born in Camden, N. J., April 29, 1875, the son of a Baptist minister, and was educated in the public schools of Norwich, N. J., later receiving a thorough mercantile training in the Loeser Clothing Company of Brooklyn, N. Y.

After leaving Colgate University, where he was a student, he came to St. Petersburg in November, 1907, and with his training and a limited capital, opened a small clothing store of 500 square foot floor space in the Wood block near Fourth street. Business grew so rapidly that today Mr. Johnson is the proprietor of two up-to-date clothing stores in the city. During the summer of 1923 he moved from his old stand in the Lewis block to 428 Central avenue, and has retained his uptown store at 842 Central avenue.

Mr. Johnson has been very active in war work and civic affairs in St. Petersburg. He acted as chairman of the War Camp Community Service fund during the World War, was a member of the Liberty Loan committee and chairman of the county publicity committee. He was also one of the organizers of the local Y. M. C. A. and the first president of its board of trustees. Mr. Johnson is also deeply interested in the Boy Scouts and has served several terms as a member of the Library and Advertising Board. He is a charter member of the St. Petersburg Yacht Club and holds the office of vice-commodore.

As chairman of the advertising committee of the Board of Trade, Mr. Johnson did some of his most effective work for St. Petersburg, originating the plan for the Festival of the States, an annual event which has become one of the greatest features of St. Petersburg's entertainment program for tourists. He has also

Arthur L. Johnson

been at the head of the "Summer Boosters" work for St. Petersburg. He is a member of the Congregational Church, having served as trustee for over twelve years.

In July, 1901, Mr. Johnson married Jessie Nash, the daughter of Henry and Alice Nash, of Pennsylvania. They have one son, Arthur Nash Johnson.

Lew B. Brown

Llewellyn Buford Brown was born in Madison, Ark., June 13, 1861, the oldest child and only son of George L. and Amelia L. (Young) Brown, the former a native of Tennessee, and the latter of Bardstown, Ky. In 1875, following the death of the father, the mother returned with her family to Louisville, Ky., where Lew Brown secured work as a printer and later as reporter on the Louisville Courier-Journal, then edited by Col. Henry Watterson. He served in nearly every deparment of that newspaper and the Evening Times.

In 1895 Mr. Brown left Louisville to buy a newspaper plant at Taylorsville, Ky., because of poor health. While there he studied law and was granted a license to practice by the Supreme Court, later serving as police judge and county and city attorney. In 1905 Mr. Brown sold out his newspaper in Taylorsville, abandoned the practice of law, and went to Harrodsburg, Ky., where he purchased the Harrodsburg Democrat.

On December 15, 1908, Mr. Brown purchased the St. Petersburg Evening Independent, then owned by Willis B. Powell. He operated both the Independent and the Harrodsburg Democrat for two years and then sold out his interests in Harrodsburg in order to devote all his time to his work in St. Petersburg.

Since coming to St. Petersburg, Mr. Brown has been actively identified with every movement for the upbuilding of St. Petersburg. Of all his achievements, however, none is more important than his work in making St. Petersburg known throughout the world as the "Sunshine City." Mr. Brown originated the nickname, and he made the nickname mean something by promising to distribute the entire circulation of the Independent free to everybody every day the sun did not shine. This offer was made effective September 1, 1910. From that date to January 1, 1924, the Independent was given away free seventy-one times. The Independent is the only newspaper in the world to make such an offer.

Although Mr. Brown would never accept a city office in St. Petersburg he has taken a deep interest in the city government. He served as chairman of the Charter Board which drafted the new charter approved by the voters on August 14, 1923.

During the World War Mr. Brown organized, financed and equipped four companies of Pinellas County Guards and commanded them with the rank of major conferred upon him by the governor by authority of the Florida Legislature.

Mr. Brown has served as president of the Board of Trade, commodore of the St. Petersburg Yacht Club, president of the Art Club, president of the Echo Club, and chairman of the City Library and Advertising Board. He is affiliated with

Lew B. Brown

the Masonic Order, Independent Order of Odd Fellows, Knights of Pythias, Red Men, and Elks, and is a member of the Baptist Church. He was instrumental in establishing the first City Hospital in St. Petersburg and originated and made good the plan for establishing the Florida Masonic Home for widows and orphans in St. Petersburg.

Mr. Brown's mother (Mrs. A. L. Cummings) is still living in St. Petersburg, 81 years of age. In 1885 Mr. Brown was married to Emma Struby who died, the mother of three children, the only one of whom now living being the son, Llewellyn Chauncey Brown. In 1898, Mr. Brown married Anna Struby and they have one daughter, Louise—now Mrs. W. Orville Ray.

L. C. Brown, now Mr. Brown's business associate and partner, was born in Louisville in 1886. After being graduated from the public schools he attended the Kentucky College at Lexington. Upon leaving college, he was for two years in business in Chicago and another two years in New York City. He became associated with his father in the newspaper business in 1912. He served as president of the Chamber of Commerce in 1921. He is a life member of the Elks Lodge.

Charles R. Hall

Charles R. Hall was born in Detroit, Mich., September 22, 1869, the son of Charles Edward and Henrietta A. (Small) Hall, the former of Detroit and the latter of Ossipee, N. H. His father died in 1872 and in 1874 Mrs. Hall moved to Philadelphia, where Charles R. Hall attended public school from the age of seven to eleven.

In 1880, Mr. Hall left school and went to work in Turner's Five and Ten-Cent Store, at Eighth and Vine streets, where he remained for one year, going to Cook Brothers & Company, Gents' Furnishings, at Eighth and Arch streets, where he was cash boy and stock boy. In 1883 he left this company to go with D. A. Hunter & Bros., wholesale millinery, at 722 Arch street. He worked there as errand boy until he was 17 years old. During the last year or so of his employment, the firm gave him an opportunity to gain his first experience in selling, taking orders from local millinery houses.

Leaving the millinery company, Mr. Hall became connected with the firm of Wm. W. Biddle & Co. He started in as stock boy, but within a few years was sent out on the road as traveling salesman. Gradually he worked his way up and at the age of thirty-eight he had become a junior member of the firm. In 1908, he severed his connections with the firm and became actively engaged in the development of New Jersey seashore property.

Mr. Hall was persuaded to come to St. Petersburg in 1909 by F. A. Davis, publisher, of Philadelphia, who was interested in many of St. Petersburg's companies. After a thorough investigation of St. Petersburg and its future possibilities, Mr. Hall in 1912 made an investment in a number of companies which at that time was considered quite heavy. In this same year West Central avenue boulevard was being agitated by H. Walter Fuller and his associates and Mr. Fuller was anxious

Charles R. Hall

that Mr. Hall should sever his connection with the New Jersey shore enterprises and become an active party in the development.

It was through Mr. Fuller that Mr. Hall made his first investment of 80 acres at Twenty-fifth street and Central avenue, purchasing the tract at $200 an acre. Within forty-eight hours after the purchase contract had been signed, Mr. Hall opened an active campaign with solid page ads in both local newspapers exploiting the West Central section. Less than a year later Mr. Hall purchased the adjoining eighty acres, extending from Twenty-eighth to Thirty-first street on Central. The land was bought from P. J. McDevitt as $500 an acre. Mr. Hall then began to exploit the two tracts as one property, and prepared a plat designating them as Hall's subdivisions Nos. 1 and 2. The first homes ever built on the bay-to-bay boulevard were the homes at Twenty-eighth and Central and Twenty-eighth and First avenue north. The homes were considered at that time as entirely too expensive for property so far from the center of the city. The lots sold rapidly and shortly afterward Hall's Central avenue subdivision Nos. 2, 3 and 4 were opened farther west on Central.

As early as 1912, after having studied the various locations about St. Petersburg quite thoroughly, Mr. Hall and his associates decided that eventually one of the most beautiful sections of Pinellas county would be Point Pinellas. Steps were taken to acquire this holding, but other developers had realized the possible future values of the property and it became very difficult to obtain all that was needed. Roy S. Hanna, F. A. Wood, Ed. T. Lewis and a number of other owners absolutely refused to sell. However, a quiet campaign of buying was inaugurated and by 1917 nearly 2,000 acres of the most desirable tracts of land had been slowly acquired and placed under one management. These tracts, together with other purchases made since that time, now are being developed by the Victory Land Company and are known as Lakewood Estates, embracing over 2,500 acres of beautiful rolling lands, including immense tracts of virgin pine timber and jungle lands.

Mr. Hall was married on September 11, 1897, to Miss Emma May Blanchette in the Presbyterian Church at Conshohocken, Pa. They have four sons and one daughter: E. Richard Hall, engaged locally in the insurance business; Charles Marvin Hall, owner of the National Show Gardens, St. Petersburg; Mildred Muriel Hall, who three years ago married C. Calvert Beall, commercial artist of New York; John K. Hall and Franklin Dudley Hall, both students in the local high school.

Al. F. Lang

Albert Fielding Lang was born in Pittsburgh, Pa., on November 16, 1870, the son of James Taylor and Harriett S. (Becket) Lang, both of Pittsburgh. He attended the public schools until fourteen years old, when he started working for the Brace Brothers Laundry, where he remained for eleven years.

In 1895, Mr. Lang founded the Lincoln Laundry, which he owned and managed

Al. F. Lang

for fourteen years, building up one of the largest laundry businesses in Pittsburgh. Ill health made it necessary for him to sell out in 1909, and in the fall of the next year he came to Florida. He had no intention originally of coming to St. Petersburg, intending to spend the winter at Fort Myers. After remaining there a few days, he made up his mind to go over to the East Coast. On the return trip, while in Tampa, he remembered how some acquaintances had boosted St. Petersburg and he decided to see the city before leaving this section of the state. He bought round trip tickets for himself and Mrs. Lang, and came across the bay. The return tickets to Tampa were never used. Both Mr. and Mrs. Lang liked St. Petersburg as soon as they saw it and within four days they had purchased a home on Beach drive. They have lived here ever since.

During the next few years, Mr. Lang took a leading part in bringing big league baseball teams to St. Petersburg for their spring training. He had always been an ardent baseball fan and his wide acquaintance with the owners and managers of major league clubs made it possible for him to work effectively. Through his efforts, the Philadelphia Nationals came here in the spring of 1915. Upon returning north, the Phillies won fourteen out of the first fifteen games played and were never headed throughout the season. St. Petersburg received a large part of the credit for this remarkable record because of the fine weather which the Phillies had while training.

Aside from his work in bringing major league clubs to St. Petersburg, Mr. Lang has been active in promoting the game in the city and state. During the past two years he has served as president of the Florida State League.

In 1914, Mr. Lang was elected mayor of St. Petersburg, and in 1916 he was re-elected for another two-year term. While he was mayor, St. Petersburg emerged from the village class and became a full-fledged city, and Mr. Lang helped materially in this change. Through his efforts, push carts and peanut wagons were barred from Central avenue and the merchants were compelled to take their wares off the sidewalks. He also forced through an ordinance prohibiting overhanging signs, and "Sign Pulling Down Day" was one of the outstanding events of his administration. Mr. Lang also was responsible for an ordinance standardizing the benches in shape and size and establishing green as the only color the benches could be painted.

Mr. Lang was one of the founders and most loyal supporters of the St. Petersburg County Club and was elected as its first president. He was re-elected in 1923.

Mr. Lang was president of the West Coast Telephone Company for two years prior to its purchase by the Peninsular Telephone Company. He is a thirty-second-degree Mason and a Shriner, and a member of the St. Petersburg Rotary Club, the St. Petersburg Yacht Club, and the St. Petersburg Country Club. He has been a member of the Chamber of Commerce ever since coming to the city.

Mrs. Lang, before her marriage, was Miss Katherine Marie Fagen, daughter of John Edward and Clara (Hatch)

Fagen, of Philadelphia. She is a member of the Woman's Club and the Daughters of the American Colonists.

A. F. Thomasson

A. F. Thomasson was born in Union City, Tenn., on April 24, 1869, the son of George F. and Alice (Wilson) Thomasson, the former of Lewisburg, Tenn., and the latter of Union City. Mr. Thomasson was educated in the grammar schools and high school of Union City and Eastman's Business College in Nashville, Tenn.

Upon leaving school, Mr. Thomasson worked in the banks of Union City for several years. He was assistant cashier in the First National Bank of that city at the time that F. O. Watts, now president of the First National Bank of St. Louis, was cashier.

In 1898, Mr. Thomasson left Union City to reorganize a bank in Scranton, Miss. He remained there a year and then was asked to become assistant cashier in the First National Bank of Nashville, Tenn., of which Mr. Watts was then cashier. He left the Nashville bank in 1901 to take charge of the First National Bank of Hattiesburg, Miss., as cashier. He remained there for seven years, becoming vice-president. While in Hattiesburg he was prominent in the organization and construction of the street railway and gas plant, and was elected president of the Four States Immigration League, with headquarters in New Orleans.

In 1909, after spending a year in the West, Mr. Thomasson came to St. Petersburg at the solicitation of F. A. Wood, then president of the Central National Bank, and became cashier of that institution. At that time the bank's capital stock was $25,000 and the deposits amounted to $260,000. On January 1, 1924, the bank's deposits totaled $5,019,117 and its capital stock was $200,000.

Mr. Thomasson was elected vice-president of the bank on January 14, 1913, and on January 12, 1915, he was elected president to succeed F. A. Wood, who retired from active management.

In addition to his work at the bank, Mr. Thomasson has taken an active part in many projects for the development of St. Petersburg. He was instrumental in building the St. Petersburg Country Club and is now treasurer of the St. Petersburg Golf Development Company. He is treasurer of the Pass-a-Grille Bridge Company and a director in the West Coast Title Company, of which he formerly was president.

Mr. Thomasson is a member of the St. Petersburg Rotary Club, the St. Petersburg Yacht Club, St. Petersburg Country Club, and the Art Club. He is a Mason and Shriner and a member of the Elks and Knights of Pythias. He is also a trustee of the First Christian Church.

Mr. Thomasson was elected as a member of the city commission on April 4, 1916, and served until 1923, when he resigned. He served as chairman of the School Board from 1914 to 1922. He has been a contributing member of the Chamber of Commerce since coming to St. Petersburg. During the war he was Pinellas County chairman in the Liberty loan drives.

On February 17, 1892, Mr. Thomasson was married to Miss Marguerite Alice Posey, daughter of W. A. and Marguerite Posey, of Aberdeen, Miss. The marriage ceremony was performed in Chattanooga, Tenn. Mrs. Thomasson is a talented musician. She received her musical education at the Ward-Belmont Seminary, in Nashville, Tenn., the Boston Conservatory of Music in Boston, Mass., and studied for some time under Madame Murio Calli, in New York City. Mrs. Thomasson served one term as president of the Careno Club.

Mr. and Mrs. Thomasson have five children, one daughter and four sons: Mrs. Helen T. Dann, Floyd A., assistant cashier in the Central National Bank; Ferdinand W., in the credit department of the bank; Alfred P., now attending Lafayette College, in Easton, Pa., and William F., now attending school in St. Petersburg. Floyd A. Thomasson during the war was a first sergeant in the Coast Artillery Corps and served a year in France.

Dr. H. A. Murphy

Dr. H. A. Murphy was born in Wabash County, Indiana, on April 9, 1845. He was attending the schools of Wabash County at the outbreak of the Civil War, and in 1862, at the age of seventeen, he joined Company I, Thirty-fifth Regiment, Indiana Infantry, and served for three years.

After the war ended, Dr. Murphy returned to his studies, receiving his medical education in the University of Cincinnati and the Louisville Medical College. In 1869, after completing his medical course, he was married to Miss Emma E. Kingsbury, and afterwards he practiced medicine in Sumner, Lawrence County, Illinois, until 1905, when his wife's poor health made it necessary for the family to go to a milder climate. Mrs. Murphy became better for a time, but died on March 31, 1909.

Upon coming to St. Petersburg, Dr. Murphy took an active interest in all city affairs until the time of his death. In 1905 he joined with C. A. Harvey in forming the Bayboro Investment Company, and he was identified with the company for a number of years in its work of reclaiming the lands around Bayboro Harbor. On March 3, 1908, he was elected mayor of St. Petersburg as the candidate of the Citizens Protective League. He received 158 votes and A. P. Avery 131.

Dr. H. A. Murphy

During his administration, many civic improvements were gotten under way.

Dr. Murphy was one of the first members of the hospital board for the hospital established by Dr. J. P. Peabody and A. P. Avery. He was a member of the St. Petersburg Land & Loan Company and a director of the Central National Bank. He also was actively connected with the St. Petersburg Post of the G. A. R. He retired in 1912 and died on December 7, 1920.

Dr. and Mrs. Murphy had five children: Mrs. Carrie L. Cooper, of St. Petersburg; Dr. Hugh K. Murphy, Mulberry, Fla.; Milton F. Murphy, Spokane, Wash.; Mrs. Mary G. Sutton, Mulberry, Fla., and Dr. Ralph D. Murphy, of St. Petersburg.

Dr. Ralph D. Murphy was born in Sumner, Ill., on August 16, 1887. He received his early education in the public schools of Sumner and later entered Winona Academy at Winona Lake, Ind., from which he was graduated in 1907. In the next fall he entered the University of Colorado, where he studied for two years, and then entered the University of

Illinois, from which he was graduated in 1912 with the degree of Doctor of Medicine. In preparing himself further for his profession, Dr. Murphy spent two years in special work in the University Hospital, Chicago, and in 1914 came to St. Petersburg, establishing himself in practice.

During the World War Dr. Murphy was commissioned in the Army Medical Corps and served for two years in various military camps throughout the country. After his discharge he returned to St. Petersburg and established himself in offices in the First National Bank building.

Dr. Murphy is a member of the Pinellas County Medical Society, in which organization he served as secretary in 1919, vice-president in 1921, and president in 1922. He also belongs to the Florida State Medical Society, the American Medical Association, and the Alpha Kappa Kappa medical fraternity. He is a member of the St. Petersburg Yacht Club, the St. Petersburg Country Club, the Chamber of Commerce, and the Rotary International.

On October 14, 1916, Dr. Murphy was married to Hazel Elise Rowland by the Rev. Dr. George Houghton in the "Little Church Around the Corner" in New York City. Mrs. Murphy is a graduate of the University of Chicago, and was born in Detroit, Mich. She is a granddaughter of John Constantine Williams, the founder of St. Petersburg.

W. F. Smith

Wilbur F. Smith was born in Battle Ground, Ind., on August 10, 1867, the son of George M. and Sarah A. (Snyder) Smith, both natives of Ohio. The families of both the father and the mother had moved to Indiana when the children were very young and were among the pioneers of the state.

After attending the public schools of Battle Ground, Mr. Smith learned the painter's trade, while yet a boy, and later went into business for himself as a painting contractor. In 1899 he gave up this kind of work and established a nursery near Lafayette, making a specialty of growing fruit trees, shade trees and ornamentals and formed a great love for this kind of work.

W. F. Smith

On December 31, 1893, Mr. Smith was married to Miss Rozella B. Ridgeway, daughter of Lorenzo D. and Nancy Jane (Ransdall) Ridgeway. Late in 1908, the ill health of their son, Sherman, made it necessary for them to seek a milder climate and they came to St. Petersburg, arriving here January 1, 1909. The climate had a beneficial effect upon the son and he regained his health.

Upon coming here, Mr. Smith intended to establish a nursery but he was advised against it and instead went back to his old work. He bought the business of the West Coast Decorating Company, owned by R. H. Sumner, and changed the name to the W. F. Smith Paint & Wall Paper Store. This store has been expanded until it now is one of the largest retail paint establishments in the state and carries one of the largest stocks of paints south of Atlanta. As a side line, Mr. Smith has been engaged in the buying and selling of real estate, handling some of the largest deals made in the city, particularly in business properties.

Mr. Smith served as a member of the city commission for four years, from 1917 to 1921, and was chairman for the last year. In 1921, on account of his knowledge and love for nursery work, he was appointed chairman of the City Park Board and is now serving on his fourth year. During his term of service on the Park Board the band shell was built in Williams Park, facilities were provided for the various pleasure clubs in Williams Park, water front, and at Mirror Lake, and many improvements were made in all the parks throughout the city. Largely as a result of Mr. Smith's insistence, Crescent Lake Park was acquired by the city, fifty-six acres being purchased from C. Perry Snell for $30,000. At the present time this land is easily worth $150,000. Plans are now being perfected to drain and develop this park and to make it one of the most beautiful in the South, the soil being particularly adapted for the growing of semi-tropical plants. A city nursery, which is under Mr. Smith's personal supervision, has been established at the park and it now has plants and palms valued at more than $20,000. All the parks in the city will be planted and beautified from this nursery.

Mr. Smith is a Mason and Shriner and is a member of the Knights of Pythias, Elks, St. Petersburg Yacht Club, and Rotary Club. He has been a contributing member of the Chamber of Commerce ever since coming here. He is a member of the First Avenue Methodist Church.

Mr. and Mrs. Smith have two children, a son and a daughter. Sherman K. Smith is a musical manager in New York City. Vora M. Smith is attending Martha Washington Seminary in Washington, D. C.

E. B. Willson

Edward B. Willson was born in Maryland August 20, 1874, the son of Richard B. Willson and Ella A. McAdam Willson. He was the eldest of his parents' nine children, and was educated in the public schools until the age of seventeen, when he left home to make his own way in the world.

Mr. Willson went to New York City, where he secured a position in the packing department of E. J. Denney—now John Wanamaker's establishment. Later, he entered the employ of the H. B. Claflin

E. B. Willson

Company, where he was given the position of stock boy at a salary of $150 a year. He served here until 1901, when he was given the opportunity to act as traveling salesman for the company. For eight years thereafter he remained on the road.

During his travels Mr. Willson became convinced that splendid opportunities awaited the business man in the South, and in 1909 he and a fellow employe, L. B. Irwin, came to Florida to find a location for a store. The men became connected with the business of Miss Lena Chase and Miss Beulah Chase, who were conducting a small dry-goods store in St. Petersburg, and the four formed what was known as the Willson-Chase Company. Miss Beulah C. Chase was president of the new company, Mr. Irwin was vice-president, Miss Lena Chase was secretary, and Mr. Willson was treasurer and general manager.

The business continued to grow under the able direction of this combination of business people, and Mr. Willson's experience in the dry-goods line was of inestimable value to him. The new store grew from an establishment employing five clerks—including three of the proprietors—to a store employing sixteen clerks, before it was enlarged. Constant additions were necessary, until in 1914 a handsome, modern structure of five stories was erected, containing 22,000 feet of floor space. And in the summer of 1922 further extensive alterations were made to take care of the increasing trade.

Besides his interests in the Willson-Chase Company, Mr. Willson is a director in the First National Bank, and is a member of the Woodmen of the World, the Royal Arcanum, the Knights of Columbus, the Elks, the St. Petersburg Yacht Club and the St. Petersburg Country Club. He is a member of Rotary International.

In 1899, Mr. Willson was married to Ida Newcomb, of Maryland. The couple have had six children, four of whom are now living.

Paul R. Boardman

Paul R. Boardman was born in Pittsburgh, Pa., January 28, 1882, son of James L. and Rebecca J. (Hall) Boardman, both natives of Pennsylvania. Both parents are now living in St. Petersburg. He was the seventh child of a family of eight, and after receiving a public school education he became an employee of the Carnegie Steel Company.

Mr. Boardman later was employed by the American Sheet Steel Company, until 1903, when he became associated with the real estate firm of Gault & Giffen, which firm was later taken over by the Land Trust Company of Pittsburgh, Mr. Boardman remaining as a salesman. Subsequently, he became auditor of the real estate and title departments of the Land Trust Company, and during the same period became secretary and treasurer of the Bessemer Securities Company, also of the Federal Realty Company, both of Pittsburgh. He was also associated with the Penn Real Estate and Development Company.

In 1908 the firm of Gault & Giffen was reorganized, with Mr. Boardman in complete charge of all accounting and as auditor. In 1909, Gault & Giffen took over the general agency of the Florida Association's holdings, located in Pinellas county, Florida. Mr. Boardman became a salesman, and after selling a large amount of acreage for the company, decided to locate in Florida.

In 1910 he came to St. Petersburg and established the real estate business known as Boardman & Getts. In 1916 he established the automobile business known as Boardman & Vogel, which business was later entered by George A. McCrea and incorporated as Boardman, Vogel & McCrea, with Mr. Boardman as president.

After serving for several years on the board of governors of the St. Petersburg Chamber of Commerce, Mr. Boardman was elected and served as president of that organization for the year 1917. In 1918 he was elected president of the Pinellas County Board of Trade and served until he entered the government service.

Mr. Boardman was appointed vice-chairman in Pinellas county in the war savings campaign, and had complete charge of the organization of the county during this campaign. In July, 1918, he disposed of his interest in the Boardman,

Vogel & McCrea Company to Mr. McCrea and went to Washington.

Mr. Boardman was appointed by the United States Shipping Board Emergency Fleet Corporation as manager of the town of Harriman, Pa., which was being constructed by the government in connection with the Bristol Shipyards on the Delaware River. Here he had complete charge of the housing facilities for about 10,000 people, as well as the operation of all municipal departments. He continued this work after the armistice was signed and until the fall of 1921. He handled millions of dollars of government money during this period.

Mr. Boardman maintained his home in St. Petersburg in the meanwhile, and when his work at Harriman was finished returned to this city and embarked in the real estate and insurance business. After being in business a year for himself, he organized the Boardman-Frazee Realty Company, Inc., of which he is president. This corporation is the general selling agent of the Shore Acres development—a section fronting Tampa Bay north of St. Petersburg, on the Gandy Bridge boulevard, being one of the largest developments in the St. Petersburg district.

Mr. Boardman also organized the Shore Acres Construction Company, Inc., of which he is president. This company is engaged in the building of homes at Shore Acres.

In 1922 Mr. Boardman was appointed city commissioner to fill the unexpired term of A. F. Thomasson, resigned, and in April, 1923, was elected to serve the regular two-year term.

In April, 1905, Mr. Boardman was married to Ada A. Kemble, of Pittsburgh, and they have two children, Paul K. and Helen Ada.

He is a member of St. Petersburg Lodge No. 1224, B. P. O. E.; the St. Petersburg Yacht Club, the St. Petersburg Tarpon Club, and a director of the St. Petersburg Motor Club.

W. McKee Kelley

W. McKee Kelley was born in New Castle, Pa., in 1878, the son of Samuel R. and Mary M. (McCracken) Kelley, and received his early education in the city of his birth.

W. McKee Kelley

Prior to coming to Florida, Mr. Kelley received training in the real estate business in some of the largest real estate firms in Pittsburgh, Pa. He was connected with the Real Estate Trust Company of Pittsburgh for more than four years, and with the Samuel W. Black Company for two years. He had also been connected with the Samuel Kelley Company, the W. L. Scott Company and the firm of A. B. Hay, Jr., and had conducted a real estate firm under the name of Frazer & Kelley and the W. McKee Kelley Company for four and one-half years.

Mr. Kelley came to St. Petersburg in 1910, having heard of the wonderful climate of the city and the opportunities for investing in and selling real estate in the vicinity. He organized the Sunshine City Land Company, of which he is now manager and vice-president, and the W. McKee Kelley Real Estate Company, which conducts a real estate, rental, loan and insurance business, and has built up one of the largest strictly brokerage businesses in St. Petersburg.

Mr. Kelley is also the president of the Fourth Street Heights Company, Inc., and president of the Bay View Heights Company, Inc.

He is a member of the Masonic lodge, the Selama Grotto and the St. Petersburg Country Club. He is a member of the First Avenue M. E. Church.

Mr. Kelley has served as a director of the Chamber of Commerce, and on various civic committees.

On December 24, 1903, he married Annie Lee Dishman at Pineville, Kentucky. Mrs. Kelley is a graduate of Stanford University, and an accomplished musician. They have one son, William McKee Kelley, Jr.

Soren Lund

Soren Lund was born in Rander, Denmark, on April 1, 1871, the son of Soren and Johanna Lund, both natives of Denmark. After going to the school in Rander for a few years, Soren Lund emigrated to America, at the age of fourteen. He arrived in New York with only $13 to his name, and no friends or relatives upon whom he could call for assistance.

Within a short time, however, he secured work in a hotel, and he has been engaged in the hotel business almost ever since, having served in all capacities from bell boy up to manager and owner. His long and varied experiences include two trips around the world as cabin boy on schooners.

Mr. Lund bought his first hotel in 1902. It was The Oaks, in Daytona, Fla. During the next eight years he purchased the following hotels in the order named: The New Grand House, Stamford-in-the-Catskills, New York; the Sunset Park Inn, North Coneway, N. H.; the Hotel Clinton, East Orange, N. J., and the Hotel Munnatawket, Fishers Island, N. Y.

During the summer of 1910, Mr. Lund was advised by his New York broker that the Huntington Hotel in St. Petersburg was for sale. He had wanted for some time to buy a hotel here, and when he learned of the chance, he came at once. He arrived on the morning boat from Tampa. He looked at the hotel, looked at the city, and then looked at his bank account. He found everything satisfactory, and within two hours had arranged to buy the hotel, starting back North again on the noon boat.

Mr. Lund owned the Huntington until May, 1920, when he sold it to J. Lee Barnes. He took a six months' rest and then started working on the plans for St. Petersburg's first million-dollar hotel. The plans were completed and the financing arranged during the winter of 1922-23, and in the spring of 1923 construction work was started. The hotel—the Soreno—was completed and open to its guests by January 1, 1924, one of the most beautiful hotels in the entire Southland. It was filled to capacity by February 1, 1924.

Mr. Lund is a Mason and a member of the Kiwanis Club. He also is a member of the Congregational Church.

On March 27, 1898, Mr. Lund was married to Miss Bertha Mickse, in Poughkeepsie, N. Y. They have one child, Soreno Lund, Jr., born September 18, 1899. He is joint owner and director of the Soreno Hotel.

John P. Lynch

John P. Lynch was born in New York City, January 23, 1879, the son of John and Harriet (Blackwell) Lynch, the former a native of Ireland and the latter of England. The parents came to this country shortly after their marriage in Eng-

John P. Lynch

land. They had six children, of whom only John Lynch and his sister, Mrs. Emily Knoener, of St. Petersburg, are now living.

Mr. Lynch attended the primary schools of Toms River, N. J., and the high school at East Orange, and then was for nine years engaged in business at Hamburg, N. J. Recognizing the desirability of further educational training, Mr. Lynch in 1904 entered Lehigh University, and in 1908 he was graduated with the degree of chemical engineer.

Upon leaving school he became assistant superintendent in the crucible steel department of the Bethlehem Steel Company. He remained there about nine months and then took charge of the Hamburg & McAfee plants of the New Jersey Lime Company. Foreseeing the possibilities for development in Florida, Mr. Lynch came here in 1910, first locating at Manatee. After staying a short time in Manatee, Mr. Lynch came to St. Petersburg, believing that this city offered better opportunities. He established himself in business as a real estate operator and loan broker, as well as a dealer in insurance. He has built up an important business in this line and also has done much building.

Mr. Lynch took a leading part in the prohibition campaign in St. Petersburg, being chairman of the city and county dry forces. He has been a contributing member of the Chamber of Commerce for many years and served as a member of the board of governors in 1915 and 1916. He has been a member of the Presbyterian Church since he was fourteen years old. He served for four years as superintendent of the Sunday school and is now an elder. In 1920 he was elected a county commissioner from District No. 2 and is now serving his second term.

On June 23, 1908, Mr. Lynch was married to Mary Ryerson Linn, in Hamburg, N. J. They have four children, John P., Jr., 15; Elizabeth K., 14; Mary Linn, 10, and Harriet Theodora, 2. The three oldest children are now attending school.

A. R. Welsh

Albert Ransom Welsh was born in Enfield, Ill., on May 4, 1860, the son of W. W. and Hannah (Deemer) Welsh. Mr. and Mrs. Welsh were married in Hope, Ind., and in 1859 moved to Illinois. Mr. Welsh, a blacksmith by trade, opened a drug store in Enfield and conducted a successful business until he retired in 1900. In 1904, he came to St. Petersburg and became such a booster for St. Petersburg that in one year he induced fifty-two other persons to locate in the city.

A. R. Welsh was educated in the public schools of Enfield and in the Southern Illinois Academy. Having learned telegraphy, he entered the employ of the Louisville & Nashville Railroad as telegraph operator when he left school. He remained with the railroad for nearly twenty-five years, serving part of the time as railroad and express agent. During this period he also owned a brick and tile factory at Omaha, Ill.

Mr. Welsh served two years as a member of the town council in Enfield and eleven years as mayor.

Coming to St. Petersburg for the first time in December, 1910, Mr. Welsh liked the city and decided to make it his per-

A. R. Welsh

manent home. He has taken an active part in the affairs of the city ever since. He is president of the Welsh Development Company, president of the R. M. Hall Development Company, president of the Realtors Association, and chairman of the City Hospital Board. Since holding this last office, the city has completed the new negro hospital and added a new addition to the city hospital now known as the Mound Park Hospital.

When Mr. Welsh came to St. Petersburg he saw the need of two political parties and called a meeting of the Republicans. This meeting resulted in the formation of the Republican Club, which carried the city for Harding in the presidential election of 1920. Mr. Welsh served as the first president of the club and holds Membership Card No. 1.

Mr. Welsh has been a member of the Chamber of Commerce since coming to St. Petersburg and has served as a member of the board of governors. He is a member of the Modern Woodmen of the World. He is also a member of the Methodist Episcopal Church and represented the state of Florida at the general conference of the church held in Des Moines, Ia., in May, 1920.

On October 26, 1885, in Enfield, Ill., Mr. Welsh was married to Miss Mattie L. Hall, a sister of R. M. Hall, of St. Petersburg. They have three children: Frank Burtis Welsh, secretary and treasurer of the Welsh Development Company; Verne Hall Welsh and Helen Natalie.

Frank Fortune Pulver

Frank Fortune Pulver was born in Rochester, N. Y., November 12, 1871, the son of N. B. Pulver and Susan Bennett Pulver. He was the youngest of five children and it was necessary for him to earn a living from a very early age.

While still in the public schools he sold newspapers and at the age of fourteen he became apprenticed in the jewelry store of Augustus Stritt in Rochester and served his apprenticeship. After leaving this establishment he worked a year in Springfield, Mass., for the Hampden Watch Company. In 1888 he was employed with the Elgin Watch Factory.

While in Elgin, Mr. Pulver purchased a formula for the manufacture of chewing gum and at once started the production of Spearmint chewing gum. This business was successful and his novel advertising attracted the attention of Wm. Wrigley, Jr., Company, who bought out his formula and business in 1913.

Mr. Pulver was actively interested in the J. R. White Jewelry Company, the F. F. Pulver Celluloid Novelty Works, both of Rochester, N. Y., and the Toothill-McBeen Silverware Company, of Oswego, N. Y., and the Harry Hall Wrecking Company, of Buffalo, N. Y. He also placed on the market what was known as the Pulver vending machine.

Mr. Pulver first came to St. Petersburg as a winter visitor in 1911 and returned from time to time until 1917, when he decided to make his permanent home here.

During the depression of 1919, he purchased the Detroit Hotel and the Pass-a-Grille bridge, and later the Hollenbeck Hotel and Elks' Club property. He also owns considerable real estate in other sections of the city and has property interests in Rochester, Troy and Geneseo. He is interested in the Fidelity Loan and Trust Company, the Soft Water Laundry

Frank Fortune Pulver

and the Florida Bond and Mortgage Company.

Mr. Pulver helped in no small measure to start the ball rolling which has resulted in the recent prosperity of the city. The increased number of visitors and investors from his native state and city testify to his popularity, New York State now leading all the states in the number of tourists.

Mr. Pulver was elected mayor of St. Petersburg December 20, 1921, to fill out the unexpired term of Noel A. Mitchell, who had been recalled November 20 of that year. On April 15, 1922, he was re-elected, running against Noel A. Mitchell and George W. Fitch.

During the year which followed, a political faction opposed to Mayor Pulver sought to get him out of office by the recall route. The first two attempts resulted in failure, the first being prevented by the courts and the second by the will of the people.

During the summer of 1923, the opposing political faction pushed through a new charter which robbed the mayor of all of his powers. In the fall, upon his return to St. Petersburg, when the mayor attempted to prove that many sections of the charter were illegal, another attempt was made to recall him. This time his opponents were successful and Mr. Pulver was recalled from office.

The wearing of a white suit and his original methods of gaining publicity have been very effective in gaining free publicity for St. Petersburg in the North.

Mr. Pulver is a thirty-second-degree Mason and a Shriner, a member of the Elks' Lodge, the Rotary Club, the St. Petersburg Golf Club and Yacht Club, and other social organizations. He has served as a director and is a member of the Florida Hotel Men's Association.

Charles R. Carter

Charles R. Carter was born April 30, 1878, in Lowndes County, Georgia, and is the son of Rufus T. Carter and Martha Coleman Carter. His family came to Florida in 1902 and to Pinellas County in 1909.

Mr. Carter was the only child of his parents, and received his public school education in the county in which he was born. In his youth he entered the employ of the Atlantic Coast Line Railway, and was passenger conductor on a run between Jacksonville and St. Petersburg for a number of years.

In 1912, Mr. Carter left the train service to engage in the real estate business in St. Petersburg with John A. Larson, a railroad engineer in the same service as himself. During a lull in the real estate business in 1914 he purchased the insurance business of Carl Ennis, and in 1917 joined with J. G. Foley to form the Foley-Carter Company to handle insurance and a bonding business.

Mr. Carter is also connected with the Brunson Dowell Land Company, extensive developers, as secretary of the organization, and is president of the Fidelity Loan and Savings Company.

Mr. Carter's first wife was Miss Gertrude Chitty, of Micanopy, Florida, who died in 1909, leaving one son, Charles R.

Charles R. Carter

Carter, Jr. In 1912, Mr. Carter was married to Miss Lula DeLoach, of Lowndes County, Ga. They have two children, Frank DeLoach and Ann Elizabeth.

Mr. Carter was active in organizing the city commission form of government in St. Petersburg, and has been a member of the commission since 1916. He also served as president of the Chamber of Commerce for two consecutive years.

Mr. Carter served as Exalted Ruler of the Lodge of Elks in 1919, and was a delegate to the national convention in Chicago in 1920. He is also a member of the Independent Order of Odd Fellows, the Modern Woodmen of America, the St. Petersburg Yacht Club and the St. Petersburg Country Club, and the Rotary International.

Bradford A. Lawrence

Bradford A. Lawrence, Jr., was born in Chicago, Ill., on May 7, 1887, the son of Bradford A. and Julia (Lane) Lawrence, the former a native of New York City and the latter of Chicago. He was educated in the public schools of Milwaukee, Wis., and Lawrence College, at Appleton, Wis.

After leaving school, Mr. Lawrence entered the bonding department of the Marshall & Illsley Bank in Milwaukee. Three years later he engaged in the life insurance business in that city, and shortly after was made state superintendent of agents. In 1912, he left Wisconsin and came to Florida, believing that there were better opportunities in this state.

During the year following Mr. Lawrence leased a site on the North Mole from the city and constructed the Spa.

Mr. Lawrence has taken an active part in the work of the Chamber of Commerce for a number of years. He was elected president of the organization in 1918 and

Bradford A. Lawrence, Jr.

again in 1924. He also has been secretary, vice-president and member of the board of governors. He is a member of the St. Petersburg Lodge No. 139, F. & A. M., Knights of Pythias, St. Petersburg Yacht Club, Rotary International, and University Club.

On April 6, 1916, Mr. Lawrence was married in St. Petersburg to Virginia Wagner, the daughter of George Byron and Ann Elizabeth (Hendren) Wagner. Mr. and Mrs. Lawrence have one daughter, Julia Ann.

Paul Poynter

Paul Poynter was born in Eminence, Morgan county, Indiana, March 29, 1875, the son of Jesse A. and Loutisha (Bennett) Poynter. He received his education in Indiana, where he was graduated from DePauw University in Greencastle, in 1897. After his graduation, Mr. Poynter became engaged in newspaper work, and subsequently became publisher and owner of several newspapers.

Mr. Poynter acquired the Sullivan Democrat in 1897; established the Sullivan Daily Times in 1903, and owned and published newspapers in Noblesville, Ind., Seymour, Ind., and Columbus, Ind. He is now also publisher of the Kokomo Dispatch at Kokomo, Ind.

In August, 1912, Mr. Poynter came to St. Petersburg and bought the St. Petersburg Times and has published it continuously since. He is also connected with the Solray Investment Company, as vice-president.

Mr. Poynter is a member of the Masonic lodge, the Elks, the St. Petersburg Yacht Club, and the country clubs at St. Petersburg, Fla., Kokomo, Ind., and Sullivan, Ind. He is a member of the Christian Science Church. He has also held the position of president of the Indiana Democratic Editorial Association, and has been director of the Chamber of Commerce of Kokomo, Ind.

Mr. Pointer was married in April, 1900, to Alice Wilkey, in Sullivan, Ind. They have two children, Eleanor Allen Poynter, twenty-two years old, and Nelson Paul Poynter, twenty years old. Miss Eleanor was graduated from Indiana University in 1922, and in the following year took post-graduate work at Wellesley College, Boston, Mass. Nelson Poynter will be graduated from Indiana University with the class of 1924.

Mrs. Poynter is a member of the board of trustees of the Indiana woman's prison and has served in that capacity for the past thirteen years.

Paul Poynter

W. L. Watson

William L. Watson was born in Portland, Maine, on August 8, 1879, the son of Jerome L. and Isabella (McDonald) Watson, the former a native of New Hampshire and the latter of Maine. He attended the grade schools in Portland and was graduated from the Portland High School in 1898. In the fall of the same year he entered Bowdoin College, from which he was graduated in 1902 with the degree of Bachelor of Arts.

After leaving college, Mr. Watson engaged in the retail coal business with his father in Portland. He came to St. Petersburg for the first time in February,

290   HISTORY OF ST. PETERSBURG

W. L. Watson

1912, to escape a severe Maine winter, and to visit his parents, who had been living here during the winter months for a number of years.

In October, 1913, Mr. Watson was engaged in the bookkeeping department of the Central National Bank. His intention was to work only during the winter and to return to Maine in the spring. However, he remained with the bank through the summer, and later became receiving and paying teller, and assistant cashier. In July, 1918, he was appointed cashier, a position he holds at present.

Mr. Watson was president of the Chamber of Commerce in 1920 and is at present a member of the board of governors. He belongs to all the Masonic bodies, is a Shriner, an Odd Fellow, and is a member of the St. Petersburg Country Club, the St. Petersburg Yacht Club, the Rotary Club, the University Club and the Delta Kappa Epsilon Fraternity. He is also a member of the First Avenue Methodist Church.

Mr. Watson was married on February 12, 1902, in Portland, Me., to Belle F. Blackden, the daughter of Mr. and Mrs. William D. Blackden. They have one son, Jerome L. Watson, second, who is at present in school.

Herman A. Dann

Herman A. Dann was born on September 18, 1889, in Titusville, Pa., the son of Phillip C. and Ida (Meeks) Dann, the former a native of Denmark and the latter of Kentucky. He was educated in the public schools of Titusville and Lafayette College at Easton, Pa., from which he was graduated in 1912 with the degree of Bachelor of Philosophy.

After leaving school, Mr. Dann was engaged for a time in newspaper work and later was employed by general contracting firms in Philadelphia. He came to St. Petersburg on January 1, 1913, and became identified with the St. Petersburg Investment Company. He remained with that company a year and then bought a controlling interest in the Southern Con-

Herman A. Dann

struction Company, a corporation of which he was made president. In 1916 he bought out the building supplies business of W. S. McCrea & Son, and incorporated the Dann-Gerow Company, of which he is president. This company at the present time is one of the largest of its kind in Florida.

Mr. Dann is also a director of the Central National Bank, a director of the Mason Hotel Company, a director of the Scanlan Company, vice-president of the Central Investment Company, and a director of the Tampa Northern Railroad Company.

Since coming to St. Petersburg, Mr. Dann has been actively identified with all organizations working for the development of the city. He has been a member of the board of governors of the Chamber of Commerce since 1918 and in 1922 was elected president of that organization. As a direct result of his efforts, the annual convention of the American Traveling Passenger Agents' Association was brought to St. Petersburg in November, 1923.

Mr. Dann is a director of the Florida Development Board and the Southeastern Builders' Supplies Association. He is a member of the Rotary Club, of which he was elected president in 1923. He is also a member of the Elks' Lodge, the Masonic order, the Shrine, and the St. Petersburg Yacht Club.

Mr. Dann was married to Miss Helen Thomasson, of St. Petersburg, in 1916. They have three children, Phoebe Hutchison, Thomasson Philip, and Nancy Wilson.

C. C. Carr

Charles Carl Carr was born in Lebanon, Ind., January 11, 1884, the son of Finley T. and Annie (Quiett) Carr, of Carlisle, Kentucky. He received his education in Indiana, graduating from high school in 1902 and from Indiana University in 1909, with the degree of Bachelor of Arts. During his student days he acted as reporter for several newspapers, and was for a time employed as reporter on the Chicago Inter-Ocean.

Upon his graduation from the university, Mr. Carr went to the Canal Zone, where for four years he was a member of the civil administration staff of the United States government. At this time he was

C. C. Carr

also superintendent of the high schools in the Panama Canal Zone, from 1909 to 1913. While in South America he wrote "The Story of Panama," which was published in 1912 by the Silver-Burdett Company.

When his work for the government was ended, Mr. Carr returned to Indiana, where, in 1914, he owned, together with Paul Poynter, the Daily Times of Sullivan. In that same year he came to St. Petersburg to buy into the St. Petersburg Times and take over its management. He was manager and part owner until May 1, 1923.

Mr. Carr next established the C. C. Carr Advertising Agency, of which he is now president — an organization with offices in St. Petersburg and at 141 West Thirty-sixth street, New York, which handled more than twenty accounts and placed more than $100,000 worth of business the first year of operation.

In addition to the advertising agency, Mr. Carr is interested in real estate and is president of the Solray Investment

Company, vice-president of the Soft Water Laundry Company, and the Fidelity Savings and Loan Company, being director in the latter. He is also a stockholder in several companies.

Mr. Carr is past president of the Rotary Club, a member of the Masonic Lodge, and the Delta Tau Delta college fraternity. He served two terms as a member of the county school board, being chairman for four years, and has been active in Democratic politics for a number of years. He also served as governor of the Chamber of Commerce board for several years.

Mr. Carr was married in New York City, September 17, 1912, to Marian Sukeforth. They have one child, Marjorie. Mrs. Carr is a graduate of Adelphi College, Brooklyn, and has been active in the Kappa Alpha Theta college sorority.

Mr. Carr is also the author of a survey on newspaper composing room page costs, which was published in trade journals throughout the country.

Freeman P. Lane

Freeman P. Lane was born at Eastport, Washington County, Me., on April 20, 1853, the son of Charles W. and Almira B. (Coulter) Lane. His father was a seafaring man, and served as first mate on a vessel of which Freeman Parker was captain. Freeman Lane was named for his father's friend.

When Freeman Lane was nine years of age the family moved to Minnesota, where his father was one of the pioneer settlers of Minneapolis. His father engaged in the carriage repair business, and became a prosperous business man, living the remainder of his life in the city he had helped settle.

Upon the removal of the family to Minneapolis, Freeman Lane obtained work as a bootblack and newsboy, attending school in the intervals of this employment. He left school when he had attained the eighth grade, and was subsequently employed in a mill, as clerk in his father's grocery store, and in 1869 as clerk in the Northwestern Telegraph Company, which was later absorbed by the Western Union.

During his service with this company Judge Lane assisted in the construction of the company's line in Minnesota and the territory of Dakota. In 1872, he became an employe of the United States government, the Northern Pacific Railroad Company, and the Northwestern Telegraph Company. In November, 1872, Judge Lane entered the office of Albee Smith, a lawyer in Minneapolis, and the following year left for the east, where he entered the Albany Law School in Albany, N. Y. He was admited to the bar May 6, 1874, and immediately returned to Minneapolis, where he engaged in his profession for more than forty years. He was a specialist in insurance litigation, and was adjudged one of the ablest attorneys of Minneapolis.

For a number of years Judge Lane was chairman of the Republican County and City Committee of Minneapolis, and was elected to the legislature in 1889, but in 1893 left the Republican party because of its attitude toward the tariff, the trusts and financial matters, and became a Populist.

In July, 1875, Judge Lane was married to Miss Mollie Lauderdale, the daughter of William H. Lauderdale, of Minne-

Freeman P. Lane

apolis. They had four children: Bessie, Ina, Mabel and Stuart.

In 1914, Judge Lane came to St. Petersburg, and in 1916 began to practice law in this city. He served as judge of the municipal court from April, 1922, to November, 1923, when he retired from this office. Judge Lane is a senior member of the Lane and Bussey law firm, director of the Associated Refining Company of Oil City, Pa. He is also a member of the St. Petersburg Yacht Club and the Chamber of Commerce.

Robert R. Walden

Robert R. Walden was born January 26, 1887, in Plant City, the son of S. Walden and Roxie (Simmons) Walden. He received his early education in the public schools of Plant City and later was graduated from the Turkey Creek High School. Upon his graduation from high school Mr. Walden left for Tampa, where he entered the Tampa Business College for a commercial training. He was graduated from this institution in 1907.

Robert R. Walden

Mr. Walden first started work in the business world as an employe of a hardware store, and later taught school for a period of three years.

Believing in the business opportunities to be had in St. Petersburg, Mr. Walden came to this city on June 8, 1915, and engaged in the retail hardware business. Today Mr. Walden is president and manager of the Walden Hardware Company, which he established upon reaching St. Petersburg, and which has been a very successful undertaking. Mr. Walden is also president of the St. Petersburg Merchants' Association.

On May 19, 1915, Mr. Walden was married to Miss Sarah Gordon in Tampa, Fla.

Mr. Walden is actively interested in the civic organizations of St. Petersburg and has held office in many of them. He is a deputy commissioner of the Boy Scouts, secretary of the Rotary Club, secretary of the City Advertising and Library Board, and a member of the Chamber of Commerce.

Mr. Walden is also a member of the Masonic lodge, the Modern Woodmen, the Selama Grotto, and the Woodmen of the World. He is also a member of the Tarpon Club, and former president of the Pinellas County Sportsmen's Association.

Mr. Walden is also actively interested in church work, being affiliated with the First Baptist Church of St. Petersburg, of which he is superintendent of the Sunday School.

O. R. Albright

O. R. Albright was born in Preston County, West Virginia, March 25, 1888. He is the son of A. S. and Zourie (Falkenstein) Albright, who are now living retired at Lakeland, Fla., the family having come to the state in October, 1904.

Mr. Albright was educated in the public schools of West Virginia, and shortly after his parents came to Florida he entered the State University at Gainesville, where he studied a course in mechanical engineering. Upon leaving the university he was apprenticed in a garage, in 1909, where he remained until 1911. At this time he started a machine shop of his own in Gainesville, and was awarded some six months later the agency for the Ford

O. R. Albright

automobile in that locality. In 1912 he took a partner in the sales end of the busines, and conducted this business until August, 1914, when he sold out his interests and gave his time to assisting his father in promoting and putting on the market a patented type of automobile jack.

In June, 1915, Mr. Albright married Ada V. Hoover, of Muscatine, Iowa, and went for a honeymoon trip to California and return in an especially equipped Ford car. This transcontinental trip covered 10,000 miles, and to California and as far back as Kansas City, Mr. and Mrs. Albright drove with Florida air in their two rear tires.

On Christmas Day, 1915, Mr. Albright received a contract from the Ford Motor Company for the agency of the Ford car in St. Petersburg. In 1920 Mr. Albright built the plant he occupies at present, a building 100 by 120 feet, fully equipped for the repair, assembling and supply of stock parts for the Ford car. During the first year of business in St. Petersburg Mr. Albright's sales totaled 28 cars. In 1923, 569 cars were sold and distributed.

Mr. Albright was elected city commissioner in St. Petersburg in April, 1921, and served for two years, when he was re-elected to the same office.

He is a charter director of the Young Men's Christian Association, a trustee and financial secretary of the Lutheran Church, and a church counsellor. He is also a stockholder in the Ninth Street Bank and Trust Company and a charter member of the St. Petersburg Motor Club.

Mr. and Mrs. Albright have one son, Russell George, and a daughter, Mary Jane.

Edwin E. Naugle

Edwin E. Naugle was born September 13, 1883, in Greencastle, Ind., the son of William E. and Mary (Bivin) Naugle. He received his early education in the public schools and high schools of Indiana and Indiana University at Bloomington, Ind., where he studied a course in journalism.

Mr. Naugle was reared in a newspaper

Ed. E. Naugle

office, having spent his early life in newspaper work in Indiana, where he was employed on every paper in Indianapolis at various times. From Indianapolis he came to Florida, and served as managing editor of the Jacksonville afternoon paper for nine years.

In September, 1916, Mr. Naugle came to St. Petersburg, attracted by the opportunities for growth and development which he saw in the city, and also because he sought a congenial business relationship with his university classmate, C. C. Carr.

From 1916 until May, 1923, Mr. Naugle was managing editor and editor of the St. Petersburg Times, and while holding that position had many opportunities for supporting projects for the development of St. Petersburg.

Since leaving the Times, Mr. Naugle has been advertising, publicity and promotion director for E. M. Elliott and Associates of the Boulevard and Bay Land and Development Company.

Mr. Naugle is a member of the Rotary Club, the University Club, the Jungle Golf Club, the Elks, and the Boy Scouts Council. He was a member of the advertising committee and chairman of the advertising committee of the St. Petersburg Chamber of Commerce for two years, and also a member of the Municipal Advertising Board for three years.

Mr. Naugle was married September 15, 1908, to Miss Mary Alma Cotter, in Jacksonville, the daughter of the late William T. Cotter, famous among the early builders of Florida, having been chief of the construction forces of the old Plant Railway system, and the builder of the Tampa Bay Hotel.

Mr. and Mrs. Naugle have four children, Mary, Marjorie, Alma and Edwin E., Jr.

Bayard S. Cook

Bayard S. Cook was born in Talbot County, Maryland, May 22, 1882, the only child of his parents, Peter and Augusta (Pippin) Cook, his father a native of Delaware and his mother of Maryland.

He was reared in his native state, and was educated in the public schools there. He was graduated from the Easton High School and from the Temple University Law School in Philadelphia in 1907. He was admitted to the bar the same year, and from 1915 to 1917 practiced law in Philadelphia.

In 1917, Mr. Cook moved to St. Petersburg, where he has been associated with the firm of Cook and Harris since November 1, 1919. From 1918 to 1922 he served St. Petersburg as city attorney.

In 1917, Mr. Cook married S. Jane Beryman, of Ohio, and they have three sons: Bayard, Jr., Douglas and James.

Mr. Cook is a member of the First Methodist Episcopal Church of St. Petersburg. He is also a member of the St. Petersburg Yacht Club, the St. Petersburg Country Club, the University Club and Rotary International.

J. Harold Sommers

J. Harold Sommers was born in Chicago, Ill., February 5, 1894, the only child of his parents, Charles F. and Bird M. (Stanfield) Sommers. His father was connected for about thirty years with the Continental Commercial Bank of Chicago, and after retiring from the bank

Mr. Sommers is president of the Tourist News Publishing Company and editor of the Tourist News magazine. He is a Rotarian and a member of the National Association of Advertising Clubs. He is a member of the St. Petersburg Yacht Club, the American Legion, the Chamber of Commerce and the University Club.

Mr. Sommers also served as chairman of the program committee for the thirty-ninth district conference of Rotary International for 1924, and is at present president of the St. Petersburg Athletic Club. He has served as vice-chairman of the advertising committee of the Chamber of Commerce for three years.

John Harris Lodwick

"A city press agent for St. Petersburg . . . . with a reasonable fund at his command, could be of more real service to our city—get more results—than any other official we have; and the funds he would expend would accomplish a great deal more than the same amount would in any other fund."—St. Petersburg Times, December 8, 1906.

J. Harold Sommers

came to Florida, where he has lived in St. Petersburg ever since.

Mr. Sommers was educated in Chicago, in the grammar schools of that city and later in Northwestern University. He received his first newspaper experience while in Montana, in 1915, when he ran a small newspaper in the town of Joliet. The years that followed were spent in advertising work and in contributing to magazines and newspapers of the country.

He was also identified with the motion-picture industry on the Pacific Coast.

As a member of the National Guard, Mr. Sommers served in the government service on the Mexican border, and later during the World War helped handle the war exposition in Chicago.

On January 8, 1918, Mr. Sommers came to Florida as a tourist, for a rest, returning the following year to put into execution his idea of the Tourist News—a magazine published in the interest of the St. Petersburg tourist. Mr. Sommers established the business, which has since developed into the largest publishing house in southern Florida. He has also established the Pinellas County Real Estate and Industrial Record.

John Harris Lodwick

Twelve years after this editorial opinion was expressed, St. Petersburg employed its first press agent; or, to use a different term, its first publicity director. John Harris Lodwick, of Cleveland, Ohio, was the man selected. The results accomplished by Mr. Lodwick have more than justified the optimistic opinion of the editor of the Times. Each year since being employed Mr. Lodwick has sent out thousands of stories regarding St. Petersburg and they have been published in newspapers everywhere throughout the North. Without exaggeration, it can be said that Mr. Lodwick has put St. Petersburg upon the news map of the country.

Mr. Lodwick was born in Cleveland, Ohio, on December 16, 1890, the son of John Reese and Bessie (Harris) Lodwick, both natives of Wales. He was educated in the Cleveland public schools and the Cleveland School of Art. Shortly after leaving school he was employed as a messenger boy for the Associated Press. In the next year, 1905, he became copy boy for the Cleveland Press. Gradually he worked his way up in newspaper work and for a number of years was sport writer on the Cleveland Leader. From 1910 to 1912, he was assistant director of sports and entertainment of the city of Cleveland. Later, he became sport editor of the Akron (Ohio) Times. During the next few years he devoted much of his time to handling important publicity campaigns.

Mr. Lodwick came to St. Petersburg in December, 1918, and was employed by L. H. Whitney, then secretary of the Chamber of Commerce, to handle the publicity for the city. He has been employed as publicity director ever since. Mr. Lodwick is a member of the Rotary Club, the University Club, the Cleveland Press Club and the Masonic Lodge. He is also a member of the Baptist Church.

On June 28, 1919, Mr. Lodwick was married to Miss Margaret R. Guinter, of Akron, Ohio.

Franklin J. Mason

Franklin J. Mason was born in Little York, New York, on April 1, 1871, the son of George S. and Loretta (Dayton) Mason, both of New York State. He was educated in the grammar schools of Brooklyn and the Long Island Business College of Brooklyn, from which he was graduated in 1886.

After leaving school, Mr. Mason commenced his business career in his father's office in Wall street. Later he was employed for five years as a bookkeeper with Boardman & Gray Piano Company, of Albany, N. Y. Leaving Albany, Mr. Mason was engaged in the granite business in Brooklyn, and later in the architectural concrete and building business in Long Island.

Following this, Mr. Mason acquired an interest in the Standard Concrete Steel Company of New York and was made general manager. He was with this company for ten years and during this period spuervised the construction of scores of large buildings, ranging from one to twenty stories in height. He left the company in 1918 to go into business for himself.

Mr. Mason came to St. Petersburg in March, 1920, seeking a change and a rest from his strenuous work. Upon coming here, Mr. Mason intended to do nothing more than to build two or three bungalows a year. However, he immediately started the erection of eight bungalows. A neighbor, attracted by the character of the work being performed on the bungalows Mr. Mason was erecting for himself, asked him to build a home for him. This started his contracting business in St. Petersburg. From this start the business grew to large proportions. During the years 1921, 1922 and 1923, Mr. Mason erected sixty to seventy-five buildings, ranging from modest bungalows to a modern hotel. His first large undertaking was the erection of a $50,000 addition to the St. Petersburg Yacht Club in 1922. In the spring of 1923, Mr. Mason started the construction of the Mason Hotel, at First avenue and Fourth street north. The hotel, which cost a million and a half dollars and is one of the finest in the South, was completed in time for the 1923-24 tourist season.

Besides being the head of Franklin J. Mason, Inc., Mr. Mason is a heavy stockholder and president of the Mason Hotel Company, Inc.; is a director in the Lakewood Development Company, and a stockholder in the Central National Bank & Trust Company and the Victory Land Company.

Mr. Mason is a thirty-second-degree Mason, being a life member of the Ancient Arabic Order of Nobles of the Mystic Shrine. He is a member of the Rotary Club, the Chamber of Commerce, the St. Petersburg Yacht Club, the Council of Boy Scouts, the Memorial-Historical Society, the St. Petersburg Art Club, the Bayboro Harbor Commission and the St. Petersburg Motor Club. He is one of the early members of the American Automobile Association.

On February 26, 1896, Mr. Mason was married to Miss Emma R. Reohr, daughter of William and Wilhelmina Reohr, of Albany, N. Y.

Jack Taylor

Jack Taylor, president of Pasadena Estates, Inc., was born in Tilton, N. H., on August 13, 1876. After attending the schools of his home town, Mr. Taylor became private secretary to Gov. C. A. Busiel of New Hampshire. Later he was engaged in the banking business in Boston and New York and became a member of the Boston, New York and Chicago stock exchanges.

Mr. Taylor visited St. Petersburg for the first time late in October, 1921, immediately after the worst storm the city had ever experienced. Although he saw St. Petersburg in the worst light possible, he was impressed with its possibilities for development, and began making arrangements at once for acquiring property. With Fred G. Aulsbrook of New York and Innes Henry of Boston, he purchased the properties now known as Pasadena-on-the-Gulf, including approximately 2,100 acres of land.

Under Mr. Taylor's direction, the development of Pasadena has progressed rapidly and it now ranks with the best developments of the South. Several million dollars have been spent in beautifying the parks and boulevards with palms, shrubs and flowers, paving streets, and numerous other improvements. Plans for the near future include the establishment of a university at Pasadena and an exclusive golf club, to be known as the Bear Creek Country Club.

Mr. Taylor is a member of the Whitehall Club and Metropolitan Club of New York City, the Boston and New York Athletic Clubs, and a number of others. He is a Thirty-second degree Mason.

E. M. Elliott

Eugene M. Elliott was born on December 18, 1882, in Topeka, Kansas, the son of Charles P. and Olive M. (Munson) Elliott. After receiving a college education he served for a time in the United States Steel Corporation as special apprentice and later took up the sale of securities and engaged in development work. He aided in the financing of a number of large companies in the automobile industry and held various important offices.

During the World War Mr. Elliott was connected with several departments of the government in organization work.

Since attaining manhood, Mr. Elliott has been affiliated with the Republican party. He has been connected with the National Republican Committee for sixteen years and was personally attached to Roosevelt, Hughes and Harding. He helped to organize the Harding Front Porch Campaign in 1920 and later was called to Washington to help in organization matters.

Mr. Elliott came to St. Petersburg on September 12, 1922, to put over the financing of the Gandy Bridge. After the sale of Gandy Bridge securities was completed, Mr. Elliott and associates purchased and began the development of the Weedon Island properties, known as the Florida Riviera.

Mr. Elliott was married on September 26, 1905, to Elsie Fortier. They have two children, E. Munson Elliott, aged 16, and Madeline Elliott, aged 13, both of whom are now attending school in St. Petersburg.

Mr. Elliott is an Episcopalian.

E. M. Elliott

INDEX

A

Ainslee, Geo.: 32.
Ainslee, W. L.: 24.
Albright, O. R., Life of: 293; 89.
Allen, Edw. C.: 86.
Allen, Charles M.: 78.
Allison, W. E., Life of: 244; 58, 82.
Anderson, A. T.: 89.
Anderson, G. W.: 20.
American Bank & Trust Co.: 176.
Armistead, Capt. J. A., Life of: 224, 131.
Armistead, Mrs. Sarah, Life of: 224, 121.
Arnold, A: 95.
Art Club: 192.
Arter, M.: 28.
Artesian Wells: 151.
Atlantic Coast Line Railroad: 32, 50.
Atkins, J. N.: 90.
Audubon Society: 191.
Aulsbrook, Fred G.: 134.
Avery, A. P., Life of: 249; 24, 56, 64, 83, 86, 91, 99, 114, 149, 171, 176, 179.
Aviation: 35, 38.
Axline, Dr. M. H.: 61, 84.

B

Banks: 173.
Barden, Fred: 32.
Barr, Pauline: 31.
Bartlett, A. F., Life of: 250; 30, 32, 54, 71, 84, 96, 100, 120, 121, 146, 163, 174.
Baseball: 183.
Baum, Jacob, Life of: 227; 11, 20, 152.
Bayboro: 57, 129.
Bayboro Investment Co.: 58, 75,129.
Beach, Dr. E. C.: 90.
Beard, John: 32.
Bell, Judge J. D., Life of: 260; 100, 145.
Benoist Company: 38.
Benton, Judge Wm. H.: 20, 24.
Bethell, John C., Life of: 226; 4.
Big Bayou: 4.
Bishop, John A.: 29.
Blanc, C. M.: 90.
Blocker, A. T., Life of: 242; 35, 58, 81, 84.
Blocker, J. C.: 83.
Blodgett, G. W.: 59, 84.
"Blue Sunday": 35, 40, 87.
Board of Trade: 30, 99.
Boardman, Paul R., Life of: 282; 91, 106, 183.
Boardwalk: 16.
Bodman, S. E.: 83.
Bond, Frank E.: 49.
Bond Issues: 23, 24, 31, 60, 65, 81, 116, 121, 153, 157.
Bonifacia: 5.
Bonney, L. W.: 35.
Boyer, Geo.: 32.
Braaf, Chas.: 84.

Bradshaw, J. G., Life of: 245; 24, 85, 153.
Branch, E. J.: 32.
Brantley Pier: 70.
Bridges: 155, 160, 162.
Bright, Mary: 148.
Brown, Carl: 32.
Brown, J. N., Life of: 264; 54, 61, 84, 86, 177.
Brown, Lew B., Life of: 274; 59, 91, 104, 112, 181.
Brown, L. C.: 106, 274.
Brown, Tom: 32.
Budd, D. W., Life of: 253; 36, 110, 156, 165.
Budd, Capt. W. O.: 109, 135.
Buhner, Mary: 43.
Burnett, Geo.: 91.
Burnside, Mrs. Virginia: 88.
Burrier, S. A.: 24.
Bussey, H. P.: 24.

C

Carley, Frank C.: 112.
Carr, C. C., Life of: 291; 106, 180.
Carreno Club: 189.
Carter, Charles R., Life of: 287; 86, 106.
Cashwell, W. Roy: 182.
Catholic Church: 207.
Celebrations: 163.
Census: 202.
Central Avenue: 81, 125, 130; when named, 30.
Central Land & Title Co.: 132.
Central National Bank: 174.
Chamber of Commerce: 28, 20, 99.
Chancellor, T. A., Life of: 269; 64, 81, 100, 165, 174, 214.
Chapman, T. R.: 24, 81.
Chase, Beulah: 145, 246.
Chase, Capt. J. F., Life of: 246, 28, 31, 76.
Chase, Lena M.: 246.
Chase, J. Frank: 32.
Childs, L. D.: 88.
Christian Church: 210.
Churches: 203.
City Charter: 84, 88, 91.
Civitan Club: 194.
Clark, T. M.: 18, 24.
Coffee Pot Golf Club: 167.
Coats, W. A.: 24, 81.
Coe's Channel: 56.
Cole, F. E., Life of: 262; 24, 58, 81, 165.
Congregational Church: 204.
Cook, Bayard S., Life of: 295; 176.
Cooper's Quarters: 124.
Corrections: In Festival and Celebrations, 164, "Albert" Johnson should be Arthur Johnson. W. H. Hibbs: Biographical sketches in Who's Who section are arranged in accordance with years the

INDEX—Continued

subjects came to St. Petersburg. Therefore, sketch of W. H. Hibbs should follow Col. L. Y. Jenness and appear on 235. E. E. Naugle: On page 180, 8th line, St. Petersburg Land & Development Company should be Boulevard & Bay Land and Development Company.
County Division: 93.
County Seat: 97.
Craven, J. H.: 71.
Crescent Lake Park: 201.
Cunningham, E. G.: 89.

D

Daniel, R. T.: 24.
Dann, Herman A., Life of: 290; 107, 176.
Davis, Dr. A. B.: 71, 100, 165, 220.
Davis, A. H.: 57.
Davis, F. A., Life of: 220; 27, 28, 30, 65, 67, 99, 132, 153.
Davis (F. A.) Companies: 67.
Davis, J. S.: 54.
Davidson, R. Lee: 86.
Davista: 77.
Demens, Peter A., Life of: 218; 7, 9, 11, 45, 121.
Dent, H. C.: 130.
Depots: 50, 53.
De Soto Celebration: 164.
Detroit Hotel: 11, 12, 32, 39, 121, 286.
Dew, Roy L.: 91.
Dunlap, A. R.: 88, 105.
Durant, C.: 18, 24, 120.
Disston City: 4.
Disston, Jacob S., Life of: 224; 67, 71, 74, 79, 132.
Disston Land Company: 46.
Divine, W. F.: 49.

E

Eddins, S. M.: 59, 82.
Edwards, George, Life of: 254; 24, 81.
Eiland, J. J.: 32.
Electric Light Plant: 20, 27, 67, 73, 154.
Electric Pier: 70.
Electric Railway: 68, 74.
Elliott, E. M., Life of: 299.
English, W. H.: 56, 102, 110, 165.
Episcopalian Churches: 203.

F

Farmer, H. A.: 64, 86.
Favorite: 72.
Festivals: 163.
Festival of the States: 164. (See corrections.)
First Avenue Methodist Episcopal Church: 205.
First Baptist Church: 206.
First Church of Christ, Scientist: 213.
First Methodist Church: 209.
First National Bank: 173.
First Presbyterian Church: 209.
Fishing: 16, 109.
Fire Department: 32.
Fisher, A. W.: 35, 114.
Fitch, George W.: 88, 90.
Florida Bank & Trust Co.: 174.
Florida Land & Improvement Co.: 46.
Florida West Coast Co.: 31, 76, 125, 165.
Foster, E. J.: 90, 182.
Freeman, A. F.: 83, 129.
Fuller, H. Walter., Life of: 272; 72, 132, 159, 166.
Fuller, Walter P.: 89.

G

Gandy Bridge: 160.
Gandy, George S., Life of: 266; 37, 69, 88, 114, 160.
Garvin, E. C.: 64.
Gas: 153.
Gerner, A. B.,: 91.
Gilbart, H. W., Life of: 229; 203.
Gill, C. M.: 20.
Good Roads: 35, 96.
Goodwin, C. P.: 58, 81.
Goodwin, Verne: 32.
Golf: 137, 165.
Gore, J. Ira: 179.
Grace Baptist Church: 212.
Grace, David R.: 91.
Granada Terrace: 128.
Green Benches: 87, 129.
Grismer, Karl H.: 182.
Gulf Beach Resort Co.: 126.
Gulfport: 34.

H

Hackney, Dr. James Sarvent: 5.
Hall, Charles R., Life of: 275; 106, 125, 133, 137, 166.
Haines, George B.: 36, 64, 156.
Hamlett, J. C.: 32, 50, 124.
Hammond, C. D., Life of: 270; 85, 135, 153.
Hanna, Roy S., Life of: 236; 32, 33, 51, 54, 71, 100, 110, 120, 142, 145, 165, 174, 197.
Harbor: 130.
Harris, S. D., Life of: 271; 61, 86, 90, 95, 102, 172.
Harris, Rev. J. W.: 149.
Harrison, J. Frank., Life of: 247; 30, 54, 71, 86, 96, 100.
Harrison, Edgar, Life of: 247; 24, 51, 81.
Harrison, E. P., Life of: 248; 121.
Harrod, G.: 32.
Harvey, C. A., Life of: 267; 58, 72, 100, 125, 129, 165.
Harvey, C. L.: 267.
Hayward, Bainbridge: 91.
Health City: 14.
Hearn, J. T.: 24.
Heathcote, W. E.: 51, 64, 71, 95.

INDEX—Continued

Henry, Innes: 134.
Henry, W. C., Life of: 251; 24, 71, 121, 148, 158.
Henschen, Josef: 8, 45.
Hibbs, H. W., Life of: 257; 18, 20, 24. (See corrections.)
High School: 118.
Hill, George A.: 49.
Hillsborough County: 93, 155.
Hines, E. A.: 89.
Holshouser, W. A., Life of: 252; 99.
Holy Spirit Church: 203.
Hospitals: 136, 149.
Howell, J. E.: 32.
Hoxie, Albert: 32, 50, 124.
Hoxie, J. C.: 18, 24, 81.
Hoyt, Rev. J. P.: 28, 31, 34, 76.
Hunt, A. L.: 9, 49.
Hurricane: 41.

I

Incorporation: 19, 24.
Independent: 180.
Independent Line: 72.
Indians: 1.

J

Jannus, Tony: 38, 213.
Jenkins, Margaret: 146.
Jenness, Col. L. Y., Life of: 234; 12, 49, 99, 121, 173.
Johns Pass Realty Co.: 132.
Johnson, Arthur L., Life of: 273; 104, 112, 164. (See corrections.)
Johnson, D., P.: 95.
Jones, W. J.: 32.
Jungle: 75, 132.
Jungle Country Club: 167.

K

Kellam, H. A.: 83.
Kelley, W. McKee., Life of: 283; 107.
Kennedy, Dr. George: 141.
Kimball, Ray: 91.
King, George L.: 18, 20, 24, 56.
King, Wm. G.: 86.
Kletts, Joe: 32.
Klowie, Said: 32.
Klutts, F. P.: 24, 81.

L

Lake Butler Villa Co.: 46.
Lakewood Estates: 136.
Lane, Freeman P., Life of: 292.
Lang, Al. F., Life of: 276; 86, 140, 164, 166, 184.
La Plaza Theatre: 37.
Lassing, Robt. B.: 110.
Lawrence, Bradford A., Jr., Life of: 288; 38, 91, 107.
Lee, Young A.: 179.
Lewis, D. M.: 59.

Lewis, Ed. T., Life of: 233; 9, 35, 57, 64, 71, 82, 86, 88, 109, 112, 141, 174.
Lewis, Fred: 11.
Lewis, Col. J. M.: 32, 57.
Library: 145.
Lindelie, A. H.: 179.
Livingston, C. F.: 24.
Lodwick, John H., Life of: 296; 107, 164.
Loehr, Mrs. Nellie R.: 88.
Long, Henry C.: 63.
Longman, Will: 32.
Ludwig, R. E.: 152.
Lund, Soren, Life of: 284; 44.
Lynch, J. P.: Life of: 284; 106, 135, 172.
Lynching: 39.

M

McCall, Cot: 110.
McCall, T. F.: 18, 24.
McAdoo Bridge: 162.
McAdoo, W. J.: 162.
McClatchie, Dorothy: 42.
McClung, C. B.: 84, 95.
McDevitt, P. J.: 35.
McIntosh, S. R.: 91.
McCleod, Wm.: 49.
McMullen, Don C.: 94.
McNabb, J. C.: 86.
McPherson, Wm. J.: 20.
McQuiston, H.: 99.
McRae, Mrs. Annie, Life of: 241; 145.
Martin, H.: 20.
Mason, Franklin J., Life of: 297; 44.
Mason Hotel: 44, 297.
Massie, Frank: 20, 24.
Matchett, E. R.: 32.
Maximo, Antonio: 3.
Mears, George W.: 95.
Measy, Benj. F.: 68.
Meeker, D. W.: 141.
Memorial Historical Society: 190.
Michael, Miss A. A.: 28.
Midwinter Fair Association: 163.
Mirror Lake: 84, 151, 200.
Missing Link: 78.
Mitchell, Noel A., Life of; 268; 35, 54, 86. 98, 102, 127, 133, 139, 164, 165, 180.
Mitchell, Robt.: 32.
Moffett, David., Life of: 228; 20, 24, 59, 82, 100, 115, 152, 169.
Morgan, Rev. L. J.; 179.
Municipal Advertising: 29, 30.
Municipal Pier: 62.
Murphy, Dr. Ralph D.: 279.
Murphy, Dr. H. A., Life of: 279; 59, 64, 83, 129, 149.
Murray, David., Life of: 235; 20, 24, 56, 99, 185.

N

National Bank: 174.
Naugle, E. E., Life of: 294; 180. (See corrections.)
Negro Section: 124.

INDEX—Continued

Newspapers: 179.
Ninth Street Bank & Trust Co.: 177.
Ninth Street Section: 11, 124.
North Shore: 127.
Northrup, T. J., Life of: 256; 58, 81, 85, 95, 146.
Norton, James S.: 86.
Norwood, Arthur, Life of: 230; 20, 24, 31, 59, 71, 88, 99, 145.

O

Odom, A. C., Jr.: 86, 172, 174, 176.
Orange Belt Investment Co.: 7, 12, 16, 32, 45, 121.
Orange Belt Railway: 7, 45, 55, 121.

P

Park Day: 185.
Park Improvement Association: 185, 197.
Parker, Thornton: 90.
Parks: 197.
Pasadena: 130, 134.
Pass-a-Grille: 236, 237.
Pass-a-Grille Bridge: 162.
Passenger Depots: 50, 53.
Patterson, W. E.: 32.
Paving Streets: 30, 81.
Peabody, Dr. J. D.: 121, 149.
Pearce, R. R.: 90.
Pellerin, Fred: 32.
Pepper, J. P.: 22.
Perry, Judge Wm. H.: 5.
Pheil, A. C., Life of: 243; 38, 54, 58, 64, 81, 84, 132, 153.
Phillips, Capt. Zephaniah, Life of: 237.
Pier: 48, 50, 55, 62.
Pinellas: 4.
Pinellas Bank & Trust Co.: 176.
Pinellas County: 93.
Pinellas County Medical Society: 194.
Pinellas County Power Co.: 154.
Pinellas Park: 78.
Pinellas Post: 182.
Pinellas Special: 54.
Plant System: 28, 50, 56.
Plaza Theatre: 37, 266.
Plaskett, Mrs. M. L.: 182.
Pope, W. P.: 61, 84.
Population, 202.
Porter, Mrs. E. G.: 88.
Postoffice: 141.
Potter, Cramer B.: 64.
Powell, W. B.: 102, 180.
Powell, W. P., Life of: 255.
Poynter, Paul, Life of: 289; 180.
Prather, G. C.: 35.
Presbyterian Churches: 204.
Prohibition: 20, 169.
Public Library: 145.
Public Utilities: 151.
Pulver, Frank Fortune, Life of: 286; 90, 162.

R

Race Track: 19.
Railroads: 7, 9, 45.
Railsback, B. T.: 24, 81.
Ramm, F. W.: 95.
Raymond, R. L.: 59.
Recall Elections: 86, 89.
Red Cross: 214.
Renfroe, H. H.: 32.
Reservoir Lake: 84, 151.
Richardson, H. H.: 49, 64.
Roads: 155.
Roberts, W. A.: 32.
Roser, C. M.: 35, 133, 135.
Roser Park: 135.
Ross, Walter S.: 91.
Rotary Club: 193.
Royal Scotch Highlanders Band: 198.

S

St. Bartholomew's Church: 203.
St. Petersburg: How named, 8; Revised plat of, 13, 121.
St. Petersburg Gulf Electric Ry.: 30, 154.
St. Petersburg Airboat Line: 38.
St. Petersburg Art Club: 192.
St. Petersburg Country Club: 166.
St. Petersburg Electric Light & Power Co.: 67, 73.
St. Petersburg Investment Co.: 69, 76, 132.
St. Petersburg Land & Improvement Co.: 16, 32, 58, 121.
St. Petersburg Reading Room and Library Association: 31.
St. Petersburg State Bank: 29, 173.
St. Petersburg Times: 179.
St. Petersburg Transportation Co.: 72.
St. Petersburg Water Front Co.: 59, 83.
St. Petersburg Yacht Club: 111.
St. Peter's Church: 203.
Sanford & St. Petersburg Ry.: 28, 50.
Sarven, G. N.: 84, 86.
Schools: 23, 115.
Seaboard Air Line Railroad: 72.
Seminole Bridge: 155.
Sharp, Jos. A.: 89.
Shell Mounds: 1, 18.
Shell Mound Park: 201.
Sibley, Joseph C.: 31, 71.
Sidewalks: 18.
Singlehurst, F. R.: 71.
Sixth Avenue: 30.
Smalley, Bob C., Life of: 261.
Smiley, P. K.: 91.
Smith, J. Bruce: 104.
Smith, W. F., Life of: 280; 87.
Snell, C. Perry, Life of: 259; 32, 50, 57, 124, 128, 162, 167.
Snell & Hamlett: 128.
Sloan, W. A.: 12, 20, 22, 24, 141.
Societies: 185.
Sommers, J. Harold, Life of: 295, 181, 184.

INDEX—Continued

Soreno Hotel: 44, 284.
Spa: 38.
Spaniards: 2.
Sparkman, S. M.: 56.
Sperling, W. F.: 5, 6, 121.
Springstead, C. W., Life of: 238; 59, 82, 88, 112, 174.
Stoner, M. L.: 71.
Storms: 41.
Straub, W. L., Life of: 258; 56, 71, 84, 93, 100, 105, 110, 112, 143, 147, 165, 179.
Straub, Mrs. W. L.: 28.
Street Improvements: 18, 158.
Suffrage: 88.
Sullivan, J. J.: 61, 84.
Sumner, R. H., Life of: 249; 133.
Sunshine City: 35.
Sunshine Pleasure Club: 199.
Sweetapple, Henry: 7, 45.
Sykes, R. E.: 84.

T

Tampa Bay Transportation Co.: 71.
Tampa & Gulf Coast Railway: 53.
Tampa West Coast Railway: 52.
Tanner, Dr. W. J.: 88.
Tarpon Club: 33, 110.
Taylor, A. M.: 45.
Taylor, Glenn: 35.
Taylor, Ira: 32.
Taylor, Jack, Life of: 298; 134.
Taylor, John S.: 94.
Taylor, Joseph W.: 35, 49, 84.
Thomas, R. H., Life of: 240; 24, 30, 58, 71, 81, 88, 100, 130, 145, 174, 180.
Thomasson, A. F., Life of: 278; 86, 162, 175.
Thorn, John N.: 88.
Times: 179.
Tippetts, Kath. B., Life of: 265; 191.
Tomlinson, E. H., Life of: 239; 31, 109, 116, 142, 149, 163, 203.
Torres, J.: 20.
Tourist News: 181.
Tourist Societies: 28, 195.
Trolley Lines: 68, 74, 128, 130, 154.
Trice, John: 29, 173.
Trinity Evangel. Lutheran Church: 212.

V

Van Bibber, Dr. W. C.: 14.
Van Deventer, G. W.: 86.

Veillard, R.: 51, 58, 83, 95, 147.
Veteran City: 31, 76.
Victory Land Co.: 137.

W

Walden, Robt. R., Life of: 293.
War: 213.
Ward, E. R.: 8, 11, 115, 141.
Ward & Baum Addition: 11, 82, 124, 131.
Washington Birthday Celebration: 116, 163.
Water: 32, 151.
Waterfront Improvements: 28, 31, 55, 75, 82, 102.
Waterfront Park: 55, 199.
Watson, W. L., Life of: 289; 88, 107, 176.
Weedon's Island: 2, 299.
Weicking, C. W.: 96.
Weller, A. P., Life of: 256; 24, 67, 99.
Weller, Mrs. A. P.: 28.
Welsh, A. R., Life of: 285; 88.
Welsh, O. B.: 91.
Welton, A.: 24, 64.
West Central: 75, 77, 125.
West Coast Bank: 173.
White Way Lights: 35.
Whitney, L. A.: 38, 106, 164.
Whitted, Albert: 232.
Whitted, T. A., Life of: 231; 18, 20, 24.
Wilder, C. C.: 24.
Williams, B. C.: 24, 57, 82, 109.
Williams, Emma Moore: 148.
Williams, Horace, Life of: 226; 156.
Williams, Gen. J. C., Life of: 217; 5, 9, 20, 45, 115, 121, 169.
Williams, J. C., Jr.: 20, 24.
Williams Park: 197.
Williamsville: 125.
Willson, E. B., Life of: 281; 106.
Wilson, T. K.: 71, 130.
Wimer, Edmund C.: 104.
Woman's Club: 188.
Woman's Town Improvement Association: 28, 186, 197.
Wood, F. A., Life of: 263; 28, 30, 35, 61, 64, 94, 96, 100, 128, 130, 180.
Woodside, John J.: 89.
World War: 127, 213.
Wright, J. B.: 24, 81.
Wright, J. W.: 99.
Wylie, Dr. Leroy: 150.
Wyman, Dr. W. E. A.: 88.